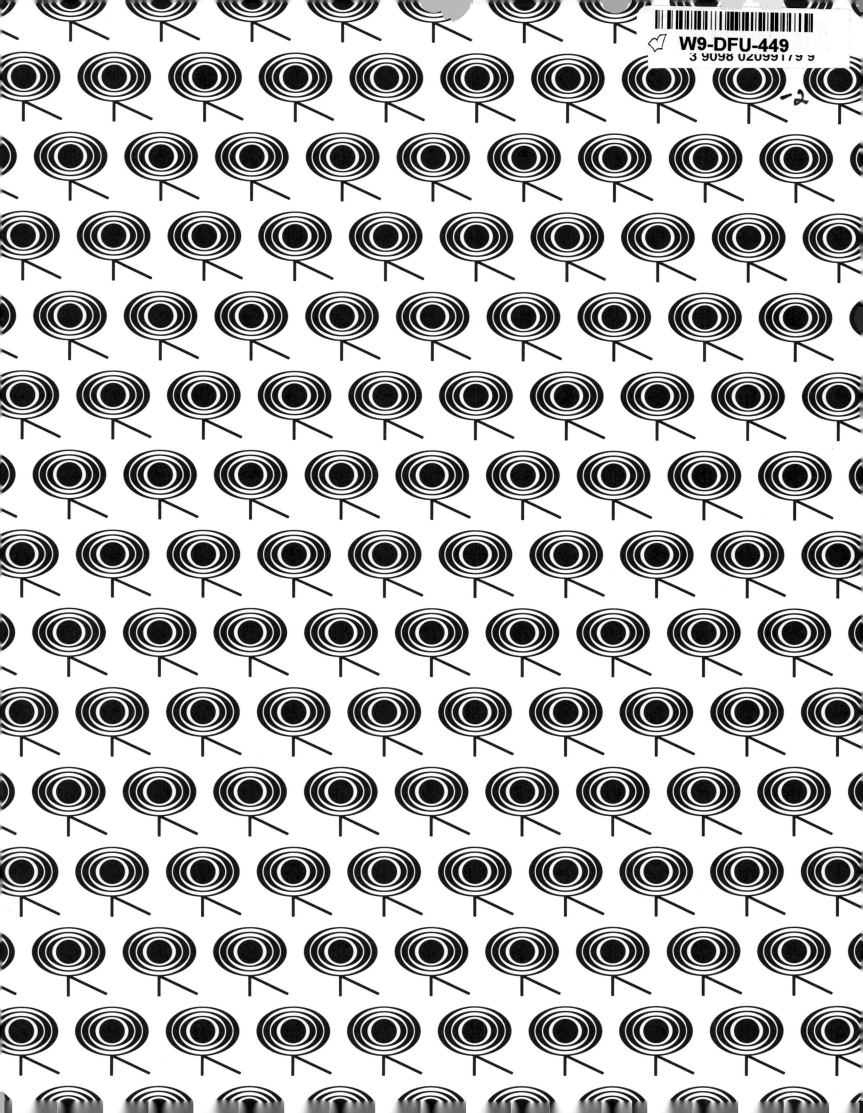

W9-DFU-449

3 9098 02099179 9

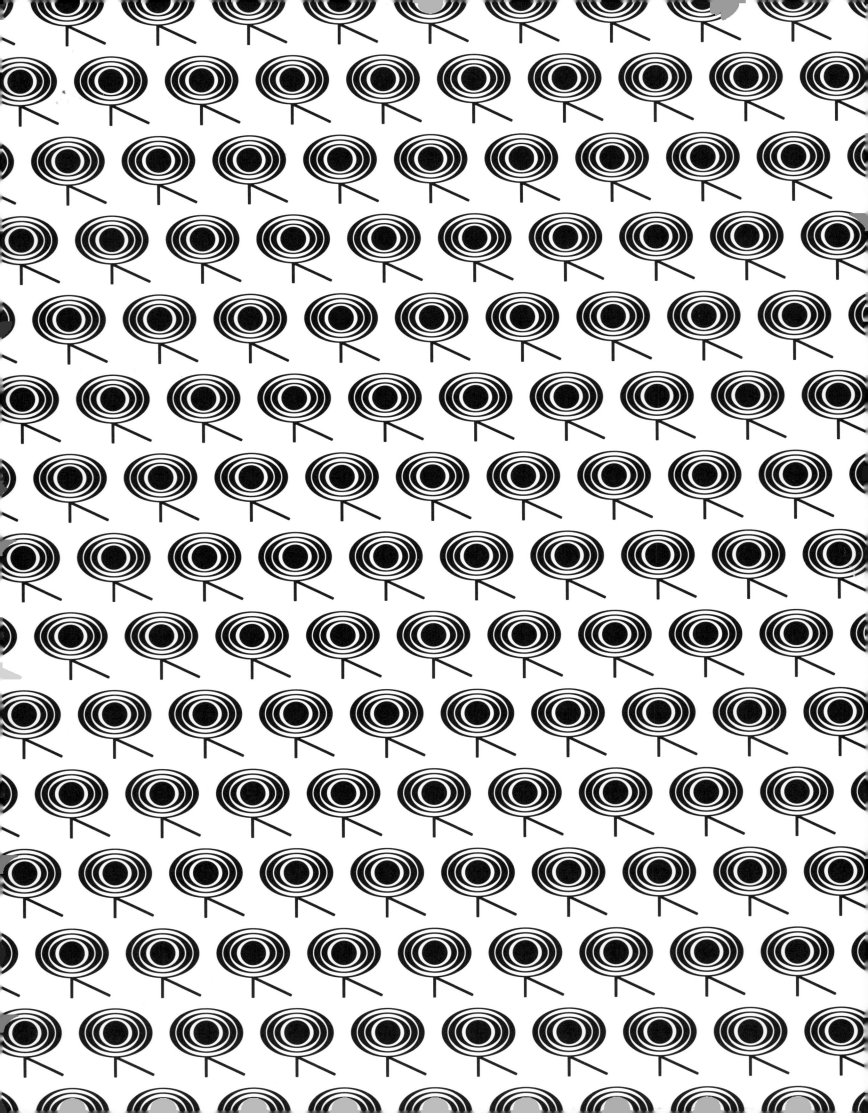

360 Sound

360 Sound
The Columbia Records Story
Sean Wilentz

CHRONICLE BOOKS

SAN FRANCISCO

Copyright © 2012 by Sony Music Entertainment
Text Copyright © 2012 by Sean Wilentz

Individual components of this book are copyrighted to individual photographers
and artists as indicated on pages 331 and 336, which constitute a continuation of
the copyright page.

All rights reserved. No part of this book may be reproduced in any form without
written permission from the publisher.

Every effort has been made to trace the ownership of all copyrighted material included
in this volume. Any errors or omissions that may have occurred are inadvertent and
will be corrected in subsequent editions, provided notification is sent to the publisher.

Foreword written by Bob Dylan, copyright © 1964, 1965 by Warner Bros. Inc.;
renewed 1992, 1993 by Special Rider Music.

Library of Congress Cataloging-in-Publication Data

Wilentz, Sean.
 360 sound : the Columbia Records story / Sean Wilentz.
    p. cm.
 Includes index.
 ISBN 978-1-4521-0756-1
 1. Columbia Records, Inc.--History. 2. Sound recording industry--History.
 I. Title. II. Title: Three hundred sixty sound. III. Title: Three hundred and
 sixty sound.

 ML3792.C65W55 2011
 384--dc23

                            2011044359

Manufactured in China.

Design and Art Direction by Farrow.
Project Management by Peter Fletcher at Plan R Marketing.
Photo Editing by Mary Maurer / 2310 Design.

This book has been set in Sabon, Univers, and Futura.

10 9 8 7 6 5 4 3 2 1

Chronicle Books LLC
680 Second Street
San Francisco, California 94107

www.chroniclebooks.com

Contents

Foreword

Then take me disappearin' through the smoke rings of my mind

Down the foggy ruins of time, far past the frozen leaves

The haunted, frightened trees, out to the windy beach

Far from the twisted reach of crazy sorrow

Yes, to dance beneath the diamond sky with one hand waving free

Silhouetted by the sea, circled by the circus sands

With all memory and fate driven deep beneath the waves

Let me forget about today until tomorrow

Hey! Mr. Tambourine Man, play a song for me

I'm not sleepy and there is no place I'm going to

Hey! Mr. Tambourine Man, play a song for me

In the jingle jangle morning I'll come followin' you

Bob Dylan from "Mr. Tambourine Man"

CS 8377 · OSCAR BROWN JR · SIN AND SOUL

BFC 40964 · TERENCE TRENT D'ARBY · INTRODUCING THE HARDLINE ACCORDING TO TERENCE TRENT D'A

ABYSSINIAN BAPTIST · GOSPEL CHOIR; PROF. ALEX BRADFORD, DIRECTOR

CS 8609 · ANDY WILLIAMS · "MOON RIVER" AND OTHER GREAT MOVIE THEMES

CL 1721 · JOHNNY HORTON · HONKY-TONK MAN

M 37779 · J.S. BACH: GOLDBERG VARIATIONS · GLENN GOULD, PIANO/KLAVIER

CS 8810 · DION · RUBY BABY

CS 8853 · JOHNNY CASH · RING OF FIRE

CS 8901 · PETE SEEGER · WE SHALL OVERCOME

CS 9015 · BARBRA STREISAND · PEOPLE

IC 33795 · BRUCE SPRINGSTEEN · BORN TO RUN

MONGO SANTAMARIA · EL PUSSY CAT

SON HOUSE · FATHER OF FOLK BLUES

BILLY JOE ROYAL · DOWN IN THE BOONDOCKS

KCS 9943 · JOHNNY CASH · HELLO, I'M JOHNNY CASH

BOB DYLAN · BRINGING IT ALL BACK HOME

CS 8198 · LAMBERT, HENDRICKS & ROSS · "THE HOTTEST NEW GROUP IN 'JAZZ'"

KCS 9701 · MIKE BLOOMFIELD-AL KOOPER/STEVE STILLS · SUPER SESSION

CS 8838 · THELONIOUS MONK · CRISS-CROSS

KS 14263 · DOROTHY LOVE COATES & THE GOSPEL HARMONETTES

THE MORMON TABERNACLE CHOIR · THE PHILAD...

PORGY AND BESS · MILES DAVIS WITH ORCH. UNDER THE DIRECTION OF GIL EVANS

OC 40995 · JULIO IGLESIAS · NON STOP

CL 1771 · THE CLANCY BROTHERS AND TOMMY MAKEM · HEARTY AND HELLISH

CS 8219 · JOHNNY MATHIS · FAITHFULLY

GRAND CANYON · ANDRE KOSTELANETZ AND HIS ORCHESTRA

ETHEL MERMAN AND THE ORIGINAL BROADWAY CAST

CS 9522 · BARBRA STREISAND · FEATURING THE WAY WE WERE AND ALL IN LOVE IS FAIR

32801 · THE CHAMBERS BROTHERS · THE TIME HAS COME

JS 38000 · ANNIE · ORIGINAL MOTION PICTURE SOUNDTRACK

BFC 40239 · L.L. COOL J · RADIO

OC 40285 · WHAM! · MUSIC FROM THE EDGE OF HEAVEN

M2S 676 · MAHLER · SYMPHONY NO. 9 · BRUNO WALTER/COLUMBIA SYMPHONY

KS 32265 · ORIGINAL BROADWAY CAST ALBUM · A LITTLE NIGHT MUSIC

THE FABULOUS JOHNNY CASH

SYMPHONY NO. 3 · KINDERTOTENLIEDER — LEONARD BERNSTEIN / N.Y. PHILHAR...

Introduction

In 1887, a group of investors formed the American Graphophone Company, the beginning of what would eventually become Columbia Records. A century and a quarter later, Columbia endures as the oldest label in the history of the recording industry. The intervening story is as fascinating as it is central to any account of the evolution of musical entertainment.

Columbia's list of major performers, past and present, is unsurpassed, and it fills the annals of modern music, popular and classical. The company has either sponsored or advanced major innovations in sound technology, the most important of which was the invention of the LP. Columbia's fitful and sometimes improbable growth from a local marketing franchise into an enormous corporation nestled in a multinational corporate empire is a remarkable case study in the history of business. And, within all these stories, there remains the lasting fact of the music itself.

Columbia has helped to transform the country's musical culture. The United States has always been a musical nation, not just in its churches, music halls, and opera houses, but also in its homes, town squares, and workplaces. At the end of the nineteenth century, the great symbols of America's musicality were the village bandstand and the parlor piano, the latter being played with greater or lesser skill by some member of the household. But the introduction of the player piano and, even more decisively, the phonograph changed everything.

What had once been a culture of amateur performance now involved purchasing and listening to the performances of professionals, including some of the greatest virtuosos in the world—a startling new form of everyday experience. Performances did not instantly vanish when the performers finished; they could be retrieved and replayed, over and over, and for decades to come. As the sounds of recorded music filled the air, together with the new clamor of automobiles, heavy industrial plants, and the crowds of burgeoning cities, the nation's aural environment changed profoundly. By the 1920s, the historian David Suisman has written, "American society *sounded* different than it had a generation earlier."

The nation's soundscape has continued to change since then, and America's sounds have spread across the globe. Composers and performers have, of course, contributed the most to the renovations of America's musical sounds. But the changes have also been the work of the music industry, an enormous congeries of businessmen, engineers, producers, arrangers, song pluggers, talent scouts, disc jockeys, artists' managers, and more. And while industry has brought the music to a mass public and shaped that public's musical tastes, its technological innovations— from the introduction of disc recordings at the end of the nineteenth century to the digital breakthroughs of recent decades—have strongly shaped the evolution of musical styles. Columbia Records has played a vital and at times essential role in this larger musical history.

Columbia has also had important connections to America's social history, especially the history of the country's turbulent race relations. The label began operating a decade after the overthrow of Reconstruction, amid a resurgence of white supremacy that would soon usher in the long era of rigidly enforced racial segregation. In 1887 alone, seventy African Americans are known to have been lynched, mainly in the South. Early cylinder recordings by Columbia of so-called "coon" songs fully reflected the racist spirit of the times. Yet these recordings also reveal a fascination with African American culture that dates back at least as far as the blackface minstrel shows of the pre–Civil War years—a strong and abiding sense among some white listeners that black music was emotionally more authentic and gratifying than the sentimental parlor songs of the genteel mainstream.

This fascination across the color line could be scornful, but it could also be empathic or envious; sometimes it was all three at once. The resulting tensions energized American culture. Later generations of record producers—looking mainly to make money for their companies but also goaded by a deeper and more sympathetic understanding of African American life—would record the work of some of the greatest African American musical artists of the last century. Columbia helped to lead the way, releasing breakthrough recordings by, among many others, Bert Williams, Bessie Smith, and Louis Armstrong. The work of Columbia producers such as Frank Buckley Walker, John Hammond, Don Law, and George Avakian, along with their colleagues and successors, aided in popularizing every variety of African American music and thereby helped to establish its centrality to the national experience. Those successes helped Columbia endure economic adversity, but they also contributed to the myriad of cultural changes that would help transform American race relations after 1945.

Columbia has also affected and been affected by the play of various other ethnic currents in American business and American music. Beginning with Asa Yoelson—who took the stage name Al Jolson—Columbia has recorded major stars who brought to bear immigrant styles, traditions, and sensibilities on existing forms of American popular music. Jolson's recording of the young George Gershwin's first hit song, "Swanee," in 1920 was an early symbol of the importance of immigrants and the children of immigrants among the distinguished composers whose work appeared on Columbia. The impact of the great wave of immigration from central and southern Europe from 1880 until World War I, especially of Jews and Italians, lasted into the twenty-first century, in the work of first- and second-generation immigrants ranging from Frank Sinatra and Tony Bennett to Barbra Streisand and Bob Dylan. The recording industry also opened opportunities for ambitious businessmen and producers who were either immigrants or the offspring of immigrants, including, at Columbia, Goddard Lieberson and Mitch Miller. And in recent decades, the success of Columbia artists such as Ricky Martin, Wyclef Jean, and Maxwell has reflected the cultural impact of newer waves of immigration from Latin America and the Caribbean.

Columbia has likewise had an enormous influence on American mass culture, particularly the continually evolving youth culture that has come to drive so much of modern life. Columbia and its subsidiary label, OKeh Records, stood at the artistic forefront of commercial popular music during the Jazz Age of the 1920s. Although the company fell on extremely hard times during the Great Depression, it did release some important records by the big bands of the jitterbugging swing era, including some key recordings in the late 1930s and early 1940s by Benny Goodman and Count Basie. Columbia then became the label of the first American teen idol, Frank Sinatra, during the bobby-soxer uproars of the 1940s. After initially abjuring rock and roll, Columbia supported the recording careers of Bob Dylan, Janis Joplin, Blood, Sweat & Tears, Santana, and others in the 1960s and 1970s as they revolutionized rock and popular music; Columbia soon became the foremost rock label in the world. At the century's end—again after some hesitation—Columbia released, coreleased, or distributed some of the most significant recordings in contemporary youth-oriented pop and hip-hop.

Yet Columbia has not confined itself to the latest trends. Unlike those specialist labels whose passion for a particular kind of music has challenged and diversified the recording industry, Columbia has tried to cover the entire spectrum, more like an emporium than a boutique. Although it is known chiefly for its popular recordings, for example, the label has long been an important source of classical music. Its releases of works by American classical performers and composers, including émigrés as well as native-born Americans, have elevated the nation's cultural prestige around the world. And, in popular music, Columbia has maintained a broad range of styles. Many of the best-loved and most influential artists in country and western music have recorded for Columbia, from Gid Tanner and Charlie Poole in the 1920s to Johnny Cash and the Dixie Chicks in our own time. Long after the musical revolutions of the 1960s, Columbia has stayed loyal to such performers of the standards as Tony Bennett and Barbra Streisand—commercial and critical favorites whose success flies in the face of claims about the increasing homogeneity of the musical marketplace.

Columbia's eclecticism and its involvement in the rise of American musical culture to global prominence have also been closely entwined with the history of the nation's cultural capital, New York City. Although it was founded in the District of Columbia—from which it took its name—Columbia moved its executive offices to Manhattan in 1897, the year before Manhattan and the Bronx merged with Brooklyn, Queens, and Staten Island to form the consolidated City of New York. Thereafter, Columbia emerged as one of the metropolis's major commercial cultural institutions, and the company's heart and soul would always be tied to New York. The link was particularly evident during the two decades after 1945, when Goddard Lieberson and Mitch Miller guided Columbia's fortunes, and when recordings of original Broadway productions and Leonard Bernstein's New York Philharmonic became bulwarks of Columbia's catalog. To be sure, Columbia never fell into the trap of New York provincialism, the conceit that little of the United States west of the Hudson holds much that is of cultural value. The label's forays into the South and Southwest, in particular, built extraordinary Columbia catalogs in blues, early jazz, and country and western music, and many of Columbia's landmark recording sessions over the years have occurred in such important musical centers as Chicago, Dallas, Los Angeles, and, above all, Nashville; those achievements are essential features of Columbia's story. Still, throughout the twentieth century and beyond, Columbia excelled in drawing from the steady supply of talent showcased in New York's auditoriums, theaters, and nightclubs, from Carnegie Hall to the Village Vanguard to Sin-é. It also evinced an ineffable style of urbanity, elegance, innovation, and exuberance inseparable from the city where it was, and still is, headquartered.

360 Sound appears in conjunction with the commemoration of Columbia's 125th anniversary. Its title means to convey the expansiveness of Columbia's history and of its artistic contributions. Working in conjunction with its then owner, the Columbia Broadcasting System, Columbia coined the slogan "360 Sound" in the early 1950s in order to help market its efforts in so-called "high-fidelity" recording. Between 1962 and 1970, "360 Sound" appeared on Columbia's record labels, bracketed by two arrows, which quickly became one of the company's better-known trade emblems. Insofar as technology and marketing are important parts of Columbia's story, the title fits well. But *360 Sound* also alludes to Columbia's efforts to provide a broad range of musical entertainment—while also posting profits.

Those last two words are, of course, all important. Columbia's original directors decided in 1889 to record a variety of musical performances not because they loved music but because they loved making money. From the sharp-elbowed, litigious maneuvering of the firm's early years to the multimedia strategizing of the present, Columbia has always been a cash-conscious enterprise in a highly competitive industry. The company's financial choices point to numerous trends, from the early concentration on popular recordings to the reduction in the label's classical and jazz programs over the last forty years. Columbia has offered a wide selection of music chiefly for business reasons, not artistic ones.

Still, the demands of the bottom line have not been the only demands at Columbia, where the pursuit of profit has meshed with the pursuit of musical excellence. During the crucial decade from 1956 through 1966, Goddard Lieberson, a trained composer, led the label with a conscious and highly sophisticated musical agenda. Subsequent top executives with strong musical opinions, including Clive Davis and Tommy Mottola, involved themselves heavily in the creative process. Columbia's producers have included a long list of musical visionaries including, most famously, the jazz and blues pioneer John Hammond. "We had a responsibility for the business because we were a part of CBS," the longtime Columbia artists and repertoire (A&R) man and executive Bruce Lundvall recalls of his salad days at the label in the early 1960s, "and we had a responsibility to a certain art form called music, and if you get the music right, the business comes right." Columbia's story is about commerce but also about commerce connected to art.

Telling Columbia's capacious story in a book of limited length has required making some painful and arbitrary decisions. Because Columbia's musical artists and its artistic directors have been chiefly responsible for securing the label's raison d'être, they receive the most attention, along with the executives who have forged Columbia's corporate identity. Contributors to major chapters of the company's history, including the stories of Columbia's engineering innovations and adaptations, receive considerable but less copious treatment. Other important and even essential figures, however—Columbia's graphic artists and designers, for example, as well as the marketing and public relations staffs so vital to the label's success—get less attention than they deserve. Indeed, even the extensive coverage of Columbia's recording artists perforce either slights or omits hundreds of significant individual performers and ensembles, including some that have been quite illustrious. Entire genres—above all, film soundtracks—turn up only in passing. The book likewise compresses important passages in the company's business history. Within these constraints, though, the book strives to highlight the major developments and themes in Columbia's history. Fortunately, some of the material either omitted from or slighted in the text receives attention in the book's sidebars and, in the deluxe package, Dave Marsh's *Legends and Legacy.*

Columbia's story involves the entire history of the American recording industry and its impact on modern life. No other record label can claim that distinction. Commemorating Columbia's anniversary invites an appreciation of a century and a quarter of musical virtuosity, technical ingenuity, and business craftiness. That appreciation in turn reveals how the culture and society of a bygone age fitfully evolved into the bewildering digitized world of the present. For now, though, let us enter the years when Columbia began—and when sound recording meant scratching impressions of spoken words on cylinders made of wax.

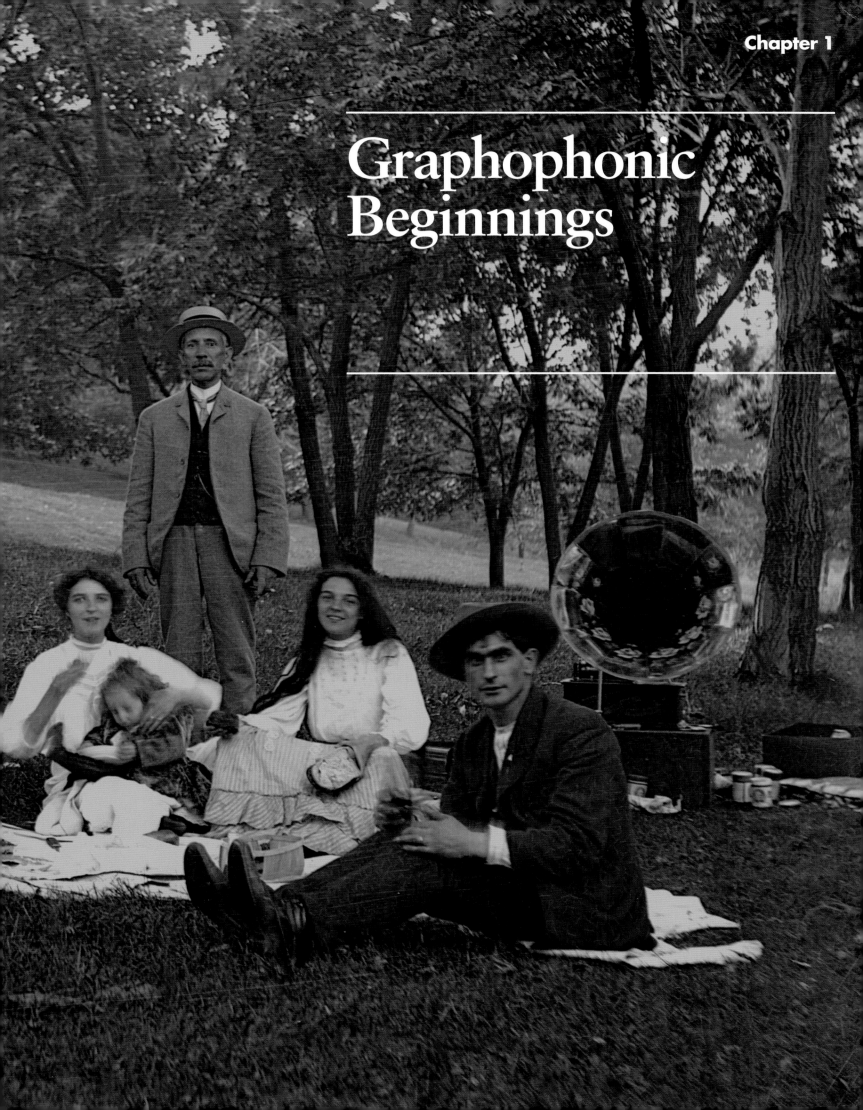

Chapter 1

Graphophonic Beginnings

The early history of Columbia Records turns on some fateful calculations and miscalculations by the renowned inventor of the phonograph, Thomas Alva Edison. Edison was of course a giant during the last quarter of the nineteenth century, which has been called the "age of inventions." Among all his creations, he would later call the phonograph his favorite ("my baby"), and he worked very hard, and for many years, on perfecting it. Yet had Edison concentrated more steadily on developing his invention, had he been less disdainful of music in favor of the spoken word, had he been more flexible and less prideful in his approach to the business and technology of recorded sound, the entire history of the recording industry might have turned out differently. Instead, Edison left room for other innovators to improve on his breakthrough and, sometimes ruthlessly, surpass his efforts at reaping the full commercial rewards. One of the chief results of Edison's wavering attention to his "baby" was the success of the enterprise that became Columbia Records, under the leadership of the shrewd, dogged, deceptively mild-visaged businessman Edward Denison Easton.

Edward Denison Easton

In 1877, while at work on refining the telegraph, Edison hit upon the idea of transcribing sounds on a cylinder wrapped in tinfoil, and the patent for his "phonograph" was issued on February 19, 1878. The discovery struck a chord far and wide. Soon afterward, a small, anonymously authored book, *All About the Telephone and Telegraph*, appeared in London and declared that Edison's phonograph "promises to be one of the most remarkable of the recent marvels of science." Excited commentators imagined the phonograph as best suited not to recording music but to capturing spoken messages and aiding in stenography, especially for legal proceedings. There were also thought to be potential literary uses: "authors, too, may perhaps be saved the trouble of writing their compositions," the little London book remarked. Edison himself listed "reproduction of music" as the fourth item on a list of ten possible uses for the phonograph, behind dictation, phonographic books for the blind, and the teaching of elocution.

After he secured his patent, Edison issued licenses to entrepreneurs who, for a nominal fee, exhibited the astounding talking machine to crowds around the country and recorded a few of the onlookers' voices. But the device proved difficult to operate, the tin foil lasted for only a few playings, and the novelty of phonographic reproduction soon wore off with the public. Edison moved on to other projects, in particular the development of incandescent lighting—the lightbulb—and he sold his patent rights to the phonograph in 1878, against 20 percent of all future profits.

In this age of inventions, though, no promising idea lay dormant for too long, as the burst of scientific and engineering innovation was hastening the rise of mass production and mass consumption. Adaptations of Edison's work with electric lighting, many initiated by Edison himself, would soon permit the illumination of entire cities; breakthroughs in metallurgy enabled the construction of the first so-called "skyscrapers." Such developments led to further innovations in science and engineering, which in turn created new opportunities for commercial investment. And so the phonograph and its possible uses, laid aside by Edison, quickly attracted attention from the associates of another of the era's greatest inventors.

In 1880, the French government awarded its Grand Volta Prize, worth a princely 50,000 francs (the equivalent of more than $100,000 today), to Alexander Graham Bell in honor of his invention of the telephone four years earlier. Bell invested the prize money in a new laboratory in Washington, DC, where his cousin, Chichester A. Bell, a chemical engineer, and a scientist and instrument maker, Charles Sumner Tainter, began conducting further experiments in acoustics and recording. At first, they worked on inscribing sounds on one side of a flat disc, but the results were unsatisfactory. Instead, on May 4, 1886, Tainter and Chichester Bell gained a series of patents for what they called a "graphophone," using a cardboard cylinder coated in ozocerite (a kind of wax) instead of tin foil, and employing a floating stylus instead of Edison's rigid needle. Unlike Edison's tinfoil strips, the wax-coated cylinders could be removed from the Bell-Tainter machine, stored away, and heard again on a later occasion.

Bell and Tainter approached Edison about combining forces, but Edison threw them out, outraged at what he considered the theft of his invention. Bell and Tainter and some associates then formed the Volta Graphophone Company of Alexandria, Virginia (created on January 6, 1887, and incorporated on February 3), to oversee commercial development of their new product. Among Volta Graphophone's original stockholders was Edward Denison Easton.

Edward Denison Easton, Stenographer and Father of Columbia Phonograph

Easton was a self-made, hard-charging, unsentimental businessman of the Gilded Age. Born in Gloucester, Massachusetts, in 1856, and raised in Arcola, New Jersey, he first worked as a reporter for a Hackensack weekly newspaper. He then mastered stenography—at the time a highly valued (and highly paid) specialty, performed mostly by men—and combined it with his newspaperman's skills to become one of the nation's premier legal reporters. In 1881 and 1882, having

Charles Sumner Tainter

Chichester A. Bell

Thomas Edison

Alexander Graham Bell

relocated to Washington, Easton covered the trial of Charles Guiteau, the assassin of President James Garfield. A year later, he reported the celebrated Star Route graft trials, involving high officials in the US Post Office. According to an article later published in the *New York Times*, Easton received an astounding $50,000 for this work, described as the largest sum ever paid for such services. Well heeled but restless, Easton then enrolled at Georgetown Law School where, nearing the end of his studies, he became fascinated with the new field of phonograph recording, which he had first encountered when he witnessed a demonstration of Edison's tinfoil device several years earlier. The great improvements introduced by Bell and Tainter apparently convinced Easton that sound recording might revolutionize every aspect of stenography, and he did not want be left in the dust.

In 1887, Easton joined a syndicate of investors that bought from Volta Graphophone the rights to the Bell-Tainter patents, founded its own American Graphophone Company to produce office dictation machines, and started in business on G Street. After leasing one wing of an enormous abandoned sewing-machine factory complex in Bridgeport, Connecticut, American Graphophone hired a dozen workmen. The company began turning out machines at a rate of three or four per day, at first, with the expectation that the federal offices in the nation's capital would prove to be its primary market. Within a year, in February 1888, Easton, while remaining a major shareholder in American Graphophone, had taken on some new partners and secured from the company its exclusive sales rights for Delaware, Virginia, and the District of Columbia. The merchandising outfit would take the name Columbia Phonograph Company, after its base of operations. Incorporated on January 22, 1889, the firm established offices in a brownstone at 627 E Street NW, in order to allow Easton and his partners to focus their business energies chiefly on DC. But the company, at Easton's urging, soon pressed ahead with larger ambitions.

Before it finished its first year in business, Columbia Phonograph had branched out beyond the marketing of office dictation machines, and with good reason. Resistance to the devices had been growing. The equipment was expensive—$150 per machine—and it could be highly unreliable. More important, stenographer specialists, fearing imminent unemployment, despised the new technology and sometimes sabotaged it, while businessmen found that they preferred traditional dictation and transcription to shouting into a recording horn. Meanwhile, early experiments had begun to explore the possibilities of using the machines instead for listening to prerecorded music. Then, in November 1889, Louis T. Glass, a San Franciscan working for the Pacific Phonograph Company, another marketing franchise, unveiled a machine that allowed the user to insert a nickel and listen, through elongated rubber ear tubes connected to the machine, to a brief musical selection or comic monologue. Coin-operated cylinder machines quickly began appearing in saloons, ice cream parlors, and other popular amusement spots. More than 1,250 of them were in operation around the country by 1891.

In the fall of 1889, just before Glass announced his innovation, Columbia Phonograph began producing music cylinders, and Columbia resolved to supply the "nickel-in-the-slot" trade. Soon, the company became the nation's premier producer and promoter of musical recordings. In 1890, Columbia Phonograph issued its first list of offerings. By June 1891, the list ran to ten pages, and it included marches, dance numbers, hymns and anthems, instrumental and vocal solos accompanied by piano, comic "dialect" routines, and spoken-word recordings, priced at $1 to $2 per cylinder.

Edison Returns and Columbia Commits to Music

Even before Columbia Phonograph's parent company, American Graphophone, was up and running, Thomas Alva Edison, the great man who had disappeared, had regained his interest in the talking machine. In 1886, having successfully completed major advances in the distribution of electrical power, Edison repurchased his own phonograph patents and avidly resumed work on improving his

Columbia graphophone

Edison Standard phonograph

Columbia graphophone

Bell and Tainter's graphophone

invention and, in turn, manufacturing and marketing the new machines. By 1888, he had perfected a new phonograph capable of making permanent recordings on wax cylinders. The directors of American Graphophone commenced what would become a recurring pattern of aggressive litigation, charging that Edison's new work was infringing on the Bell-Tainter patents.

A courtroom confrontation seemed inevitable until a wealthy manufacturer of tableware glass tumblers from Pennsylvania, Jesse H. Lippincott, intervened. Interested in building a new monopoly along the lines of the American Bell Telephone Company, Lippincott, in 1888, bought up the stock of Edison Phonograph Works, along with its patents and exclusive sales rights to the Edison phonographs. He then forged a testy alliance with American Graphophone under the umbrella of his North American Phonograph Company, which would serve as a national sales and leasing agency for both companies' machines, working through local franchises around the country. (Pacific Phonograph, where Louis Glass worked, was one of Lippincott's franchises.) Columbia Phonograph, when finally incorporated early in 1889, retained the territorial sales rights it had secured from American Graphophone, but now it had the additional rights to sell and lease Edison's phonograph as well as the Bell-Tainter machine. Although formally licensed by North American Phonograph, Columbia operated very much on its own as it moved into producing music cylinders.

The North American Phonograph conglomerate was doomed from the start. The market for the cylinder machines, especially for the graphophones, was poor, as businessmen and stenographers continued to resist devices that were as bothersome as they were expensive. Edison had little interest in the growing preference for recorded music, believing that it demeaned his invention, and he resented it when North American Phonograph decided to provide his machines as well as the Bell-Tainter graphophones to the amusement-trade operators. Although Edison agreed to manufacture musical recordings, he did so grudgingly—"purely," he wrote, "as a matter of accommodation to the North American people." Lippincott's business plans, meanwhile, proved disastrous. Efforts to coordinate the production and merchandising of two different machines manufactured by two different companies in two different plants led to constant disputes. Heavy unpaid bills and threats of litigation mounted.

Edward Easton, meanwhile, remained one of American Graphophone's directors, and in March 1890 the other directors sent him on a fact-finding trip to discover how the public was responding to the two versions of the talking machine. Traveling the country by railroad from Florida to Oregon, Easton learned that North America's local dealers wished to sell one version or another, but not both, and that they greatly preferred the Edison phonograph, which produced clearer sound. Easton also came away more convinced than ever that the future lay in providing prerecorded music for the penny arcades, and eventually for private entertainment, not in building devices for business dictation. With live music readily available in concert halls and saloons, and with so many Americans making music in their own homes, it was not self-evident that musical recordings would prove profitable over the long haul, even after the "nickel-in-the-slot" machines began to proliferate. But Easton—who appears to have had little interest in music, let alone any aptitude for it—took the risk. Strictly as a commercial venture, he and Columbia were in the music business for keeps.

In the fall of 1890, Jesse Lippincott suffered a stroke and Edison, his principal creditor, took over direction of North American Phonograph. By the following spring, the company was clearly headed for collapse. Three years later, after a severe depression had leveled the national economy, Edison succeeded in his efforts to petition the North American Phonograph into bankruptcy. The move enabled Edison to salvage his patents and reclaim his company, but for two years, while the bankruptcy was being settled, he was not permitted to proceed with further perfecting and marketing his invention.

Easton and Columbia were poised to exploit the situation. In May 1893, after he had gained full control over the parent graphophone company (which had always retained its patents), Easton formed a new combination, with himself

"Promises to be one of the most remarkable of the recent marvels of science."

From *All About the Telephone and Telegraph* on Edison's phonograph

Phonograph cylinders

Columbia graphophone advertisement

COLUMBIA

Graphophone

Young Americans everywhere are voicing with their elders the praises of the Graphophone.

Parents find this great entertainer the best and most wholesome means of making home more attractive than the street.

Whether you spend the long summer evenings on the Porch at home or away at the Seaside or Camp, you will find the Graphophone the most valued possession—a portable Theatre, Opera and Vaudeville combined, with its side-splitting Song and Stories, and the Classic Music of the great Masters to suit all tastes and moods.

Write us at once for OUR FREE TRIAL AND EASY PAYMENT OFFER, which enables you to own a Graphophone by paying on small installments that will not be felt.

Every purchase carries with it a WRITTEN GUARANTEE backed by a TEN MILLION DOLLAR CONCERN ; the best assurance of the superiority of the Columbia goods.

Record-making is a difficult art. Unsuccessful attempts of the Columbia imitators prove this. It is comparatively simple to produce a record of one voice or one instrument. But a complex problem is presented when several voices are recorded, together with an orchestra of forty different instruments. The only Company that has mastered this problem satisfactorily is the Columbia Phonograph Co., and this explains why the Columbia Bands and Orchestras excel all others.

Grand Prix Paris 1900   Double Grand Prize St. Louis 1904
Highest Award Portland 1905

COLUMBIA PHONOGRAPH CO., GEN'L.
90-92 West Broadway, New York City
Largest Talking Machine Manufacturers in the World
Only Makers of BOTH Disc and Cylinder Machines.   Stores in all Principal Cities.
Dealers Everywhere.

FILL OUT AND MAIL THIS COUPON TO-DAY

Columbia Phonograph Co., New York City
90-92 W. Broadway. Send me complete information regarding your Free Trial and Easy Payment Offer.

Name..........

Address........

W. W 8

as president, in which American Graphophone would handle development and manufacturing of the machines and cylinders, while Columbia handled distribution and sales. (Because the company had acquired its sales rights to the graphophone before the formation of North American Phonograph, those rights would not expire when the conglomerate did; indeed, once North American Phonograph dissolved, Columbia could expand its base of operations well beyond its original sales district in and around Washington.)

Thereafter, Columbia's general attorney, Philip Mauro, launched fierce attacks on Edison's claimed patent rights, which would eventually lead to a cross-licensing of patents. Two other employees pitched in with important contributions: Thomas MacDonald, the first manager of the Bridgeport plant, invented a spring-driven motor that would help make the graphophone an everyday household appurtenance, and Frank Dorian, a champion of recorded music, laid plans for marketing Columbia's cylinders in Britain and Europe. By the mid-1890s, now focused on home entertainment as well as public amusement, Columbia had geared up to seize control of the market in cylinder recordings.

Easton and Columbia did not have the field to themselves, even with Edison once again standing on the sidelines because of the bankruptcy. Since the late 1880s, several other locally based recording companies had arisen, all of them as part of the Lippincott operation. The largest included the New Jersey Phonograph Company, the Metropolitan Phonograph Company (which was absorbed by the New York Phonograph Company in 1890), and the Ohio Phonograph Company. Columbia fought them off with aggressive marketing tactics, including extensive advertising in the two earliest trade papers, *Phonogram* and *Phonoscope*. In addition, at the start of each of its cylinder selections, Columbia inserted a little spoken advertisement— "The following record taken for the Columbia Phonograph Company of Washington, DC," or some such announcement—a tactic that helped spread the company's name around the country. In the mid-1890s, the label struck a deal with the mass retailer Sears, Roebuck and Company, whereby Sears would sell Columbia's cylinders as Sears Graphophone Records. (Neither company took much effort to disguise the cylinders' source: Sears simply pasted its labels, often carelessly, over Columbia's.) In time, Columbia also opened graphophone parlors in Washington, New York, and Atlantic City—elaborately decorated arcades festooned with electric lights and filled with scores of coin-slot machines that were loaded with Columbia cylinders.

The steady demise of North American Phonograph and then the depression of 1893 caused many of the local recording companies to fail, and it badly weakened others. Columbia, which struggled but survived, remained combative, all the more so after the collapse of North American Phonograph freed it from its sales district restrictions. In May 1894, Columbia established and incorporated a new affiliate, Columbia Phonograph Company General, to help enlarge its business outside of Washington. A year later, the company opened a branch at 1159 Broadway in New York, its first office located outside its original sales territory. By mid-decade, Columbia was adding important talent from other companies to its own growing list of artists. And by the turn of the century, much of the competition in manufacturing entertainment cylinders had disappeared. The great exception was Edison, who returned to the fray in 1896.

Cylinder players

In the Land of Popular Tastes: From Yodelers and Whistling Stars to the Marine Band

Although Easton was firmly committed to recording music, the recording technology then in existence narrowed his musical options. The process of sound recording was entirely mechanical: sounds entered a large recording funnel, which terminated in a diaphragm to which a cutting stylus was attached; the stylus then cut a groove on the blank recording cylinder. But the reproduction of the sounds thus recorded on the cylinders lost a great deal of the lower, bass frequencies. (Although the stylus actually recorded the bass tones, the cylinder

Blacking Up

Despite the demeaning caricatures [it was] an American art form

Paging through the earliest record catalogs requires confronting many songs with bigoted titles. From the Sousa Band's "Darkie's Temptation" in 1903 to the Skillet Lickers' "Run Nigger Run" in 1927 with the likes of "Heinie Waltzed 'Round on His Hickory Limb," and "When That Little Yellow Fellow Plays Piano" in between, Columbia was no exception.

Mostly, the bigoted songs ridicule African Americans. This was the era of Jim Crow, a resurgence of white supremacy that the end of slavery never killed. It was also the time when vaudeville developed out of the blackface minstrel shows.

As music, blackface minstrelsy is as important as it is disturbing. Despite the demeaning caricatures, the performing, the dancing, and the music were an American art form. In using authentic music from the black community, the minstrel shows disseminated such styles in ways Jim Crow otherwise forbade.

Columbia and its subsidiaries made records with three of the best: Bert Williams, a black blackface minstrel; Al Jolson, a vaudeville giant; and Emmett Miller, one of the fathers of country music. Williams was regarded by many as the greatest comedian in minstrelsy and in vaudeville. Some of his records, notably "Nobody" and "I Don't Like That Face You Wear," are double-edged, challenging stereotypes as well as reinforcing them.

Al Jolson, the most famous blackface performer, is best remembered now for his blackface "Mammy" in *The Jazz Singer,* the first sound movie. Jolson fought anti-black discrimination on Broadway from the time he first became a star in 1911; in 1931, he performed what amounted to an anti-racist skit with Edgar Connor, a black actor, in *Hallelujah, I'm a Bum.*

Emmett Miller was the last great blackface performer. Hank Williams's version of "Lovesick Blues" and Bob Wills "I Ain't Got Nobody" came directly from his version. Miller remained influential for decades in the work of Merle Haggard, Louis Prima, Bob Dylan, and even David Lee Roth of Van Halen.

Dave Marsh

Al Jolson in blackface

FAMOUS "RECORD" MAKERS

New York City, May 1, 1898.

TO THE COLUMBIA PHONOGRAPH CO:--

        We hereby accept the proposition you have made us, to give our exclusive services as makers of talking machine records to the Columbia Phonograph Company during the ensuing year.

THEY MAKE COLUMBIA RECORDS EXCLUSIVELY.

COLUMBIA PHONOGRAPH COMPANY.

players responded far better to treble sounds.) And until practical master molds for manufacturing cylinders were devised in 1901 and 1902, each cylinder had to be produced individually, meaning that recording was an extremely tedious process: performers had to repeat their speeches or songs dozens of times in a single session in front of multiple acoustic devices. As a result, Columbia released a good deal of what would today be considered novelty material—gimmicky recordings for middle- and working-class listeners, much of it performed by acts from Washington and the city's environs whose vocals were shrill enough for reproduction and who possessed the staying power to repeat themselves over and over.

The art of yodeling—from the German *jodeln* which means, literally, to utter the sound *jo*—had been brought to America by visiting European performers in the mid-nineteenth century and had been picked up by troupes of blackface minstrels. The yodeling sound was well adapted to transcription to cylinder and it was inexpensive to record. Consequently, one of Columbia's early recorded acts was the policeman and yodeler Eddie Giguere, whom the company promoted as "the well-known yodeler of the Washington Police Patrol." Whistling was another cylinder recording favorite, especially as practiced by John Yorke AtLee, the greatest of Columbia's individual stars in the company's early years. By day, AtLee worked at a modest clerk's job at the Department of the Treasury, but by night he showed off his talents as an artistic whistler in local theaters. Beginning in 1889, he also held private recording sessions in his own parlor, where, accompanied on a piano, he made thousands of recordings, three cylinders at a time, of such popular numbers as "The Mocking Bird," "Home Sweet Home," and "A Curl from Baby's Head."

The early cylinder singing star Len Spencer was another local talent. The son of a prominent Washington family—the slain President Garfield was his godfather—Spencer performed onstage in blackface and was skilled at inserting humorous minstrel-show-style anecdotes. After recording, unbilled, for Columbia in 1889, Spencer switched to New Jersey Phonograph, for whom he recorded exclusively in the early 1890s, until he returned to the Columbia catalog in 1895. His most popular cylinders included a rendition of "A Hot Time in the Old Town." In 1893, with great fanfare, Columbia announced the addition of tenor George H. Diamond, whose recordings of songs such as the baseball number "Slide, Kelly, Slide" made him, the label's brochure boasted, "highly appreciated by users of the phonograph throughout the country."

In 1896, Easton lured the recording manager Victor Emerson away from New Jersey Phonograph and appointed him "superintendent of records," a precursor to the producers and A&R people of today. Emerson would be a mainstay at Columbia for the ensuing seventeen years, after which he formed a recording company of his own. While at New Jersey Phonograph, Emerson had recorded the first African American recording star, George Washington Johnson, with whom he would later work at Columbia. Johnson's enormous popularity revealed anew a long-standing fascination with black performers among white listeners. It also brought a small (though certainly racist) breach of the color line just as racial segregation was about to gain validation from the US Supreme Court in the landmark case of *Plessy v. Ferguson* (1896).

Born in northern Virginia in 1846, Johnson had either been born free or, more likely, emancipated as a boy; either way, he was raised as a body servant and companion to the son of a well-to-do white farmer. Taught to read and write, Johnson also developed his musical talents and, after moving to New York in the 1870s, earned a decent living as a street entertainer, whistling the popular tunes of the day and displaying an unusual stamina. Recorded in 1890 by Metropolitan Phonograph as well as by New Jersey Phonograph (he would soon also record for Edison), Johnson whistled and sang two novelty tunes that remained his signatures for several years, "The Whistling Coon" and "The Laughing Song." The companies thought, correctly, that white audiences would delight in hearing a black man perform numbers that mocked blacks, but the songs' popularity transcended the race of the performer. Rival recording labels rushed to produce

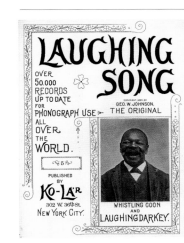

"Laughing Song" sheet music

Famous "Record" Makers, 1898

cover versions of Johnson's songs by white singers and whistlers. Not one to be left behind, Columbia had its top seller, the whistler John AtLee, record his own cylinders of Johnson's hits.

By 1895, when he first recorded for Columbia in New York, Johnson was at the peak of his stardom, and "The Whistling Coon" and "The Laughing Song" were the best-selling recordings in the United States. Columbia issued cylinders of both songs, including a version of "The Laughing Song" on which Len Spencer and his brother Henry (also a recording artist) engaged in some humorous repartee before introducing Johnson. Thereafter, Johnson continued to enjoy success on various labels until his life turned tragic. In 1899, he stood trial in New York for beating to death his common-law wife. Although the case was dropped for insufficient evidence and Johnson returned to recording, his star began to fade within a few years as the introduction of mass-produced molded cylinders negated the value of his stamina, and a new round of white performers started covering his songs. Len Spencer, who became both a successful booking agent and artist, arranged for his old friend to work as an office doorman. Johnson died in obscurity in 1914 and was buried in an unmarked grave in Queens.

Topical songs as well as pure entertainment appeared in the early Columbia catalogs. The bloody labor conflict at Andrew Carnegie's Homestead steel works in July 1892 inspired a recording that same year by a singing group, the Brilliant Quartette, called "The Fight for Home and Honor (Homestead, Pa.)." Cylinders favoring Democrats as well as Republicans appeared during the 1892 presidential campaign, with songs supporting, respectively, Grover Cleveland and Benjamin Harrison. Language instruction, comic monologues, poetry recitations, and other spoken-word recordings also appeared on the label's cylinders. One of Columbia's brief dramatic presentations, "The Mad Ravings of John McCullough," presented a supposedly crazed actor spouting disjointed bits and pieces of Shakespeare, and it became a highly reliable seller.

Columbia expanded on its campaign song cylinders in 1892 with recordings of political speeches on behalf of Cleveland and Harrison. Four years later, several recitations of William Jennings Bryan's famous "Cross of Gold" nomination speech appeared, and supporters of Bryan's Republican opponent, William McKinley, also recorded cylinders. Thus began Columbia's nonpartisan involvement in the political process, which would survive the demise of cylinder recording and last until the rise of radio. In 1908, along with other recording companies, Columbia would for the first time issue speeches recorded by the candidates themselves, getting William Howard Taft and William Jennings Bryan to speak about topics ranging from "Imperialism" to "Enforced Insurance of Bank Deposits"—campaign oratory that was more florid but also more substantive than the sound bytes that have come to dominate modern presidential politics.

Columbia enjoyed its greatest early commercial success with its cylinders by members of the US Marine Band, who performed publicly under the direction of the "March King," John Philip Sousa. Born in Washington, DC, in 1854, Sousa was the son of a trombonist in the Marine Band. A natural musician who was blessed with perfect pitch, the youngster's primary instrument was the violin, although he dreamed of running off with a circus troupe. At age thirteen, at his father's insistence, he enlisted in the Marine Corps and joined the band as an apprentice. Sousa proceeded to master all the wind instruments and started composing; in his spare time, he played violin in the pit orchestras at Ford's Theater and the Washington Theater, where he also learned how to conduct.

After completing his apprenticeship, Sousa spent several years traveling and finding work with numerous orchestras and variety shows. (One job involved playing music for a "nudie-girl" revue; another was in an orchestra led by the great French operetta composer, Jacques Offenbach.) In 1880, he was selected to head the Marine Band, and he would remain at the post for twelve years. Late in 1889 or early in 1890, Columbia secured an agreement to record members of the band, and the resulting cylinders turned Sousa into something of a recording star—although all he really did in connection with the recordings was to permit them to be made.

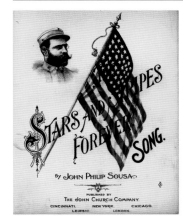

"Stars and Stripes" sheet music

John Philip Sousa

A demanding maestro as well as composer, Sousa had dedicated himself to improving the music's instrumentation and elevating performance standards, in part by placing his musicians on a strict rehearsal schedule. Stationed near Columbia's Washington offices, Sousa's ensemble combined patriotism with excellent musicianship—and it also had Sousa's rousing new military marches such as "Semper Fidelis" to offer, along with popular song favorites like "Little Annie Rooney" and "Down Went McGinty (Dressed in His Best Suit of Clothes)." Sousa was also a skilled promoter who used concert appearances and press interviews to good effect. By the end of the 1880s, the Marine Band had gained a following outside of Washington, and Sousa had become a recognized expert on patriotic music. Thanks to the Columbia recordings and an annual autumn concert tour initiated by Sousa in 1891, the band quickly achieved national fame, and its peppy rhythms sparked a popular craze for military music.

Still, Sousa's and the Marine Band's early links to Columbia were problematic. Because the recording horns used to make the cylinders could not pick up sounds from more than a few feet away, it was impossible to record the entire band at once. With only about one-third of the members actually performing, the recorded sound was greatly diminished from that of the band's actual performances. The playing time allowed on the early cylinders, ranging from two to two and a half minutes, forced the stripped-down ensemble to truncate the band's melodies. Sousa himself was delighted at the newfound publicity and was happy to see some of his band members earn some extra income ($1 an hour per man), but he was far from enthusiastic about the recordings. He deemed the repetitive recording process a form of torture and regarded the recording engineers as a nuisance; he recoiled at the cylinders' poor fidelity; and he was incensed that he did not receive any royalties for his own compositions and arrangements. The recording band was small enough that it did not require a conductor, so Sousa left an assistant in charge—and the bandleader never once set foot in the makeshift recording studio that Columbia set up across the street from the band's barracks. Columbia's advertisements boasted of "the WORLD-RENOWNED UNITED STATES MARINE BAND, which plays at the WHITE HOUSE for President Harrison"—but only a few of the band's members actually played on the cylinders, and they were recorded without John Philip Sousa.

As far as Easton and Columbia were concerned, though, the recording band's quality (to which the maestro had greatly contributed) and the Marine Band's rising reputation formed a magical combination. Fifty-nine Marine Band cylinder titles appeared in the fall of 1890, an astonishing debut. Even after the great Sousa resigned his directorship to form his own private Grand Concert Band in 1892, the public's appetite for Marine Band recordings only seemed to grow. By 1897, when Sousa's successor, Francesco Fanciulli stepped down, four hundred different titles by the Marine Band were on the market, including "The Kiss Waltz" and "The Enthusiast Polka" as well as Sousa favorites like "The Washington Post March."

The Marine Band cylinders' success solidified Columbia's business. So did the introduction in 1894 of the new spring-driven graphophones, priced at $75 and suitable for home use, which led to the recording industry's first true boom year in 1897. Sales continued to skyrocket over the succeeding years. Ironically, Columbia's prosperity due to the success of the Marine Band recordings led the company to move its headquarters in 1897 out of the nation's capital (and away from the Marine Band) to New York. Manhattan was by now unquestionably the nation's leading center for the lively arts and publishing as well as for business and finance—a city of great significance around the globe that was about to become even greater thanks to the consolidation of the five boroughs into the City of New York. From his new offices in the Tribune Building at 154 Nassau Street, in the heart of downtown Manhattan's commercial pandemonium, Edward Easton planned a business empire that would soon boast branch offices in London, Paris, and Berlin, as well as in Washington, Baltimore, Philadelphia, Buffalo, Chicago, St. Louis, and San Francisco. Music played on machines that had originally been designed for dictation was swiftly

Early recording session

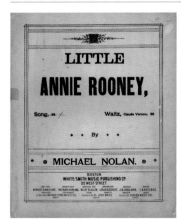

"Little Annie Rooney" sheet music

Previous page:
US Marine Band

Columbia Logos

Around 1908, someone whose identity will probably be forever unknown to us developed the company's first trademark: a pair of sixteenth notes, "Magic Notes," in a circle. Before the gramophone, there had been musical automata but a voice had never emanated from a machine, so these were indeed magic notes. The new logo appeared at the same time as Columbia's innovative "Double Disc" with sound on both sides. Label colors, fonts, and designs changed with dizzying rapidity, but the Magic Notes were almost invariably somewhere on the label until CBS assumed control of Columbia Records in 1939. At that point, the logo was reconfigured with two overlapping circles containing the CBS microphone and the Magic Notes. As part of the revamp, label colors and typefaces were standardized.

When Columbia introduced the long-playing record, it was heralded with another new logo, "Lp," enveloped in yet another circle. After Neil Fujita took over Columbia's art department in 1954, LP jacket designs became strikingly innovative, and it was possibly Fujita himself who revamped the LP label design. From 1955, "Columbia" was in serif lettering and the Magic Notes finally gave way to the Walking Eye. The CBS network had introduced its own "eye" trademark in October 1951. Designer William Golden based it on the hex symbols drawn on Amish barns to ward off evil spirits, and it was Golden who introduced Fujita to Columbia's Goddard Lieberson. Some say the legs on the modernist Walking Eye depict a stylus; others see it as a design element to differentiate it from CBS's eye. On LP labels, the new logo appeared three times to the left and three times to the right of the label copy. The "6 Eye" design was standard until 1962 when one "eye" was positioned to the left of the catalog number and another to the right of the record number. "Stereo" (and later "Mono") was prefixed and suffixed by another Columbia slogan, "360 Sound."

Overseas, EMI owned the name "Columbia" for most countries except Japan, and persevered with the Magic Notes until it discontinued Columbia in 1972. In 1987, Sony acquired Columbia Records from CBS and then acquired the overseas rights to the Columbia name and trademarks from EMI. Currently, Sony employs adaptations of old logos and trademarks on both new and reissued records, underscoring its connection to Columbia's rich history.

Colin Escott

A progression of the Columbia Logo

becoming a part of American life, and Easton and Columbia deserved by far the most credit. But new and grave challenges soon arose that eventually drove Easton to a near-fatal nervous breakdown.

The Rivalry Begins: A New Format, the Birth of the Victor Talking Machine Company, and Columbia's Two-Sided Disc

The first hurdle Columbia faced involved shifting from cylinder recordings to discs. In 1887, a young Prussian immigrant named Emile Berliner had applied for (and, four years later, secured) a patent on a hand-cranked machine he called a "gramophone." Berliner's invention played recordings that had been photoengraved on one side of a plate-glass disc covered in lampblack and fixed with varnish. This was the first flat disc record, which he also patented and called a "phonoautogram." Berliner's early discs introduced a new level of sound distortion, and their tonal quality was thus inferior at first to the best of the cylinders. But Berliner, who always envisaged his invention as a medium of home entertainment, worked steadily on improvements, and thanks to a forceful advertising campaign the gramophone began winning customers as the century came to an end.

For music lovers, the discs not only contained as much as 50 percent more music than the cylinders and were much easier to store but also sounded as good as or even better than the cylinders. The discs' greatest comparative advantage, though, lay in how they were manufactured. In 1901–1902, both Edison and Columbia introduced the new cylinder mold process, which turned out duplicate cylinders by pouring wax into master metal molds—a far more efficient method than recording the cylinders one by one, but still cumbersome and time-consuming. By then, though, thousands of discs could be pressed relatively rapidly from a single metal master. As the demand for recorded music for private entertainment soared, disc recording became practically mandatory. Berliner's invention made it possible for recording to become a major part of the music industry's emerging mass market.

Easton needed to find ways for Columbia to manufacture its own discs and graphophones that could play them without violating Berliner's patents, and he had no qualms about being devious. The main difficulty lay with discs, as selling recordings had become Columbia's bread and butter. Columbia's attorney, Mauro, helped to work out a partnership with a former Berliner employee, Joseph Jones. Columbia's critics would charge that Jones had absconded with some improvements involving electroplated wax discs that he had developed while working for Berliner and then cofounded an independent company and applied for his own patents. But whatever the truth was, as early as 1899, even before Jones won the patent for his wax disc, Columbia was surreptitiously distributing red shellac disc records, in conjunction with Jones, under the American Talking Machine label. The following year, Columbia began selling discs made by Zon-O-Phone Records of Camden, New Jersey, through its own dealer network. Thereafter, Columbia joined with the Burt Company of Millburn, New Jersey, primarily a maker of billiard balls and poker chips, to form the Globe Record Company, which produced 7-inch discs under the Climax label. Finally, late in 1901, the courts awarded Jones his wax disc process patent, and in 1902, having taken over the Burt firm and moved it to Bridgeport, Columbia began manufacturing discs under its own label.

Events seemed to be moving in Columbia's direction. Berliner's American firm, which had made great strides in the 1890s, was forced to suspend operations in 1900 as a result of costly litigation with a former sales agent. Edison, who had returned to the field with his National Phonograph Company in 1896, had surpassed Columbia in the field of wax cylinders and appeared to be flourishing, but cylinder recording was becoming outdated. Furthermore, Easton had advanced abroad as well as at home when American Graphophone organized a separate English branch, Columbia Graphophone Ltd., in London in 1899, which in turn established trademarks across Europe in the name of its American parent company. But the American Graphophone-Columbia company could not afford complacence.

"Music on both sides, two records for a single price . . . no other record is worth considering."

Columbia advertisement

Emile Berliner

Columbia advertisement for Double-Disc Records

COLUMBIA
DOUBLE~DISC RECORDS

MUSIC ON BOTH SIDES

MUSIC ON BOTH SIDES

Columbia *Double*-Disc Records! Music on *both* sides! A different selection on *each* side!

And *both* for 65 cents—practically the price of *one*—32½ cents for each selection! They may be played on *any disc machine*, no matter what make, and they give you *double value for your money*, plain as daylight—better surface, better tone and far greater durability. If you have not heard a Columbia Record issued during the last year and a half, don't say that you know what your talking machine can do. The present Columbia process of recording produces a *naturalness* and *roundness* and *perfection* of tone that is positively unequalled in any other. Send 65 cents for a sample and a catalog and the name of our dealer.

Columbia *Double*-Disc Records! Double discs, double quality, double value, double wear, double everything except price! Don't put your record money into any other!

COLUMBIA PHONOGRAPH CO., Gen'l, Box 215, Tribune Bldg., N.Y.

Prices in Canada plus duty—Headquarters for Canada—264 Yonge Street, Toronto, Ont. Dealers wanted—Exclusive selling rights given where we are not properly represented. Creators of the Talking-Machine Industry. Pioneers and Leaders in the Talking-Machine Art. Owners of the Fundamental Patents. Largest Manufacturers of Talking-Machines in the World.

In October 1901, Berliner's engineer Eldridge Johnson, who had bought the rights to Berliner's patents and combined them with his own, organized the Victor Talking Machine Company. Soon thereafter, Johnson boldly raised production levels at Victor's factory in Camden, New Jersey, operating around the clock, seven days a week, hoping to manufacture on average more than two hundred gramophones daily.

Victor also scored a marketing coup with its new trademark. As a result of Johnson's ties with Berliner, Victor enjoyed close ties with the Gramophone Company, Ltd., founded in London in 1897 as the English affiliate of Berliner's company. One of the Gramophone Company's directors had spotted a painting by the artist Francis Barraud, showing the artist's brother's terrier, Nipper, listening to a cylinder phonograph. Revised to have a disc gramophone painted over the cylinder machine, the painting became the basis for Gramophone's "His Master's Voice" logo, to which Victor, as a result of its agreements with the company, enjoyed full usage rights in the United States. The logo was an instant success and would endure as one of the most effective commercial trademarks in modern history. Soon thereafter, Columbia would devise its own "Magic Notes" trademark (later "Note the Notes"), which was bold and effective but not nearly as powerful as Nipper and the gramophone.

Victor would remain Columbia's archrival for decades to come, an important theme for most of Columbia's history. Victor established its reputation first and foremost as the record industry's prestige label, catering to refined and discriminating tastes as well as to the general record-buying public. As early as 1902, discs had overtaken cylinders as the preferred format among more sophisticated and affluent purchasers. (By now, Columbia was selling its cylinders for twenty-five cents apiece, whereas the cheapest of Victor's single-sided records cost fifty cents.) And, although Victor would always record a great deal of popular material, it excelled at winning the upscale market. In order to keep up, in 1903, Columbia launched an ambitious Grand Opera Series featuring celebrity artists like the Austrian contralto Ernestine Schumann-Heink and the Italian baritone Giuseppi Campanari, both of the Metropolitan Opera. Only a few weeks later, though, Victor began importing and marketing the Gramophone Company's Red Seal records of premier classical performers, including the greatest opera star of the era, Enrico Caruso. Soon after that, Victor began making its own Red Seal recordings and signed Caruso and other standouts to its own contracts. With Caruso and the rest of the Red Seal series performers in its catalog, Victor secured a position of artistic excellence that no other company could match.

Victor's aura of refinement was not limited to its records. In 1906, the company introduced a new gramophone, the "Victrola," with its horn placed inside the player, which turned an ungainly contraption into a compact and attractive home furnishing. (One Victor Company executive stipulated that "ladies did not like mechanical looking things in their parlor.") A new Victrola ranged in price from $22 to $100—more expensive than other standard phonograph models at the time but inexpensive enough that Victor temporarily killed off Columbia's disc-playing graphophone sales.

With Edison commanding most of the cylinder business and Victor seizing most of the disc player market, Columbia was caught in a squeeze. Easton reorganized the firm once again, establishing a new department devoted solely to manufacturing and selling graphophones as dictation machines. But a financial panic in 1907 plunged the nation's economy into a depression that devastated the recording business and prompted firings at Columbia. Easton, tormented by a multitude of pressures, started to go to pieces. In 1908, he apparently tried to commit suicide by jumping off a commuter train to New York. Although the incident was blamed on an attack of vertigo and then hushed up, Easton retreated into convalescence, sidelining him for several months.

Just before the financial panic hit, John Philip Sousa raised a different set of difficulties for the entire recording industry. Columbia had already suffered a blow when Sousa and his private band—which Sousa had organized when he stepped

"The menace of mechanical music"

John Philip Sousa denouncing recorded music over live performances

Ernestine Schumann-Heink

Pablo Casals

down from the Marine Band in 1892 and which had recorded for Columbia in the late 1890s—began recording with Victor in 1900. Now, Sousa denounced what he called "the menace of mechanical music." He complained bitterly that record companies were storing up "canned music" (a term Sousa apparently coined), thereby stealing the audiences for live concerts, including the Marine Band's shows, without sharing profits with the composers.

Sousa expressed concern that ordinary people would cease to sing on their own, which had been a great national pastime, and that this would lead to a decline in the nation's culture and physique. ("Then what of the national throat?" Sousa wrote. "Will it not weaken? What of the national chest? Will it not shrink?") He also fretted over the inferiority of recorded music to live performances. Sousa's complaints raised basic questions about the very meaning of music, and whether mechanical reproduction diminished or even destroyed the human pleasures of performing and listening. But his commercial concerns were paramount. Sousa duly joined with the popular operetta composer Victor Herbert to head a lobby that, in 1909, persuaded Congress to enact legislation that awarded composers and publishers a royalty of two cents per copy of all recordings. This reform, without endangering the recording companies, helped correct a glaring inequity in the music industry.

Columbia did manage some important feats in these years, spurred by the competition with Victor. In 1907, in response to the Victrola, the company introduced its own updated machine, the "Grafonola," with an inside horn and adjustable front louvers. Also in 1907, the two companies reached an agreement to pool their patents in order to avoid costly future litigation. More important, during Easton's absence, Columbia completed development of a new doubled-sided record model, suited to both its ten-inch and twelve-inch discs. "Music on *both* sides, two records for a single price . . . *no other record is worth considering*," Columbia's advertisements blared. The public responded eagerly.

The double-sided discs, which were the first records to feature the Magic Notes logo, probably saved Columbia from failing during the depression of 1907–1908. Victor reacted furiously, claiming that Columbia was disrupting the recording business with a gimmick that the public neither needed nor wanted. Unable to concede defeat gracefully, Victor's lawyers concocted a lawsuit by buying up a dubious 1904 patent for double-faced discs and then taking Columbia to court for infringement. But the suit failed, and Victor had to rush to begin pressing its own double-sided records. Victor's overall sales declined in 1909 amid the double-sided disc furor, and it only gradually recovered in 1910 and 1911. It is quite possible that Columbia's sales matched or even surpassed Victor's temporarily during these years. Certainly, though, Columbia's innovation triumphed in the long run, as two-sided records (and, in time, two-sided cassette tapes) remained the norm for the recording industry for the next eighty years.

Bert Williams

Columbia also enjoyed a major success on the artistic front in 1906, when it picked up from Victor the talented black musical and comedy star Bert Williams. Born in Nassau, the Bahamas, in 1874, to a couple of mixed African and European descent, Williams moved with his family back and forth to the United States, before winding up in Riverside, California, where he graduated from high school. He then entered show business in a minstrel troupe in San Francisco and eventually teamed up with George Walker, another young performer, billing themselves as "Two Real Coons." Walker would be his straight man, a slick, proud black dandy, the perfect foil for Williams's "dumb coon" character. Williams, who was light-skinned, appeared in blackface, a common device among black performers that was both an extension and an inversion of the familiar white minstrels' act. Williams was especially adept at using the black-on-black routine—in which a genuine black man stood behind the makeup—to befuddle the racism that lay at the heart of so much American popular entertainment at the end of the nineteenth century and the beginning of the twentieth.

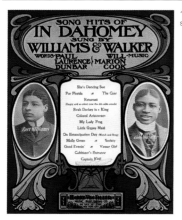

"In Dahomey" sheet music

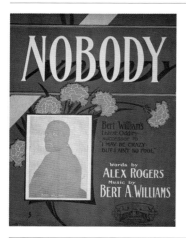

"Nobody" sheet music

Bert Williams

Walker and Williams went on to produce a succession of hit vaudeville shows, including, in 1901, *In Dahomey*, with music by the classically trained composer Will Marion Cook and lyrics by one of the seminal African American poets of the era, Paul Laurence Dunbar. That same year, the duo recorded several sides for Victor, including a rendition of Williams's composition, "Good Morning, Carrie," which numerous other artists also covered. Presumably because the records were made before disc-manufacturing methods were improved, Victor pressed only a limited number of copies and soon dropped Walker and Williams's recordings from its catalog. In 1906, though, the partners affirmed their talents when they appeared in a new show, *Abyssinia*, which was full of fine songs that broke with the usual racist conventions. Columbia stepped into the breach and signed the duo, and Williams's star would shine brightly (before and after he went solo in 1909) for more than a decade to come.

One of the songs Williams performed in *Abyssinia*, "Nobody," which he cowrote with his frequent collaborator Alex Rogers, became a top seller and served Williams as his signature number for the rest of his career. Half sung and half spoken, Williams's rendition beautifully captured the song's delicate mix of sadness and wit:

> *When life seems full of clouds and rain,*
> *And I am filled with naught but pain,*
> *Who soothes my thumping, bumping brain?*
> *[pause] Nobody . . .*
>
> *I ain't never done nothin' to Nobody.*
> *I ain't never got nothin' from Nobody, no time.*
> *And, until I get somethin' from somebody sometime,*
> *I don't intend to do nothin' for Nobody, no time.*

The recording would remain a strong seller in Columbia's catalog into the 1930s. Despite Columbia's standout success with Williams, though, the intense competition with Victor during the first years of the new century continued, and Victor was winning the fight. In one telling example, the most admired stars Columbia had signed for its Grand Opera Series in 1903, including Ernestine Schumann-Heink and Giuseppi Campanari, soon switched to Victor's Red Seal series. Still, Columbia did not give up the ghost. Early in 1911, the Scottish operatic soprano Mary Garden—whose acting abilities and nuanced use of vocal color earned her the moniker "the Sarah Bernhardt of opera," and whose work at the Manhattan Opera House and with the Chicago Grand Opera Company had made her a celebrity in America—recorded selections from *La Traviata* as well as old popular favorites like "Comin' Thro' the Rye." The young genius cellist Pablo Casals, who first recorded in 1911, was aligned with Columbia by 1915, an association that would last for the rest of Casals's long career.

On the popular side, performers like the prolific baritone Harry McClaskey (who performed as Henry Burr) had a good measure of success with Columbia. McClaskey performed as a member of the Columbia Male Quartet, which recorded, among other standards, "Let Me Call You Sweetheart." In 1911, the veteran "coon" singer Arthur Collins, who had had a number of hit cylinder songs with Edison's National Phonograph Company, teamed with Byron Harlan, and recorded Irving Berlin's new song "Alexander's Ragtime Band" for Columbia. The recording became an instant musical sensation even though its unsyncopated rhythm had nothing to do with ragtime.

Columbia's continuing efforts to promote its two-sided discs led to some wildly successful releases, including an inexpensive "demonstration" record in 1913, which featured on one side a spoken pitch for the two-sided format and on the other a recording of Henry Burr (McClaskey) singing "Good Night, Little Girl, Good Night." Later reports claimed that this recording sold three to five million copies. If true, the historian Tim Brooks notes, this "would surely make it the biggest selling record during the first half century of the phonograph."

Columbia Grafonola advertisement featuring Campanari

"Alexander's Ragtime Band" sheet music

Mary Garden as Thaïs

They All Sing

Ponselle
The supreme dramatic soprano of the Metropolitan Opera Company, New York.

Hackett
The great Metropolitan Opera Company tenor, known throughout the civilized world.

© Mishkin, N. Y.

Stracciari
The unexcelled baritone who has sung with all the greatest opera companies.

© Mishkin, N. Y.

Romaine
The Metropolitan Opera Company soprano whom London and Paris have acclaimed.

© Mishkin, N. Y.

Barrientos
The world-famous Spanish coloratura soprano of the Metropolitan Opera Company.

© Mishkin, N. Y.

More Exclus.

Operatic
Baklanoff
Garden
Gordon
Lazaro
Macbeth
Mardones
Rothier

Concert
Farrar
Gates
Graveure
Lashanska
Maurel
Meader
Nielsen
Seagle

New Columbia Reco the 10th

COLUMBIA GRAP
Ca

Columbi

Exclusively for

Columbia Artists

Instrumentalists

Eddy Brown
Casals
Grainger
Hofmann
Jacobsen
Seidel
Ysaye

Miscellaneous

Harry C. Browne
Guido Deiro
Fisk University Quartette
Yvette Guilbert
Fred Hughes
Marconi Brothers
Paulist Choristers
Frank Tinney

*at all Columbia Dealers'
every Month*

COMPANY, New York
Toronto

© Strauss Peytonke

© Apeda, N. Y.

© White, N. Y.

Harry Fox

The greatest jazz com-
edian who ever jollied
you in a song.

Al Jolson

The funniest black-
face comedian who
ever sang on the
American stage.

Nora Bayes

The most rollicking
comedienne who ever
rocked the house with
laughter.

© White, N. Y.

Bert Williams

By far the best colored
comedian who ever sang
a comic song

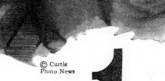

© Curtis
Photo News

Van and Schenck

The inspired singers who
mix melody with happy
mirth.

a Records

Edison Declines to Merge

These successes helped Columbia to turn a profit—its recorded earnings in 1910 exceeded a half million dollars—even though Victor boasted earnings ten times greater. Edward Easton, who had temporarily recovered his faculties and returned to the helm, duly approached Edison's National Phonograph, the lagging third company, with a merger proposal late in 1911. Easton stated that he had lost interest in the recording business, and his idea made obvious commercial sense. A merger would allow Edison to cut costs while attaching Edison's name recognition and technical expertise to Columbia's resources. Edison still sold cylinders, whereas Columbia's main business was now in discs; a combined company would cover both recording methods and be better positioned to battle Victor. Besides, as the Edison company's president Frank L. Dyer bluntly told his boss, "we cannot disguise the fact that our phonograph business is in a most unhealthy and hazardous condition."

But Edison, who had never truly warmed to recording music, still resented what he considered Easton and Columbia's vicious efforts to undercut his patents, and he never seriously considered the offer. By turning Easton down, the aging inventor all but ensured that the recording industry would largely be left to Columbia and Victor. "He would run his own company his own way," Tim Brooks writes of Edison, "eventually, into the ground." Less than two years later, Columbia Phonograph underwent a further reorganization that left its old partner company, American Graphophone, on the brink of dissolution, further paving the way for Columbia's future as a maker almost exclusively of entertainment records.

During the years immediately prior to the entry of the United States into World War I in 1917, Columbia's music program survived chiefly on its popular music titles. The label's all-purpose orchestra and band leader, Charles A. Prince, enjoyed success with medleys of patriotic tunes as well as recordings of instrumental "dance" versions of hit songs like "Glow Worm." Columbia also cashed in on a popular craze for Hawaiian music that began around 1915, issuing records by artists like the husband-and-wife team of Louise and Ferara, and the Toots Paka Hawaiian Company. And during that same decade, Columbia scored another triumph in its continuing rivalry with Victor—indeed, one of the greatest triumphs in its entire history—when it signed the rising Jewish immigrant belter of American song and the leading blackface singer in the county, Al Jolson.

Al Jolson and W. C. Handy

Born in Lithuania in 1886 as Asa Yoelson, Jolson, the son of a cantor, had earned nickels singing on street corners as a boy in Washington, DC. He started out in show business at age sixteen, performing as part of an Indian medicine sideshow in Walter L. Main's famous three-ring circus. After earning a reputation on the minstrel stage and in vaudeville as "The Blackface with the Grand Opera Voice," Jolson opened in *La Belle Paree*, his first Broadway musical revue, at the Winter Garden Theater in 1911, after which Victor released his first recording, of George M. Cohan's "The Haunting Melody." His performances in two more shows at the Winter Garden the following year made Jolson New York's latest young sensation. Just then, in 1913, Columbia snatched him away from Victor and released his rendition, accompanied by Charles Prince's Orchestra, of "You Made Me Love You," a new song from his latest show, *The Honeymoon Express*, that would become an American standard. The record began a string of hits on Columbia, including "Rock-a-Bye Your Baby with a Dixie Melody" and "April Showers," that continued until 1923, when Jolson switched to Brunswick.

During his decade with Columbia, Jolson was almost certainly the label's single most successful artist. Neither modest nor subtle, he happily proclaimed himself "the World's Greatest Entertainer." Self-promotion aside, Jolson brought to his recordings, as he did to the vaudeville stage and later to movies, an overpowering

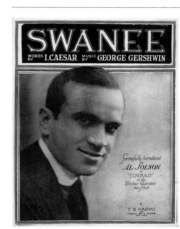

"Swanee" sheet music

Al Jolson in
The Jazz Singer

Marquee for
The Jazz Singer at
Warners' Theatre,
New York

Previous page:
"They All Sing Exlusively for
Columbia Records" advertisement

Al Jolson

yet versatile singing style, matched with an uncanny charisma. Yet today, Jolson—who is best remembered for his starring role in the first major "talkie" film, *The Jazz Singer*, in 1927—evokes reflexive scorn for his blackface performances. The reaction is understandable but also simplistic.

Coming after Williams, Jolson explored anew what the critic James Miller has called blackface's "racially coded fantasies" of freedom and spontaneity. Performing in blackface allowed Jolson to perform with a passion and kinetic intensity that was still thought unseemly for white performers, much as it had for minstrels since the 1830s. Yet Jolson's songs contained none of the contemptuous mockery of blacks found only a decade earlier in George Washington Johnson's "The Whistling Coon" and "The Laughing Song." The lyrics to some of his most popular numbers, such as "You Made Me Love You," have no racial references at all, and even on later minstrel-style hits, such as "My Mammy," Jolson's intonation, although imitative, did not come across in a derisive "darkie" dialect. Indeed, some listeners at the time discerned in Jolson's singing a hybrid of black secular and Jewish liturgical styles. The playwright Samson Raphaelson, who would go on to write the play on which *The Jazz Singer* was based, heard Jolson at the Winter Garden in 1916 and thought, "My God, this isn't a jazz singer. This is a cantor!"

Released several years before the first popular recordings of jazz and blues, Jolson's early records also introduced most of his white listeners to an unfamiliar rhythmic energy. Paradoxically, by exploiting an old racial caricature, Jolson's recordings helped to reduce the cultural divide.

Building on Bert Williams's success, meanwhile, Columbia released some work by a few important African American artists. Williams himself continued to turn out witty hits like "You're on the Right Road but You're Going the Wrong Way." Columbia also began what would become a long though sporadic association with the composer and bandleader W. C. Handy. Eventually celebrated widely, if fancifully, as "the Father of the Blues," Handy had begun to make his national mark in 1909, when he moved his band from Clarksdale, Mississippi, to Memphis and wrote a campaign song for Edward H. Crump, a local mayoral candidate who courted black voters. Handy later rewrote this song as "Memphis Blues." The publication of the sheet music for "Memphis Blues" in 1912 is credited as the inspiration for the invention of the foxtrot, by the fabulously successful white New York City dance team Vernon and Irene Castle—the latest cultural breach of the color line.

Handy went on to compose "Yellow Dog Blues" and the music for "The Girl You Never Have Met." Those titles, along with a disc of "Memphis Blues," accounted for the lion's share of the nearly $40,000 in author royalties that Columbia paid Handy in 1915 alone. Then, in 1917, Handy recorded ten sides for Columbia with his Orchestra of Memphis, including his own "Ole Miss Rag." The label eagerly promoted these records by proclaiming "W. C. Handy Week" throughout the United States. Meanwhile, the Castles' enthusiasm and commercial savvy had sparked a dance craze that Columbia exploited with several foxtrot recordings by Charles Prince. In 1917, after initial prompting by Al Jolson, Columbia added to its catalog what would prove a harbinger of music and African American artists to come: "Indiana" coupled with "The Darktown Strutters' Ball," as performed by a group of white musicians, the Original Dixieland Jass Band.

A different vein of African American music, and of the black historical experience, came to Columbia in 1915 when the label lured the Fisk Jubilee Singers away from Victor. First organized in 1871 at Fisk University in Nashville—an institution founded five years earlier to provide higher education to former slaves—the group originally consisted of Fisk students who specialized in spirituals (or so-called "sorrow songs"), which they sang on tours to raise funds for the financially strapped school. Now, more than forty years later, an updated version of the singing group carried forward the musical legacy of the Reconstruction era, when southern blacks' hopes for social and political advance had briefly blossomed. Along with Bert Williams's records and W. C. Handy's, the singers' Columbia discs, which included recordings of "Swing Low, Sweet Chariot" and "Steal Away to Jesus," offered another example of black performance that contradicted the "coon" song conventions.

"The Memphis Blues" sheet music

Vernon and Irene Castle

W. C. Handy

The Founding Era Ends

Columbia's broad musical tastes did not render the label immune to the super-patriotism and anti-German fervor that gripped the country once the United States actually entered World War I in April 1917—the fervor that famously caused the renaming of sauerkraut as "victory cabbage." Until then, Columbia and its subsidiaries were happily recording for the German market, both in the United States and Germany, including songs aimed specifically at German war widows. Suddenly, in April 1917, works of Bach, Beethoven, Brahms, and Wagner (performed mainly by instrumental soloists such as the violinist Francis Macmillan, or star vocalists like Swedish American diva Olive Fremsted) disappeared from the catalog. In their place, interestingly, Columbia offered an expanded range of non-German popular ethnic music, including Greek, Spanish, and Polish music, released on a new green label line. Columbia took special advantage of its proximity to Manhattan's Lower East Side to record Yiddish performers, klezmer bands, and cantors, including "the Jewish Caruso," Josef Rosenblatt. In America—or, at any rate, at Columbia—the Jews temporarily supplanted the Germans.

Fortunately for the established firms, including Columbia, the war stimulated consumer demand for lighthearted entertainment that would distract listeners from the worries of war, as well as patriotic music, so there was enough business to go around. (Portable phonographs even turned up on the battlefronts in Europe, bringing the troops some musical relief from the boredom and dread of trench warfare.) But a number of new recording and manufacturing companies also suddenly appeared, including the Sonora, Aeolian, Gennet, Vocalion, and Brunswick labels. (One of the new companies, OKeh Records, originally founded in 1915 as the American representative of the fast-growing Lindström Record group of Germany, would prove particularly important to Columbia over the coming years.) This new competition and the wartime mobilization were not the only changes Columbia would have to weather in the second decade of the twentieth century.

In 1915, the troubled Edward Easton succumbed to his demons for the last time and he died in a private asylum at age fifty-nine. Although his eldest son, Mortimer, served on the company's board of directors, he never carried much weight. The new president, Philip T. Dodge—brought to Columbia, it appears, by a business associate who had been one of the original investors in American Graphophone—was an aggressive and capable industrialist who had previously run the Mergenthaler Linotype company and, in 1914, rescued International Paper from financial collapse. As soon as Dodge took over at Columbia, labor strife at the Bridgeport factory led to a two-week closure, before the workers, affiliated with the American Federation of Labor, finally won an eight-hour day. Two years later, at the end of 1917, the new management, faced with a wartime shortage of materials, collapsed American Graphophone into the Columbia Graphophone Manufacturing Company.

The last remaining business and personal ties to the original firm had dissolved. Columbia had even moved its studio and executive offices, in 1913, to the elegant Woolworth Building skyscraper on lower Broadway, then the tallest building in America—a far cry from the brownstone in Washington, DC, where the label had started out. The founding era of Edward Easton was over; Columbia had survived its birth pangs and pioneered the field of musical recording. But new challenges just ahead included one that many feared would ruin the entire commercial recording business: the advent of radio.

Woolworth Building, New York postcard

Advertisement for Columbia Graphophone Company

The Original Dixieland Jass Band

Music Played at the White House By the President's Band.

List of Records by the U. S. Marine Band OF WASHINGTON, D. C.

Now in stock and for sale at wholesale and retail by the

COLUMBIA PHONOGRAPH CO.,
627 E Street, N. W.

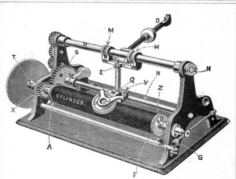

Пластинки

ROUMANIAN RECORDS   COLUMBIA GRAPHOPHONE CO. NEW YORK

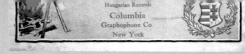

Hungarian Records
Columbia
Graphophone Co.
New York

Columbia
Servian ♫ Croatian
Records

СРПСКЕ ПЛОЧЕ
HRVATSKE PLOCE

COLUMBIA PHONOGRAPH CO. Genl

CREATORS OF THE
TALKING MACHINE INDUSTRY

OWNERS OF THE
FUNDAMENTAL PATENTS

LARGEST MANUFACTURERS
IN THE WORLD

STORES IN ALL
PRINCIPAL CITIES

DEALERS EVERYWHERE.

COLUMBIA
GOLD MOULDED
RECORDS

GRAND PRIX   DOUBLE GRAND PRIZ
PARIS 1900   ST. LOUIS 1904

CYLINDERS
1906

Columbia
Grafonola

COLUMBIA

Won the First Prize at St. Louis

The *Columbia Graphophone* was awarded the GRAND
PRIZE over all the talking machines at the ST. LOUIS EXPOSI-
TION. This is the first prize and the highest award given. The
Columbia was also awarded the Grand Prize at Paris in 1900.
This proves that the *Columbia* is the best talking machine.
It is also the greatest musical instrument in the World.

Columbia Phonograph Co.
231 North Howard Street
BALTIMORE, MD.

GOLD MOULDED
25 COLUMBIA 25
CENTS   ## RECORDS.   CENTS

We lead. Others attempt to follow.

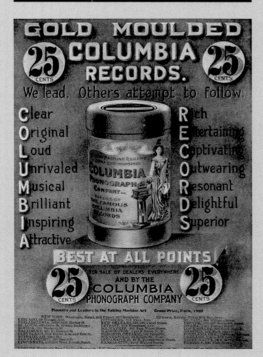

Clear   **R**ich
Original   **E**ntertaining
Loud   **C**aptivating
Unrivaled   **O**utwearing
Musical   **R**esonant
Brilliant   **D**elightful
Inspiring   **S**uperior
Attractive

BEST AT ALL POINTS

FOR SALE BY DEALERS EVERYWHERE.
AND BY THE
25   COLUMBIA   25
CENTS   PHONOGRAPH COMPANY   CENTS

Pioneers and Leaders in the Talking Machine Art   Grand Prize, Paris, 1900

Columbia
Indestructible
Cylinder
Records

Columbia
Records
FOR
Graphophones
and Phonographs

1898

DESTROY ALL PREVIOUS LISTS.

The
GRAPHOPHONE

1902

HAN

Columbia
Double-Disc

COLUMBIA

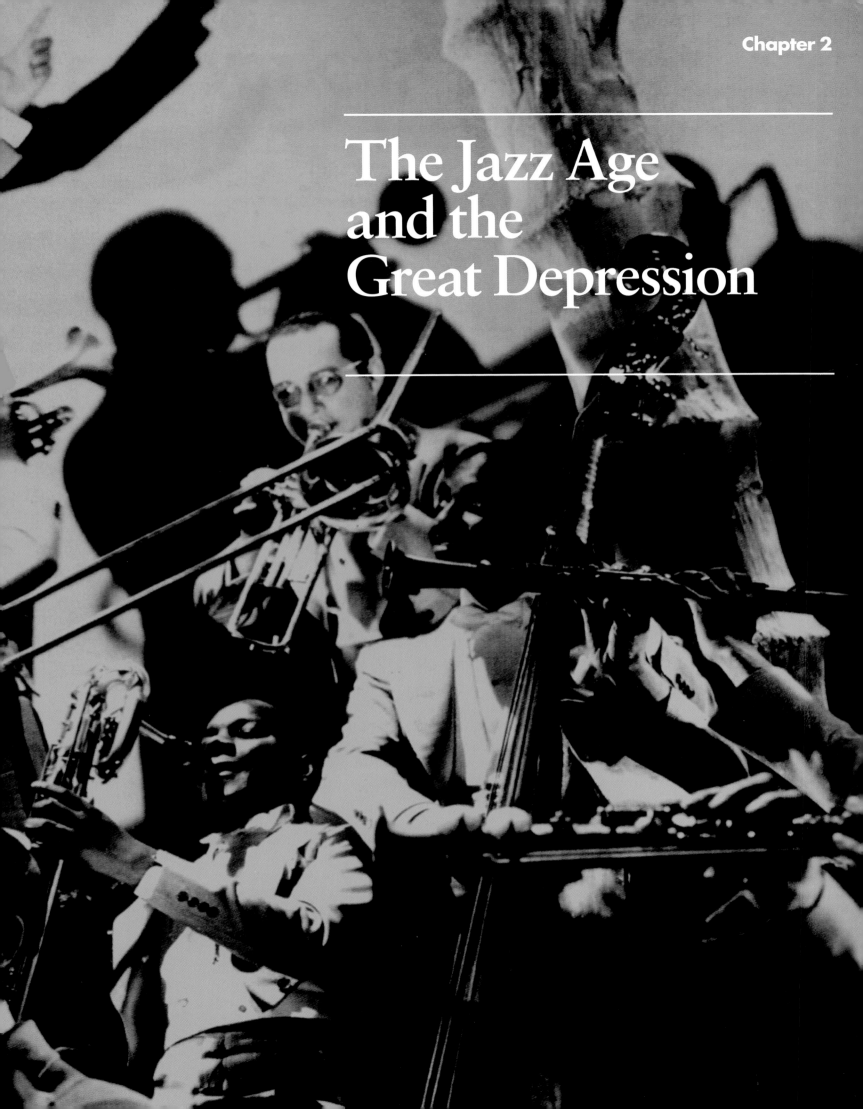

The Jazz Age and the Great Depression

The conclusion of World War I brought Columbia bright hopes in the very short run. Record sales were strong amid a brief postwar economic boom, and the label began signing new artists, classical as well as popular. Yet even then, the company continued to lag behind Victor. The story of Rosa Ponselle was a case in point. Ponselle, a young woman from Meriden, Connecticut, had an untrained but opulent soprano voice that had carried her from vaudeville to a stunning, historic debut with the Metropolitan Opera, opposite Enrico Caruso, in *La Forza del Destino* in November 1918. At the coaxing of her manager, Ponselle immediately signed with Columbia, for whom she recorded her first release only two weeks after her debut. Over the ensuing five years she would record nearly fifty more sides for the label. But Ponselle never had much enthusiasm for Columbia—one critic described her early recordings as "dutiful"—and she came to dislike the recordings' quality, saying that she sounded as if she had been "put in a box." In 1924, she departed to join Caruso on Victor, which, despite Columbia's best efforts, remained the premier label for opera and classical music in general.

Rosa Ponselle advertisement

Columbia Records

Photo by Lumiere

ROSA PONSELLE
Newest Columbia Star

In one splendid evening this young American girl of Italian parentage took her admitted place among the world-famous artists of the Metropolitan Opera Company. Rosa Ponselle makes records exclusively for Columbia. Her first four are:

La Forza Del Destino—La Vergine Degli Angeli (Verdi)
Rosa Ponselle and Chorus - - - - - 49558—$1.50
"Good-bye" (Tosti) - - - - - - - 49560—$1.50
Madame Butterfly—"Un Bel di Vedremo" - - - 49571—$1.50
Cavalleria Rusticana—"Voi Lo Sapete, O Mamma" - 49570—$1.50

Ask any Columbia Dealer to let you hear these wonderful records
COLUMBIA GRAPHOPHONE CO., NEW YORK

In the popular music field, Columbia did anticipate trends that would come to be identified with the Jazz Age of the 1920s and its exuberant, urbane rebellion against traditional cultural mores. In 1918, the Original Dixieland Jass Band left Columbia to return to Victor, the label that had released its first record. Columbia quickly tried out several other jazz bands, and scored a hit when it landed Wilbur Sweatman, the first African American to make recordings labeled as "jass" or "jazz." A performer of ragtime early in his career, Sweatman had altered his band's instrumentation dramatically in 1917, inspired by the Original Dixieland Jass Band's commercial success. After cutting six sides for Pathé, Sweatman and his Jazz Orchestra began recording for Columbia early in 1918 and spent three productive years on the label, issuing its own version of "The Darktown Strutters' Ball" along with other popular numbers like "Kansas City Blues" and "Lonesome Road."

In a very different vein, Columbia also hired the New York bandleader Ted Lewis, who began recording late in 1919. Best remembered for his catch phrase, "Is everybody happy?" Lewis would go on to become an important proponent of the big band jazz that captured much of the mainstream white audience in the 1920s; his ensemble would feature such exceptional musicians as the young clarinetists Benny Goodman, Jimmy Dorsey, and Don Murray. Al Jolson, by now Broadway's greatest star, enjoyed his latest recording smash with his rendition, recorded in January 1920, of the young composer George Gershwin's "Swanee," with lyrics by Irving Caesar. Gershwin's first hit record, "Swanee" marked the start of the brief but spectacular career of one of America's greatest composers.

By then, though, the heady postwar mood had disappeared. In 1919, a combination of labor strife and government repression of radicals in the country's first "red scare" signaled a sharp conservative political shift. The labor turmoil touched Columbia directly: amid a rash of walkouts across the country, the firm's management successfully broke a strike at the Bridgeport plant over the summer, agreeing to take back strikers without prejudice, but with wages and working conditions unchanged.

The specter of prohibition reared its head as well: in October, President Woodrow Wilson vetoed the Volstead Act, which approved measures to enforce the recently ratified Eighteenth Amendment, which banned the manufacture, import, or sale of alcoholic beverages. Congress then overrode the veto and Prohibition began. The possibility loomed that, with alcohol consumption driven to the black market, criminal elements would take over large portions of the nation's entertainment industry, including Columbia. The fears proved unfounded in Columbia's case. But in the latter months of 1920, the national economy fell into a sharp deflationary recession, which would nearly destroy the label.

"Is everybody happy?"   Ted Lewis

Commercial Radio, Jazz Fever, and Near Extinction

Record company executives blamed their new troubles less on the sweeping forces of politics, law, and economics than on the arrival of commercial radio, and with good reason. In 1920, KDKA of Pittsburgh established itself as the nation's first major commercial radio station. Over the next two years, the number of stations around the country reached two hundred, and, by the start of 1923, there were said to be 3 million radios in American homes. Sales of phonographs crashed, industry wide, from 2.2 million in 1919 to 596,000 in 1922. Sales of discs from the major labels likewise fell: Victor's business dropped 20 percent between 1923 and 1924, and another 20 percent the following year. Columbia probably fared even worse.

The radio's programming format featured live classical and popular music as well as news and drama, and in time it included more ambitious music programming. In 1925, WSM in Nashville began broadcasting its *WSM Barn Dance*, which was renamed the *Grand Ole Opry* in 1928 and went on to become an American institution. By the late 1920s, new radio networks were broadcasting programs such as *The Voice of Firestone*, bringing classical music performances to listeners around the country. The louder, cleaner, and richer sound of the radio broadcasts, with much

Wilbur Sweatman

Ted Lewis

rounder bass tones, was deeply attractive; the entire listening experience, with live announcers and artists speaking and performing, was more sociable and dynamic. And, of course, once the radio was purchased, the music was free.

The record companies claimed that existing copyright law permitted them to ban the radio stations from broadcasting commercially recorded music and, in effect, stealing their product. Records appeared with labels warning that they were not licensed for radio broadcasting, and, even though the claim lacked formal legal sanction, live music did remain the rule on radio through the 1920s. Record company executives took heart when, just as the postwar recession eased during the second half of 1921, the new mania for jazz began sweeping the country.

The jazz craze further exposed abiding cultural tensions over race. Most record buyers were white, and they could not get enough of music by white band leaders like Columbia's Ted Lewis. However, during the very early 1920s, recordings by black jazz and blues performers, including Joe "King" Oliver and Mamie Smith, also enjoyed great success, proving that whites would buy the work of black performers and also that a significant number of blacks could afford to purchase records. Buoyed by this good news, W. C. Handy's sometime collaborator Harry H. Pace founded in 1921 what would become the black-owned and directed Black Swan Records, to market African American music as a means to advance the uplift of "the race." The following year, OKeh Records hired the jazz pianist and combo leader Clarence Williams to oversee a new blues and jazz recording program. The established larger labels also began, tentatively, issuing records by African American musicians. In 1921, Victor released a medley of songs (including "I'm Just Wild About Harry") from the Broadway hit *Shuffle Along* by Noble Sissle and Eubie Blake, as performed by the pit band Eubie Blake and His Shuffle Along Orchestra.

The biracial appeal, though, disturbed Southern record distributors who, proclaiming the need to adhere to the rule of Jim Crow in every facet of life, bridled at catalogs that intermingled black and white artists. At the same time, the advent of radio heightened the record companies' interest in recording blues (as well as so-called hillbilly music) aimed specifically at black and poor white listeners who did not have radios because they did not have electricity. And so, in 1923 and 1924, just as black music was winning mass popularity, the major companies initiated their "race records" lines for black performers of blues and gospel music as well as of jazz. These delineations were supposed to help market the work of black performers to black audiences, thereby extending the mission of Pace and Black Swan Records while also reaching poorer rural blacks, but they further reinforced the color line. Columbia's new 13000 series (later changed to "14000" after superstitions about the number thirteen apparently damaged sales) became its race records line.

Paradoxically, by affirming segregation, the record companies also helped sustain certain forms of black performance. In jazz, for example, musicians, listeners, and critics alike were coming to distinguish between hot jazz, played by combos in the traditional New Orleans style, and sweet or hybrid jazz, played by the larger jazz orchestras. In clubs, cabarets, and concert halls, as well as on the radio, sweet jazz was all the rage, whereas hot jazz faded into the background. But recordings of hot jazz groups such as Clarence Williams's Blue Five proved popular enough for the record companies to continue to release them, thereby keeping alive, inside the studio, a style that would become the matrix for profound jazz innovations in the second half of the 1920s.

It would take more than the early enthusiasm for jazz, though, for Columbia to outlast the postwar slump and the competition from radio. In October 1923, after selling off its office dictation business (now called Dictaphone), the company filed for bankruptcy and was placed in receivership. Although its recording programs continued and new Columbia records appeared, the label was on the brink of extinction—when it was saved by an American émigré to Britain, Louis Sterling. An ambitious young Jewish immigrant who had been raised on New York's Lower East Side, Sterling had traveled by cattle boat in 1903 to London, where he found work at Columbia's English subsidiary and began to climb the company ladder. Sterling quickly learned everything there was to know about the recording industry; in 1909, he became chief executive of the English Columbia branch; by the 1920s,

"Mean Blues"
The Whispering Pianist
(Art Gillham)

Art Gillham

Chapter 2 : The Jazz Age and the Great Depression

he was a premier figure on the English musical scene, best known for his recordings of classical music conducted by, among others, Thomas Beecham. In 1922, when other record executives were more terrified than ever of radio, Sterling bought Columbia Graphophone Company Ltd. and its European trademarks for $500,000. At the end of 1924, he and a group of partners sailed to New York, where they purchased the remains of American Columbia for $2.5 million.

Electrical Recording and a New Intimacy

Sterling had good reason to be sanguine. He had purchased American Columbia chiefly to gain access to a revolutionary new recording process, the most important innovation in recorded sound since its invention. Beginning around 1920, engineers at the research bureau of the American Telephone and Telegraph monopoly had been pursuing innovations in electrical recording. In place of the recording funnel, diaphragm, and cutting stylus, the researchers substituted a condenser microphone, vacuum tube amplifier, and stylus controlled by electromagnets. By stimulating the stylus with electrical impulses rather than mechanically transmuted sound waves, technicians could capture high and low tones that completely eluded conventional acoustic recording equipment. No longer would recording be confined to small groups; the new electrical microphones could handle entire symphony orchestras. They could also capture subtler sounds with great fidelity.

AT&T's manufacturing division, Western Electric, offered Victor exclusive rights to the new process, but Victor, put off by the price, dithered. Sterling did not hesitate, and, in order to comply with Western Electric's demands that its licensees be American companies, he bought American Columbia. Columbia then became the first recording company to embrace electrical recording entirely. (The label did continue to use its acoustic recording machinery for a time, but strictly for producing its new lines of budget records, initially released under the Harmony label.) Showing off part of the technology's potential, Columbia released an electrical recording of "Adeste Fideles" sung by 850 members of the Associated Glee Clubs of America at the Metropolitan Opera House in 1925. That same year, the mellow-voiced Art Gillham, also known as "the Whispering Pianist," recorded Columbia's first pop release that used the new electrical process, "You May Be Lonesome."

Eventually, electrical recording would transform American musical style—a turning point in the history of American culture as well as recording. For the moment, though, Sterling's confidence in the recording business and its new sound helped to deflect the threat from broadcasting—for, instead of competing, radio and records wound up reinforcing each other's appeal. The radio programs brought listeners into a new kind of imaginary intimate contact with performers, the next best thing to being there—either in the broadcasting studio, a fictive hayloft, or some high-toned metropolitan night spot. Now, though, something resembling that intimacy could come across on records as well, as could the full musical dramatics of large ensembles. Encouraged by radio and the movies, meanwhile, a new kind of celebrity spread across the breadth of American entertainment in the 1920s—recording artists who appeared on live radio broadcasts. Radio, which was expected to kill the recording industry, became the industry's greatest publicist. Phonograph companies even began offering radio-phonograph combinations. And so, as the Twenties roared, the recording business enjoyed a rebound. Sterling's reorganized and renamed Columbia Phonograph Company, now boasting two offices in Manhattan, helped lead the way.

Expanding Popular Genres: Blues and OKeh Records, "Hillbilly" Music and Columbia

The 1920s brought an expanding awareness of musical genres to Columbia and the music-buying public that foretold the shape of things to come. On the lookout for new ventures, Columbia acquired the OKeh label along with its catalog

Radio, which was expected to kill the recording industry, became the industry's greatest publicist.

"Beale Street Blues" sheet music

Victoria Spivey

Lonnie Johnson

Charlie Poole

in 1926. After venturing into recording ethnic music for immigrant communities, OKeh had dipped into jazz with recordings like "Ja Da" in 1919, performed by the New Orleans Jazz Band featuring one Jimmy Durante. But the label had shifted direction dramatically in 1920, after its production director, Fred Hagar, and his new coproducer Ralph Peer (who had earlier worked for Columbia) supervised Mamie Smith and Her Jazz Hounds' recording of "Crazy Blues." The record became a surprise smash hit, and OKeh immediately began tapping into the market for African American blues and jazz, which led to its hiring of Clarence Williams to oversee its blues and jazz recording programs. In 1924, having already begun intensively recording black artists in New York and Chicago, OKeh began sending Peer, accompanied by two engineers and equipped with a portable recorder, on regular tours of the South in search of new talent.

The exact nature of the link between Columbia and OKeh would remain somewhat murky and even problematic until the mid 1930s. The two companies did not, for example, share master recordings of their respective artists. In their separate advertising, they appeared to be more like competitors than allies. Still, OKeh, which Columbia now owned, continued to enlarge its existing offerings of jazz, blues, and other "race record" fare, as well as recordings of white country, hillbilly, and Western music (to which Peer and OKeh had also drawn attention, in 1923, with another surprise hit, Fiddlin' John Carson's "Little Old Cabin in the Lane"). The energetic Thomas G. Rockwell, who had worked for Columbia in San Francisco, provided the impetus for OKeh's growth. Sent by Columbia to serve as general manager of OKeh's Chicago office, Rockwell began signing up new acts as well as traveling across the South in search of undiscovered talent, building on Peer's example. (Peer, who would leave OKeh in 1925 and move on to Victor, went on to oversee for Victor the famous 1927 field recording sessions in Bristol, on the Virgina–Tennessee state line, that turned up both the Carter Family and Jimmie Rodgers.)

The brash, hard-drinking Rockwell had no musical knowledge and could barely carry a tune, but he was nevertheless a discerning listener. He expanded OKeh's established 8000 "race" series to release scores of important blues and jazz records from a range of artists that included Sippie Wallace, Victoria Spivey, and Lonnie Johnson. On one of his scouting trips in 1928, he stumbled upon, in tiny Avalon, Mississippi, a splendid guitar player and singer named John Hurt, for whom he quickly arranged recording sessions in Memphis and New York. Given the name "Mississippi" John Hurt as a sales gimmick by OKeh, Hurt enjoyed a brief moment in the sun before fading back into obscurity amid the Great Depression. Decades later, during the folk revival of the 1960s, his music was rediscovered and his reputation and influence blossomed, but Rockwell and OKeh had been there first, thereby giving to Columbia the masters of Hurt's finest recordings—part of a rich vault of original material by important artists that would become one of Columbia's chief assets in future years.

All along, Rockwell's colleagues at the parent Columbia label, led by Columbia's head of artistic production, Frank Buckley Walker, were recording other exceptional singers and musicians whose work would shape American music for decades to come. A Georgia duo made up of fiddler Gid Tanner and guitarist Riley Puckett began recording for Columbia in 1924 as the label's first "hillbilly" act. Joined two years later by another fiddler, Clayton McMichen, and the banjoist Fate Norris, the group, under the name Gid Tanner and His Skillet Lickers, would produce (with various changes in personnel) more than eighty sides for Columbia, keeping alive old-time traditions that would eventually enjoy a major revival in the 1950s and 1960s. In July 1925, a string band newly signed to Columbia, the North Carolina Ramblers, featuring the hard-living vocalist and banjo picker Charlie Poole, recorded "Don't Let Your Deal Go Down Blues," which became one of the first hits in country music. Poole and his band played in a distinctive, at times quirky, style and were unequaled, the music historian Bill C. Malone writes, for their "controlled, clean, well-patterned sound." The Ramblers' subsequent career on Columbia, cut short by Poole's death from heart failure in 1931, would later become a musical template for the bluegrass vocalizing and instrumentals of Bill Monroe.

Crazy Blues

Whatever the style or quality of "Crazy Blues," it changed everything

Mamie Smith's 1920 "Crazy Blues" has been described as the first blues recording or the first commercial blues recording, or the first commercial blues recording by a black performer. Actually, it's not even Smith's first release on OKeh Records, the now-famous, although defunct, label that Columbia purchased six years later. Arguably, it's barely a blues.

As a record company, Columbia Records is 125 years old. But its identity contains a repository of other record labels, because the company grew by acquisition not only by accumulating stars, particularly in the volatile period from World War I through the Great Depression. These include OKeh, which Columbia bought outright in 1926, but also such important labels as Brunswick and Vocalion, which became linked to Columbia in the mid-1930s, and many of whose masters ended up in Columbia's vaults.

"Crazy Blues" is particularly important, even though its appearance predates Columbia's ownership of OKeh. The record was a smash hit, selling 75,000 copies in its first month, a million in the first year. Although OKeh had been threatened with a boycott by racist groups, it never happened. "Crazy Blues'" real achievement was making the market for blues plausible to record companies, including Columbia.

As blues, Mamie Smith's "Crazy Blues" isn't much, but neither are the first jazz records, and for about the same reasons. Nevertheless, this is where the record business made a leap toward the center of black taste and toward discovering that it was a mainstream taste, as well. The lineage is direct from Mamie Smith's "Crazy Blues" to Bessie Smith (no relation), whom Columbia would begin recording in 1923, and also to Victoria Spivey and from there to the entire stream of blues records. And OKeh's early forays into the blues became a literal prologue to Columbia's own blues recording. Whatever the style or quality of "Crazy Blues," it changed everything.

Dave Marsh

Mamie Smith with Willie "The Lion" Smith on piano and her Jazz Hounds

Bessie Smith and the Blues

African American blues and jazz also became Columbia mainstays, thanks again in part to the efforts of Frank Buckley Walker. In 1917, while on active service with the naval National Guard and stationed near Selma, Alabama, Walker had chanced to hear a young singer named Bessie Smith in a local gin mill. Early in 1923, Clarence Williams of the still-independent OKeh Records mentioned to Walker that he had recently worked with Smith on a recording of "I Wish I Could Shimmy Like My Sister Kate" for OKeh, but that the record had languished, unreleased. Seizing on the opportunity, Walker instantly asked Williams to look up the singer and bring her to New York so that she might record for Columbia.

Williams did not have to travel very far. Smith, who had been born in Chattanooga in 1894, was already a well-known performer on the black theater circuit by the time Walker had heard her. At the very beginning of 1923, she had joined the cast of a Broadway-bound show featuring clarinetist and saxophonist Sidney Bechet called *How Come?* A dispute with the show's producer, though, had caused Smith to leave the troupe for Philadelphia, which was where Williams found her. In February 1923, under Walker's protective wing and accompanied by Williams on the piano, Smith began cutting her first sides for Columbia Records at the label's studio on Columbus Circle. She would continue to record for Columbia into the 1930s.

Smith's debut recording for Columbia, "Downhearted Blues," written by Alberta Hunter (coupled with "Gulf Coast Blues," which Walker originally thought would be the more popular side), became an enormous hit. Today many critics regard it as one of the most important popular recordings ever made, a timeless lament of a mistreated woman, sung in an overpowering voice that is at once passionate and carefully measured. Soon thereafter, Smith recorded additional landmark songs, including "Baby, Won't You Please Come Home," and "'T'aint Nobody's Biz-ness If I Do." By the end of 1925, she had made one hundred sides, among them another enduring masterpiece, her slow, sorrowful, and majestic version of W. C. Handy's "St. Louis Blues," superbly accompanied by the young cornet player Louis Armstrong. The electrical recording techniques introduced in the mid-1920s only enhanced Smith's vocals on powerful records like "Empty Bed Blues."

Dubbed the "Empress of the Blues," Smith became the dominant female recording star of her era, at the height of her career commanding from Columbia $250 apiece for each of her usable recordings. Although she dismissed Walker as her manager in 1928, placing her financial affairs in the hands of the man she had married shortly after signing with Columbia, Walker continued to supervise her recording until 1931.

The 1920s saw the rise of numerous other female blues stars, including Ma Rainey, Mamie Smith, Sippie Wallace, and Alberta Hunter—a trend that contradicts later histories that emphasize male blues singers and guitarists. Indeed, the sales, popularity, and even pay scales of the female performers dwarfed those of most of the famous men who have since become honored as blues legends, including Blind Lemon Jefferson, Charlie Patton, and Robert Johnson. Yet even though the pool of talented blues women was large, Bessie Smith came to define female blues in those years and for decades thereafter.

Another Columbia artist, meanwhile, Ethel Waters, excelled in the blues and in a wider range of genres as well. Two years younger than Smith and raised in Philadelphia and Camden, New Jersey, Waters first gained attention in the early 1920s in Harlem, and then in Atlantic City, as the vampy songstress "Sweet Mama Stringbean." Bert Williams spotted her talent and steered her away from the independent black-owned Black Swan Records, where she was the star performer, and toward Columbia. Waters arrived at the label just as the new electronic recording techniques were being introduced. Although she was no prude when it came to singing and recording numbers like "Birmingham Bertha," Waters was also harmonically more sophisticated than most of the blues singers, which allowed her to perform many other kinds of material. Her hit recording in 1925 of "Dinah," first recorded that same year by Eddie Cantor, quickly made her a top-ranked singer

"The size of her voice was tremendous, and the spirit marvelous."

John Hammond on Bessie Smith

Bessie Smith "Race Records" flyer

Bessie Smith

at Columbia. During the ensuing decade, appearing in films and stage productions as well as on records, Waters would become a major star with her versions of what have become standards in the great American songbook, including "Heat Wave," the showstopper from Irving Berlin's 1933 Broadway stage production, *As Thousands Cheer*, as well as "Stormy Weather" and "Am I Blue?"

A few years before, far from Broadway, in a barber shop on Beale Street in Memphis in early 1929, a Columbia talent scout, whose name has been lost to posterity, heard a man-and-woman duo singing for dimes, accompanying themselves on guitar. By the summer, the two were recording in New York. Their original names, Joe McCoy and Lizzie Douglas, had been discarded in favor of their new recording label pseudonyms, Kansas Joe McCoy and Memphis Minnie. Their first record included "When the Levee Breaks," sung by Joe—the latest in a string of songs describing the catastrophic floods in Mississippi and Louisiana two years earlier. The couple would split up in 1935, but decades later, Led Zeppelin and then Bob Dylan would create their own versions of that song. Memphis Minnie would go on to become one of the foremost blues stylists of the 1930s and 1940s.

Columbia recorded important solo bluesmen as well. In 1927, Dan Hornsby, a Columbia talent scout in Atlanta, got wind of one Bob Hicks, who was working in a barbecue restaurant on the northern edge of the city. Dubbed "Barbecue Bob," Hicks saw his first recording, "Barbecue Blues," sell an astounding fifteen thousand copies. His next, "Mississippi Heavy Water Blues"—one of the first of the musical commentaries on the 1927 floods—established him as a major blues singer. Columbia had already released four sides by another important Atlanta bluesman, Peg Leg Howell, and would go on to release two dozen more. The most accomplished of the Georgia blues performers, Blind Willie McTell, recorded for Columbia and OKeh under the names Blind Sammie and Georgia Bill, most auspiciously a coupling of "Southern Can Is Mine" and "Broke-Down-Engine Blues," released in 1931. Also in Atlanta in 1931, the premier black string band, the Mississippi Sheiks, having already appeared on OKeh, recorded four sides for Columbia, including "I've Got Blood in My Eyes for You."

From Texas, came the guitar evangelist, Blind Willie Johnson. It is technically a mistake to call Johnson a blues singer, as he never recorded (and, it seems, never performed) anything but religious music. Yet Johnson's singing and playing blurred the border between spirituals and blues. His astonishing bottleneck guitar playing, in open-D tuning, set what is still the highest standard in blues performance; his finger-picking style, with its heavy bass runs, was enormously influential. Johnson's harsh-voiced way with the songs he recorded, sometimes with female vocal accompaniment—"If I Had My Way I'd Tear the Building Down," "Keep Your Lamp Trimmed and Burning," "John the Revelator"—conveyed biblical parables and prophecies with a haunting anguish. Blues music would never be the same after he came along, thanks to the thirty sides which he recorded for Columbia between 1927 and 1930.

Johnson, who was born in East Texas in 1897 and blinded as a boy, apparently hoped to become a preacher and a minister, among the few ways a sightless young black man could scratch out a living. He would never completely escape poverty, spending much of his adulthood singing and preaching in the streets of his home base, Beaumont, Texas, where he would die of malaria in 1945.

How Johnson came to record for Columbia in Dallas in early December 1927 remains a little mysterious, although the surviving evidence strongly suggests that the man responsible was Frank Walker, who by now was supervising almost all Columbia's field recording. Regardless of how it came about, Johnson plainly impressed Columbia's producer in Dallas, who had him record six sides at that first session. He impressed enough listeners for the label to invite him back into the studio in Dallas a year later, and then to successive recording dates in New Orleans and Atlanta.

Johnson also appears to have had something of a touring career as a busker. According to McTell—whom he befriended in Atlanta and whose guitar-playing style he deeply influenced—the two of them played together in "many different parts of the states and different parts of the country from Maine to Mobile Bay."

OKeh Record label

Blind Willie Johnson advertisement

Ethel Waters

But it would be through his recordings that Johnson left his legacy, not least the startling, soulful bottle-neck instrumental (with wordless, almost moaning vocal accompaniment) that he recorded at his first session, "Dark Was the Night, Cold Was the Ground"—a recording that is three and a half minutes of terrifying beauty that transcends all genres.

Louis Armstrong, Bix Beiderbecke, and Duke Ellington

What many critics consider Columbia's greatest musical contributions during the Jazz Age came via the OKeh connection. In 1925, Louis Armstrong, age twenty-four, was an enormous talent who had risen from his boyhood in the New Orleans Colored Waif's Home for Boys to play in some of the hottest jazz ensembles of the day. OKeh had noticed that some of its titles recorded by Clarence Williams's Blue Five were selling better than others; Columbia, too (which would not take over OKeh for another year), had noticed that Fletcher Henderson and His Orchestra's version of "Sugar Foot Stomp" was unusually popular. Why? Armstrong was playing on all of them.

In 1924, Armstrong had left Joe "King" Oliver's Creole Jazz Band in Chicago in favor of Henderson's New York–based ensemble, the most popular African American dance band of the day. While in New York he had also recorded with Bessie Smith. Then he returned to Chicago, where—with the encouragement of Tommy Rockwell and intense prodding from his wife, the pianist Lil Hardin Armstrong—he began recording under his own name for OKeh late in 1925. Backing him up were the combos that became commonly known as his "Hot Five" and "Hot Seven" groups. Brought together strictly for studio work, the Hot Five and Hot Seven would make a musical revolution entirely on records, unsupported by club or concert performances. The sessions affirmed that hot jazz had become relegated to the recording studio, but their success was also a breakthrough in recorded music never quite equaled since, even by the best studio bands.

The Hot Five consisted originally of Lil on piano along with three New Orleans musicians with whom Armstrong had been playing for more than a decade—Kid Ory on trombone, Johnny Dodds on clarinet, and Johnny St. Cyr on guitar and banjo. The combo continued the New Orleans jazz tradition of collective improvisation but opened up more space for Armstrong's brilliant solos, as well as for his inimitable vocalizing. One of the group's early sides, "Heebie Jeebies," recorded in February 1926, included Armstrong performing the first recorded example of "scat" singing. Armstrong did not invent the style, but after "Heebie Jeebies," the group's first popular hit, it caught on with singers and audiences—and the recording showed that Armstrong was a superb vocalist as well as a dazzling horn player. The story that Armstrong dropped his lyric sheet and had to scat instead of sing is apocryphal, but, as the jazz scholar and curator Phil Schaap observes, the performance has "the marvelous ring of spontaneous creation"—that is, of the heart and soul of jazz.

During a single week in May 1927—augmented by two, Baby Dodds on drums and Pete Briggs on tuba (and with John Thomas sitting in for Kid Ory)—the ensemble dubbed the "Hot Seven" recorded what would become twelve classics, including "Wild Man Blues" and, best of all, "Potato Head Blues." Then, in 1928, recording with a thoroughly revamped Hot Five group (actually a sextet) that featured members of the Carroll Dickerson Orchestra, including Earl "Fatha" Hines on piano, Armstrong set a new standard for virtuosity and originality in jazz, performing startling compositions like "West End Blues." Had Armstrong never recorded again after the Hot Five and Seven sessions, the critic Gary Giddens writes, "he would still be regarded as the single most creative and innovative force in jazz history."

In 1927, the great cornet player Bix Beiderbecke enjoyed what was probably the most fruitful year in his tragically foreshortened life. Having broken into the business in 1923 with the Wolverine Orchestra, with whom he recorded for

Duke Ellington

Louis Armstrong

Gennett, Beiderbecke, a native of Davenport, Iowa, spent a brief period enrolled at Iowa State University, then held intermittent jobs playing with, among other groups, the band led by the Greek-born pianist Jean Goldkette. In 1925, he recorded two songs, including his own "Davenport Blues," for Gennett, with a combo he called his Rhythm Jugglers—which included, on trombone, one Tommy Dorsey. He was on to something.

While working for Goldkette, Beiderbecke started collaborating with Frank Trumbauer, a master of the soon-to-be extinct C-melody saxophone, and Trumbauer grew to become Beiderbecke's father figure and closest friend. From the autumn of 1925 through the following spring, Beiderbecke played in a combo that Trumbauer had formed and called, somewhat grandly, Frankie Trumbauer and His Orchestra. Then, in October 1926, at New York's Roseland Ballroom, Goldkette's group, pushed by Beiderbecke's solos, bested Fletcher Henderson and His Orchestra in a legendary "battle of the bands." Beiderbecke's playing left the audience—including Henderson's musicians—astonished. "All of a sudden, comes this white boy from out west, playin' stuff all his own," Rex Stewart, Henderson's cornet player and a great admirer of Louis Armstrong's, later recalled of that night. "Didn't sound like Louis or anybody else. But just so pretty. And that *tone* he got. Knocked us all out."

A year later, under financial pressure, Goldkette disbanded his group, and both Beiderbecke and Trumbauer ended up joining Paul Whiteman and His Orchestra, in which Beiderbecke would gain his greatest public exposure both on the bandstand and on records. In the interim, though, Beiderbecke also started cutting records with smaller groups for OKeh—sessions that produced what most critics agree is his best recorded work. In February 1927, Beiderbecke took his place at OKeh's New York studio with the Trumbauer group, playing superbly on several numbers including the breathtaking, frenetic "Clarinet Marmalade," and, in a timeless take, the moderate tempo ballad "Singin' the Blues." In May, also with the Trumbauer group, Beiderbecke recorded two of his best-known solos on "I'm Coming, Virginia" and "Way Down Yonder in New Orleans," and he performed even better on the band's rendition of Hoagy Carmichael's "Riverboat Shuffle."

Beiderbecke's work for OKeh continued through the summer of 1928. In a July 5 session in Chicago, once again with the Trumbauer orchestra, Beiderbecke played strongly on two songs, "Bless You! Sister" and "Dusky Stevedore." Two days later, the latest permutation of a group formed a year earlier, Bix Beiderbecke and His Gang, recorded two sides, including "Ol' Man River," from Jerome Kern's and Oscar Hammerstein II's new Broadway musical, *Show Boat*. Beiderbecke and this band would record their final side for OKeh, "Rhythm King," in New York in late September. But by then Beiderbecke's inner demons were starting to get the better of him, and he soon began to succumb to the alcoholism that would kill him three years later at age 28.

Beiderbecke did not win much appreciation during his lifetime outside of a relatively small circle of fans and fellow musicians. Only with the publication in 1938 of Dorothy Baker's novel loosely based on his life, *Young Man with a Horn* (followed, twelve years later, by the movie version, which starred Kirk Douglas), did the Beiderbecke cult begin to emerge. Admired widely for his lyricism, Beiderbecke now ranks as a Jazz Age icon, his subtle finesse a brilliant complement to Armstrong's blasting resonance. And his enduring musical reputation stands largely on the recordings he made, over a span of eighteen months in 1927 and 1928, for OKeh Records.

Also in 1927, yet another major American artist began a long-term, on-again, off-again connection to Columbia and its associated labels. Edward Kennedy "Duke" Ellington had been a rising star for several years when he and his orchestra, the Washingtonians, recorded his "East St. Louis Toodle-Oo" for Columbia in March. Later that year, Ellington accepted an offer from Harlem's Cotton Club to become its house band (after King Oliver turned the job down). On the strength of weekly radio broadcasts from the club, aired first on New York's WHN, next on the CBS radio network, and then on the NBC network, Duke Ellington and His Cotton Club Orchestra became national favorites.

Paul Whiteman
and His Orchestra

Bix Beiderbecke

Ellington and his ensemble were just shifting from their "sweet" dance band sound to the hotter style, heavily influenced by the young trumpeter Bubber Miley, which became known as Ellington's "jungle" sound. Under a variety of names, the group recorded mainly for Victor at the end of the 1920s and the start of the 1930s. But Ellington's orchestra also completed some classic sides for OKeh, many of them under the pseudonym the Harlem Footwarmers, including "Black and Tan Fantasy" and "Mood Indigo"—numbers that would be associated with Ellington for the remainder of his career. He would continue to make recordings with Columbia, OKeh, and other labels connected with Columbia from the 1930s to the 1960s.

On the Eve of the Great Depression

By 1927, with OKeh adding income as well as excitement to the firm, Columbia was back on its feet, having just posted its first profitable year since 1920. Louis Sterling had returned to England (leaving the management in New York to now-president Harry Cox, the label's former treasurer), and there he cultivated the new Columbia Masterworks series, featuring electrical recordings of complete symphonic and operatic works by Schubert, Wagner, and others, all issued on multidisc sets. The first of the complete symphony sets appeared in grand style in 1927, a collection of all nine Beethoven symphonies, released to commemorate the one-hundredth anniversary of the composer's death. In popular music, vaudeville made itself known as well. Eddie Cantor (born Edward Israel Iskowitz on the Lower East Side), a young star in Ziegfeld's *Follies*, released in 1925 his hit number, "If You Knew Susie." Two years later, the veteran vaudeville singer Sophie Tucker's "Some of These Days," recorded with Ted Lewis and His Orchestra, became a major success. In 1929, Jimmy Durante, performing with his act Clayton, Jackson, and Durante, issued a memorable recording of "Can Broadway Do Without Me?"

The significance of Columbia's Jazz Age vaudevillians should not be slighted. There is always a danger, when looking back at any aspect of cultural history, of celebrating great artists at the expense of more popular troupers. Louis Armstrong and Bix Beiderbecke, for instance, made outstanding, innovative music in the 1920s, but their records sold modestly. The runaway seller of the decade for Columbia was recorded instead by the blackface comedy duo of Moran and Mack.

George Moran and Charles Mack, both natives of Kansas, had teamed up in 1917 and made their reputation performing in several vaudeville shows, including George White's *Scandals* and Florenz Ziegfeld's *Follies*. Working within the traditional "coon" sketch format—with the clever Mack playing off the slow-witted straight man Moran—their act was at once a throwback to the nineteenth-century minstrel stage and a model for the enormously popular *Amos 'n' Andy* series, which debuted on radio in 1928 and would remain in syndication as a television show as late as 1966. Some at Columbia thought that Moran and Mack's racial burlesque was offensive, but Louis Sterling loved them and they got their chance to record for the label. Released in 1927, *Two Black Crows, Parts I and II* sold more than a million copies, a figure that is certified by credible records in Columbia's files. The duo's follow-up recordings did nearly as well.

Listening to Moran and Mack today is a trial, in part because of the racial stereotypes and in part because of the corniness of so many of their jokes. But the act was a popular favorite—far more popular at the time than the musical intricacies of Armstrong's Hot Five and Hot Seven records, or the pathos of Bessie Smith's blues. And we should not simplify and dismiss Moran and Mack any more than we should Al Jolson (who had by now switched from Columbia to Brunswick). Their dialogue stayed away from the casual hatefulness of the old minstrel show banter. Within the old racist "coon" show format, their typical jokes used irony to poke caustic fun at the follies and injustices of the world:

MACK. On our farm, we had a thousand chickuns, an' 999 o'em laid eggs.
MORAN. What was wrong with de udder one?
MACK. Uh, he was de head man.

"... [has] the marvelous ring of spontaneous creation"

Phil Schaap on Louis Armstrong's scat performance

The Louis Armstrong Story, Louis Armstrong and His Hot Five

Previous Page:
Louis Armstrong and His Hot Five

Louis Armstrong, Bing Crosby, Frank Sinatra

These three singers, singly and all together, changed the world of popular music

Louis Armstrong, who recorded for OKeh and Columbia, did more to change popular singing than any other American. His Hot Five and Hot Seven tracks, progressive for many reasons, feature emotionally heated vocals at levels not previously heard, and mark the advent of scat singing, in which nonsense syllables replace words in a way that seems spontaneous. Armstrong also had almost as great a knack for comedy, usually comedy with teeth, as he did for joy. The combination was unprecedented and unsurpassed.

Bing Crosby, who recorded for Columbia with Paul Whiteman's band and solo for Brunswick, studied Armstrong, but his greatest achievement was his understanding of the electric microphones that appeared in the late twenties. Crosby was the first hugely popular singer who not only crooned but almost whispered, who worried not about the back rows of the theater but the erogenous zones in each individual's ear. Compared to Crosby, even the best previous crooners sound emotionally vacant, even when they're equipped with superb lyrics. Every singer after him, from Connee Boswell to Elvis Presley, including the later Armstrong, uses this innovation in ways similar to Bing.

Sinatra, who spent the first ten years of his solo career at Columbia, built something new on these foundations. Sinatra had an even more conversational tone than Crosby. More important, his Columbia records from the forties take Armstrong and Crosby's emotionalism and turn it to a darker, more fatalistic purpose, even on numbers like "Saturday Night (Is the Loneliest Night of the Week)" and "You'll Never Walk Alone." For Sinatra, it seemed, the whole world was at stake in each glance across the room, embrace, or kiss, and the outcome never escaped the shadow of doubt.

These three singers, singly and all together, changed the world of popular music, especially in America and, ultimately, worldwide.

Dave Marsh

Louis Armstrong

Here was material, the music historian Gary Marmorstein writes, that was "coated in minstrelsy but also dipped in the sly wit that black performers (notably Bert Williams) often employed to subvert the tradition."

While Moran and Mack rose to the top in the latter half of the 1920s, the new electrical recording methods began having their profound effects on musical style. The improved technology of the mid-1920s quickly became a boon to singers with weaker voices. But talented newcomers, beginning with Art Gillham, also discovered how to use the electrical microphone—first on radio, then on records—to create the warmer sound that would become known as crooning. Rudy Vallée—who worked with Victor for most of his career but recorded briefly for Columbia and its associated smaller labels in the late 1920s and early 1930s—became the first great crooner sensation with hits such as "Deep Night."

The singer and musical historian Ian Whitcomb has suggested that Vallée and the other early crooners, including Al Bowlly and Gene Austin, were the first mass-media pop idols, working with what later became a formula of "squeezing diversity through a strainer of familiarity." Vallée in turn helped inspire the young Bing Crosby, who recorded his first side, "I've Got the Girl," with vocalist Al Rinker for Columbia in 1926. Crosby returned to Columbia in 1928, singing chiefly with Paul Whiteman and His Orchestra (including Bix Beiderbecke) after Columbia temporarily stole Whiteman from Victor. A new generation of recording stars, with a style all their own, was coming to the fore.

Then, suddenly, the stock market crashed in October 1929. And the economic emergency deepend into a long and grinding depression. Columbia and the rest of the recording industry collapsed, ending the recovery that had follwed the advent of electrical recording. Radio now almost thoroughly supplanted recordings as the public's preferred form of home entertainment.

The Edison recording operation was already hampered by the old inventor's special aversion to jazz—he thought it was music for "the nuts" and likened one jazz performance to "the dying moan of dead animals." Now, the operation reverted to producing nothing but office dictation machines, Edison's original limited goal for his "baby."

Desperate to break out of the slump, Victor (which had been bought up by the Radio Corporation of America, to become RCA Victor in 1929) rushed an experiment in 1931 and 1932: the company began manufacturing records that could include up to fifteen minutes of music, to be played at the slower speed of 33⅓-rpm. Five years earlier, Edison's firm had tried a similar experiment and introduced a disc with thinner grooves that could play up to twenty minutes on each side using an improved phonograph, but the sound quality was poor and the public balked at having to buy new equipment. The new RCA Victor records sounded better than Edison's had; indeed, one report in the *New York Times* praised the tone as "incomparably fuller" than the conventional 78s. But the new records appeared as now outmoded one-sided discs on a flexible plastic that, unless played with a new lightweight needle, would be ripped to shreds after several plays. Faced with customers less willing than ever to buy any new equipment at the outset of the Depression, Victor hastily abandoned the project.

Columbia, meanwhile, was so depleted that it had to rely on England for the lion's share of its supply of new recordings. Finally, in 1931, Louis Sterling allied his Columbia Gramophone Ltd., the Columbia operation in England, with the RCA Victor-owned HMV Gramophone Ltd. to form the largest record conglomerate in the world, Electrical and Musical Industries Ltd. (EMI)—and thereby making RCA Victor part owner of American Columbia. Concerned that the merger might cause him trouble with American antitrust laws, though, and convinced that American Columbia had become dead weight, Sterling dumped the struggling firm on a banker's holding company in May 1931, which in turn sold it several months later to the Grigsby-Grunow company of Chicago, the manufacturer of Majestic radios, refrigerators, and washing machines. The label had landed in a kind of economic and financial purgatory. The Jazz Age was over and so, very nearly—once again—was Columbia.

Record sales in the United States in 1930 dropped to a total of about ten million discs.

Moran and Mack with director Richard Wallace and actor Walter Weems on the set of *Two Black Crows in the AEF*.

Sophie Tucker

Duke Ellington and His Band, Cotton Club, Harlem, New York

The Jukebox Helps Save the Day

Looking back at the Depression era forty years later, the great producer John Hammond recalled the grimness that pervaded the firm just after the precocious twenty-year-old completed his first recording for Columbia: "In 1932, Columbia Records was selling about one hundred thousand units a year, hardly as much as a single hit record sells today. Labels included Columbia Masterworks for classical music, Columbia for popular records, and OKeh for country music and anything by and for the Negro." Columbia did enjoy some success selling recordings by smooth hotel bandleaders like Guy Lombardo and Anson Weeks. And, in 1931, just before its demise, Columbia's budget label Clarion Records released "When the Moon Comes Over the Mountain," sung by Kate Smith, who would go on to have an enormous radio career. But apart from these successes, lacking the guidance of Louis Sterling, the label was drifting along through the crushing hard times. Its prospects only worsened over the coming years; in the mid-1930s, Columbia's pop program would be cut down virtually to nothing, while the Masterworks catalog would consist mainly of imports. And still, the crippled Columbia and Columbia Masterworks, informed by the blues and jazz orientation of OKeh, would survive just long enough to revive under new ownership at the end of the 1930s, after things in the recording business had taken a turn for the better. One reason for that was the growing popularity of the jukebox.

With the election of Franklin D. Roosevelt to the White House and the end of Prohibition in 1933, thousands of bars and cocktail lounges opened around the country, creating a new opportunity for providers of inexpensive recorded music. Foreshadowed by the nickel-in-the-slot cylinder machines that had helped launch the recording industry in the 1890s, the jukebox, first introduced in 1927 by the Automatic Musical Instrument Company, permitted customers to choose from a variety of selections automatically. At the same time, it brought low-cost entertainment to customers and extra profits to the saloon owners just when both were needed badly. Soon, jukeboxes could be found in diners, drugstores, pool halls, bus stations, and beauty parlors—wherever people sat down and had to wait for anything. Equipment manufacturers had to meet a new demand for improved playback needles, which could be used for hundreds of playings without having to be changed—an innovation that also enhanced home entertainment. Making the most of electrical amplification and oversized speakers, jukeboxes provided the highest-quality sound reproduction heard outside of the movie theaters.

Above all, the jukebox trade provided a ready market for the recording companies as well as a powerful promotional tool for their artists. By the mid-1940s, jukeboxes would absorb 60 percent of all the records produced in the United States. Once the entertainment trade journals *Billboard* and *Variety* began tracking jukebox sales returns, record executives and radio music producers could get a sharper bead on the public's preferences and anticipate new hit records. (Jukebox operators, *Billboard* would remark in 1941, "have a much better judgment of what the public will take to than many of the execs at the production end of the business.") Recording artists looked to the jukebox charts to discern which new song titles were catching on and might be worth covering themselves.

For Sale Again, and Going Cheap

Just as the jukebox was beginning to reinvigorate the industry, Columbia went through another change of owners. In 1934, the now-failing Grigsby-Grunow company negotiated the sale of Columbia for $75,000 to a new English firm, Decca, which specialized in producing budget records. (The price tag indicates the state of the business, coming eleven years after Louis Sterling bought Columbia for $2.5 million.) Yet when the head of Decca, E. R. Lewis, landed in New York harbor, he learned that another firm, the American Record Company, had snuck in and bought Columbia for nearly $5,000 less than the price he had offered. ARC, as the company was known,

Jukebox operators "have a much better judgment of what the public will take to."

Billboard magazine on music industry executives vs. jukebox operators

Guy Lombardo

Gene Autry with jukebox

had been formed out of a merger of several smaller companies in 1929. Headed by the cut-rate-movie entrepreneur Herbert Yates, who had purchased the firm in 1930, ARC was adept at buying up failed and failing labels and leasing portions of others. These included Brunswick (its lead label) and Brunswick's subsidiary Vocalion, both of which ARC had bought from Warner Bros. in 1931, with licenses to use the labels' names and produce records from their previously recorded masters. John Hammond later contended that Yates and ARC had been party to the original deal to buy Columbia, supposedly arranged on a 50-50 basis with Decca. But whatever the case was, the outcome infuriated E. R. Lewis, and Lewis's anger would have additional consequences for Columbia and the recording industry at large.

Yates's purchase delivered Columbia from the netherworld of Majestic refrigerators and radios into a hungry and dynamic if down-market recording consortium, whose profits came chiefly from low-priced discs sold through chain stores and to the jukebox operators. But the deal also prompted the outraged Lewis to establish an American Decca company by buying from Warner Bros. the Brunswick Radio Corporation, which owned those portions of Brunswick (including a pressing plant) not owned by or leased to ARC. Under the guidance of Jack Kapp, the former creative director at Brunswick Records, Decca slashed prices and built an all-star lineup that included Bing Crosby as well as Tommy and Jimmy Dorsey. The other record companies began to quaver.

Columbia, meanwhile, had to adjust to Herbert Yates's emphasis on minimizing costs, as well as his somewhat haphazard approach to building a catalog. As ARC's latest acquisition, Columbia was relegated mainly to overseeing the slower-selling acts like Andy Iona and His Islanders, who blended Hawaiian steel guitar sounds with big-band jazz. Then, from 1936 to 1938, the label went virtually dormant, offering no sales catalogs and hardly any new popular releases, while it issued classical titles licensed from Columbia Gramophone, Ltd. Brunswick, more than ever, would be ARC's principal label. But, even as it sat at the bottom of the heap, Columbia was surrounded by some artistic standouts, a few of them truly exceptional, who would end up gracing the label's roster in future years. It was also in the company of some enormously talented and ambitious record producers.

Thanks to a contract worked out by Duke Ellington's manager, Irving Mills, Ellington and his orchestra recorded almost exclusively for Brunswick during most of the 1930s, and, through the connection to ARC, the masters would eventually end up in the Columbia vaults. These included important multisided releases of "Diminuendo and Crescendo in Blue" (which took up two sides on one record, with the record format shaping the dynamics of the music itself) and "Reminiscing in Tempo" (which took up four sides on two records). Also on Brunswick, the "Hi-Dee-Ho" bandleader Cab Calloway, whose ensemble had established itself as a sometime house band at the Cotton Club, recorded what would become his most famous song, "Minnie the Moocher," in 1931. Apart from a brief stint on RCA Victor, Calloway would remain on ARC labels and then on Columbia through the mid-1940s.

In 1932, Art Tatum, a young, nearly blind, but highly touted pianist from Toledo, Ohio, arrived in New York. He soon cut his first sides for Brunswick, which included his cascading reimagining of "Tea for Two"—the song that would remain Tatum's signature tune for the rest of his career. Less remembered today were the Boswell Sisters, one of Brunswick's most popular and innovative acts in the early 1930s, who recorded a startlingly fresh style of close-harmony vocalizing. Recasting popular melodies with quirky rhythms, the trio became the major inspiration for the Andrews Sisters.

Cab Calloway

Art Tatum

The Boswell Sisters

Art Satherley and Don Law, Cowpokes and Country: Gene Autry, Patsy Montana, Bob Wills, and Roy Acuff on ARC

ARC's most important producers included two English émigrés who were passionate about American folk and "hillbilly" music and the blues, and who were destined to become legendary A&R men for Columbia. Arthur Satherley would in time be known affectionately by his numerous grateful recording stars as "Uncle Art."

Talent Scouts: Don Law and Art Satherley

Each produced records as well as discovering talent

Columbia's most famous talent scout was John Hammond in New York. But in the South, it had two equally adept scouts in Don Law and Art Satherley. Both were immigrants from England who came to America because they were fascinated by its lore. Each produced records as well as discovering talent. Satherley was Law's mentor, and Law replaced Satherley when the former retired in 1952.

Art Satherley, born in 1889, came to the United States sometime in the 1910s. By the mid-twenties, he was a salesman for Paramount Records who spent most of his time producing old-time country and black blues records. He joined the American Record Company in 1929, five years before ARC bought Columbia.

Don Law came to the United States in 1924, and got a job in Dallas with the local office of Brunswick Records. He met Satherley when ARC bought Brunswick in 1931. In 1936 and 1937, Law did sessions with Robert Johnson and in 1938, along with Satherley, made "San Antonio Rose" with Bob Wills.

Satherley worked especially closely with Gene Autry. One or both of them signed Lefty Frizzell, Ray Price, Johnny Horton, Tex Ritter, Red Foley, Spade Cooley, Johnny Bond, Bill Monroe, Roy Acuff, and Marty Robbins, and that isn't all.

Both were beloved by artists. Satherley became "Uncle Art." Law recorded Johnny Cash from 1956 to 1964 without a written contract. Cash sent the signed papers back with a note that ended: "My only regret is that I wasn't with Columbia Records, and Don Law, for the very first." When CBS corporate regulations forced Law to retire at age 65, Ray Price, who had been rejected by Law twenty times before he was signed in 1951, insisted on keeping him as his record producer. Over the next five years, they made eight top ten country hits, including Price's biggest pop record ever, "For the Good Times."

Dave Marsh

Gene Autry with Don Law, Columbia Studios

He had arrived in the United States in 1913 at age twenty-four, and eventually worked his way up at the Paramount label, before he was hired in 1928 by the cut-rate Plaza Music Company, one of the dime-store record suppliers that was folded into ARC in 1929. As ARC's Southern music producer, Satherley undertook his own field recording trips and established himself as the nation's premier figure in recording new western as well as country singers. Don Law, thirteen years younger than Satherley, had worked as a bookkeeper at Brunswick Records, where he gradually ventured into working with artists on their recordings. After ARC bought the label in 1931, he became Satherley's assistant and, soon enough, his protégé.

Satherley had been employed by ARC for three months when a young man dressed in a business suit and carrying a guitar case walked into his office and introduced himself as Gene Autry. Hailing from Tioga, Texas, near the Oklahoma border, Autry initially recorded songs in a style close to that of the popular "hillbilly" singer Jimmie Rodgers, mixed with more sentimental pop fare. His first big hit, released on Vocalion in 1931, was "That Silver Haired Daddy of Mine," a song rooted musically and emotionally in the genteel parlor ballads of the late nineteenth century. Satherley, though, thought Autry ought to scrap both Rodgers and pop, capitalize on his western background, and present himself as a cowboy singer. Autry initially spurned the idea. "That sort of stuff didn't sound very glamorous to me," he later recalled. "My recollections of ranch life included aching muscles and endless days in the sun and dust. I wanted to be a dreamy-eyed singer of love songs like Rudy Vallée." But Satherley prevailed, and Autry, in his new persona, became one of the nation's premier entertainers.

In 1932, Autry won a featured slot on the enormously popular *National Barn Dance* show broadcast by WLS in Chicago, where he appeared with the nickname the Oklahoma Yodeling Cowboy. Two years later, he appeared in his first Hollywood western, and over the coming years he turned out more than forty popular B western films for Herbert Yates's Republic Pictures. All the while, Autry sold millions of records on ARC's various labels, culminating in what would become his signature cowboy song "Back in the Saddle Again," released on Vocalion in 1939 and later rereleased on Columbia. Baby boomers may remember Autry best for his long-running television series, broadcast by CBS beginning in 1950. But by then, Autry had already built upon his early extraordinary success at ARC to become something of a national institution, on radio and in the movies as well as on records, reinventing an entire national mythos of the steadfast cowboy by adding to it a great singing voice.

One year after Autry debuted on WLS's *National Barn Dance* another rising country star joined the show. Born Ruby Blevins and raised near Hope, Arkansas, Patsy Montana took her stage name from the silent film actor and champion roper Montie Montana. After breaking in on radio in Chicago, Montana and her group, the Prairie Ramblers, recorded for RCA Victor, then took a radio job in New York, where they began recording for ARC with Art Satherley. At Satherley's prompting, Montana finished up a recording session in the summer of 1935 with a song of her own, "I Want to Be a Cowboy's Sweetheart," which became the first smash hit by a female country recording artist. Montana would remain on ARC and its surviving labels, turning out hits that included "Rodeo Sweetheart" and "Montana Plains," until 1941, when she switched to Decca.

Bob Wills offered a different kind of western musical entertainment. Wills, a Texan, started out as a fiddler and (for a time) blackface performer. In 1932, he and a band he had assembled landed a regular radio show, sponsored by the Burris Mill and Elevator Company, broadcast from Fort Worth all over Texas. The Burris company—managed by W. Lee O'Daniel, who would later have a major political career—was the manufacturer of Light Crust Flour, and Wills's group duly renamed itself the Light Crust Doughboys. Two years later, after a series of disputes with O'Daniel, Wills formed a new band which wound up playing a regular radio gig in Tulsa, under the name Bob Wills and His Texas Playboys. Wills added new instrumentalists, including horn players and an eighteen-year-old electric steel guitarist named Leon McAuliffe, whose style would help set the standard for steel guitar performance in country and western music.

Bob Wills

Patsy Montana

Gene Autry

Satherley signed the group to ARC in 1935 and oversaw its first recording sessions in Dallas and, a year later, in Chicago. After showing some initial resistance, Satherley allowed Wills and the band to play in an uninhibited hybrid of jazz and western music that was gradually evolving into a style known as western swing. The sessions produced, among other hits, the classic "Steel Guitar Rag," and in 1936, Wills and his band sold more records on ARC's Vocalion label than any other artists it released—including ARC's other new western sensation, Gene Autry. Over the decade to come, Wills and the Playboys would record regularly in Dallas, with Don Law as well as Satherley producing. The band shifted its style yet again during these years, performing music that reflected the influence of Benny Goodman, Tommy and Jimmy Dorsey, and the other big swing bands. Yet even as Wills altered styles, he never repudiated his older music, including fiddle tunes. At one session in late November 1938, Wills played for Satherley a reworked fiddle number, and Satherley suggested he call it "San Antonio Rose." The tune would remain one of the band's most popular long after Wills switched to MGM in 1947.

Neither Satherley nor Law had anything to do with signing yet another great country star on ARC, Roy Acuff, although Satherley would be responsible for keeping Acuff with Columbia in the late 1930s and beyond. Acuff, from rural East Tennessee, had learned to play the fiddle as a young man and eventually joined the Tennessee Crackerjacks, who had a regular show on WROL in nearby Knoxville. Another Knoxville radio performer, Charlie Swain of the group the Black Shirts, sang a fundamentalist hymn, "The Great Speckled Bird," and Acuff, who was also a singer, added it to the repertoire of his band, renamed the Crazy Tennesseans. As it happened, one of ARC's field music scouts, William R. Callaway, loved the song and was searching for someone to record it when he found out about Acuff.

During two separate groups of sessions in 1936 and 1937, supervised by Callaway, Roy Acuff & His Crazy Tennesseans recorded more than thirty sides for ARC. They included two versions of "The Great Speckled Bird," the second consisting in part of new verses based on scripture written by Acuff. But Acuff became convinced that Callaway and ARC were cheating him out of royalties and he abruptly ceased recording. Finally, late in 1938, Art Satherley, now working strictly for Columbia, offered Acuff a new deal which included the privilege of examining the books. Earlier that same year, Acuff had auditioned for *The Grand Ole Opry* and was an enormous hit. He was now poised to become a major star, which he quickly did in the early 1940s.

Acuff's work for ARC appeared chiefly on the Vocalion and the OKeh labels, as did Montana's and Wills's. Other important artists on Vocalion included the brilliant jazz violinist and vocalist Stuff Smith (who with his Onyx Club Boys enjoyed a big hit in 1936 with "I'se a Muggin'") and the sophisticated blues pianist Leroy Carr (who, although alcohol abused killed him at the age of thirty in 1935, would prove a strong influence on the styles of later masters such as Nat King Cole and Ray Charles). Vocalion would also be the home of a great blues artist—arguably the greatest of all time—whom Satherley's assistant, Don Law, recorded almost by happenstance. Working with Satherley, Law had, by the mid-1930s, gained enormous experience while helping to oversee sessions with the likes of Bob Wills. But Law's most legendary sessions at ARC, at least in retrospect, came with a performer who at the time impressed a few knowledgeable listeners but barely caused a ripple with the public.

Robert Johnson

So much mythology has accumulated around Robert Johnson that it is easy to lose sight of some of the simpler, generally agreed upon facts. In 1936, the itinerant bluesman, then in his mid-twenties, sought out a white music store owner and local music scout in Jackson, H. C. Spier. He ended up recording for the Vocalion label through the efforts of another part-time scout for ARC, a traveling salesman named Ernie Oertle. Well known in the Delta jook joints of Arkansas and Mississippi, the young performer—later described by Law as of "medium height, wiry, slender, nice looking boy, beautiful hands"—yearned to make records, and he would prove a revelation.

Johnson transformed blues melodies into complex yet searing compositions.

Roy Acuff

Johnson transformed blues melodies (some of which he had heard on records by Leroy Carr and others) into complex yet searing compositions; then he added lyrics filled with desperation and foreboding, and rich in old-time religion resonance. Compared to the gruff, at times undecipherable singing of Delta blues masters like Charlie Patton, Johnson's clear, versatile voice was well matched to the recording studio. His guitar playing—and especially his left-hand construction of what the critic Peter Guralnick has called his "iron chords"—would captivate later generations of aspiring guitarists.

At the time, though, Johnson was not treated as anything special. In November 1936, Oertle took him to a group recording session in San Antonio. During three sessions spread over five days, with Law (by now the regional manager for ARC) overseeing the proceedings, he recorded sixteen numbers in a makeshift studio at the Gunter Hotel. The other recording acts included a pair of Mexican singing duos and their musicians, and a cowboy band, the Crystal Spring Ramblers. The sessions were twice delayed, first when Johnson got picked up by the police, falsely charged with vagrancy, and Law had to bail him out of the Bexar County jail, and then when the singer called Law asking for money to pay a prostitute.

Vocalion immediately released twelve of his sides. His first records sold modestly, although "Terraplane Blues" enjoyed some success in the South and Southwest, selling approximately five thousand copies. Six months after his first set of sessions, Johnson recorded again with Law, in another group session, this time in Dallas at the Brunswick Records Building. (Johnson's fellow performers this time included the Light Crust Doughboys—the same Texas band Bob Wills had left four years earlier—and Zeke Williams and His Rambling Cowboys.) Out of these sessions came two of Johnson's most terrifying songs, "Hell Hound on My Trail" and "Me and the Devil Blues," along with "Love in Vain," which the Rolling Stones would reproduce thirty years later. These recordings sold in even smaller numbers than Johnson's first batch, but Law fully intended to record him again. The logic of recording company economics was such that it was acceptable to sell in small numbers in as many niche markets as possible with performers like Johnson: add them all up, and the total would be all that mattered.

Back in New York, though, the young producer John Hammond heard Johnson's recordings and wrote that he made the recently discovered Louisiana ex-convict singer and guitarist, Leadbelly—who had become the rage among white blues aficionados and released four sides on ARC's Banner label—"sound like an accomplished poseur." Hammond had been planning for a concert of black music at Carnegie Hall and he asked Law about inviting Johnson to perform. But through Oertle, Law learned that Johnson was dead. Now lying in an unmarked grave in Greenwood, Mississippi (most likely at the Little Zion Church), Johnson was the unfortunate victim of (depending on whom you believed) a jealous husband, an angry woman, or the devil himself.

Another quarter of a century would pass before Johnson's music reached a mass audience and exerted its singular influence on contemporary rock and blues—thanks chiefly to Columbia producer Frank Driggs but also to his boss, John Hammond, who finally fulfilled his wish to present Johnson to a large public. By then, though, Hammond himself had become something of a legend.

John Hammond

Born in New York in 1910 to a family of great wealth—his mother's family was descended from the Vanderbilts—Hammond attended prep school, where he was drawn to left-wing politics, and entered Yale. While still in his teens, he acquired a fascination with the black dance music being performed in Harlem, not far from the Hammond home on upper Fifth Avenue. After three semesters of indifferent studies, he dropped out of Yale and, backed by a $12,000-per-year trust fund (the equivalent of about $160,000 today), moved back to Manhattan to become a record collector and critic, one of the many young white men searching for emotional and aesthetic authenticity who found it in black music. "The jazz I liked best was played by

"... the most effective and constructive form of social protest I could think of"

John Hammond on bringing recognition to the role of African Americans in jazz

Benny Goodman with Count Basie and John Hammond

John Hammond

Negroes," he later recalled. "To bring recognition to the Negro's supremacy in jazz was the most effective and constructive form of social protest I could think of." In 1931, Hammond began to champion the Harlem-based pianist Garland Wilson. Attracted to Columbia because of Frank Walker's work with Bessie Smith, he bought and paid for a recording session, with an additional guarantee to buy 150 copies of the resulting record. Wilson's renditions of "St. James Infirmary" and "When Your Lover Has Gone" were unmemorable, but Hammond's career as a record producer was launched.

Later that year, upon turning twenty-one, Hammond picked up part of his inheritance and moved to Greenwich Village, where he wrote radical journalism for, among other publications, *The Nation* and *The New Republic*, including reports on the trial of the Scottsboro Boys, a left-wing cause célèbre. In 1932 his friend Ben Selvin, a bandleader and longtime Columbia producer, introduced Hammond to Columbia's top executives. Because the label's fortunes had severely ebbed under Grigsby-Grunow, Selvin persuaded Hammond to make jazz records with New York musicians for the livelier English market, and particularly for the EMI conglomerate. Hammond duly recorded three numbers with Fletcher Henderson and His Orchestra, which had been recording on and off with Columbia since 1923, at Columbia's studios on Fifth Avenue near Union Square. Soon after, Hammond became the American correspondent for the British periodical *Melody Maker*. He went on to record in 1933 additional up-and-coming jazz musicians for Columbia in England, including Benny Goodman, Coleman Hawkins, Benny Carter, and Joe Venuti.

A proud and willful man, Hammond was not above calling attention to his own accomplishments and those of the artists with whom he worked—and in the process, by various accounts, he sometimes stretched the truth. But Hammond, the record hunter turned talent scout, certainly had a knack for timely moves and discoveries. In a small coup, he traveled to Philadelphia and persuaded Bessie Smith, who had not been inside a studio in two years, to come back to New York and record for OKeh. The session took place on November 24, 1933, with a lineup that included the clarinetist Benny Goodman, trombonist Jack Teagarden, and tenor saxophonist Chu Berry. This all-star combo produced several numbers, including a song that would prove a lasting Smith favorite: "Gimme a Pigfoot." "The size of her voice was tremendous, and the spirit marvelous," Hammond later remarked about the session, but it would be Smith's last recording date. Convinced that Depression-weary listeners wanted their spirits raised, Smith refused to record any traditional blues songs; unfortunately, her upbeat new efforts did not sell.

Over the next four years, after Grigsby-Grunow sold Columbia, the persistent Hammond badgered ARC to sign Smith to a regular recording contract. Finally, he made a deal for her to sing for Brunswick, he reported later. But, in September 1937, before any agreement had materialized, Smith was critically injured in a gruesome nighttime accident on US Highway 61 just north of Clarksdale, Mississippi, where the automobile in which she was riding collided with a truck. Hammond later told an apocryphal story of how racist medical attendants refused to admit her to a "whites only" hospital in Clarksdale. In actuality, she was taken to the local black hospital, where she died the next day, having never regained consciousness.

Hammond's rediscovery of Smith ended tragically, but he would never stop finding superior talent for Columbia and then ARC—sometimes as if he were a magnet for future musical stars. Early in 1933, months before he recorded Smith, Hammond visited an uptown club called Covan's, hoping to hear a singer he admired, Monette Moore. Instead, he heard her last-minute replacement—the seventeen-year-old Billie Holiday. Deeply impressed, Hammond oversaw Holiday's recording debut on some sessions with Benny Goodman, whom Holiday was dating at the time, that began on November 27 of that year, just three days after Bessie Smith's last session. The young Holiday was intimidated, but the sessions produced a halting yet promising version of "Your Mother's Son-in-Law," as well as Holiday's first hit, "Riffin' the Scotch."

Coming so soon after Bessie Smith's last session, Holiday's first recording date appears, in retrospect, to have been a symbolic passing of the torch from one generation's black female musical star to the next. It was also the beginning of Holiday's fabled

Billie Holiday with Ben Webster, unknown guitar player, and Johnny Russell, Harlem

Billie Holiday

association with Hammond, the ARC consortium, and a shifting ensemble of top musicians—above all, the elegant, classically trained pianist Teddy Wilson (whom Hammond had also first recorded in 1933). That association would produce, over the rest of the decade and into the early 1940s, one of the most important bodies of work in jazz, despite Holiday's deepening dependence on drugs and alcohol.

Holiday, to be sure, did not always see eye to eye with Hammond and his colleagues. In 1939, after the label had been sold once again, Columbia declined to release her hair-raising rendition of the anti-lynching song "Strange Fruit," which Hammond deemed at once too lurid, too didactic, and, musically, too tame. The record was eventually released by the small Commodore label, run by Milt Gabler.

But Holiday continued with ARC's various labels, leading to recordings that included Holiday's coauthored masterpiece, "God Bless the Child," released on OKeh in 1941. Almost all Holiday's recordings through the early 1940s appeared on Brunswick, Vocalion, or OKeh. Her sole Columbia release, apart from the first record cut with Goodman, would be "I Cover the Waterfront," which, coupled with "Until the Real Thing Comes Along," appeared in 1942—well after ARC had left the picture, as we will see.

Hammond, still in his twenties, could discern gifted performers and composers even at great distances. One night in 1936, sitting in his automobile and listening to the radio in wintertime Chicago, he picked up an experimental station in Kansas City, which was presenting a band led by the pianist Count Basie, whom Hammond had heard in New York three years earlier. The development in Basie's style astonished Hammond: "I couldn't believe my ears," he later recalled. He returned to his car at the same time the next night, and the next, in order to listen to Basie. Then, he drove to Kansas City and, at the Reno Club, found not just Basie but also Lester Young, Hot Lips Page, Jo Jones, and the rest of Basie's band, including its singer, Jimmy Rushing. Basie had already signed to record with the band for Decca, but soon enough they would be working with Hammond at Columbia.

Hammond would also soon be working once again with Benny Goodman. Having first recorded with Hammond in 1933, Goodman and his band signed with RCA Victor, experiencing thereafter some spectacular highs in popularity and equally spectacular lows. A three-week engagement at the Palomar Ballroom in Los Angeles, however, in the late summer of 1935, changed the band's fortunes mightily, as Goodman scrapped his stock arrangements in favor of fresh hot ones—and tore up the place. Reports soon spread of an exciting new music and of a new dance that went along with it, the jitterbug. Sometimes called the "birth of the swing era," the Palomar shows became a pivotal moment in the rise of big-band swing. Victor's release of a string of Goodman band hits, including "King Porter Stomp" coupled with "Sometimes I'm Happy," and "Christopher Columbus" coupled with "Get Happy," spread the frenzy. "It is clear in retrospect that the Swing Era had been waiting to happen," the critic Donald Clarke writes, "but it was Goodman and his band that touched it off."

Goodman was helping to revolutionize the music business socially as well as artistically, by breaking with the taboo that disallowed black and white musicians from playing together. In 1935, he organized the Benny Goodman Trio, including the pianist Teddy Wilson and the drummer Gene Krupa; thereafter, the vibraphonist Lionel Hampton joined the group, now the Benny Goodman Quartet. Goodman had become so popular that he even managed to tour the South in defiance of Jim Crow. Then, in mid-January 1938, Goodman, newly dubbed "the King of Swing," further solidified his public standing with a spectacular sold-out concert at Carnegie Hall. Goodman was still recording for Victor, but in short order he would switch to Columbia.

A little less than a year after Goodman's momentous concert, Hammond staged his "From Spirituals to Swing" concert, also at Carnegie Hall, two days before Christmas in 1938. Billed as "an evening of American Negro music" and formally dedicated to Bessie Smith, this was the event that Hammond had hoped would include the New York debut of Robert Johnson. Another blues singer, Big Bill Broonzy, performed in the late Johnson's place, and the rest of the bill for the sold-out show was a stunning collection of performers, including Count Basie, Helen Humes, Sidney Bechet, Sister Rosetta Tharpe, and Big Joe Turner. Sponsored by the

"It's clear in retrospect that the Swing Era was waiting to happen."

Donald Clarke on Benny Goodman's impact

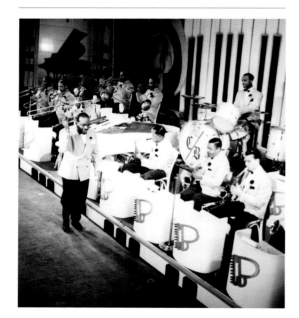

Count Basie and His Orchestra

Count Basie

Communist Party–aligned cultural organ *New Masses*, for which Hammond wrote, the concert quickly came under attack as a subversive affair, but Hammond brushed off the attacks as further evidence of the righteousness of his cause. A follow-up show was held at Carnegie Hall a year later.

There were other negative perceptions of Hammond as well. Inevitably, the fact that a well-connected, albeit youthful, white record producer was recording black artists for white-owned labels prompted charges of covert and not-so-covert inequality and exploitation. And some in the business continued to find Hammond's tendency toward dramatic exaggeration hard to take.

Although he has rightly become a predominant figure in most histories of Columbia, Hammond was, of course, hardly the only important figure in promoting and recording popular music at ARC during the Depression. Tommy Rockwell, late of OKeh and then Brunswick Records, oversaw the entire program as the firm's general manager; Art Satherley and Don Law were turning up and recording some monumentally important country and western as well as blues performers out in the field. Back in New York, the songwriter, band leader, and A&R man Morty Palitz was an essential force, especially in connection with big band recordings. However, as a producer and impresario, Hammond had begun to advance some of the most vital popular musical trends of the time and for decades to come, including swing, boogie-woogie, and the folk blues revival. His musical contributions were enormous, as were his efforts at knocking down racial prejudice in the music industry.

The Corporate Turning Point: Ted Wallerstein, William Paley, and the Purchase by CBS

Thanks to the public's enthusiasm for swing music and the spread of jukebox culture, the recording companies had climbed out of the worst depths of the Depression, but all the energy, acumen, and idealism at ARC could not keep the company from running a distant third behind a resurgent RCA Victor and the phenomenal new Decca. In 1938, Victor and Decca were competing neck and neck, with sales totals of thirteen million and twelve million records respectively. ARC sold only seven million. Still, what ARC lacked in sales it made up for in quality and musical innovation. Some connections were brief but intense, like the week of recording by the great Carter Family country ensemble in New York in May 1935 that yielded more than forty tracks for ARC. Others mixed ingenuity and happenstance. A famous article in *Life* 1938 listed thirty "Good Hot Records," of which more than one-third either had been made by or were owned by ARC, including Louis Armstrong's original "West End Blues" and Stuff Smith's "You'se a Viper." "Decca and Victor seemed more conservative, Columbia more daring," the music critic George T. Simon later wrote. Simon was referring specifically to big band recordings, but the assessment held true for the American Record Company generally. The excitement and expertise around the company made ARC more than a mishmash of cheap record labels.

Then the intervention of two men changed everything, initiating the emergence of Columbia, under its own name, as one of the giants of American entertainment. Like Jack Kapp at Decca, Edward Wallerstein, the head of RCA Victor, had done a great deal to carry the troubled recording business through the Great Depression. Wallerstein specialized in turning adversity into opportunity: he led Victor to abandon its fiasco with long-playing records, tapped into what had become a neglected classical recordings market, promoted the label's extensive back list, and introduced inexpensive turntables that could be adapted to play through radio speakers. But by 1938, Wallerstein—who had just recovered from a heart attack and was sensing that his authority at RCA Victor was declining—was looking to make a change.

There are a number of different stories about how and why Wallerstein came to find now-lowly Columbia a promising alternative. Without question, the label, although severely reduced, still had an established and imposing trademark, a pressing plant in Bridgeport, and the rights to sell English Columbia's recordings, all of which made it inviting. That Columbia's status had sunk so low inside ARC also suggested

Benny Goodman Sextet

Benny Goodman

that it might be easily obtainable. It remains unclear whether Wallerstein tried to raise money himself to buy Columbia from ARC or simply suggested that someone else take it over. But, whatever actually happened, Wallerstein helped to excite the interest of one of the most successful of the new radio moguls, William S. Paley—who, as it happened, had had his own dalliance with Columbia a decade earlier.

Born in Chicago in 1901, the son of a fabulously successful Jewish immigrant cigar maker, Paley had attended the Wharton School at the University of Pennsylvania with the expectation that he would enter the family business, which had since moved to Philadelphia. In the late 1920s, he became involved instead with radio and one of the offshoots of Louis Sterling's then-expanding Columbia Phonograph Company. In 1927, a talent agent and concert manager named Arthur Judson approached David Sarnoff, the chief of the Radio Corporation of America, with a roster of clients and plans for a new radio network, but Sarnoff turned him away. Defiantly, Judson and his partners founded a network on their own—United Independent Broadcasters—with backing from Columbia Phonograph (whose leaders were already nervous about an impending merger of RCA and Victor and hoped to use UIB to promote Columbia artists). The new enterprise went on the air in September 1927 as the Columbia Phonograph Broadcasting Company. Within a year, though, the network was suffering heavy losses that necessitated a fresh infusion of cash, and Columbia Phonograph wanted out. The owners of the network's Philadelphia affiliate, WCAU, an attorney named Ike Levy and his brother, Leon, a dentist, came to the rescue. (Leon Levy happened to be the husband of Bill Paley's sister Blanche.) Ike was willing to put up $50,000 to salvage the struggling radio network, and he persuaded Bill Paley's cigar-maker father, Sam, to match his stake.

Sam Paley had been impressed by how advertising on WCAU had increased his cigar sales, and he helped push Bill into running the UIB enterprise, assured that if the radio turned out to be a bust, the young man could still take over the family's cigar business. Before long, the son had moved to New York, learned as much as he could about radio, and become the de facto head of both UIB and Columbia Phonograph Broadcasting.

Finally, in 1928, Paley bought a majority share of the network, which by now consisted of sixteen affiliates, for $400,000, and he quickly reorganized it under the name Columbia Broadcasting System. Although he still had only scant experience in broadcasting, Paley proved an able radio executive. Among the singers he booked were Bing Crosby, Kate Smith, and Morton Downey. By the end of the 1930s, CBS also had the makings of a first-rate news division, which included a fledgling reporter, Edward R. Murrow.

By purchasing ARC, Paley would become the proprietor of the recording company that had originally given his rapidly growing radio network its name, and of the other labels that had energized ARC since the start of the Depression. (In 1940, the Brunswick and Vocalion labels would revert to Warner Bros., as would all Brunswick and Vocalion masters recorded before 1931, but Paley would keep the masters from the 1930s.) Yet the price Paley negotiated, $700,000, was nearly ten times the amount that Herbert Yates had spent to buy lowly Columbia from Grigsby-Grunow barely four years earlier. Wall Street insiders thought Paley had taken leave of his senses to pay so much for any recording company or even combination of recording companies, and Paley had to overcome deep skepticism among the radio network's board of directors before the sale could be approved. But on January 1, 1939, the deal was sealed, and in May, Paley completed the reorganization of ARC as the Columbia Recording Corporation, a subsidiary of CBS, with Ted Wallerstein as its president.

Under a variety of owners and directors, the company Edward Easton and his partners had formed forty years earlier had somehow survived numerous crises, and along the way it had helped make musical history. Columbia's glory years were yet to come.

"Decca and Victor seemed more conservative, Columbia more daring."

George T. Simon

Kate Smith

Bing Crosby

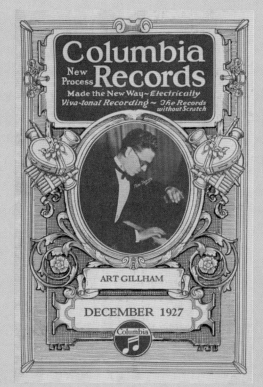

Columbia Records
June 1920

"Magic Notes"
TRADE MARK

Columbia

Copyright, patented Record. Not to be publicly performed
without licence nor sold below price fixed by patentees.

61188
SPEED 78   FB 1513

STOMPIN' AT THE SAVOY
(GOODMAN, WEBB & SAMPSON)
THE INK SPOTS

LONDON
FRANCIS
DAY
BERLIN · PARIS

HANSEN
BIEM

Columbia Records
November   1921

COLUMBIA
Symphony
Records

Grand Opera and
Concert Selections:
the very soul of im-
mortal music at its
imperishable best!

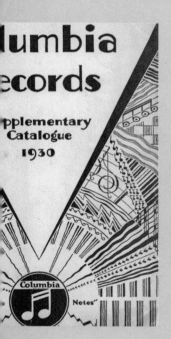

**lumbia
Records**

upplementary
Catalogue
1930

Columbia
Notes

COLUMBIA
Columbia
Grafonola
SCANDINAVIAN   RECORDS
SWEDISH · DANISH   NORWEGIAN

Viva-tonal
Recording

Electrical
Process

Columbia

Paul Whiteman
AND HIS
Orchestra
Waltz

THE MERRY WIDOW
(LA VIUDA ALEGRE)
(Lehár)

50069-D
(98536)

MADE AND PAT'D IN U.S.A. JAN.31'13 AND RE 16588
COLUMBIA PHONOGRAPH COMPANY, INC. NEW YORK,U.S.A.

COLUMBIA
Columbia
Grafonola
SPANISH   RECORDS

Columbia Records
New Process—No scratching sound from the needle!

Columbia

World's Most Famous Race   Comedienne-Columbia Artist

ETHEL WATERS

MISS WATERS

has been
playing to packed houses
and will appear at
ROYAL
THEATRE
ALL NEXT WEEK
Beginning Monday, July 11th

Buy Her Records
From These Authorized
Dealers

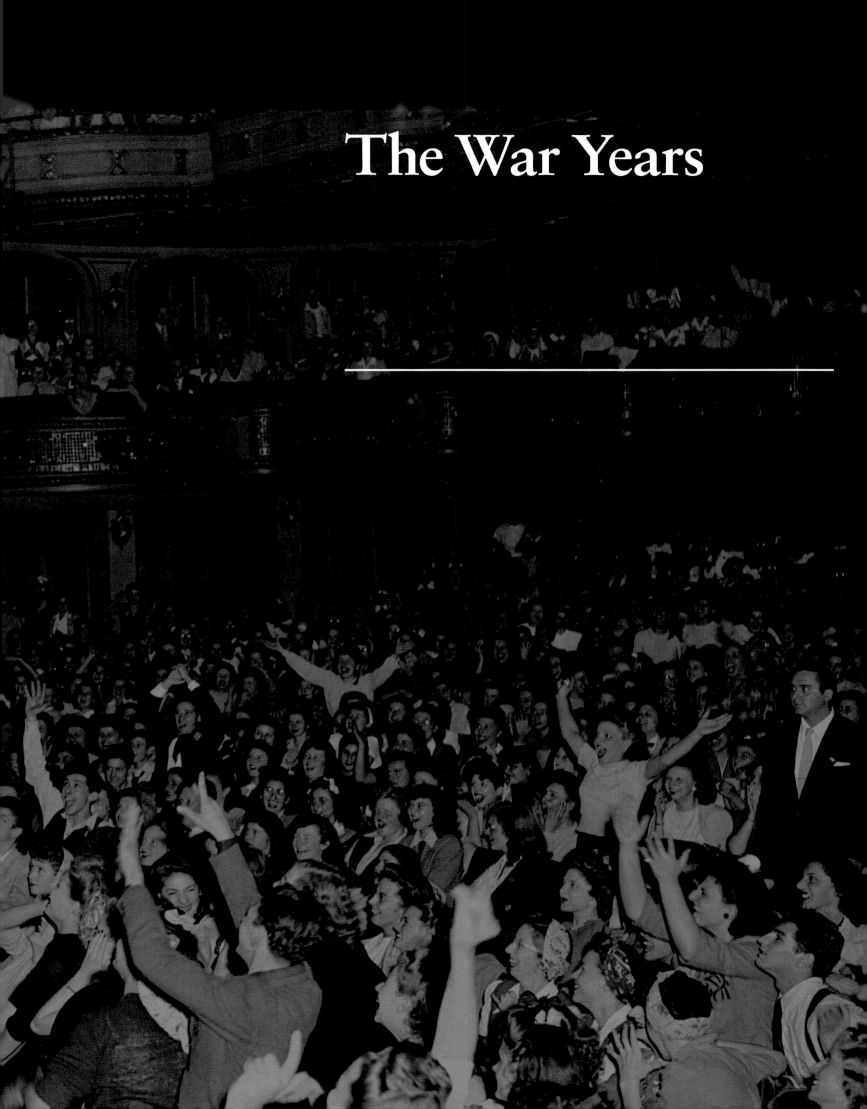

The War Years

Paley's purchase immediately injected energy as well as cash into Columbia, as shown by CBS's decision to move its new recording subsidiary to enlarged quarters in a seven-story building, 799 Seventh Avenue, on the corner of Fifty-second Street. Columbia would now operate in the newest center of New York's bustling commercial entertainment scene, convenient to Times Square and Tin Pan Alley and adjacent to what would become, in the 1940s, the renowned, neon-lit Fifty-second Street jazz clubs. With Ted Wallerstein in charge, the label would seek every opportunity to expand its artistic reach.

Yet the nation was dramatically shifting gears, moving from continuing battles against the Great Depression to total war against the Axis powers after Japan's attack on Pearl Harbor in 1941. As Americans mobilized for war, the recording industry, not least the Columbia Recording Corporation, faced daunting hurdles of its own.

Fifty-second Street, New York

Much of Columbia's story during the war years revolves around Wallerstein. Born in Kansas City in 1891 but raised in Philadelphia, he graduated from Haverford College, served stateside in the Army during World War I, and worked in the Oklahoma oil fields before he entered the recording industry, rising to become the east coast manager of Brunswick by the time he was thirty. His work at Brunswick and later RCA Victor, prior to the sale of ARC to CBS, won him a reputation as a master of the business side of the recording industry—"the greatest record salesman of his day," John Hammond later called him. A polite and somewhat distant man, Wallerstein took up the presidency of Columbia Recording burning to improve the company's position in every category of musical entertainment—yet he did so with a gift for delegating authority and responsibility that paid off in quality as well as profits. He also knew the operations of Columbia's nemesis, RCA Victor, inside out, something that Paley the sharp businessman thoroughly appreciated. "We bought, in buying him, a lot of expertise and certainly bought our competitor," the CBS executive (and eventually its president) Frank Stanton later recalled of Wallerstein. "Or the man who ran our competitor."

Wallerstein immediately hired Hammond as associate director of popular recording, charging him specifically (or so Hammond later recalled) with signing to an extended contract Benny Goodman, whose work Wallerstein admired. Hammond did so, and would thereafter work closely with Goodman (who married Hammond's sister, Alice, in 1942), although the two men forged a complex relationship that did not lack mutual suspicion and rivalry. Wallerstein also encouraged Hammond to bring Count Basie and His Orchestra, who were recording for Decca, into the Columbia fold.

Columbia had inherited from its ARC days the comic bandleader Kay Kyser (with his trumpeter, Merwin Bogue, who called himself Ish Kabibble), the moonwalking bandleader Cab Calloway, and the society-orchestra leader Eddy Duchin. The immensely popular cowboy singer and movie star Gene Autry had also moved to Columbia. Bob Wills and His Texas Palyboys would hone their western swing style on OKeh and Columbia in the 1940s. Having been retained by Art Satherley for OKeh and renamed his band the Smoky Mountain Boys, Roy Acuff began an ascent that would eventually win him the popular title of "King of Country Music." After a public fight with Goodman in 1938, the fiery drummer Gene Krupa formed his own band and recorded several superb records for Columbia, backed with vocals from Anita O'Day and the trumpeter Roy Eldridge. Columbia's roster also briefly included Duke Ellington, who switched to RCA Victor in 1940.

Hammond, with his love of black music, enriched the mix. Shortly after the first "From Spirituals to Swing" concert, on a tip from the pianist Mary Lou Williams, Hammond heard the young black electric-guitar wizard Charlie Christian and signed him up. Christian would record superb sides for Columbia with the Benny Goodman Sextet as well as the Goodman band, until his untimely death from tuberculosis, at age twenty-three, in 1941. Then, at the second "From Spirituals to Swing" concert in December 1939, Hammond showcased an excellent gospel jubilee group from North Carolina, the Golden Gate Quartet, and signed them to record for OKeh. As always, Hammond knew musical talent when he heard it: the group would move on to the Columbia label, perform at New York's pioneering racially integrated club, Café Society, secure its own nationwide radio program, and sing at Franklin D. Roosevelt's third inauguration, in 1941. And, in 1939, Big Joe Turner, who had also appeared at the first "From Spirituals to Swing" concert, began a residency at Café Society and recorded several sides for Columbia, including "Cherry Red," which appeared on the Vocalion label.

Building Classical and Jazz

Ted Wallerstein, for his part, was more of a businessman than a music connoisseur but he arrived from RCA Victor determined to break Victor's domination of the classical music market. He undertook the task with clever

Benny Goodman

Ted Wallerstein (right) on the cover of *Tide* magazine

Benny Goodman

salesmanship. Columbia had kept a toehold in classical music with its imports from the British Columbia branch, but Victor enjoyed an overwhelming advantage, holding contracts with the Philadelphia Orchestra, the New York Philharmonic, and the Boston Symphony Orchestra. Above all, Victor recorded Arturo Toscanini and the NBC Symphony, almost certainly the most listened-to orchestra in the nation. Columbia Masterworks did have its own major conductor, Gustav Mahler's protégé Bruno Walter, who had fled Germany after the Nazis took power in 1933. (Adolf Hitler sometimes mentioned Walter specifically in his venomous speeches berating the Jewish influence on German culture.) If Walter's recordings lacked the popularity of Toscanini's, they gave the Columbia catalog, before and after CBS took over, undeniable weight and stature.

Still, Wallerstein knew that Columbia would not seriously challenge RCA Victor simply by trying to improve its supply of classical music. Instead, he aimed to increase consumer demand for Columbia's recordings with a clever new marketing strategy. In August 1940, a full page ad appeared in *Life* magazine announcing that Columbia had suddenly cut in half the price of all its classical recordings. (Wallerstein's sales department assured retailers that Columbia would make up the difference in any revenue they lost due to the sale, a minor cost to the label since most retailers kept so few of Columbia's classical recordings in stock.) The strategy succeeded. Price-conscious classical music buyers now eagerly sought out Columbia recordings, and once they had done so they became loyal to the label. RCA Victor, suddenly under pressure, had to reduce the unit price of its Red Seal classical line in order to compete—but, because so many of its records were already in the stores, Victor was in no position to offer retailers compensation, a fact that only deepened the retailers' attachment to Columbia. The payoff for Columbia was immediate. At the end of 1941, the label reported an elevenfold increase in the sales of its classical records. Not since the turn of the century had Victor's classical line faced such competition.

Wallerstein was also skilled at poaching performers whom he knew from his days at RCA Victor felt neglected. In particular, he set his sights on landing the disgruntled popular conductor André Kostelanetz, who had already left Victor for Brunswick, where his lot had not improved. Having originally signed Kostelanetz to Victor, Wallerstein now persuaded him to switch to Columbia, and there the conductor went on to enjoy a long and successful career. Wallerstein also snapped up the New York Philharmonic, which debuted on Columbia in 1940 with a recording of Igor Stravinsky's *Le Sacre du Printemps*, conducted by the composer. Additionally, Columbia Masterworks, now run by the Boston music critic Moses Smith, added several opera stars, veterans and newcomers, to its catalog. Among these was the tenor John Carter, who had come to the Metropolitan Opera after winning its Auditions on the Air competition in 1937 and 1938, which was broadcast on CBS's great rival, RCA's National Broadcasting System.

Although Wallerstein preferred classical music and was wary of popular music fads, he trusted John Hammond's judgment and recognized a powerful new musical trend when he saw it. While working at RCA Victor, he had also come to understand the immense value of returning to the company's back list instead of focusing solely on the latest recordings. Remarking on how the report in *Life* magazine in 1938 on "Good Hot Jazz" had mentioned so many older recordings owned by Columbia, such as Louis Armstrong's "West End Blues," Wallerstein asked Hammond about the possibility of reissuing some of them. Hammond suggested that Wallerstein contact a twenty-year-old Russian-born Armenian immigrant and jazz enthusiast then studying at Yale, George Avakian, whom he had run into in New York jazz circles and whose writing for *Tempo* magazine had begun winning him admirers.

A precocious promoter of jazz, both old and new, Avakian had already persuaded Decca to release three compilation collections of jazz reissues, dedicated to the music's three major centers, Chicago, Kansas City, and New Orleans. (All three were released along the lines Avakian had drawn, although, given the small amount that Decca was willing to pay him, he wound up focusing only on the *Chicago Jazz* collection, which appeared while he was still in his junior year in New

André Kostelanetz conducting on the set of *Music In My Heart*

George Avakian

André Kostelanetz

Haven.) Now working for $25 a week, he researched old masters for Columbia at the Bridgeport plant, not far from Yale—"a dream come true," he later remarked. His greatest find among the stacks—which filled three large rooms, from floor to ceiling—was a trove of unreleased masters of Louis Armstrong and the Hot Five and Hot Seven, some of which had been languishing for more than a decade. Avakian received Armstrong's permission to release the recordings on Columbia, and they became one of the foundations of Columbia's Hot Jazz Classics series. Avakian skillfully annotated the Armstrong release, as he had his Chicago collection for Decca, providing commentary that combined musical expertise with an easy, accessible style—an archetype for the liner notes that would become standard for record covers. (The effort led to an enduring enmity between Avakian and Hammond, who tried to grab credit for the notes.) Columbia then released additional reissues from Duke Ellington and Bessie Smith masters. Although his college grades suffered as a result, Avakian, at age twenty-two, had become an accomplished professional producer as well as a genuine scholar of jazz, and his future seemed unbounded, until World War II got in the way.

War, the Industry, and the Petrillo Ban

The United States' entry into the war in 1941 had quick and dramatic repercussions for the entire recording industry. Recalling the events of World War I, record executives initially imagined that the public, deprived of entertainers and entertainment, would start buying records in droves. But, only five months after Pearl Harbor, the federal government declared that shellac was a material vital to the nation's defense and that it would permit the recording companies to use no more than 30 percent of what they had used earlier. By 1943, no new shellac could be used at all, which forced the companies to grind and recycle old recordings. Federal agents padlocked warehouses that contained record-pressing materials; production of radios, phonographs, and jukeboxes ended; and both the record business and the listening public were effectively forced to go on a wartime footing, using machinery already to hand. The constrained circumstances forced recording companies to be more selective in their releases, which in Columbia's case meant jettisoning, among other performers, almost all its traditional string-band country and folk musicians apart from proven stars like Roy Acuff, as well as almost all its blues singers.

The wartime strains also exposed rifts within the recording industry that echoed the "canned music" controversies raised by John Philip Sousa at the turn of the century, about the displacement of concert musicians. Under the wartime mobilization, the radio networks severely curtailed their expenses, which left them not only with limited time and money for programming their established musical stars like Kate Smith, but also left lesser-known talents by the wayside. Despite efforts by the record companies and individual artists to preempt playing records on the radio, stations went ahead and filled up empty time by airing recorded music, introduced by a relatively new species of radio personality, the disc jockey. The news columnist Walter Winchell had coined the term in 1935 to describe Martin Block, the host of *The Make-Believe Ballroom* on New York's WNEW. Then, in 1940, in the case of *RCA Manufacturing Company v. Whiteman*, the United States Court of Appeals for the Second Circuit ruled that records purchased by the radio stations were the stations' property and could be broadcast however the stations desired. Recorded music, presented by the disc jockeys, would soon be on the airwaves day and night.

Consequently, as the expanding ranks of DJs broadcast more recorded music, opportunities for musicians to perform live evaporated. (*Time* magazine had already reported, five years earlier, that there were eleven thousand permanently unemployed musicians around the country, and many more who were subject to sporadic layoffs.) To make matters worse, the composers and music publishers were already well organized as the American Society of Composers, Authors, and Publishers (ASCAP), and the broadcasters were represented for copyright matters by

Kay Kyser with
His Orchestra

Billie Holiday

The Golden
Gate Quartet

the new Broadcast Music, Inc. (BMI). Caught between these powerful organizations, the musicians' American Federation of Musicians (AFM) began to feel deprived of any consideration.

The AFM's president, a colorful, sometimes surly ex-trumpeter, originally from Chicago, named James Caesar Petrillo, decided that enough was enough. Looking back to a golden age before jukeboxes and DJs, when thousands of musicians performed live in restaurants and dance halls as well as radio, Petrillo demanded that the recording companies cease manufacturing records except for home entertainment until they provided compensation for the displaced musicians and underwrote free concerts around the country. Only records for private enjoyment would be permitted. If the recording companies balked, Petrillo would order his members out on strike, despite a wartime no-strike pledge honored by other major unions.

Petrillo was putting the record executives in a difficult bind. Since the mid-1930s, the jukebox operators had been providing the labels with an irreplaceable source of revenue. The recording industry could not simply abandon jukeboxes without inviting its own destruction. Under the law, moreover, the labels were powerless to prevent disc jockeys from playing the abundance of records they already had on hand, let alone any new ones. The recording companies refused to yield and, on August 1, 1942, the musicians' strike began.

In their efforts to find ways around the so-called Petrillo ban on recording with instrumentalists, the recording companies, including Columbia, discovered loopholes and turned to gimmicks that had odd effects on recorded music, not all negative. As the strike loomed (Petrillo had made the tactical error of putting the industry on notice about his intentions) the companies feverishly recorded melodies by their top performers, including Goodman, Basie, and Kyser at Columbia. Once that supply ran out, the companies relied on reissues and material known in industry slang as "iceboxes"— music that had been recorded but remained unreleased. Among the most successful of the reissues was a number recorded in 1939 by Harry James and his fledgling orchestra, "All or Nothing at All," fronted by one Frank Sinatra—a singer obscure enough that his name did not appear on the label of the original release. The record sold poorly (although Sinatra's performance did help persuade the bandleader Tommy Dorsey to lure him away from James), but by the time it was rereleased in 1943, Sinatra was a phenomenal star. With Sinatra's name now prominently displayed, "All or Nothing at All" spent eighteen weeks on the *Billboard* best-seller chart, peaking at number two.

Another revenue-generating tactic for the recording companies was to issue new spoken-word records, of which the most notable example was Columbia's full-length recording of a successful Broadway production of *Othello*, starring Paul Robeson as the Moor, Uta Hagen as Desdemona, and José Ferrer as Iago. (Robeson had first appeared on Columbia in a revival cast production of *Showboat* in 1932.) Major singing stars, including Sinatra and Bing Crosby on Decca, and Perry Como on RCA Victor, recorded songs backed by vocal groups instead of musicians. In one of the quirks of union politics, harmonica players were excluded from the ban, which allowed Columbia's dazzling Larry Adler to add to the celebrity he had built during the late 1930s.

Musicians appeared despite the strike on discs sent to the troops to boost morale, through the V-Disc program, organized by the War Department. Billie Holiday, Frank Sinatra, Glenn Miller, and scores of other leading entertainers took part in the program, which would last until 1949. The War Department further encouraged the troops overseas—and sustained the entertainers' popularity—with radio broadcasts on the American Forces Network. These included the network broadcast segments of *Grand Ole Opry*, which proved especially popular with the GIs. The war correspondent Ernie Pyle reported that Japanese troops at the Battle of Okinawa screamed, "To hell with Roosevelt! To hell with Babe Ruth! To hell with Roy Acuff!"

Due to the Petrillo ban, however, never again would the big bands like Goodman's and Basie's enjoy the kind of adulation they had known before 1942; instead, public fascination began to focus on the vocalists instead of the musicians, an important further step in the history of celebrity moving toward the single

Public fascination began to focus on the vocalists instead of the musicians, an important further step in the history of celebrity moving toward the single charismatic star.

Larry Adler

Paul Robeson as Othello with José Ferrer as Iago in a scene from Shakespeare's *Othello*

V-Discs

Virtually every American popular singer participated in the program

Among those most troubled by the American Federation of Musicians strike that lasted from August 1, 1942, to November 11, 1944, was the United States military, which wanted recorded music for recreation and morale-building. The union, performers, and record companies came together in wartime solidarity to make one kind of record only. They were called V-Discs: twelve-inch (rather than the standard ten-inch) 33 RPM (rather than the standard 78 RPM) records that contained up to six and a half minutes of music (and often spoken introductions).

Virtually every American popular recording artist participated in the program, from Glenn Miller and Frank Sinatra to Louis Jordan and Billie Holiday. Much of the music was made at special recording sessions (Columbia used CBS Playhouse No. 3—now the David Letterman theater—and No. 4, which later became Studio 54.) Columbia was one of the companies that took on the job of pressing the V-Discs. Until October 1943, when the AFM

granted an exception to the strike on condition that the V-Discs never be sold commercially, the military used concert and recital recordings, radio broadcasts, movie soundtracks, and old 78s as source material.

Soldiers loved the V-Discs so much that the program continued through the occupation of Germany and Japan into 1949. After that, because the union had demanded that the discs never be sold commercially, the military discarded and destroyed all copies on bases, and even attempted to confiscate those that servicemen had smuggled home. Fortunately, copies of most V-Discs were kept in the Library of Congress and the National Archives. More recently, CD compilations of the V-Discs have been issued, and labels like Columbia Legacy have used some of the material for legitimate reissue.

Dave Marsh

Frank Sinatra with a V-Disc recording

charismatic star. And, the ban helped insure that the very earliest phases of the bebop revolution in jazz that began with the experimentation of Charlie Parker, Dizzy Gillespie, and their associates in the early 1940s went unrecorded until 1944, when small independent labels jumped in.

Decca came to terms with the AFM in September 1943, as did the recently launched label Capitol Records a month later. Columbia and RCA Victor held out for another year, but they finally reached an agreement, fittingly enough on Armistice Day, November 11, 1944. The union won the creation of a fund, into which the recording companies would place a portion of their royalties, specifically for assisting hard-pressed musicians and funding live public performances.

The battle was over, but it had been bitter and it left lasting scars. When, in October 1944, President Roosevelt, prompted by an appeal begun by Ted Wallerstein, had urged the union to allow the musicians to return to the studios, Petrillo refused angrily, comparing the hold-outs at Columbia and RCA Victor to pre–Civil War slaveholders. After Columbia acceded, Wallerstein said the company had had no choice but to give way, lest it go out of business, and he chided the government for not taking more forceful action against the union. At one level, the AFM's fight against recorded music was a classic case of trying to ward off the impending realities of technological obsolescence. Yet Petrillo and his union were not opposed to records or recording per se, but rather to how the recording industry was profiting from the destruction of an entire culture of musical performance. The AFM's musicians' fund, by redistributing a nominal portion of the recording companies' profits, would bring the displaced performers a measure of dignity as well as financial security—and also sponsor thousands of free concerts in parks and schools across the country, at the record companies' expense.

Having normal recording activity disrupted for two years was without question demoralizing as well as costly to the recording industry. Yet the strike did not permanently reduce the public's appetite for recorded music, and the industry recovered quickly. In 1941, the last full year before the ban, American recording companies sold a total of 120 million records; the figure was roughly comparable in 1945. In 1946, two years after the strike ended, the figure had more than doubled, to 275 million.

Billie Holiday's Departure, Eugene Ormandy's Arrival, and the Rise of Frank Sinatra

Columbia's greatest artistic loss during the war years came in 1944, when Billie Holiday defected to Decca. "God Bless the Child," released in 1941, won Holiday acclaim and would go on to be her most popular and most covered song. But the following year, never entirely at home either at ARC or Columbia, she recorded the melancholy "Trav'lin' Light" with Paul Whiteman and His Orchestra for release on the new Capitol label, and the record sold well. (To avoid contractual conflict with Columbia, Holiday was credited under the soon-to-be famous nickname given to her by Lester Young, "Lady Day.") After a brief intermediary period during which she performed with Eddie Heywood and His Orchestra on Milt Gabler's Commodore label (which had earlier released "Strange Fruit" after Columbia turned it down), Gabler finally lured Holiday to Decca, where he had since become an A&R man. Over the next three years, her releases included "Lover Man" and "Good Morning Heartache."

Along with Holiday's departure, though, the early 1940s also saw two extraordinary additions to the Columbia fold. The first signing was in classical music. According to one version of the story, Ike Levy, the lawyer who had been instrumental in getting William Paley involved in the recording business, was also a member of the Philadelphia Orchestra's board of directors, and he had become dissatisfied with RCA Victor's handling of the orchestra's recordings. With a new conductor and music director, Eugene Ormandy, about to replace Leopold Stokowski, Levy supposedly got his brother's brother-in-law, Paley, to buy Columbia in order to poach Ormandy and

Charlie Christian with Benny Goodman

William Paley

the orchestra from Victor. It took years to complete the switch, but in May 1943, in the middle of the Petrillo ban, the Philadelphia Orchestra and its new conductor finally joined Columbia—one of the most important acquisitions in classical music in the company's history.

Ormandy had been born in Hungary in 1899 as Jenö Blau. A violin prodigy who went on to earn a university degree in philosophy, he moved to the United States in 1921 and changed his name. Thanks to a former Budapest friend and fellow émigré, the conductor Erno Rapee, he quickly found work as violinist at Major Bowes's Capitol Theater in New York, a major silent movie palace. It was an excellent job, and Ormandy made the most of it, eventually rising to become one of the ensemble's conductors. In 1931, Arthur Judson (who had started the broadcasting company that would evolve into CBS) secured Ormandy to stand in for an ailing Arturo Toscanini in a performance with the Philadelphia Orchestra. That appearance led to Ormandy's appointment as conductor of the Minneapolis Symphony, with which he made several successful recordings of relatively unfamiliar music, including works by Schoenberg and Bruckner, for Victor in 1934 and early 1935. Ormandy then moved back east to work as associate conductor under Stokowski in Philadelphia. After winning the post of music director in 1938, he conducted between 100 and 180 concerts a year.

An exceptional musical mind, able to learn scores quickly and conduct them from memory, Ormandy favored the formal, even reserved podium presence of his hero and friend Toscanini, but he retained the rich legato orchestral style that Stokowski had made famous. This lush manner, dubbed by critics the "Philadelphia Sound," was not especially effective for the standard mainstream repertoire of Haydn, Mozart, and Beethoven, but it was superbly suited to the late Romantic music of Debussy, Dvořák, Ravel, and other composers that Ormandy preferred. Ormandy also became a strong supporter of Sergei Rachmaninoff's music, conducting the composer's own recordings of three of his piano concertos in 1939–1940 as well as the 1941 premiere of his *Symphonic Dances*—a piece that Rachmaninoff dedicated to Ormandy and the orchestra.

Ormandy always considered recording as secondary to his live performances. "I would much rather give concerts!" he told an interviewer in 1961. But his version of the Philadelphia Sound translated extremely well to records. For his first Columbia session in 1944, Ormandy chose, somewhat out of character, Beethoven's Symphony No. 7 and Brahms's Fourth Symphony, as well as Richard Strauss's *Death and Transfiguration*. Over the years, he would go on to conduct and record a wide variety of material, including several symphonies by Dmitri Shostakovich, works by American composers such as Samuel Barber, Ned Rorem, and Roger Sessions, and a wildly popular collaboration with the Mormon Tabernacle Choir singing "The Battle Hymn of the Republic." Ormandy quickly became a pillar of Columbia's revived classical music program.

The other important addition to Columbia's roster, which had direct connections to the Petrillo ban, was Frank Sinatra. Sinatra had joined the fabulously popular Tommy Dorsey band in 1939 after a short stint singing with Harry James. (James, who could not afford to pay Sinatra what he was worth, gave way like a gentleman, earning Sinatra's undying gratitude.) But Sinatra's rising popularity as well as his troubled financial relations with Dorsey forced a difficult decision about whether he should set out on his own. In January 1942, with Dorsey's permission, Sinatra recorded his first solo sessions without the Dorsey band. Before the year was out, Sinatra had left the band completely.

For years, John Hammond's direct superior at Columbia, Emmanuel "Manie" Sacks, who was also one of Sinatra's cronies, had been cajoling the singer to go solo. Once Sinatra did so, Sacks talked Paley into putting the singer on CBS radio, where his voice and his name would reach a mass audience. Sinatra's talents were already recognized by much of the cognoscenti: in May 1941, he was at the top of the polls in both *Billboard* and *DownBeat*. But "Sinatrauma," as the newspapers were to dub it, was just beginning to erupt, as hordes of teenaged listeners began idolizing the singer—especially the bobby-soxers, young females nicknamed for a popular style of socks rolled down just above the ankle.

"I would much rather give concerts!"   Eugene Ormandy

Leopold Stokowski conducting the New York Philharmonic Orchestra at Carnegie Hall, New York

Eugene Ormandy

The first wave of bobby-soxer furor crested at the end of December 1942, when Sinatra appeared as "an extra added attraction" on a music and movie bill starring Benny Goodman and His Orchestra at the Paramount Theater in Times Square. As soon as Goodman brought the young singer to the stage and announced his name, torrents of shrieking came from the girls in the audience. "What the fuck was that?" Goodman wondered aloud, genuinely taken aback; until that night, he had known barely anything about Sinatra and his frenetic fan appeal. "Frank stopped the show every time," Goodman's trumpeter Yank Lawson later recalled of the Paramount run (which was extended for Sinatra from one week to eight). "The lines were four deep clear around the block with people trying to get in."

Dismissed by some critics as a fad, the Sinatra explosion turned out to be the start of an unprecedented rise to stardom, which carried the singer through a spectacular extended engagement at the Riobamba club, a return engagement at the Paramount in May, and a contract for regular appearances on the popular radio show *Your Hit Parade*. When Sinatra returned yet again to the Paramount in October 1944, riots nearly broke out. The theater could not accommodate the swarms who wanted to attend, estimated at as many as 35,000—their excitement deftly reinforced by promotional ads and gimmicks dreamed up by theater promoters and Columbia's publicity department. (Among other tricks, the promoters would hire young women to scream or even simulate fainting at the very mention of Sinatra's name.) While the decibel level from his fans became deafening, Sinatra's earnings soared, from $150 per week for the first run at the Paramount to $25,000 per week for his shows there eighteen months later. And on June 1, 1943, with the rerelease of "All or Nothing at All" in the offing, Columbia signed Sinatra to a solo contract, lending him $25,000 to help break his contract with Dorsey.

In retrospect, "Sinatrauma" looks like a forerunner of the Elvis Presley craze of the mid-1950s and the "Beatlemania" of the mid-1960s—and the emergence of a definable commercial youth culture (and, for the record labels, a fifteen- to twenty-four-year-old market demographic) that has driven much of American culture ever since. But Sinatra's breakthrough also marked a culmination of shifts in entertainment tied directly to alterations in the recording industry that began in the 1920s. With the introduction of additional budget record lines in the wake of the Great Crash, greatly augmented by the spread of the jukebox, recording companies reached teenagers and young adults as never before. By the mid-1930s, the jitterbug craze, fed by recordings by the big bands, had arisen directly from the changes in record marketing and the spread of the jukebox. All these conditions meant that the teen market was primed to welcome a star of epic proportions. During World War II, a new cohort of swooning bobby-soxers made Sinatra that megastar—his tender bel canto voice, long-breath phrasing, and shambling skinniness conveying romance, virility, and vulnerability all at once. Sinatra himself could not quite believe the reaction: "If I bent a note, looped a note, they went wild," he remembered years later. And Sinatra's emergence as a teen idol affirmed the cultural turn in which the singer, and not the bandleader and his musicians, became the focus of adoration.

Once Sinatra had signed with Columbia, he and Sacks wanted to wait out the musicians' ban so that the singer's debut on record would be as strong as possible. But, in June and July of 1943 when Jack Kapp at Decca released *a capella* records of Crosby and the up-and-coming vocalist Dick Haymes backed by choral groups, Columbia, possessing no additional Sinatra recordings to reissue, panicked. So, in a series of four studio sessions that ran from June until November, Sinatra performed with the Bobby Tucker Singers under the direction of the composer-arranger Alec Wilder. Of the nine songs recorded, seven, including "Close to You" and "People Will Say We're in Love," landed on the best-seller chart. A year later, on November 24, 1944, only thirteen days after the Petrillo ban ended, Sinatra was back in the studio with a full orchestra and his superb orchestral arranger and conductor, Axel Stordahl, recording a batch of songs that included "But a Dream," later described by the critic Will Friedwald as "the ne plus ultra of Sinatra-Stordahl, with Sinatra awash in an ocean of strings, holding notes all over the place like a long wave of sound."

Through 1945, Sinatra returned to the studio fourteen times and appeared in two films, *Anchors Aweigh* with Gene Kelly, and a brief picture for RKO, *The House*

"Frank stopped the show every time . . . The lines were four deep clear around the block."

Yank Lawson on Frank Sinatra's frenetic fan appeal

"If I bent a note, looped a note, they went wild."

Frank Sinatra

Frank Sinatra with Axel Stordahl

Previous page:
Frank Sinatra, Columbia Studios (left). Crowds waiting outside the Paramount Theater, New York City, before a Sinatra performance (top right). Frank greeting fans, Pasadena, California.

Alex Steinweiss and the Birth of the Album Cover

The new concept was commercially as well as artistically successful

Alex Steinweiss is renowned among graphic designers and commercial artists as the inventor of the record album cover, but he deserves even wider recognition. Until the early twentieth century, the presentation of music in commercial visual media did not rise above the simple vignettes that appeared on the covers of sheet music. Through the Depression years, the recording companies designed their albums of 78s as dull, book-like packages, usually unadorned with any pictures. But soon after Steinweiss, at the precocious age of twenty-two, arrived at Columbia as its first art director in 1939, he changed all of that dramatically and invented a bold new art form.

Trained in the graphic arts at Brooklyn's Abraham Lincoln High School and the Parsons School of Design, Steinweiss worked for three years with the great Austrian émigré poster designer, Joseph Binder. At Columbia, he enlivened album covers by drawing on the Modernist pictorial and typographical innovations of the Bauhaus school in Germany, the Dutch De Stijl movement, and Russian Constructivism. His first cover, for a collection of Rodgers and Hart songs, showed a high-contrast photo of a theater marquee with the album's title in lights. The new concept was commercially as well as artistically successful: sales of Bruno Walter's recording of Beethoven's "Eroica" symphony increased ninefold when graced with Steinweiss's cover.

After Steinweiss worked in a civilian job for the United States Navy during World War II, Ted Wallerstein brought him back to Columbia on a freelance basis, to develop packaging for the LP. Steinweiss's idea of placing the discs inside folded cardboard, with the art glued on front and liner notes on the back, quickly became the industry standard, as it remained until the advent of the compact disc. Steinweiss's early LP covers—complete with his personal lettering style, which was dubbed the "Steinweiss scrawl"—extended further his brilliance at visually representing the music contained within.

Columbia Records would continue to innovate and excel in its design and packaging in the 1960s and after, under the direction of such major figures as Neil Fujita and Bob Cato. Alex Steinweiss, though, was the pioneer, whose work for Columbia broke down the barriers between commercial design and high art.

Sean Wilentz

Alex Steinweiss

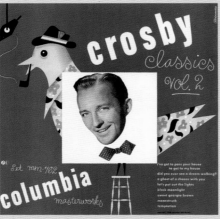

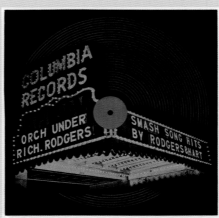

I Live In. The first established the singer—whose vocal skills at this point greatly outstripped his acting ability—as a legitimate movie performer; the second, with its song of the same name, further popularized the ideals of religious and racial tolerance that had become lodestars in the nation's struggle against the Nazis. Above and beyond raising soldiers' morale, recording stars had entered the war propaganda effort, most notably Glenn Miller's Army Air Force Band, whose repertoire mixed swing entertainment with explicitly anti-Nazi, pro-Allies material. (Miller would give his life to the cause when a plane in which he was flying disappeared over the English Channel at the end of 1944.) Sinatra would eventually shift rightward politically, but in 1945 he was still a strong liberal. Both *The House I Live In* and the song with the same title (with music composed by the talented Popular Front Communist Earl Robinson and lyrics by another talented Communist Party member, Abel Meeropol, who also wrote "Strange Fruit") exuded a wartime left-leaning liberal spirit, denouncing bigotry and celebrating America as the country of the little guy.

Peace!

The Allied victory in World War II beckoned to a bright future for Columbia and the country at large. Under the aegis of CBS, the label arguably survived the conflict (including its home-front struggle with the musicians' union) stronger than it was when the conflict began. For the company's executives, artists, and other employees (including young George Avakian, who survived his combat service in the Pacific), and for the nation, the peace amounted to a new beginning after more than fifteen years combined of economic catastrophe and world war. Unlike in 1918, the United States emerged from the war a superpower in geopolitics, its economy revived by four years of military production, whereas much of Europe lay in ruins.

The Columbia Recording Corporation wasted no time in preparing for the postwar adjustments and opportunities—and, as it did so, new leaders arose from within its ranks. In November 1945, three months after the war ended, Ted Wallerstein flew to Europe to reestablish distribution to that reviving market. On the return trip, a storm in Lisbon grounded Wallerstein, leaving a young executive named Goddard Lieberson, who had taken over as director of Columbia Masterworks, temporarily in charge. No one could have predicted it at the time, but young Lieberson would prove central to Columbia's achievements at mid-century.

An American serviceman dancing the jitterbug with a young woman

Frank Sinatra, Columbia Studios

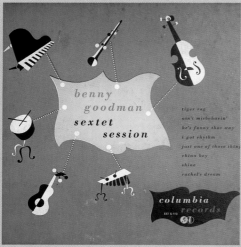

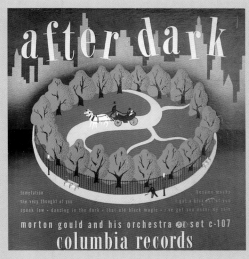

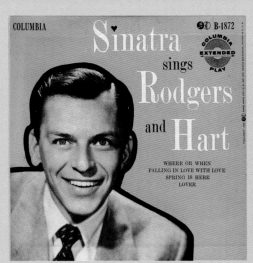

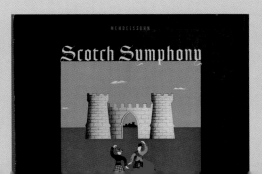

Chapter 4

The Golden Years of Mid-Century

Paris had been the international cultural capital of the nineteenth century, but after 1945 New York City became the international capital of the twentieth. While the great European cities were still recovering, physically and psychologically, from the war's devastation, Manhattan's skyscrapers glistened. Wall Street and Madison Avenue were dynamos of global finance and advertising. In every imaginable sector of literature and the arts—book publishing, radio (and soon television), art dealing, painting (in the heroic early days of abstract expressionism), museums (notably the Museum of Modern Art), academic scholarship, opera, dance, theater (ranging from Broadway musicals to experimental drama), orchestral music, jazz, and more—New York became the center of action for performers, writers, and artists as well as for the venues, entrepreneurs, and companies that presented them. Columbia Records was very much part of that heady mix. Over the decade and a half after the war's conclusion, the label acquired a new cosmopolitan prestige, a reputation for technical virtuosity, and a carefully cultivated image of refined exuberance.

Leonard Bernstein conducting vocal soloists and the New York Philharmonic at Carnegie Hall, New York

Columbia's overall record sales doubled between 1945 and 1946, but the excitement was palpable in many other ways. Notably, the company's relations with its parent corporation, Columbia Broadcasting, always in flux, were now singularly harmonious. CBS enlarged the company's offices at 799 Seventh Avenue. A new trainee program began for returning veterans, and the company augmented every department, from electroplating to sales, with fresh talent. The label increased its radio programming on CBS, sponsoring *Masterworks of Music* for the classical line and *Columbia Record Shop* for popular records. In March 1947, the company was reorganized under the name of Columbia Records, Inc., Subsidiary of the Columbia Broadcasting System, Inc. Ted Wallerstein, who had been rebuilding the company for eight years, was named a director of CBS; at the end of 1947, he was elected chairman of the board. And, as Wallerstein reached the zenith of power, a Columbia executive twenty years his junior was preparing the way for the next stage of the label's development.

Goddard Lieberson

Goddard Lieberson had arrived at Columbia in 1939, still in his twenties but already cutting an accomplished and intriguing figure. Born in England in 1911, the son of the Russian-born owner of the country's first rubber heel factory, he had emigrated with his family first to Canada and then to the United States, where he grew up in Seattle. For a time, he attended the University of Washington in Seattle and then moved, in 1932, to the Eastman School of Music in Rochester, New York. A talented young musician with broad literary interests—at age sixteen, he had set James Joyce's poem "Alone" to music—Lieberson supported himself as a nightclub pianist, newspaper music critic, and private-school music teacher. He came to epitomize what had already become a familiar figure in the musical world, the gifted, aspiring immigrant or first-generation American, often Jewish, who found opportunity in the music industry and made his mark there. And his mark would include undermining conventional discriminations between "high" (or classical) and "low" popular forms. Lieberson heard excellence in all kinds of music and stood by his standards of excellence.

Young Lieberson was socially ambitious and not shy about seeking out well-known artists whom he admired. While still a student he had befriended the great African American writer and composer James Weldon Johnson as well as Carl Van Vechten, the New York–based photographer, aesthete, and author of the scandalous novel *Nigger Heaven*. But Lieberson was also a serious and prolific composer. By the end of the 1930s, he had written more than one hundred works, several of which were performed by orchestras under the aegis of the New Deal's Works Progress Administration. WPA work was not enough, though, to make up for the financial hardships and uncertainties of the late Depression years.

Newly married, his Eastman School degree work still unfinished, Lieberson settled in Manhattan, unsure about whether he could make a living at his art, and lacking any clear idea of where his career was headed. "I guess I came to New York to see what the hell was going on," he wrote to a friend many years later. After deciding against accepting a position with a music publisher, he followed a suggestion from a new friend, John Hammond, and took a $50-a-week job at Columbia, where he was assigned a position as Moe Smith's assistant at Columbia Masterworks. Lieberson quickly won Ted Wallerstein's respect by working hard to improve the label's classical catalog. After four years, Lieberson took over at Columbia Masterworks.

Through the war years and the war's immediate aftermath, Lieberson's patrician charm helped keep the Masterworks artists happy and launched Lieberson into the highest circles of sophisticated Manhattan society. Lieberson was the consummate man about town, the guy who aimed to know everyone who was worth knowing, and who was unashamed about sprinkling impressive names into his conversation. He was famous for his wining and dining, and even more for his clever, knowing wit. (He once sent a royalty check to the pianist and art collector Rudolf Serkin, one of the classical musicians he had helped bring to Columbia,

Miles Davis with
Goddard Lieberson

Goddard Lieberson
with Dave Brubeck

Goddard Lieberson
with Leonard Bernstein

with the note, "Here is another Utrillo!") He also acted on his impatience with the conventional distinctions between "elevated" and "popular" music. Among his more inspired artistic efforts were two prototypes for what would eventually be called "crossover" classical recordings: an album of selections from George Gershwin's opera *Porgy and Bess* released in 1945 and, two years later, Béla Bartók's *Contrasts for Violin, Clarinet, and Piano*, written on a commission from Benny Goodman.

Lieberson also surrounded himself with worldly and highly talented friends whom he had met on the way up. Among them was the eccentric, gifted composer Alec Wilder, formerly a fellow student of Lieberson's at the Eastman School in Rochester. Drawn to Manhattan as Lieberson was, Wilder was also drawn to popular music and he composed numerous hits, including the Mills Brothers' "I'll Be Around." But Wilder championed contemporary classical music as well, and he recorded several of his own jazz-influenced pieces for Brunswick in the late 1930s, with an ensemble he called the Alec Wilder Octet. (The group's oboist was another former Eastman student who would soon begin an important career at Columbia, Mitch Miller.) In 1945, Columbia released a set of Wilder's chamber pieces—conducted by its new singing sensation, Frank Sinatra.

The social whirl contributed to the dissolution of Lieberson's marriage amid his prolonged affair with the renowned ballet dancer Vera Zorina, who at the time was married to the choreographer George Balanchine. After both of their divorces were finally decreed, in 1946, Lieberson and Zorina wed—at Ted Wallerstein's house in Westport, Connecticut. (Zorina was already pregnant with the couple's first child.) Earlier that year, Lieberson had been promoted to vice president of Columbia—the same corporate level as his popular music counterpart, Frank Sinatra's pal Manie Sacks, and only one step below Wallerstein in the Columbia Records hierarchy.

Changing Length and Changing Speeds

All along, in another sector of Columbia Records, a secret project was underway that would revolutionize the recording industry. The revolution was made public on June 21, 1948, at a press conference at New York's Waldorf Astoria Hotel. Columbia, Wallerstein announced, had designed a 12-inch, long-playing record, manufactured on unbreakable Vinylite, which contained up to 22½ minutes of music per side, along with a 10-inch version which played 13½ minutes per side—and the label was ready to release recordings in the new formats right away. The new longer-playing records would be more durable than the standard 78s as well as, overall, less expensive: one 12-inch long-playing record featuring an entire symphony would cost $4.85, compared to $7.25 for an album of five conventional 78s containing the same symphony.

Wallerstein then demonstrated the new record on an inexpensive long-playing adapter, manufactured by the Philco company, that consisted of a turntable, a motor geared to 33⅓-rpm, and a lightweight pickup arm, and that could be plugged into any radio or conventional phonograph. Columbia had never quite abandoned its connection, dating back to the label's inception, to producing phonographic equipment. The company continued to manufacture what it called its Viva-tonal Phonograph, marketed in tandem with its new electric process recordings, until 1928; it produced radio phonograph combinations through the 1930s and 1940s. But long-playing records required entirely new equipment, and, in alliance with Philco, Columbia was prepared to provide it to listeners at the lowest possible cost.

Wallerstein's announcement was astounding, and the public greeted the news enthusiastically. The very first long-playing recording, of Nathan Milstein performing Mendelssohn's Violin Concerto in E minor with the New York Philharmonic, Bruno Walter conducting, appeared in shops only a week after the press conference. Soon thereafter, Columbia released the first pop long-playing record, *The Voice of Frank Sinatra*, in the 10-inch format, although most of the label's new pop recordings would remain for the time being on 78s. By the end of 1948, Columbia had sold 1,250,000 long-playing records.

Engineers and the top insiders at Columbia had been laboring over [the LP], on and off, for a decade.

Bruno Walter conducting

Igor Stravinsky

The LP Era Begins

The biggest immediate beneficiary was the Broadway original cast album

The introduction by Columbia Records of the 12-inch 33⅓-rpm phonograph record—the album—benefited every kind of recorded music. Classical music derived particular benefit because many works were quite long.

The biggest immediate beneficiary, though, was the Broadway original cast album. The LP arrived in 1948, and the next year, Rodgers and Hammerstein delivered a triumphant, fully integrated musical, *South Pacific*. The show, at that time the longest-running in history, was released on 78s and EPs as well as LP, but it was the album that proved to have the longest life.

It's not hard to see why: hit songs from shows had long been a major factor in American pop, but the LP provided a way of reliving the show, especially since a show's songs now told a complete version of its story. These cast albums can be seen as the first "concept albums," ten years before *Sgt. Pepper's*, twenty-five before *Thriller*.

Cast album sales went on for years rather than the weeks or months pop music usually endured. Lerner and Loewe's *My Fair Lady* cast album spent 480 weeks on the chart (it was number one for fifteen), *The Sound of Music* spent 276, *Camelot* spent 265, *West Side Story* spent 191, *Flower Drum Song* spent 151, *Gypsy* spent 116. And movie soundtracks could sometimes do the same: the *My Fair Lady* soundtrack charted for 111 weeks and *West Side Story*'s for 198. But the cast albums and soundtracks represented more than a revolution in how music was packaged and sold—they also steered musicians, the industry, and most important, the audience toward new ways of listening.

Dave Marsh

Cast of *The Sound of Music*, Columbia Studios

The long-player revolution appeared to come out of nowhere, but engineers and the top insiders at Columbia had been laboring over it, on and off, for a decade. Precedents for long-playing records dated back to the 1920s; indeed, Wallerstein himself, as the general manager of RCA Victor's record division in 1932, had had to shut down the company's experiment with long-playing recording when it failed. Soon after Wallerstein took over as the president of the new CBS-owned Columbia, discussions began about a joint CBS-Columbia research project to make a viable long-playing record. The desired speed remained 33⅓-rpm, which radio stations had used for transcriptions and were thus equipped to play. The key problem lay in finding an effective way to fit a great deal more music per inch on each record—perfecting, both for manufacturing and listening, what became known as the microgroove.

Success has a thousand fathers, and there are contradictory stories about who deserves how much credit for inventing the long-playing record. Peter Goldmark, an engineer and refugee from Hitler's Germany, had been working at CBS laboratories since 1936. He had long wanted to displace the 78-rpm phonograph, whose sound, he later wrote, "seemed to violate what I thought the quality of music should be." According to Goldmark, he approached Wallerstein with a basic concept for a long-playing record, but Wallerstein rebuffed him. (Wallerstein, for his part, later recalled that although Goldmark would go on to oversee the LP project—and later grandly claim virtually all the credit for the LP—"he didn't actually do any of the work." Other accounts claim that William Paley later insisted that Goldmark—and, hence, CBS—receive the glory.) Goldmark then turned to CBS executive Paul Kesten, proposing what he called a "systems approach" in which a management research team would work together to solve complex problems without losing sight of the larger goal. Kesten cleared Goldmark's request for "at least a hundred thousand dollars" to see the effort through.

33⅓ Microgroove: Planning the Revolution

Beginning in 1940 (and then again in earnest after 1945, once the war was over and work could resume once more) the researchers assembled, under Goldmark's and CBS's formal supervision, on the tenth floor of CBS's headquarters at 485 Madison Avenue. One engineer, Bill Bachman, whom Wallerstein had lured away from General Electric to become Columbia's research director, is singled out in many accounts for his brains and leadership, without which, these accounts claim, the project could not have succeeded. But there were several other important participants, including Bill Savory, Ike Rodman, Jim Hunter, Vin Liebler, and, from CBS, Rene Snepvangers. Their basic goal was straightforward—finding the best way to increase greatly the number of grooves per inch on each record without injuring the recordings' fidelity—but the technical complexities were immense. Goldmark had already determined that the lightweight, unbreakable synthetic compound Vinylite, which had come into limited use by the record companies during the war due to the shortage of shellac, would be practicable for long-playing records. Although far too expensive for multidisc 78-rpm recordings of symphonic works, vinyl would be fine if the entire work could be fit on a single disc. But then came the problem of perfecting equipment, especially tone arms and styluses, and making them light enough to produce excellent sound from the microgroove.

As the engineers came up with successive experimental models of long players, Wallerstein kept throwing cold water on their ideas. Each version—first, one that ran from seven to eight minutes per side, then ten to twelve minutes, then eighteen minutes—was inadequate, Wallerstein insisted, as none was suitable to the lengths of most symphonic works, the classical standard by which Wallerstein stood. Ever cautious, Wallerstein was also quick to pounce on the slightest imperfection of sound quality.

As he later conceded, Wallerstein's stubbornness reached the point where it even upset his boss. "Mr. Paley, I think, got a little sore at me," he later recalled, "because I kept saying, 'That's not a long-playing record,' and he asked, 'Well, Ted, what in hell is a long-playing record?' I said, 'Give me a week, and I'll tell you.'" Some of the frustrated scientists and engineers thought Wallerstein impossible. ("The man was inhuman," Goldmark later wrote, although Goldmark also developed a grudging

"...seemed to violate what I thought the quality of music should be."

Peter Goldmark on 78s

Bill Bachman and Peter Goldmark

Peter Goldmark standing next to a tower of 78s holding the same amount of music as the stack of LPs under his arm, 1948

respect for his taskmaster.) Finally, by the summer of 1947, the research team had designed a microgroove long player that passed muster. Columbia had completed its arrangements with the Philco company to produce new turntables and tone arms. There were still some kinks to work out, especially regarding placement of several tracks on each side for pop music records, but Paley had by now invested $250,000 in the project and he decided that it was time to present the new product to the public. Nine months later, at the Waldorf Astoria, the LP revolution hit the market.

Nearly as remarkable as Columbia's announcement, in retrospect, was the refusal of its archrival, RCA Victor, to enter the long-playing field. CBS management had quietly apprised David Sarnoff, the head of RCA, about the breakthrough in April 1948, months ahead of the public announcement, with an offer to license the technology. Columbia presumed that if all the record companies released some version of the LP, the public's acceptance of and adaptation to the new format would proceed all the more smoothly. Wallerstein repeated the offer at the Waldorf press conference. Most of the other recording companies agreed, but RCA turned it down and, early in 1949, announced its own new development of a 7-inch unbreakable record that would play at 45-rpm. No less interested than Columbia in finding a solution to the problems in playing long-form musical pieces on 78s, RCA had developed a rapid record changer, which would allow listeners to stack a large number of records around oversized spindles above the turntable. The records, which played at 45-rpm, would then quickly and automatically drop to the turntable in ordered succession, creating a virtually uninterrupted flow of music. The goal was the same as that of CBS's microgroove LP; RCA simply pursued it with a different technology. Now, rather than switch to Columbia's long-play technology, RCA would fight.

What has since been called "the battle of the speeds" continued for more than a year. Finally, in January 1950, having lost $4.5 million as well as some valuable artists such as the opera singer Ezio Pinza (other artists including Artur Rubenstein and Jascha Heifetz were threatening to leave as well), RCA threw in the towel and announced it would market its own 33⅓-rpm long-playing records. RCA's efforts with the rapid record changer were not totally futile; indeed, for thirty years the 45 would be the industry's favored medium for pop singles, as well as for automatic jukeboxes, which benefited from RCA's new changer design. (Columbia even began issuing its own 45s in 1951.) But for most record buyers, Columbia's victory in the speeds battle provided reassurance that the 33⅓-rpm LP was not a gimmick and could be purchased with confidence for every variety of music.

The LP's impact reached far beyond the musical possibilities it offered. As so much more music could now be contained on a portable and easily stored disc made of vinyl, the process of packaging and merchandising records changed. Until now, the concept of the album had literally meant several discs bound and sold together, in the manner of a photo album. The LP rendered that sort of collection obsolete, and Columbia hired its former art director Alex Steinweiss, who was now working freelance, to come up with fresh packaging. Steinweiss had designed the first illustrated albums for Columbia in 1939, boldly drawing on avant-garde Modernist principles to produce startling and alluring new covers. For the LP, he devised what is known in the industry as the "wrap pack," consisting of paper pasted on cardboard, which would remain the label's design for its 33⅓ releases until the appearance of the compact disc. Steinweiss added his poster-like graphics and clever typography, and thereafter, the art department began hiring new crops of freelance graphic artists to illustrate the LPs. (Later in the 1950s, photographers would arrive on staff, including the artist whose album work many would consider the best in the business, Don Hunstein.) Mail-ordering, meanwhile, became much more practicable, paving the way for the eventual birth of the Columbia Record Club in 1955.

A new recording studio also had to be found to accommodate the large ensembles that would now be recording more than ever, using the magnetic recording tape introduced in the aftermath of World War II. For decades Columbia had recorded in an old German beer hall turned theater with excellent acoustics, Liederkranz Hall on East Fifty-eighth Street, for many of its major orchestral sessions as well as smaller ensembles. But the hiss and rattle of the old building's radiators got picked up on tape,

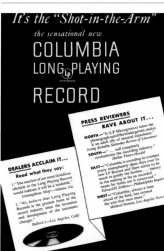

Don Hunstein, Columbia staff photographer

George Szell

Columbia Long-Playing Record advertisement

Aaron Copland

which made the place useless during the colder months of the year. (CBS would ruin the building's tonal magic in 1949 by taking over half the space and installing expensive aluminum control booths.) Early in 1949, company engineers found an alternative on East Thirtieth Street, in an immense, abandoned Greek Orthodox Church from which the radio station WLIB had been broadcasting. With a ceiling more than one hundred feet high and plenty of space to accommodate recording equipment and a walled-off control booth, 207 East Thirtieth, between Second and Third Avenues, would prove a vital asset to Columbia's continued growth.

The LP was designed chiefly with classical music in mind, and Goddard Lieberson made the most of it. Reducing Columbia's traditional heavy reliance on British- and European-made recordings, Lieberson shifted the label's focus toward American composers such as Charles Ives, Virgil Thomson, and Aaron Copland, as well as to music recorded in the United States. In his own way, Lieberson advanced the elevation of the American musical art form to the same level as its European counterpart. He also championed more recent classical music, recording the young Robert Craft conducting the works of Anton Webern as well the French composer and pianist Robert Casadesus performing the complete piano works of Maurice Ravel. Above all, Lieberson forged a relationship between Columbia and Igor Stravinsky that would last until the composer's death in 1971. And, by the mid-1950s, the label's classical catalog was so crammed with talent—such as the conductors Eugene Ormandy, Fritz Reiner, George Szell, and André Kostelanetz—that Columbia began to suffer a true embarrassment of riches, with some artists beginning to feel as if others were receiving more attention from the label's executives.

As it happened, Columbia had decided to undertake an entirely new label to supplement its mainstream label releases. In 1953, the new enterprise, Epic, was born, featuring classical and pop music along with some jazz. Intended to enlarge the company's scope, Epic also helped keep artists' egos in check: George Szell and the Cleveland Orchestra went to Epic, well out of the way of their rivals, Eugene Ormandy and the Philadelphia, who stayed with Columbia. In time, Epic proved an important incubator for new talent—and eventually became a major label in its own right.

The LP Makes Its Way: *South Pacific*, a Documentary Surprise, and Benny Goodman

Curiously, given all that it did for the classics, the LP made some of its greatest initial splashes in three other areas, two of which, Broadway musicals and spoken-word recordings, would become special interests of Goddard Lieberson's.

Back in 1943, Decca (having settled with the American Federation of Musicians in advance of Columbia and RCA Victor) had released a 78-rpm version of Richard Rodgers's and Oscar Hammerstein II's *Oklahoma!* and claimed dominance in the recording of Broadway musicals. Six years later, though, with its LP at the ready, Columbia positioned itself to take over. Early in 1949, under Lieberson's direction, the company released an original cast recording of Cole Porter's *Kiss Me, Kate* both as a bulky 78-rpm package and on a considerably less expensive and less cumbersome microgroove LP. Columbia followed up with an LP of *Finian's Rainbow*, which was nearing the end of its Broadway run. Then, spectacularly, came Rodgers and Hammerstein's *South Pacific*.

Basing their work on James Michener's *Tales of the South Pacific*, Rodgers and Hammerstein, along with the production's book author, Joshua Logan, had fashioned a compelling wartime romantic drama with one of the finest scores ever to hit the Broadway stage. Songs such as "Some Enchanted Evening," "Younger than Springtime," "I'm in Love with a Wonderful Guy," destined to become worldwide standards, populated the score. Ezio Pinza, lured out of his recent retirement from the Metropolitan Opera to star in the show, would soon leave RCA Victor for Columbia; his costar, Mary Martin would reappear on Columbia regularly over the coming decades. *South Pacific* became one of the best-selling LPs of its time. With the record's triumph, Columbia had begun establishing itself as the premier label for Broadway cast recordings.

Mary Martin with Goddard Lieberson, Columbia Studios

Mary Martin and Ezio Pinza in *South Pacific*

The success of another of Columbia's top-selling early LPs was connected to another labor conflict. In 1947, Congress approved, over President Harry S. Truman's veto, the antilabor Taft-Hartley Act, which had the effect of threatening the trust fund won by the American Federation of Musicians three years earlier. For eleven months, beginning in January 1948, James Petrillo and the AFM enforced a second music-recording ban. Although not nearly as effective as the first, the ban did shut down a good deal of musical recording. Eventually, the union and the companies found a way to skirt the law and preserve a modified, independent Music Performance Trust Fund. And the timing turned out to be lucky for CBS radio producer Fred Friendly. Just before the strike commenced, Friendly had conceived the idea of an aural history of world news events from the 1930s and 1940s, and he enlisted Edward R. Murrow to serve as narrator. Lieberson, in part to fend off the possible effects of a new suspension of recorded music, agreed to release Friendly's project as an LP on Columbia Masterworks, and gave Friendly the $1,000 advance he needed to seed the enterprise. The result, *I Can Hear It Now*, was a surprise hit that sold five hundred thousand copies and further popularized the LP format.

The two-LP release of a recording made at Benny Goodman's historic Carnegie Hall concert early in 1938, issued in 1950, showed how well LPs suited jazz. In a purely private gesture, Arthur Marx, a well-to-do friend of Goodman's (and husband of the Goodman band singer Helen Ward), had recorded two sets of acetates of the concert, one of which resurfaced twelve years later. The quality was exceptional, and Goodman (who had been recording for Capitol but was negotiating to return to Columbia) instantly realized he had a major new recording to offer Columbia, without having to step inside a studio. Transferred to LPs, the recordings offered an hour and a half of memorable material on only two discs. *The Famous 1938 Carnegie Hall Jazz Concert*, instantly a strong seller, has survived to this day as one of the most popular of all jazz releases.

At the start of the 1950s, with its catalog of LPs, Columbia was poised for a decade of exceptional growth, but it was also dealing with major personnel changes. In 1949, Lieberson won a promotion to executive vice president, which prompted an infuriated Manie Sacks to leave for RCA Victor. But Lieberson then had to swallow his disappointment when, in 1951, CBS chose Jim Conkling, the head of A&R at Capitol Records, to succeed Ted Wallerstein as Columbia's president. Frank Stanton told Lieberson that he lacked business experience, despite Lieberson's immersion in contrats and royalties with his Masterworks artists. Some observers surmised that the immigrant's son William Paley, for complicated psychological reasons, simply preferred the all-American Conkling to the cultivated arriviste Lieberson.

Mitch Miller: Enter Tony, But Exit Frank

Another important new face had arrived in 1950, when Lieberson helped to recruit as head of Columbia popular A&R a former fellow student from the Eastman School, the oboist turned record producer Mitch Miller. The son of Russian Jewish immigrants, Miller had been raised in Rochester, mastered the oboe as a boy (well enough to play as second oboist in the Syracuse Symphony while he was still in high school), and graduated from Eastman in 1932. When he moved to New York two years later, Miller found steady work for more than a decade playing on radio and in recording sessions until he turned to producing records, first classical, then popular. At the end of the 1940s, Miller was head of popular recordings at Mercury Records, where, though hampered for a time by the second Petrillo strike, he worked with Patti Page and the very young Vic Damone.

Miller's main artist at Mercury was Frankie Laine, whom he persuaded to record what would become a runaway hit in 1949, "Mule Train," complete with its famous overdubbed whip crack, the sort of audio gimmick that Miller loved. Miller himself performed oboe on the first of Mercury's two highly successful *Charlie Parker with Strings* albums, on which the bebop legend substituted a small classical section backed with a rhythm section in place of his usual quintet. Snapped up by Columbia

Doris Day

Jim Conkling
with Mitch Miller

Tony Bennett

"In three seconds I can tell talent. I signed Tony Bennett before I even met him. I heard a demo record he did."

Mitch Miller

Marlene Dietrich with Rosemary Clooney

Ray Conniff

Rosemary Clooney

in 1950, Miller was soon reunited with Laine (with whom he then recorded "Jezebel" and "I Believe") and worked with the full run of Columbia vocalists, including Arthur Godfrey and Doris Day. (Dinah Shore, who had begun a highly successful stint at Columbia, was lured away with a million-dollar deal by RCA Victor the same year Miller arrived.) Miller also quickly landed a brand new singing star.

"In three seconds I can tell a talent," Miller later boasted. "I signed Tony Bennett before I even met him. I heard a demo record he did." That demo, "Boulevard of Broken Dreams," would be reworked by the arranger Marty Manning and become the first big hit in Bennett's long and storied career. Born Anthony Dominick Benedetto in 1926 in Astoria, Queens, Bennett had begun singing early—at age ten, he performed at the official opening of the Triborough Bridge. He soon dropped out of high school to help support his impoverished family and found part-time work as a singing waiter in restaurants all over Queens. After surviving brutal combat in Europe in World War II, including at the Battle of the Bulge, he studied bel canto singing at the American Theater Wing in New York—one of a generation of veterans offered fresh opportunity by the government's GI Bill—while he scrutinized the styles of jazz musicians such as Art Tatum and Stan Getz for pointers on vocal improvisation. He also did some recording and, in 1949, got an enviable booking at Café Society in Greenwich Village, opening for Pearl Bailey. (Invited to the show by Bailey, Bob Hope, impressed, advised the young singer to change his stage name from Benedetto to Bennett.) But despite his experience and talent, Bennett came to Miller's attention a virtually complete unknown.

Under Miller's strict supervision, the singer soon turned into a formidable addition to the label. "Boulevard of Broken Dreams" was followed by "Because of You," with a lush arrangement for strings by Percy Faith (Columbia's newly-arrived chief arranger and conductor); the song hit number one on the *Billboard* chart for ten weeks. Later that year, with similar orchestration, Bennett made a number-one pop hit out of Hank Williams's country standout "Cold, Cold Heart," followed in succeeding years by "Blue Velvet," "Rags to Riches" (another number one hit), and "Strangers in Paradise," from the Broadway show *Kismet*. Bennett also took well to the LP format, starting with *Because of You*, a collection of singles hastily released in 1952. His record, *Cloud 7*, released three years later, was one of the first "concept" albums with a unified musical theme, which presented Bennett performing in a quiet, jazz-inflected mellow style.

Bennett's arrival was all the more fortunate for Columbia because the label was losing its greatest pop star, Frank Sinatra. How and why Sinatra fell out with Columbia is an oft-told and contested story. Mitch Miller caught a good deal of heat, especially from Sinatra, for steering the singer toward cheap novelty songs. Miller shot back that Sinatra had the right to refuse to record anything and besides, as he put it, "Who ever told Sinatra what to do?" (He later insisted that Sinatra "was ruining his own career.") Without question, Sinatra hit a terrible crisis in the early 1950s, personal and professional, as his marriage to film star Ava Gardner collapsed; during one excruciating nightclub engagement in New York, his voice collapsed as well. It is rare to hear artistry as lofty as Sinatra's 1940s recordings for Columbia descend to the likes of "Mama Will Bark," recorded with the early television personality Dagmar as well as a dubbed-in dog bark sound in 1951.

Yet Sinatra also recorded some strong material in his last years with Columbia, including an album issued in 1950, *Swing and Dance with Frank Sinatra*. Sinatra's move to Capitol Records and his fresh collaboration with the arranger Nelson Riddle (beginning with "I've Got the World on a String" in 1953, followed by their smash-hit recording in 1954, "Young at Heart") were certainly in order. But Sinatra had been experimenting with new musical directions before the switch, even as he endured his painful slump.

With Lieberson's go-ahead, Miller kept nurturing Columbia's pop recording stable, adding fresh talent while taking command of performers who were at the label when he arrived. The elegantly tuxedoed, flamboyant, and genuinely gifted entertainer and pianist Liberace already had scores of records and several LPs to his credit (and was about to launch his famous career on nationwide television) when Miller recorded his over-the-top rendition of "September Song," released in 1952. The record outsold all of Liberace's previous releases.

Rosemary Clooney, an excellent, microphone-savvy stylist in the Bing Crosby mold, had made her recording debut on Columbia in 1947, at age nineteen, as the singer, with her sister Betty, for Tony Pastor's big band. A great favorite at the label, she went solo in 1949—but, following Miller's arrival the following year, he effectively took over her recording career. After she had considerable success with "Beautiful Brown Eyes" in 1951 Miller brought her a new song cowritten by William Saroyan, "Come On-a My House." The seductive lark ("Come on-a my house, my house a come on") struck Clooney as beneath her, and she refused to record it—until Miller threatened to fire her. It would prove the first of a string of Clooney hits at Columbia over the rest of the decade.

Miller's style could be heavy-handed, but his touch for producing hits was sure. Through the summer of 1954, Clooney's "Hey There!" and "This Ole House," along with Liberace's middle-brow treatments of Chopin's "Polonaise" and Liszt's "Liebestraum," were among a bevy of best-selling Columbia pop records. The others included releases by Miller's charges Doris Day, Jo Stafford, and the Four Lads. The following year, Miller would be reunited with Vic Damone.

Bluegrass and Honky-Tonk: From Monroe to Frizzell

A world away from Manhattan's bustle and glamour, Columbia recorded in the late 1940s and early 1950s some new landmark pieces of what later came to be known formally as country music. The credit goes chiefly to Art Satherley and Don Law, both of whom had made the transition from ARC to Columbia. The two men worked apart during the war years—Satherley continued overseeing country and western recordings, while Law, at Columbia's behest, took over a short-lived children's record division in New York—but they teamed up again in 1945 and divided responsibility for directing Columbia's country music division, with Satherley covering the country west from El Paso, and Law scouting east. "Hillbilly" or country music enjoyed a boom after World War II, as younger performers such as Hank Williams and Eddy Arnold, with new and popular songs about drinking, loving, and losing, came to the fore. Satherley and Law did more than their part to encourage and capitalize on the excitement. Their acquisitions included the first major artists who played a variation of country music that came to be known in the 1950s as bluegrass.

Bill Monroe and His Blue Grass Boys' releases for Columbia in 1946 and 1947 are widely considered the cornerstone of the bluegrass style. Monroe, the son of a prosperous Kentucky farmer, had been orphaned at age sixteen. He first made his name singing and playing mandolin with his brother Charlie, a guitarist, performing live on one country station after another around the Southeast. Known for their relentless tempos, piercing close harmonies, and Bill's lightning-fast mandolin solos, the Monroe Brothers signed with RCA Victor in 1935 and stayed with the label until 1938, when the duo broke up. Bill then formed a new band of his own, the Blue Grass Boys, named in honor of Kentucky, the Bluegrass State, and continued to record for Victor.

Hired as regulars on WSM's *Grand Ole Opry* in Nashville in 1939, Monroe and his band quickly became country music favorites, with a fan base concentrated in Virginia, the Carolinas, Kentucky, and Tennessee. Three years later, Satherley, who occasionally visited Nashville to deal with his popular star Roy Acuff, learned that Monroe wanted to leave RCA Victor. Despite Columbia's retrenchment of its "hillbilly" offerings amid the shellac shortage, Satherley duly signed Monroe to a one-year contract—only to run into the Petrillo ban. A delayed first session in Chicago early in 1945 produced Monroe's first Columbia release, "Rocky Road Blues" coupled with "Kentucky Waltz," but Satherley's interest in Monroe and his group had waned, and the record did not appear until January 1946. Satherley did not, however, give up on Monroe entirely, and the band reassembled for two days of recording in September 1946. By then, the Blue Grass Boys included two new members, Earl Scruggs on banjo and Lester Flatt on guitar and singing lead vocals.

In those first two days of recording and two more in October 1947—all held in Chicago and all produced by Satherley—Monroe and his revamped group laid down

Art Satherley

The Stanley Brothers

Bill Monroe and His Blue Grass Boys

their new country sound. How to describe that sound—and how new it really was—caused some perplexity at Columbia. As the company had cut loose almost all its Appalachian string bands during World War II, it had become used to releasing country recordings by Gene Autry, Bob Wills, and others like them—music heavily influenced by western or cowboy styles and often played with slick instrumental arrangements. Even Roy Acuff's star had dimmed after the war, as the new crop of honky-tonk-style country singers, Hank Williams above all, made him suddenly sound old-fashioned. On a first listen, Monroe and his group sounded more outdated than Acuff did, almost like a throwback to the rougher, twangy traditional mountain music of Gid Tanner and Charlie Poole. Yet Monroe and his reformed Blue Grass Boys were powerful innovators.

Building on the rapid-fire instrumentals and close harmonies that Bill and Charlie Monroe had perfected ten years earlier, Monroe's new group offered a sophisticated updating of the old-time string band style. Their innovations included the introduction of tight vocal trios, elaborate gospel quartets, and, above all, Scruggs's revolutionary, syncopated three-finger banjo-picking technique, adapted from the playing he had grown up with in North Carolina, a rapid, lively unfolding of rolls and licks that would become synonymous with bluegrass music. The Columbia sessions also highlighted Monroe's enormous talents as a songwriter. Of more than two dozen original sides recorded by the group in 1946 and 1947, only one, Jimmie Rodgers's "Blue Yodel No. 4," was neither written nor cowritten by Monroe. Several of Monroe's numbers, including "Blue Moon of Kentucky" and "Will You Be Loving Another Man?" would eventually become bluegrass classics.

In 1948, Scruggs gave Monroe two weeks' notice, saying that he wanted to return home to care for his mother, whereupon Flatt told Scruggs that he, too, intended to leave the band. Soon thereafter, the pair joined with Monroe's bass player Howard Watts (known as Cedric Rainwater) and started a new group, the Foggy Mountain Boys. Always experimenting—they dispensed with the mandolin, for example, in favor of a Dobro—Flatt and Scruggs took the new bluegrass sound in their own direction. They initially recorded for Mercury Records, with whom they released their masterpiece, "Foggy Mountain Breakdown," in 1949. (Eighteen years later, they would rerecord the number as the theme to the film *Bonnie and Clyde*.) But in 1950, they signed with Columbia and would remain on the label as a duo until 1969, pursuing new musical experiments while releasing brilliant bluegrass versions of old numbers like "Salty Dog." Statistically if not artistically, their "The Ballad of Jed Clampitt," composed for the television series *The Beverly Hillbillies*, remains the greatest hit in the history of country and western music.

Shortly after Flatt and Scruggs left the Blue Grass Boys in 1948, Art Satherley signed an up-and-coming group from southwestern Virginia, the Clinch Mountain Boys, led by the brothers Carter and Ralph Stanley. Formed as a group in 1946, the Stanleys and their band had their radio debut at the end of that year on WCYB in Bristol, Virginia, a premier country music station, with Carter Stanley playing guitar and Ralph singing high tenor vocals and playing clawhammer-style banjo. In 1947, they recorded with the small Rich-R-Tone label and began gaining a considerable regional reputation. Although they drew their inspiration initially from both the recordings of the Carter Family and from the unusual minor-key singing style of their local Primitive Baptist Universalist church, the Stanleys were avid fans of Monroe, Flatt, and Scruggs, and they quickly adopted much of the Blue Grass Boys' style to their own playing. (In 1948, for example, Ralph Stanley dropped his clawhammer banjo playing in favor of Scruggs's style.) Receiving the call from Satherley, Monroe's own producer, was an enormous thrill: "We knew Columbia was the best label there was, same way Cadillac was the best car," Ralph Stanley later recalled.

Having just lost Flatt and Scruggs, Monroe hit the roof when he heard that Columbia had signed the Stanleys, whom he considered imitators as well as rivals—and with some justification. In 1948, during the second Petrillo ban, Monroe and his group had played on the *Opry* broadcast what would become one of Monroe's signature numbers, the racehorse song "Molly and Tenbrooks." The Stanleys heard the broadcast and, impressed, recorded the song for Rich-R-Tone, which was operating outside the musicians' union, and the label released the Stanleys' version before Monroe had even

"We knew Columbia was the best label there was, same way Cadillac was the best car."

Ralph Stanley

Jimmy Dickens (center) and His Country Boys

Lefty Frizzell

Flatt and Scruggs

had the chance to record his own. As soon as he learned that Satherley had come to terms with the Stanleys and the Clinch Mountain Boys, Monroe defected to Decca.

The Stanleys and their band helped Columbia make up for the loss by recording some excellent sides in their three years with the label, including Carter Stanley's songs "The White Dove" and "Little Glass of Wine" and superb arrangements of the traditional numbers "Pretty Polly" and "Man of Constant Sorrow." In time, the Stanleys repaired the breach with Monroe; Carter Stanley even joined the Blue Grass Boys as a guitarist while the brothers were briefly separated in 1951. The Stanleys and the Clinch Mountain Boys would themselves move to Mercury Records in 1952, to be followed by a succession of other labels, until Carter's untimely death, at age forty-one, in 1966. Columbia, meanwhile, having pioneered the recording of bluegrass music, still boasted the exceptional talents of Flatt and Scruggs. And, all the while, the label had been making strides in other branches of country music.

In 1950, Columbia's hottest country act was neither Bill Monroe nor Flatt and Scruggs, nor the Stanleys, but the diminutive *Grand Ole Opry* star "Little" Jimmy Dickens, who possessed an enormous talent for turning novelty songs such as "Take an Old Cold 'Tater (And Wait)" into major hits. One day, Dickens and a group of music-industry notables were gathered in a hotel room in Nashville, listening to demos of songs that Dickens might want to record. A studio owner from Dallas, Jim Beck, showed up with a song that he thought would suit Dickens perfectly, "If You've Got the Money, I've Got the Time." Among those in the room was Don Law, who knew Beck from Dallas. Law, like Dickens, cared little for the song but was greatly impressed by the singer on the demo. He and Satherley duly travelled to Dallas and signed up their new prospect, the twenty-two-year-old Lefty Frizzell.

Born in Corsicana, Texas, but raised in Arkansas, Frizzell had been gaining popularity performing on the honky-tonk nightclub circuit throughout the Southwest. Deeply influenced by the records of Jimmie Rodgers, the young singer invented a distinctive style that smoothed the rougher edges off of honky-tonk music while remaining true to its gritty spirit. Unlike the full-throated Appalachian style of Hank Williams or Roy Acuff, Frizzell's tone and phrasing were nuanced, making full use of the stylistic shadings of the electronic microphone. If anyone could be described as the Bing Crosby of honky-tonk, it would be Lefty Frizzell. And once he signed with Columbia, Frizzell became an instant national star. His first record, a remake of "If You've Got the Money, I've Got the Time," hit number one on the country music chart upon its release—and then its B-side, "I Love You a Thousand Ways," also hit number one. A string of additional smash singles followed in 1952.

Suddenly, though, Frizzell's career, plagued by disputes with his manager and disordered personal finances, began to unravel. The hit records became more sporadic; by the late 1950s, Frizzell had cut back on his recording schedule; in the 1960s, he began a fitful descent into alcoholism that would hasten the stroke that killed him in 1975, at the age of forty-seven. But Frizzell did manage to produce, in 1959, an extraordinary recording of a new song that sounded ancient, "Long Black Veil," written by Danny Dill and Marijohn Wilkin, which remains a standard in the American country and folk repertoires. And for decades to come, his early hits and singular style would influence major country artists, including Roy Orbison, Merle Haggard, Willie Nelson, Keith Whitley, and Dwight Yoakam. "No one could handle a song like Lefty," Haggard has said. "He would hold on to each word until he finally decided to drop it and pick up the next one. Most of us learned to sing listening to him."

Jazz Revives under Avakian: From Brubeck to Armstrong

While country music continued to thrive at Columbia, the label's pop list conspicuously lacked the successors to the jazz and blues masterpieces that had been the company's main claim to artistic fame in the 1920s and 1930s. The absence had to do, in part, with John Hammond. After he concluded his wartime military service, Hammond was expected to return to Columbia and oversee its jazz department, but it was not to be. Very quickly, he ran into serious conflict with Ted Wallerstein over some

Sarah Vaughan

Mahalia Jackson

Erroll Garner

Louis Armstrong,
Columbia Studios

Louis Armstrong
Plays W. C. Handy

Louis Armstrong
with W. C. Handy
and George Avakian

Johnny Mathis

recording and editorial work he had undertaken outside Columbia. And Hammond was indifferent to the bebop revolution then sweeping through the jazz world, so much so that he asked Goddard Lieberson about switching his focus from jazz to classical music, which Lieberson thought was a terrible idea. On the outs with Columbia, Hammond worked for several years at some smaller labels until he took a job at Vanguard Records in 1953. He would not return to Columbia until 1959.

Not that jazz completely disappeared from Columbia with Hammond. Early in 1945, the popular bandleader Woody Herman, attracted in part by the acoustic wonders of Liederkranz Hall, had signed with Columbia, and over the next two years recorded some excellent material for the label, including a soaring arrangement of "Caldonia." The great Duke Ellington returned to Columbia in 1947 to record his first 10-inch LP, *Liberian Suite*, issued in 1948. Two major 12-inch recordings released on Columbia Masterworks soon followed, *Masterpieces by Ellington* and *Ellington Uptown*, before Ellington departed for several years, first for Capitol and then, very briefly, Bethlehem Records. Having dissolved his orchestra in 1949, Benny Goodman regrouped and recorded for Columbia with a revamped sextet. From 1948 through 1953, Columbia also recorded numerous excellent sides by the stylish young singer Sarah Vaughan, who reached crossover stardom with hits like "Black Coffee" and "I Cried For You" before she switched to Mercury. But apart from these artists—and its superb backlist recordings of Louis Armstrong, Bessie Smith, Benny Goodman, and the other prewar greats—Columbia's presence in jazz was not what it had been. Columbia was also slow to release jazz and blues in LP format, lagging well behind smaller independent labels such as Bethlehem, Clef (later Verve), Prestige, Riverside, and, above all, Blue Note. At Columbia, the LP was used chiefly for classical music and pop singers like Sinatra and Bennett.

In time, George Avakian helped turn the situation around. After his discharge from the army in 1946, Avakian rejoined the Columbia production staff. With Hammond gone, he resumed his work on the Hot Jazz Classics series and later adapted some of his reissues to LP. But when he was appointed director of the pop music department in 1947, Avakian became immersed in preparing an extensive pop catalog of 10-inch LPs. "Jazz was really an afterthought and came later," he would recall. "There really wasn't much of a strategy with the 10-inch LP for jazz at Columbia."

The change began in 1954, when the popular sui generis pianist Errol Garner cut his debut album for Columbia with Avakian. (Avakian would soon go on to produce Garner's *Concert by the Sea*, a hit that became a classic.) That same year, well outside the white-bread pop mold, Avakian recorded Mahalia Jackson's first album for Columbia, *The World's Greatest Gospel Singer*, a title that reviewers were happy to affirm. Dave Brubeck, developing the cooler jazz sound that was taking hold, also turned up on Columbia's doorstep in 1954, looking for a recording company more powerful than his home base, Fantasy Records in San Francisco. Avakian produced Brubeck and his quartet, including the brilliant alto sax player Paul Desmond, for three more years. And Brubeck came to appreciate Columbia's clout when his face appeared on the cover of *Time* magazine on November 8, 1954. He formed a connection with Columbia that would last until the late 1960s, with many musical highlights, above all the landmark *Time Out* in 1959, which included Desmond's "Take Five" and Brubeck's "Blue Rondo à la Turk."

With Brubeck about to join Columbia, the label's president, Jim Conkling, gave Avakian carte blanche to produce an album of anything he'd like to record. Still only thirty-five years old, the one-time jazz history whiz kid chose the music of W. C. Handy, to be performed by Louis Armstrong. The only difficulty was that Armstrong, who had no long-term contractual deal, had been tending to record for Decca. But Armstrong's no-nonsense manager, Joe Glaser, negotiated a deal in which Armstrong would finally receive royalties for his old Hot Five and Hot Seven recordings. The project would bring together the gifts of two of Columbia's greatest musicians, overseen by the much younger man who had become the major force in Columbia's jazz recording program.

So, over three days in mid-July 1954, Louis Armstrong and His All-Stars (Trummy Young on trombone, Barney Bigard on clarinet, Arvell Shaw on bass, and Barrett Deems on drums, with Velma Middleton contributing additional vocals) gathered in Chicago. They recorded eleven Handy numbers, ranging from standards

such as "St. Louis Blues" and "Yellow Dog Blues" to the more obscure "Chantez-les Bas." When Handy, now past eighty and blind, heard the playback in New York, he nearly wept with pleasure and gratitude.

Louis Armstrong Plays W. C. Handy is widely admired as Armstrong's best record of the 1950s and one of the finest of all jazz recordings. The LP format lent itself to the appreciation of jazz improvisation: the album's version of "St. Louis Blues," which ran to more than eight minutes, is arguably the best ever recorded of Handy's most famous composition, rivaled only by the one recorded thirty years earlier for Columbia, with Bessie Smith backed by Armstrong. The album also led to a fresh surge of public interest in Armstrong, which Columbia was happy to feed. In May 1955, Avakian gathered the All Stars in New York to record *Satch Plays Fats*, a dazzling collection of Fats Waller songs. Three months later, Columbia recorded Armstrong and the All Stars' rendition of "Mack the Knife," which would introduce Kurt Weill and Bertolt Brecht to the American hit parade. (Weill's widow, Lotte Lenya, had just recorded the song for Columbia as well, for an album of Weill's Berlin theater songs that would appear in 1956.) Concert appearances by Armstrong at the end of the year and in January 1956, in Milan, Amsterdam, and Hollywood, yielded material for Columbia's *Ambassador Satch*, a recording that was several notches below the Handy and Waller albums. Nevertheless, the record led to broadcasts of Armstrong playing in concert on Edward R. Murrow's top-rated CBS television show *See It Now*, which further consolidated Armstrong's hold on the public's imagination. With his infectious, exuberant smile and good-natured humor, as well as his blazing talent, Armstrong was able to win over mainstream white audiences of the mid-1950s as the embodiment of jazz style.

Jazz had truly returned to Columbia, with Avakian fully involved. New albums appeared from Buck Clayton and Eddie Condon. The annual Newport Jazz Festivals, directed by the pianist-turned-impresario George Wein, arranged for Columbia to record at the third gathering in 1956. Several fine albums resulted from these live recordings, above all *Ellington at Newport*, featuring Paul Gonsalves's stunning saxophone solo of twenty-seven choruses on "Diminuendo and Crescendo in Blue." (Technical snafus required Ellington to rerecord portions of the performance, including Gonsalves's dizzying salvos, which upset some jazz sticklers, but Ellington was undisturbed, as long as he could offer a listenable version of what he called "the rhythmic groove of the century." A tape of the original did turn up years later, though, and the original performance was restored.) The album reinvigorated Ellington's career, and several projects with Columbia ensued, including the landmark recording of the soundtrack for Otto Preminger's *Anatomy of a Murder*, one of the first feature films to showcase jazz.

On a trip to San Francisco in 1956, Avakian was introduced to the singing of a talent who would blossom under Mitch Miller's tutelage. The lean, boyishly handsome Johnny Mathis, born John Royce, possessed a light, appealing voice unlike any Avakian had ever heard. Recruited to Columbia as a jazz singer, Mathis recorded an album of standards, which flopped. Miller took over and called in musical director Ray Conniff (who had previously worked with Rosemary Clooney and Frankie Laine, among others) to supply arrangements of soft romantic ballads. Mathis's career took off in 1957 with his recordings of "Wonderful! Wonderful!" which would reach number fourteen on the Billboard chart, "It's Not for Me to Say," which would reach number five, and "Chances Are," which would reach number one.

Miles Davis

At the 1955 Newport Jazz Festival, Avakian heard the sound of jazz's future. Columbia's slowness to rev up its jazz program after 1948 had left it bereft of the bebop musicians who were remaking the genre. One of the youngest beboppers, the prodigious trumpeter Miles Davis had emerged from St. Louis and moved to New York in 1944 at the age of eighteen, to study at Julliard—but he left the school after he latched on to the jam sessions at Minton's Playhouse on West One Hundred and Eighteenth Street in Harlem, the general headquarters of the bebop revolution. He went on to play for two

> "I heard and saw jazz's first modern superstar."
>
> George Avakian on Miles Davis

John Coltrane, Cannonball Adderley, and Miles Davis recording *Kind of Blue*, Columbia Studios

Miles Davis with Gil Evans

stints in Charlie Parker's combo. During the early 1950s, Davis embarked on his own and conducted historic experiments in "cool" jazz and bluesier hard bop.

Davis had already approached Avakian about possibly joining Columbia, but Avakian had demurred, put off by Davis's disabling heroin addiction and his long-term contract entanglement with Prestige Records. But hearing a sober Davis at Newport perform Thelonious Monk's "'Round Midnight," with a combo that included Monk, persuaded Avakian to think again. "I heard and saw jazz's first modern superstar," Avakian later recalled. "What struck me was that Miles was the best ballad player since Louis Armstrong. I was convinced that his ballad playing would appeal to the public on a very large scale." While Davis was still rapidly finishing several albums he owed to Prestige, he also completed for Avakian, in three sessions in 1955 and 1956, the hard bop album *Round About Midnight*, which Columbia released in March 1957. As part of the deal, Davis made sure that his accompanists were the other members of the quintet with whom he was then playing at the Café Bohemia in Greenwich Village: John Coltrane on tenor saxophone, Red Garland on piano, Paul Chambers on bass, and Philly Joe Jones on drums.

Davis's Columbia recording output during the remainder of the decade was a steady buildup of beautiful performances that led to an astounding culmination. After Avakian teamed him up with the arranger Gil Evans, who wrote charts for larger ensembles, Davis recorded *Miles Ahead*, which would lead to the masterpieces *Porgy and Bess* and *Sketches of Spain*. In April 1958, working with a new sextet, Davis issued *Milestones*. Jazz musicians including Davis had been looking for fundamental changes in form that would let them break free of the chord structures of even the most advanced hard bop, or the new synthesis of jazz and classical music called "third stream." Davis worked with these new approaches, but on some of his records in the late 1950s he also experimented with modal composition, scrapping the conventional major and minor chord structure in favor of simple scales or a series of scales for improvisation. It was modal composition that he would use to create his definitive masterpiece.

In two sessions at the Thirtieth Street studio in March and April 1959, Davis recorded the landmark all-modal album *Kind of Blue*. He was accompanied by a sextet that included Coltrane, Chambers, pianist Wynton Kelly (later replaced by Bill Evans), alto saxophonist Cannonball Adderley, and drummer Jimmy Cobb. Davis had not spent much time composing the album's numbers—"Miles conceived these settings only hours before the recording dates," Evans recounted on the album's liner notes—and, as had become typical with Miles, there was little rehearsal, and the musicians had hardly any idea of what they were to perform. But beginning with its first cut, "So What"— consisting of a mode based on two scales—the relaxed improvisations and melodic freedom of *Kind of Blue* sounded a direct contrast to the rigid chord structures of bebop.

The result immediately won plaudits from critics and enthusiasm from fans. The album's influence would prove profound, shaping jazz masterpieces such as John Coltrane's *My Favorite Things* and *A Love Supreme*, but also inspiring a later generation of rock and roll improvisers ranging from Pink Floyd to the Allman Brothers' Band (whose popular concert number from the early 1970s, "In Memory of Elizabeth Reed," is Duane Allman's version of Davis's "All Blues"). More than fifty years after its release, critics cite *Kind of Blue* as one of the greatest of all jazz albums. According to the music historian Ashley Kahn, "*Kind of Blue* is the premier album of its era, jazz or otherwise."

Stringing and Singing Along with Mitch

One popular musical innovation that Columbia largely spurned in the 1950s was rock and roll, along with the rhythm and blues that preceded it. Addressing the first annual trade convention of disc jockeys in Kansas City in 1958, Mitch Miller lambasted "the juvenile stuff pumped over the airwaves these days [that] hardly qualifies as music." A year earlier, at a CBS stockholders' meeting, a songwriter named Gloria Parker demanded that the larger corporation divest itself of any links with companies that promoted "this rock and roll junk which is creating juvenile delinquency." Columbia's top management would not go quite that far. When he was

Mitch Miller,
Columbia Studios

Dave Brubeck Quartet,
Time Out

Previous Page:
Miles Davis,
Columbia Studios

Charles Mingus

invited to join a committee of prominent music-industry executives in denouncing rock and roll's depravity, Goddard Lieberson (who disliked the music) refused on the inviolable principle of free expression. Yet Columbia remained unreceptive.

As Parker's remarks suggested, the attacks on rock and roll, above and beyond the music's character, were part of a powerful, wider anxiety that arose in the early 1950s about youth culture in general. The public was so concerned about the supposedly wayward morals of the evolving teen demographic that the Senate Subcommittee on Juvenile Delinquency was established in 1953. This was followed, a year later, by the formation of the Comics Code Authority to rein in gory comic book content. Finally, in 1959, the House of Representatives Subcommittee on Legislative Oversight and the Federal Communications Commission began investigations into alleged bribery schemes (dubbed "payola") involving payoffs by independent record companies to DJs, which allegedly was the sole reason why radio stations were promoting rock and roll.

"Pay-to-play" arrangements had in fact long been part of the music industry, dating back well before radio to the days when vaudeville performers quietly took money to perform and make hits out of songs for certain publishers. But the allegations of criminality ruined some careers, most notably that of the pioneer rock and roll DJ Alan Freed, and for a time the outcry had a chilling effect on the entire entertainment industry. CBS, in particular, exerted additional pressure on Columbia to avoid rock and roll, out of fears that the FCC might eventually start revoking the licenses of radio and television stations that played the offending music. Mitch Miller would later tell the music historian Colin Escott, somewhat disingenuously, that CBS's concerns were the basic reason why Columbia shied away from rock and roll. "I wanted to make a profit for Columbia, and I could have hired guys to cut rock 'n' roll," Miller recalled, "but you had to pay to get played."

With CBS growing anxious and Miller standing guard, Columbia made no better than indifferent efforts to sign artists who sounded too much like Elvis Presley or Buddy Holly—two artists whom Columbia actually had opportunities to record. In 1957, Columbia released instrumental material recorded by Holly's producer Norman Petty, but, pointedly, it was not rock and roll. The label did occasionally make big inroads into the rock and roll–dominated youth market with major releases by country singers like Ray Price, Marty Robbins, Johnny Horton, and Jimmy Dean, but they, too, were not rock and roll performers.

Columbia's continuing commitment to country and western music did sometimes pull the label closer to rock and roll. After the up-and-coming country singer Marty Robbins, working with Don Law, enjoyed a country hit with "Singing the Blues" in 1956, Mitch Miller had the pop singer Guy Mitchell cover the song for the crossover market—and Mitchell's version topped the pop charts, selling two million copies. Robbins was incensed, and Miller duly handed him over to the arranger Ray Conniff, who helped Robbins release a string of pop country hits that sounded close enough to rock and roll, beginning in 1957 with "A White Sport Coat and a Pink Carnation." As a concession to get a young Memphis country singer named Johnny Cash to sign with Columbia, the label also recorded Cash's friend, the rockabilly star Carl Perkins. Having already recorded "Blue Suede Shoes" for Sun, Perkins had barely survived an automobile accident in 1956. In 1958, after he had recovered and returned to live performing, he began working with Columbia and recorded a dozen singles over the next five years, notably "Whole Lotta Shakin' Goin' On" (already made a hit by Jerry Lee Lewis).

There were also some important releases for young listeners on Columbia's subsidiary label, OKeh Records. During the war, Columbia had ditched almost all of its blues artists, and it shut down the OKeh line in 1946. Thereafter, though, the success of independent rhythm and blues labels including Atlantic and Savoy persuaded Columbia to revive OKeh in 1951, as an outlet for R&B as well as pop and jazz. "Because of tremendous sales revenue realized by rival waxeries from their race departments," *Billboard* reported in its flashy show-biz slang, "CBS is now understood to be willing to change its concepts of dignity in favor of dollar volume."

OKeh enjoyed colossal success in 1951 with Johnnie Ray, whose R&B-influenced, hyperemotive performance of the pop song "Cry," coupled with "The

Johnnie Ray

Big Maybelle

Screamin' Jay Hawkins

Previous page:
Dave Brubeck Quartet,
Columbia Studios

Mitch Miller

Little Cloud That Cried," sold a million copies in only its first two months on the market. After Epic took over OKeh's pop list in 1953, OKeh focused on R&B, hoping to get an inside track on what might turn into pop hits for Columbia when recorded by pop artists. At times, OKeh's releases crossed into the emerging rock and roll market. The label released several singles by Big Maybelle, including her version of "Whole Lotta Shakin' Goin' On" in 1955—two years before Jerry Lee Lewis's version appeared. In 1956, Screamin' Jay Hawkins released his enormous hit, "I Put a Spell on You," on OKeh. But OKeh's modest efforts—it released between fifteen and twenty 45-rpm singles annually—made it practically an afterthought at Columbia, more of a vestige of the label's old race record line than anything else. And Columbia utterly failed to see the potential of releases such as "Whole Lotta Shakin'" and "I Put a Spell on You," both of which actually became enormous pop hits—but not on Columbia.

Looking back, we might view Columbia's first take on rock and roll as commercially as well as artistically foolhardy. But considered purely in terms of profits and loss, the decision, at the time, seemed to be a no-brainer. Columbia had emerged after 1950 as the preeminent label of the LP. Columbia's initial victory in the battle of the speeds had made 33⅓-rpm albums its bread and butter. Early rock and roll, however, was sold to teenagers chiefly on 45-rpm singles. Although RCA produced two Elvis Presley albums in 1956, the label's real success came from the millions of 45s of "Hound Dog" and "Love Me Tender" it sold. It was a similar story at the dozens of smaller independent rock and roll labels.

The success of the rock and roll 45s, to be sure, flew in the face of Columbia's early success with the LP in the speeds battle. But the economics of record merchandising meant that the sudden shift posed no threat to Columbia. The profits for selling LPs, with their higher list prices, were obviously much greater than the profits for selling 45s. The higher list prices also made retailers relatively cautious in buying LPs, as opposed to 45s, which meant that the recording companies could count on the retailers actually selling the LPs they stocked. With 45s, however, distributors would order bulk quantities in case a record caught on, knowing they could return the bulk of those singles that did not sell. Millions of 45s sold to the public, but millions were returned at tremendous cost to the companies in lost recording and manufacturing costs.

So long as Columbia ruled the LP charts, the company retained an enormous commercial advantage. Only in the mid-1960s, when rock and roll performers and producers reoriented themselves to recording albums, would Columbia's accountants have reason to take rock and roll seriously. Until then, no matter how artistically cramped Columbia, and especially Mitch Miller, might seem in retrospect, the label's rebuffing of rock and roll made perfect sense.

Miller himself, meanwhile, preferred nostalgic sing-along Americana, which he began recording with a twenty-five-man chorus that he called "the Gang." Released in 1958, the album *Sing Along with Mitch* struck a chord with listeners who favored smooth, familiar, upbeat material, like "You Are My Sunshine" and "Down by the Old Mill Stream." The record would sell more than eight million copies, and Miller and the Gang would release ten more smash hit albums over the next two years—the prelude to their long and successful television career. Columbia, meanwhile, which had battened on "Sinatrauma" nearly twenty years earlier, had largely abandoned the latest youth craze, rock and roll, to its competitors. But the company also made a great deal of money, which strengthened its commitment to producing highly successful LPs of mainstream popular music.

Leonard Bernstein and Glenn Gould: Flavors of Genius

In mid-1956, Jim Conkling, who had presided over Columbia since 1950 but had never felt entirely comfortable in New York, resigned. Into the office, at last, stepped Goddard Lieberson, for whom the job had long seemed tailor made. Among his numerous projects, Lieberson had just completed a Broadway triumph that would greatly advance the label's prestige as well as its commercial stature. For many years

Isaac Stern

Glenn Gould

Leonard Bernstein

before that, Lieberson had been instrumental in expanding Columbia's reach and heft, in and out of his favorite field of classical music.

Under Lieberson's aegis, and headed by David Oppenheim and, beginning in 1959, Schuyler Chapin, Columbia Masterworks boasted a roster of classical artists unsurpassed in quality and range. Its leading stars included the pianists Rudolf Serkin and Philippe Entremont, the violinists Isaac Stern and Zino Francescatti, the composer and conductor Igor Stravinsky, the Philadelphia and Cleveland Orchestras, the Budapest String Quartet, the Julliard String Quartet, and the Mormon Tabernacle Choir. A crucial renewal of an important connection began in 1957 when the New York Philharmonic, attached to Columbia since 1940, replaced its music director, Dmitri Mitropoulos, with Leonard Bernstein, the first American-born maestro to lead a major orchestra. Masterworks valued Mitropoulos for his interpretations of Mahler and Schoenberg, but in Bernstein, both Columbia and the Philharmonic obtained an exceptional new force. Bernstein already had a relationship with Columbia—the label had recently released the original cast recording of his *Candide*, and he was good friends with Oppenheim—but now the bond, with CBS as well as Columbia, became much closer.

Bernstein, although not yet forty, was establishing himself as a phenomenal musical polymath—an educator and composer as well as conductor—and his vitality burst all over the place in the mid- and late 1950s. In September 1957, *West Side Story*, his breakthrough Broadway musical (with a script by Arthur Laurents, lyrics by the young Stephen Sondheim, and choreography by Jerome Robbins), opened to spectacular reviews. The Columbia original cast album appeared soon after, and would hold the number one position on the Billboard popular music chart for fifty-four weeks. Just after taking over the Philharmonic, Bernstein also began broadcasting on CBS his Young People's Concerts, the first and still the most successful music appreciation series in television history.

In 1959, with the Cold War at its height, Bernstein took the orchestra on a tour of Europe and the Soviet Union, filmed in part by CBS. The highpoint of the Soviet leg was a performance of Shostakovich's Fifth Symphony in the presence of the composer, who came to the stage at the conclusion to congratulate Bernstein and the musicians—a symbolic step toward reducing Cold War tensions through cultural understanding. Bernstein and the Philharmonic duly recorded the symphony for Columbia. Bernstein then turned his attention to Mahler's symphonies, which he would record with the approval of the composer's widow. The next year, Columbia released a new studio version, with Bernstein conducting, of Bernstein's musical *On the Town*, which he had written with Betty Comden and Adolph Green and which had been originally released on 78s by Decca fifteen years earlier.

The pianist Glenn Gould, another force of nature, joined Columbia Masterworks in 1955. Born in Toronto in 1932, Gould had completed work at the Royal Conservatory of Music at the age of twelve. He had been appearing in concert for a decade when Sasha Schneider of the Budapest String Quartet tipped off David Oppenheim about his exceptional talent. Oppenheim heard Gould perform at Town Hall and signed him right away. However, once Gould began recording at the Thirtieth Street studio, Columbia's management recognized that the pianist had some distinct oddities: in one instance, a writer for *Esquire* magazine, sent to the studio by Columbia's publicity department, found him plunging his hands in scalding water.

Gould's reputation for oddness would grow over the years to come. But beginning with his incandescent debut recording of Bach's *Goldberg Variations*, one of the best-selling classical music albums of its time, Gould would spend a long career at Columbia. Eschewing much of the standard, showy, high-Romantic piano repertoire, Gould combined formidable virtuosity with a keen inventiveness. While he explored anew the polyphony of earlier composers, Bach above all, he also recast the music of twentieth-century composers including Arnold Schoenberg and Paul Hindemith. Gould's genius would become all the more important to Columbia in 1964, when the pianist retreated to his home base in Toronto and ceased making concert appearances completely in favor of recording, broadcasting, and writing.

Cast of *West Side Story*, Columbia Studios

West Side Story Original Cast Album

Previous page:
Glenn Gould, trying out pianos, Columbia Studios

Cast of *West Side Story*, Columbia Studios

Lieberson's Broadway

With Columbia Masterworks in safe hands, Goddard Lieberson, as Columbia's president, indulged two special interests he had developed since the mid-1940s. Based on his involvement during the Petrillo bans with *Othello* and *I Can Hear It Now*, Lieberson had become fascinated with the possibilities of spoken word LPs. In 1952, he recorded a Broadway production of George Bernard Shaw's *Don Juan in Hell*, starring Charles Boyer, Charles Laughton, Agnes Moorehead, and Sir Cedric Hardwicke, released with critical notes by the Columbia University scholar Jacques Barzun. Lieberson then launched what he called his Literary Series, in which well-known authors including Katherine Anne Porter and Edith Sitwell read from their own works. The project sold poorly, and some critics thought that it reeked of pretension, but Lieberson's literary interests were genuine: in 1947, he had authored a novel, *Three for Bedroom C*. He also advanced work on an LP recording of *Waiting for Godot* featuring E. G. Marshall, Bert Lahr, Kurt Kaznar, and Alvin Epstein, graced with liner notes by William Saroyan. Lieberson took such enormous pride in this project that he carried an advance copy to Paris to get the approval of Samuel Beckett, whom he had never met, prior to the recording's release. Beckett enjoyed the album and he also enjoyed Lieberson, and the two became good friends.

Lieberson's absorption with Broadway, by contrast, brought Columbia riches as well as artistic satisfaction, and in many ways it epitomized the label's postwar, New York–based glamour. In the early 1950s, Lieberson had produced, in addition to recordings of new shows, a series of studio versions of older works, in which, Gary Marmorstein writes, he "discovered his deepest musical passion." The series began in 1951 with a sumptuously packaged release of a full-length recording of *Porgy and Bess*, starring Lawrence Winters and Camilla Williams, complete with a libretto. New recordings of *Anything Goes*, *Babes in Arms*, *The Bandwagon*, and *Girl Crazy*, all starring Mary Martin, soon followed. A new version of *Pal Joey* came along that was sparkling enough to spur Richard Rodgers to mount a revival of the show. Lieberson-produced releases of major new productions included *Kismet* in 1953 (with "Strangers in Paradise" recorded by Tony Bennett in advance of the cast album's release), and *The Pajama Game* in 1954.

Then, in 1956, came *My Fair Lady*. Adapting George Bernard Shaw's *Pygmalion* to the musical stage had been giving Frederick Loewe and his lyricist Alan Jay Lerner fits until they brought in director Moss Hart, who subtly adjusted the story of the Cockney girl and the phonetics professor—but even then the show was no sure thing. The lead producer, Herman Levin, looked to his friend William Paley for financial backing, but it was Lieberson who persuaded Paley to provide the necessary funds, about $400,000, for which CBS received a 40 percent interest in the show. *My Fair Lady*, starring Rex Harrison and Julie Andrews, opened on March 15, 1956, to smashing reviews, and it would run for 2,717 performances—a record run at the time, which produced a handsome return for Columbia. Three days after the premiere, meanwhile, Lieberson supervised the recording session at the Thirtieth Street studio, and the LP was rushed into stores. For fifteen weeks, the recording was the best-selling album in the nation, and it would remain on the charts for another eight years, its shelf life prolonged when Lieberson produced a newly recorded stereo version in 1959. The album was still selling well when, in 1962, Warner Bros. purchased the film rights for the then-unheard-of price of $5 million.

Nothing could top *My Fair Lady*, but with Lieberson as president, Columbia continued to excel in Broadway original cast recordings. *The Most Happy Fella*, *L'il Abner*, *Bells Are Ringing*, and Bernstein's *Candide* followed in swift succession, all in 1956. The cast recording of *West Side Story*—about which Lieberson was initially leery, given *Candide*'s relatively brief Broadway run—came in 1957. The next season brought *Goldilocks* and *Flower Drum Song*, and in 1959 there was *Gypsy*, which featured Ethel Merman belting out the showstopper "Everything's Coming Up Roses." A few important musicals —including *The Music Man* and *Fiorello!*—eluded the label's grasp, but Columbia was undeniably at the top of the heap in Broadway LPs. Its dominance was affirmed when it recorded what would turn out to be Rodgers and

Jack Klugman with Ethel Merman during a recording session for *Gypsy*, Columbia Studios

Robert Coote with Julie Andrews and Rex Harrison during a recording session for *My Fair Lady*, Columbia Studios

Kind of Blue and *Time Out*

In 1959, Columbia Records became a center of the commercial *and* the artistic jazz world as the result of two albums: *Kind of Blue* by Miles Davis and *Time Out* by Dave Brubeck. Each of these albums was very popular on release and remained so for decades; each of them heralded new horizons.

Kind of Blue was the most successful application of George Russell's *Lydian Chromatic Concept of Tonal Organization,* a 1953 work that was based on a 1944 conversation in which Davis, then eighteen, told Russell that he wanted to find a way to "play every chord." Russell's theory, far too complex to summarize briefly, led to a fundamental shift in jazz improvisation and composition, one based not on chord changes, as bebop was, but on scales. The theory propelled the future work of Davis, Bill Evans, and John Coltrane—all three played on *Kind of Blue*—as well as many others. Working with modes gave *Kind of Blue* a droning but open sound, and a refocus on melody without reference to major or minor keys, and also allowed an appealing dissonance.

Time Out isn't far behind it. Dave Brubeck, a student of Darius Milhaud and (briefly) Arnold Schoenberg, based the entire album on odd time signatures: 5/4, 9/8, 7/4, 6/4. Sometimes the time isn't clear until well into a piece. Sometimes the beats and the melodies are deliberately representative of Turkish music. The effect resembles both "cool" jazz (which Davis pioneered) and the West Coast jazz that had emerged in the early fifties.

Of the two, *Time Out* was undoubtedly more controversial but Goddard Lieberson committed Columbia to it, and it paid off, even on the singles charts, where "Take Five" had considerable success. *Kind of Blue* is almost certainly the best-selling jazz album of all time.

Dave Marsh

Dave Brubeck Quartet, Columbia Studios

Hammerstein's final collaboration, *The Sound of Music*, in 1959, followed a year later by Lerner and Loewe's Arthurian romance, *Camelot*.

By the end of the 1950s, Columbia Records was firing on all cylinders, generating profits and exercising influence beyond anything imaginable during even the most hopeful early postwar years. Despite its spurning of rock and roll, the label's popular music division was a powerhouse, led by such perennial hit makers as Tony Bennett and Johnny Mathis—success that belies the common impression that rock and roll came to dominate American popular music in the 1950s. The profits from the pop singers allowed Columbia to record albums by important jazz artists such as Charles Mingus and Gerry Mulligan, the established stars Ellington and Armstrong, and the new star, Miles Davis.

Columbia Masterworks gave the company enormous prestige. Goddard Lieberson's musical theater releases added enormous profits as well as Broadway class. Columbia's invention of the LP certainly had had a great deal to do with its extraordinary success. But without the talents of Ted Wallerstein, Goddard Lieberson, Mitch Miller, George Avakian, and dozens of producers, engineers, art directors, marketers, and more, the artistic advantages the LP offered never would have materialized. By the end of the decade, the potential for the LP had expanded even further thanks to fresh technological innovations.

"360 Sound": High Fidelity and Stereo Innovation in the 1950s

During the war, Adrian Murphy, who had lately headed CBS's early efforts to develop television, served on active duty in Europe as a member of the Signal Corps. While stationed in Luxembourg, Murphy saw one of the Magnetophon reel-to-reel tape recorders, developed by the German electronics firm AEG, which the Allies had captured from Radio Luxembourg. First introduced in the mid-1930s but much improved since then, the machines were capable of recording sound with exceptional fidelity on a magnetic tape that consisted of a long acetate strip coated with metal oxide particles. Murphy arranged to have one of the machines sent to CBS early in 1947, but electronics firms, notably the Ampex company in California, were already developing their own versions. In October 1947, Bing Crosby, who was helping to fund Ampex's work, broadcast the first radio program ever prerecorded on magnetic tape. Within two years, Columbia was using the new technology for recording and editing. The latest revolutions in sound technology—there would be more than one—were underway.

Beginning in the mid-1920s, electrical recording had greatly improved the sound quality of recorded music. Yet as long as the performance captured by the microphone was transferred directly to a master copy, called an acetate master— which was in fact a lacquered aluminum disc —recording engineers could do nothing to erase distortions or to fix mistakes made by the performers. Magnetic tape, however, permitted engineers to alter and improve performances in any way they liked simply by editing and splicing the tape. Tape did not require as much space to store; unlike acetates, it could be reused; it did not degrade. And the introduction of the first commercial two-track tape recorders by Ampex in the late 1940s opened up the possibility for making commercial recordings available in stereophonic sound.

The impact of these innovations would in time profoundly alter the recording industry. But the changes to home listening as well as to recording techniques unfolded gradually, in a series of stages. The first stage involved the refinement of so-called high-fidelity monaural phonographic sound, or what would soon be known popularly as "hi-fi."

At roughly the same time as magnetic tape was adapted to recording, the Columbia microgroove LP significantly reduced surface noise on records and reproduced nuances more effectively, giving listeners a cleaner and richer sound. Improvements in amplifier design further enhanced fidelity, especially by allowing audio peaks to be reproduced without distortion. These improvements, combined with magnetic recording, raised the possibility of capturing a sound so true to life that

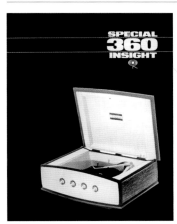

Columbia 360 advertisements

listeners might begin to imagine they were sitting in a concert hall rather than in their living rooms. Columbia, having helped develop the LP adaptor turntables in 1948, now turned to marketing early hi-fi equipment. During the summer of 1952, the "Columbia 360" phonograph hit the market, a mass-produced combination of high-quality phonograph components, manufactured by CBS. The sets included two speakers in order to create an illusion of stereophonic sound. The following year, CBS added a third speaker to the "360" set—and the "360" hi-fi, accommodated to play both 33⅓- and 45-rpm records, quickly became the most popular preassembled phonograph set on the market. The name "360 Sound" in turn became linked to Columbia's efforts to provide genuine stereophonic recordings.

The research and development of stereo sound reproduction had originated in the 1920s and 1930s, with the movie companies at the forefront. The first commercial film released with a stereo soundtrack, Walt Disney's *Fantasia*, appeared in 1940. After the arrival of the two-track tape recorders, though, the recording companies began moving in earnest toward stereo recording. RCA Victor beat Columbia to the punch, making experimental two-track recordings in October 1953. Four months later, Victor taped, on both monaural equipment and Ampex two-track recorders, the Boston Symphony Orchestra performing Berlioz's *The Damnation of Faust*. By 1956 Columbia, too, was recording in stereo, focusing chiefly on classical works; these sessions included a taping of the New York Philharmonic's energetic new maestro, Leonard Bernstein, conducting a performance of Handel's *Messiah*. It would take another two years before stereophonic phonographic equipment for home listening would be widely available. (Along with the other recording companies, Columbia did begin marketing stereo-tape editions of select titles in 1957.) Finally, though, in 1958, Columbia released its first stereo albums, including Bruno Walter conducting Mahler, Bernstein conducting Stravinsky, and more popular material performed by Johnny Mathis and Dave Brubeck.

There was skepticism at first about the glories of stereo, especially among record buyers. "Let's face it—the craze for stereo has not been as intense as expected," Ward Botsman, a nay-saying A&R man for Vox Records told the *New York Times* early in 1959. Even classical music audiophiles, for whom most of the early stereo records were intended, had the impression that stereo would be effective only for the grandest of choral works and for opera, which was not necessarily reason enough to justify buying new stereo equipment. Inside the recording companies, to be sure, critics like Botsman were in the minority. When Columbia announced its new line of stereo records (which offered "the only Guaranteed Stereo Fidelity"), its ads spoke of them as the latest of Columbia's technical triumphs—the result "of the same long years of pioneering research that gave you the original Long Playing record and the fabulous 360 High Fidelity Phonograph." But the introduction of stereo did not appear to usher in as dramatic a change in listening habits as the one the LP had initiated a decade earlier. Even the record companies, despite their inevitable commercial hype, did not push too far, too fast.

In 1958, Columbia released a specially packaged demonstration stereo album called *Listening in Depth*. The album, meant to celebrate the wonders of the new sound, was a musical sampler designed to appeal to all tastes, including an excerpt from Tchaikovsky's Pathétique symphony, a composition, entitled "Track 360," that Duke Ellington had written and arranged for the occasion, and the Kirby Stone Four singing "Baubles, Bangles, and Beads." Bill Bachman, still working for Columbia, contributed a difficult but rewarding set of liner notes on the technical aspects of stereo recording and reproduction. Goddard Lieberson's brief introductory remarks, though, were measured: although Lieberson referred to "the new listening" and to "a dimension probably not experienced before," he concluded quietly that "the new refinement of stereophony is, in the final analysis, eminently worth all of our whiles." Stereo recordings would take a long time to become the unquestioned norm, especially outside classical music. Columbia and the other major recording companies did not complete the shift to so-called compatible stereo, which could be played on mono equipment, until 1968. In that same year, the industry phased out producing mono albums, but mono singles continued to appear through the 1970s.

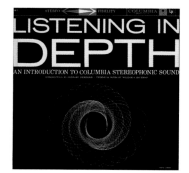

Listening In Depth

Duke Ellington

Still, Columbia was very proud of its "360 Sound," and the term would appear on its stereo record labels from 1962 to 1970 and on its mono labels from 1963 to 1967. And even in the late-1950s, the hi-fi and stereo innovations left lasting impressions, including some that had little to do with the actual sound being reproduced. The new hi-fi components, and then the pair of (carefully placed) stereo speakers, at once reflected and contributed to the 1950s consumerist romance with the latest technology, a fascination most commonly associated with television's conquest of the middle-class living room. Encouraged by publications like *High Fidelity* magazine, a middle-brow culture of hi-fi expertise flourished, blending up-to-the-minute technical knowledge with a quest for the truest sound. Like the television— or, for that matter, like the old Victrolas and Grafonolas—the hi-fi console and stereo speaker set became important home furnishings: The look of the equipment, as well as its tonal quality, could be as strong a statement about its owner's taste, expertise, and disposable income as the music being played on it. What Lieberson described as stereo's new aural dimension came to be associated with deeper psychological dimensions. Advertisements for the latest Columbia Phonographs in national magazines such as *Life* contained Freudian touches like the claim that the new high-fidelity recordings and equipment opened up "the whole universe of human hearing, both subconscious and conscious."

Finally, although the new listening appealed to status seekers, Columbia and CBS also offered it to the masses, in accord with the dictates of mass-market consumerist democracy. By 1957, there were more than thirty-five Columbia Phonograph models on the market, ranging in price from $29.95 to $1,995—each designed, the ads said, to "embody the characteristics of 360 Sound." Two years later came new "Big Stereo" units that ran the gamut from a lightweight portable with a list price of $39.95 to a heavy, fruitwood stereo console, with FM radio included, that sold for $399.95. The consoles became a new marker in the attainment of the American Dream. The portables became fixtures in the bedrooms of the ermerging generation of baby boomers who would soon have a great deal to say about the future of popular music.

Rising to the Top

At the fateful private meeting in April 1948, when William Paley, CBS president Frank Stanton, and the Columbia Records team unveiled the LP to David Sarnoff of RCA, Sarnoff, with wounded arrogance, observed how remarkable it was that "little Columbia Graphophone" had bested mighty RCA Victor in developing a long-playing format. Of course, Columbia Graphophone was now Columbia Records, Inc. But the company that had for so long been the weak sister among the major recording labels while Victor lorded it over everyone still had a great deal to prove, even after it began releasing its LPs. By 1960, the proof was in, as far as Goddard Lieberson was concerned. "For fifty years," the *New York Times* reported in February, "the Victor record division of the Radio Corporation of America has been the undisputed leader in all phases of phonographic disc sales and production." But Lieberson, the report continued, now emphatically disputed Victor's leadership. Independent market research, he claimed in the *Times*, confirmed that Columbia had captured 21 percent of total market sales in 1959, which placed it higher than Victor and Capitol, with Decca lagging behind in fourth place. A spokesman for Victor said his company was "confident" that Lieberson was mistaken. Yet the fact that Lieberson could plausibly make such a claim showed how far Columbia had risen over the previous decade and a half. And market share could not begin to describe the singular esteem accorded the label's artists and its recording program.

Columbia's glory years would continue into the 1960s. But the new decade would also bring national trauma and cultural upheavals that challenged Columbia Records just as they challenged every other American institution.

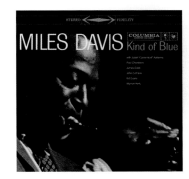

Miles Davis,
Kind of Blue

Miles Davis,
Columbia Studios

ROSEMARY CLOONEY
MIXED EMOTIONS · THIS OLE HOUSE · TENDERLY · BEAUTIFUL
BROWN EYES · BOTCH-A-ME · HEY THERE · WHY DON'T YOU
HAUL OFF AND LOVE ME · MAMBO ITALIANO · COME ON-A MY
HOUSE · HALF AS MUCH · I COULD HAVE DANCED ALL NIGHT
BLUES IN THE NIGHT

Columbia
masterworks

CL 608   Columbia
DIXIE BY DORSEY

JIMMY DORSEY and his ORIGINAL "DORSEYLAND" JAZZ BAND

from Beethoven to Blues...

Lp brings you a new standard of record perfection

"the record that plays up to 45 minutes"

I LIKE JAZZ

America's most wanted phonographs

High Fidelity Columbia "360"
with eXtra-Dimensional sound

NEW, LOW COST COLUMBIA
"HEMISPHERIC SOUND" PORTABLES

COLUMBIA
RECORDS
799 Seventh Avenue, New York 19, N.Y.

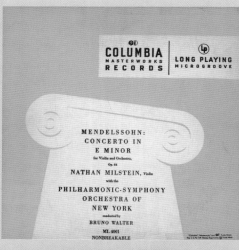

COLUMBIA
MASTERWORKS
RECORDS   LONG PLAYING
MICROGROOVE

MENDELSSOHN:
CONCERTO IN
E MINOR
for Violin and Orchestra,
Op. 64
NATHAN MILSTEIN, Violin
with the
PHILHARMONIC-SYMPHONY
ORCHESTRA OF
NEW YORK
conducted by
BRUNO WALTER
ML 4001
NONBREAKABLE

Columbia's DISC DIGEST

a preview of new records for February, 1946

MINGUS AH UM / CHARLES MINGUS
BETTER GIT IT IN YOUR SOUL   GOODBYE PORK PIE HAT   BOOGIE STOP SHUFFLE   SELF PORTRAIT IN
THREE COLORS   OPEN LETTER TO DUKE   BIRD CALLS   FABLES OF FAUBUS   PUSSY CAT DUES   JELLY ROLL

CL 1370   COLUMBIA   Lp

MARY MARTIN · EZIO PINZA
SOUTH PACIFIC
Music by RICHARD RODGERS · Lyrics by OSCAR HAMMERSTEIN 2nd
with original B'way cast
COLUMBIA   Lp   masterworks

George Gershwin's   COLUMBIA   Lp
MILES DAVIS – PORGY AND BESS
orchestra under the direction of Gil Evans

CL 1274

COLUMBIA
MASTERWORKS
I CAN HEAR IT NOW
Edward R. Murrow–Fred W. Friendly·
EDWARD R. MURROW, Narrator
ML 54095   SIDE 1
NONBREAKABLE   (XLP 543)
LONG PLAYING   Lp

ML 5060
BACH:
THE GOLDBERG VARIATIONS
GLENN GOULD, PIANO
COLUMBIA MASTERWORKS

THE ORIGINAL BROADWAY CAST
DAVID MERRICK and LELAND HAYWARD
ETHEL MERMAN
COLUMBIA MASTERWORKS Lp

No more broken-up Beethoven
Enjoy the world's greatest music without interruption on Columbia LP Records

COLUMBIA MICROGROOVE **RECORDS**

$40 library of Columbia High-Fidelity LP Records
when you buy a Columbia High-Fidelity Phonograph

LISTENING IN DEPTH

from $29.95 to $1,995... **COLUMBIA PHONOGRAPHS**

We're all signed up with **COLUMBIA RECORDS!**

THE RECORD OF THE STARS
COLUMBIA RECORDS INC.

alfred **DRAKE**
with the original broadway cast

KISS ME KATE

COLE PORTER

patricia **MORISON**

columbia LP long playing

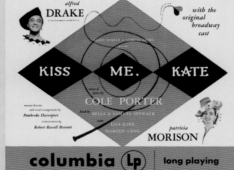

STEREO COLUMBIA MASTERWORKS
LEONARD BERNSTEIN
Rhapsody in Blue
An American in Paris
New York Philharmonic and The Columbia Symphony

LP *is in!*

public acceptance proves it
trade acceptance proves it

LP

CBS
THE
COUNT
BILLIE H
HENRY
THE JIM
JIMMY
MAL WA

COLUMBIA EXTENDED PLAY B-308

Selections:
STAR DUST
LIEBESTRAUM
CARIOCA
POLISH DANCE

LIBERACE at the piano

MOONLIGHT SONATA
WARSAW CONCERTO
AS TIME GOES BY
MALAGUENA

Orchestra conducted by
GEORGE LIBERACE

COLUMBIA RECORDS

CL 1028   **COLUMBIA**
JOHNNY MATHIS
WONDERFUL
WONDERFUL
WONDERFUL
WONDERFUL
WONDERFUL
WONDERFUL
WONDERFUL
WONDERFUL
WONDERFUL

STEREO FIDELITY **COLUMBIA LP**

COLUMBIA LP
CL 552
the new Benny

Chapter 5

Musical Revolutions

In March 1965, a little more than five years after Goddard Lieberson proclaimed Columbia Records' supremacy, CBS moved into a formidable new skyscraper at Fifty-second Street and Sixth Avenue and took the record label with it. The parent company's coffers were swollen with television advertising revenues, and its headquarters at 485 Madison had grown too shabby for the company's new status. Now CBS would operate in the most impressive edifice imaginable, with enough room to house its subsidiaries. Designed by the eminent architect Eero Saarinen, its façade constructed out of specially quarried dark Quebec granite (for which the building was dubbed Black Rock), the building was a monument to power and elegance but also to imperious and immaculate corporate order. It was a far cry from the record label's cluttered old quarters down Fifty-second Street on Seventh Avenue, where Columbia had also stood apart, at least physically, from CBS.

Andy Williams

Even as it moved its offices, the label embodied the primacy, established by Lieberson, of identifying and supporting superior artists. As it happened, though, Columbia Records moved to Black Rock just as new cultural revolutions were overturning any settled view of excellence, especially in music. Associated with the frenzy that surrounded the arrival of the Beatles in 1964, these revolutions originated in the deeper political and social unrest caused by President John F. Kennedy's assassination, the continuing struggles for civil rights and racial equality, and the fierce divisions over America's escalating war in Vietnam. From its perch on the twelfth floor at Black Rock, Columbia would have to respond to startling new trends and changing tastes, some of which clashed with its own highly developed musical preferences—and clashed with the corporate grandeur of Black Rock.

Tranquility at the Top

Columbia began the decade in serene confidence. Gifted, reliable pop singers, including Tony Bennett, Johnny Mathis, and Doris Day, remained essential to the label's commercial success, and the list of Columbia's pop stars was growing. Ray Conniff, the superb arranger, had devised an interesting sound using an orchestra and a choir singing wordless melodies, and in 1959 the Ray Conniff Singers released the first of a series of successful albums. Percy Faith's recordings firmly established the sound of easy listening or "mood" music. Jerry Vale, born Gennaro Luigi Vitaliano in the Bronx, would never be Tony Bennett, but after he released a number of strong-selling singles in the 1950s, his career blossomed in the early 1960s. Robert Goulet, having broken through performing in Lerner and Loewe's *Camelot* in 1960, embarked on a solo career that earned him a Grammy in 1962 as Best New Artist.

Andy Williams arrived at Columbia in 1961. A smooth-voiced Midwesterner, Williams broke in with the New York-based label, Cadence Records, whose roster included the Everly Brothers. Through the end of the 1950s, Williams recorded several top-ten hits for Cadence, including, with Peggy Powers, "I Like Your Kind of Love." Still searching for a style that would eventually become identified with easy listening, he then moved to Columbia, but before the switch he recorded, for Cadence, Johnny Mercer and Henry Mancini's "Moon River," from the film *Breakfast at Tiffany's*. Cadence slighted the record because it seemed to lack appeal with teenagers, and it never reached the charts. Williams released another version with Columbia as the title track of a new album in 1962, the album was a major hit, and Williams had found his theme song.

Williams broke through again in 1963 with a youth-oriented Mort Shuman–Doc Pomus number, "Can't Get Used to Losing You," which reached number two on the Billboard pop chart. But his rendition of Mercer and Mancini's "Days of Wine and Roses," also in 1963, would become an American standard, while the LP of the same name topped the pop album charts for sixteen weeks. And the success of *Days of Wine and Roses* following that of *Moon River* was part of what had become a trend at Columbia, home of the original LP, where a successful pop album could be as important as a hit single, if not more so. Albums would be the main vehicles for breakthrough artists in genres old and new, including the label's newest female star.

Barbra Streisand

Barbra Streisand came to Columbia in 1962, in connection with her arresting debut in the small part of Miss Marmelstein in the Broadway musical *I Can Get It for You Wholesale*. Goddard Lieberson produced the cast recording; Streisand would go on to win a New York Drama Desk Award and a Tony nomination. Barely out of Brooklyn, she had just turned twenty, but she had been hard at work for years, singing in nightclubs, performing in summer stock, and landing television spots. Even while she was creating a sensation in *Wholesale*, Streisand booked separate midnight-show engagements in two clubs where she had worked earlier, Bon Soir on Eighth Street in Greenwich Village and the Blue Angel on Fifty-fifth Street.

"It takes a big man to admit a mistake, and I made a mistake. I would like to record Barbra."

Goddard Lieberson, President, Columbia Records

Robert Goulet

Tony Bennett, Las Vegas

Barbra Streisand

Friends and colleagues advised Lieberson to sign her to Columbia right away, but Lieberson was not sold on Streisand as a solo recording act. Her voice was interesting, he thought, but too large for contemporary tastes, and her choice of material, which was heavy on Broadway show tunes, was not commercially viable for a pop singer. Streisand might be fine on stage or in a cabaret, but not in a recording studio, he supposed. Only after hearing her sing before an adoring crowd at the Blue Angel did Lieberson relent. "It takes a big man to admit a mistake, and I made a mistake," he told Streisand's manager, Marty Erlichman. "I would like to record Barbra."

Erlichman, for his part, thought that Columbia was perfect for Streisand—so much so that he got her to turn down a more lucrative offer from Capitol Records. Columbia had prestige as well as commercial clout, but there was something more to the label's mystique. "It was a feeling I had for them," Erlichman recalls. "They weren't as dogmatic about having a hit single . . . they were an album company." Still unsure whether Streisand would ever actually record a hit single, he wanted to relieve her of that pressure and give her the room to grow as an artist. As it happened, Streisand would have a big hit with "People" in 1964, but she would make her reputation with albums—and she would not record a number one pop single until the mid-1970s.

Signed in October 1962, Streisand recorded with a small combo before live audiences at Bon Soir, but Columbia decided to shelve the material in favor of an album recorded with a studio orchestra over three days in January 1963. Columbia nearly burdened the record with the title *The Sweet and Saucy Streisand*, but Streisand and Erlichman shot that down in favor of *The Barbra Streisand Album*. Having secured the contractual privilege of complete creative control, Streisand skillfully chose and recorded eleven standards by the likes of Rodgers and Hart. She also had the benefit of working with an excellent producer, Mike Berniker. Released in late February to critical acclaim, the album eventually won Grammy Awards for Album of the Year (Other Than Classical) and Best Vocal Performance, Female (as well as Best Non-Classical Album Cover, for Columbia designer John Berg). The album also reached number nine on the *Billboard* chart and earned Streisand her first gold record. Four months after the album's release, Streisand recorded another eleven tracks, a selection this time heavy on the music of Harold Arlen. *The Second Barbra Streisand Album*, released in October, topped at number two. A star was born.

New Trends and Falling Profits Catch Up with Columbia

Even as it added Williams and Streisand, though, Columbia's pop division detected shifts in the market. Some of its sure-fire sellers were running into trouble. Mitch Miller's immense success with the *Sing Along* albums had permitted him to retire from Columbia A&R, but suddenly, in the early 1960s, Miller and the Gang's string of eleven consecutive gold albums ended as sales figures per album plummeted from five hundred thousand to three hundred thousand to a meager seventy-five thousand. At the same time, sales figures for recordings of new Broadway shows—which had come to represent as much as 20 percent of Columbia's revenues from popular music—tumbled. Excellent and popular shows were still being produced. But despite some exceptional successes, including RCA Victor's *Hello, Dolly!* and *Fiddler on the Roof*, Broadway recordings lacked the sales magic they had enjoyed in the late 1940s and 1950s.

Losing the lucrative Broadway market was one sign that Columbia was receding from the leading edge of popular music. But the deeper problem lay elsewhere—for even after Mitch Miller retired from A&R, the label remained largely unreceptive to rock and roll. By now, Columbia's hostility placed it completely at odds with the popular music market. This was reinforced by the fact that the market was shaped by radio, where the number of mainstream traditional pop stations was dwindling while new rock and roll stations proliferated. With its performers receiving less air play, Columbia's pretax profits in 1965 fell to less than 5 percent of total sales, which put enormous pressure on the company's popular records division to improve its commercial performance. But there was only so much the label could do with its long-established priorities intact. "It was as if Columbia had collected a vast vault

"It was a feeling I had for them. They weren't as dogmatic about having a hit single . . . they were an album company."

Martin Erlichman on Columbia

Barbra Streisand

Mitch Miller

Barbra and Broadway

In "People," the featured number in the show, Streisand found her first hit single

Barbra Streisand's career in Broadway theatricals came to a crescendo with *Funny Girl* in 1964, and it also came to a crashing end. *Funny Girl* and *I Can Get It for You Wholesale* (in which she appeared from 1961 to 1963) are the only two stage plays in which she's ever acted on Broadway. But in "People," the featured number in *Funny Girl*, Streisand found her first hit single.

Streisand didn't need Broadway. Her previous three albums received gold records for selling more than 500,000 copies each, and gold was then the highest standard in the recording business. Additionally, her contract specified that she chose all the material for her records, which gave her an almost unheard of control and the ability to ensure the development of a personal style.

Streisand's career remained music-centered until the early seventies. Columbia released two albums each year from 1963 to 1967. From 1965 to 1968, she made a television special every year, always music-centered. She even did a concert tour in 1966 (and no more until 1994). Streisand made her first movie in 1969, but her first four films were musicals.

The original cast album market dwindled quickly after the British Invasion, so fast it's doubtful that even a star of Streisand's magnitude could have saved it. Columbia, which made the most and the most important original cast albums from the forties through the mid-sixties, wasn't spared. After 1964, Columbia never had a top-ten cast album again; only *Mame*, in 1966, cracked the top forty or stayed on the charts for as much as a year. The last hurrah was *A Chorus Line* (1975), which sold two million copies, although it did so without ever charting higher than ninety-eight.

Dave Marsh

Barbra Streisand as Miss Marmelstein
in *I Can Get It for You Wholesale*

of gold," the label's then administrative vice president Clive Davis later wrote, "and then the country disavowed the gold standard."

Columbia did try to keep up to date. The company enjoyed great success with three country singles that became major Top 40 radio hits, Johnny Horton's "The Battle of New Orleans" and Marty Robbins's "El Paso" in 1959 and, two years later, Jimmy Dean's "Big Bad John." Late in 1962, the label signed Dion diMucci of Dion and the Belmonts, and released several hits, including "Donna the Prima Donna." Otherwise, Columbia's attempts to latch on to coming musical trends were uneven, as borne out by two stories connected to John Hammond.

Aretha Franklin

At Lieberson's invitation, Hammond had returned to Columbia in 1959 although his reputation had faded somewhat. About a year into his new tour with the label, he heard an unreleased single, "Today I Sing the Blues," by an eighteen-year-old Aretha Franklin, and it bowled him over. Franklin, the daughter of the Detroit-based Baptist minister and civil rights activist C. L. Franklin, had released her first album, a gospel collection called *Songs of Faith*, with the Checker label, based on recordings made when she was only fourteen. Now, after a troubled period in which she gave birth to a child out of wedlock, she had resumed her career and landed at Columbia, thanks to Hammond. "I'm happy to say that Aretha Franklin looks as if she is going to become a very big star," he wrote excitedly. But Hammond and Franklin were an unhappy pairing: he thought her immature and in need of supervision, which turned her off. And, even though Franklin enjoyed some success, Hammond, along with everyone else at Columbia, was unsure about where her talents lay, so they tried a little of everything, shifting from jazz styling along the lines of one of her idols, Dinah Washington (which Hammond favored), to girl-group tunes. Franklin made a name for herself as a talented vocalist, but she would only begin to soar when in 1966 she left Columbia to work with the famed producer Jerry Wexler at Atlantic Records. Wexler tapped into her full talent by taking advantage of her church background in what he called "the secularization of gospel," turning black sacred rhythms and feelings into songs of love, heartbreak, and defiance.

Bob Dylan

The very different story of Bob Dylan's successful early years with Columbia has been told many times, best of all by Dylan himself in his memoir, *Chronicles: Volume One*. Having grown up in Hibbing, Minnesota, listening to and playing rock and roll, young Robert Zimmerman had become caught up in the folk music bohemia in Minneapolis and been transfixed by the recordings, writing, and mythic persona of the Oklahoma troubadour Woody Guthrie. Early in 1961, he traveled to New York, both to meet Guthrie (who was bedridden with Huntington's chorea in a New Jersey hospital) and to undertake a serious music career. A folk music boom had begun in the late 1950s, in two distinct varieties: an "authentic" folk movement that built on the 1930s and '40s left-wing singing of Guthrie, Pete Seeger, and others and identified closely with the civil rights movement, and a more commercial, clean-cut style epitomized by groups like the Kingston Trio. Dylan, four months shy of his twentieth birthday and burning with ambition, set out to make his way among the less commercial folkies, although soon enough he would fix his sights on broader musical frontiers.

In late September 1961, having taken the burgeoning Greenwich Village folk scene by storm, Dylan got a big break when the critic Robert Shelton wrote a rave review of one of his appearances at Gerde's Folk City in the *New York Times*. The same day that the review appeared, Dylan arrived for a Columbia recording session to accompany the folk singer Carolyn Hester on harmonica, and Hammond, having met Dylan briefly in Hester's apartment, offered him a Columbia Records contract—chiefly because of his skillful harmonica playing. Dylan—already passed over by other record labels as too rough and derivative of Guthrie—eagerly agreed.

Aretha Franklin

Bob Dylan, Columbia Studios

Previous page: Barbra Streisand

Bob Dylan

Hoping to make good on all fronts of the folk craze, Columbia also signed the more polished and commercial groups the Brothers Four and the New Christy Minstrels. Somewhere between the bohemian and the mainstream stood the execptional Irish folk quartet the Clancy Brothers and Tommy Makem, who made their name downtown before they broke through, and would go on to record fifteen albums for Columbia. But thanks to Hammond, Dylan, too, had hit the big time. His fit at Columbia was not easy. His first album, *Bob Dylan*, consisting largely of traditional folk songs and blues, sold poorly, and the scuttlebutt around the label's office called him "Hammond's Folly." But Columbia stuck with him and Dylan stuck with Columbia. Their relationship continued through his rapid evolution into and of out of the topical, politically charged songwriting of *The Freewheelin' Bob Dylan* and *The Times They Are A-Changin'*, to the more personal, inwardly reflective songs on *Another Side of Bob Dylan* in 1964, to his merging of poetry and electric rock and blues on the classic albums *Bringing It All Back Home*, *Highway 61 Revisited*, and *Blonde on Blonde* in 1965 and 1966.

Columbia stood behind Dylan but did not try to forge a new star in its own image, as the company had attempted with Aretha Franklin. Dylan knew what he wanted to do, and Columbia, having taken him on at Hammond's direction, ultimately had sense enough to allow him to do it. Historians have often pointed out that Dylan's combination of writing and performing heralded the demise of the longstanding Tin Pan Alley professional structure, in which tunesmiths provided singers with their songs. But, not unlike Barbra Streisand, Dylan, by insisting on self-direction, also helped end the era in which recording companies could treat their singers as mere performers instead of as the central creative presence.

There were, to be sure, more bumps along the way for Dylan early on. In September 1962, during the recording of *The Freewheelin' Bob Dylan*, his manager, Albert Grossman, along with Grossman's lawyer, attempted to repudiate Dylan's recording contract, claiming the artist had signed it while still a minor. Columbia, for its part, asserted that because Dylan had recorded for the label after he turned twenty-one, Grossman did not have a leg to stand on. Only after tense negotiations and reassurance from Columbia did Dylan repudiate his repudiation, after which he won a new, more favorable contract. Then Grossman, who had long been at loggerheads with Hammond, persuaded Columbia to substitute Tom Wilson, a jazz producer, as the supervisor of Dylan's future recordings. Soon after that, in May 1963, CBS executives barred Dylan from singing his biting satirical song "Talking John Birch Blues" on the *Ed Sullivan* television show, and Dylan walked off the set. (Columbia duly pulled the song off *Freewheelin'*.) Dylan cried "censorship" over the Sullivan show, but CBS contended it was a simple legal matter, as one verse of the song linked the right-wing Birchers to Hitler, which the company's lawyers decided was libelous. Despite the drama, Dylan's relationship with Columbia survived the walkout. And although there would be additional rocky times down the road, these, too, would pass, to be followed by Dylan's numerous artistic landmarks on Columbia over the decades to come.

Johnny Cash

"Hammond's Folly" did have an all-important fan at Columbia in Johnny Cash, whose very presence connoted Columbia's enduring importance in country and western music. The label's rich tradition in recording country artists continued into the 1950s and 1960s thanks chiefly to Don Law, who took over sole directorship of the country division after Art Satherley retired in 1952, and who then held the reins until his own retirement in 1967. Along with Chet Atkins at RCA Victor, Owen Bradley at Decca, and Ken Nelson at Capitol, Law played a major role in building upon the music's postwar boom and in making Nashville the national headquarters for country music recording.

Before World War II, country music consisted of many different styles recorded in many different locations, principally Chicago, Dallas, and Los Angeles. As late as 1945, Nashville had just one music publisher and no studios or session men. But the situation was rapidly changing. After 1939, when NBC began broadcasting a portion of WSM's *Grand Ole Opry*, performers from across the nation began moving to

"[Cash] made it known he thought Dylan was a giant."

John Hammond

Johnny Cash

Previous page:
Bob Dylan with (on right) Suze Rotolo

Johnny Cash

Johnny Cash

Johnny was and is the North Star; you could guide your ship by him

I was asked to give a statement on Johnny's passing and thought about writing a piece instead called "Cash Is King," because that is the way I really feel. In plain terms, Johnny was and is the North Star; you could guide your ship by him—the greatest of the greats then and now. I first met him in '62 or '63 and saw him a lot in those years. Not so much recently, but in some kind of way he was with me more than people I see every day.

There wasn't much music media in the early sixties, and *Sing Out!* was the magazine covering all things folk in character. The editors had published a letter chastising me for the direction my music was going. Johnny wrote the magazine back an open letter telling the editors to shut up and let me sing, that I knew what I was doing. This was before I had ever met him, and the letter meant the world to me. I've kept the magazine to this day.

Of course, I knew of him before he ever heard of me. In '55 or '56, "I Walk the Line" played all summer on the radio, and it was different than anything else you had ever heard. The record sounded like a voice from the middle of the earth. It was so powerful and moving. It was profound, and so was the tone of it, every line; deep and rich, awesome and mysterious all at once. "I Walk the Line" had a monumental presence and a certain type of majesty that was humbling. Even a simple line like "I find it very, very easy to be true" can take your measure. We can remember that and see how far we fall short of it.

Johnny wrote thousands of lines like that. Truly he is what the land and country is all about, the heart and soul of it personified and what it means to be here; and he said it all in plain English. I think we can have recollections of him, but we can't define him any more than we can define a fountain of truth, light, and beauty. If we want to know what it means to be mortal, we need look no further than the Man in Black. Blessed with a profound imagination, he used the gift to express all the various lost causes of the human soul. This is a miraculous and humbling thing. Listen to him, and he always brings you to your senses. He rises high above all, and he'll never die or be forgotten, even by persons not born yet—especially those persons—and that is forever.

Bob Dylan in *Rolling Stone* magazine (September 26, 2003)

Bob Dylan with Johnny Cash

Nashville. Thus, as country music thrived in the late 1940s and early 1950s, Nashville became the focal point of the industry.

Law, who like Satherley had begun in the field recording era, and who had been visiting Nashville regularly for years, made the adjustment. From the mid-1950s on, he oversaw most of his recording in Nashville and Los Angeles. He was one of the first producers to use Owen Bradley's famous Quonset Hut studio, the very first studio on what would become Nashville's famous Music Row. (In 1962, he would convince Columbia to buy the Quonset Hut outright.) Through the 1950s and early 1960s, Law continued to record Columbia's established country stars including Flatt and Scruggs, Lefty Frizzell, "Little" Jimmy Dickens, and Ray Price (who hit the top with his mammoth hit "Crazy Arms" in 1953). Law also oversaw a stable of rising stars, including Marty Robbins, Johnny Horton, Jimmy Dean, and Johnny Cash.

Cash came out of a different part of the country music world than the emerging Nashville mainstream, closer to rockabilly and rock and roll than to bluegrass or honky-tonk. After a difficult, hardscrabble boyhood as the son of an Arkansas cotton farmer, he enlisted in the United States Air Force in 1950, at the height of the Cold War, and, after his discharge, moved to Memphis, nurturing musical ambitions. His early successes with Sun Records led him to record that label's first album in 1957. He departed for Columbia in 1958, bringing Carl Perkins with him. Recording for the label in Nashville, he quickly produced a crossover hit, "Don't Take Your Guns to Town," backed with "I Still Miss Someone."

As his career took off, Cash became mired in heavy drinking and an addiction to amphetamines and barbiturates, dependencies that would continue until the late 1960s. With his private life in disarray, Cash would fail to record a major hit from 1957 until 1963. But then, his single "Ring of Fire" topped the country charts for seven weeks, and it would prove one of the biggest hits of Cash's career. The crucial idea for recording the song with a mariachi song arrangement reportedly came to Cash in a dream (fueled by what, nobody knows); Cash's producer, Don Law, instead of telling the singer he was crazy, urged him to do it. Over the next two years, Cash passed through something like his own folkie protest period, which included recording, in 1964, a landmark concept album, *Bitter Tears,* bemoaning the plight of Native Americans. And, although Nashville and Greenwich Village seemed worlds apart, Cash praised Dylan as a superb songwriter, hung out with him when he was in New York, performed his work in concert, and generally, as Hammond later recalled, "made it known he thought Dylan was a giant"—a judgment that, by 1963, carried considerable weight at Columbia.

Neither Cash nor country and western music nor the early Bob Dylan, though, would be sufficient to bring Columbia fully into the new mainstream of contemporary popular music. Nor would their sales figures—which in Dylan's case finally did match his growing celebrity—overcome the label's financial difficulties. Columbia's classical and jazz recordings, although as high in quality as ever, were not going to do the trick either. Indeed, commercially, they were part of the problem.

Classical Achievements Amid Financial Uncertainty

In February 1962, Bruno Walter, a giant of Columbia's classical music program for nearly three decades, died. Leonard Bernstein had by now become the leading conductor at Columbia—and the most famous conductor in the country— and Eugene Ormandy and the Philadelphia Orchestra retained their large following. Still, upon losing Walter, Columbia decided to invite George Szell and the Cleveland Orchestra back to Columbia from the Epic label. Szell was widely admired as a musician's musician—yet Columbia initially tried to persuade him to record popular classical fare like Ravel's *Boléro.* The austere, even autocratic Szell, who as a young man had worked with Richard Strauss, refused. Instead, he said he would record *Symphonie Domestica,* a relatively obscure piece of Strauss's that was not yet in the Columbia catalog, to help mark the composer's centenary in 1964. Szell prevailed— and his version of *Symphonie Domestica* won general critical acclaim as the outstanding recording of the Strauss commemoration. Szell would continue to make

Jimmy Dean and
Johnny Cash
with Don Law

essential recordings for Columbia until his death in 1970, including a splendid collection of the four Brahms symphonies.

The rest of the classical roster at Columbia was as impressive as the ones that Goddard Lieberson and his successors at Columbia Masterworks had built in the 1940s and 1950s. The violinist Isaac Stern recorded with several orchestras; he also played with a trio consisting of himself and two other Masterworks artists, the cellist Leonard Rose and pianist Eugene Istomin, and they turned out outstanding recordings of Beethoven and Mendelssohn. Pablo Casals, a Columbia artist for more than fifty years, conducted and released a vibrant new version of Bach's *Brandenburg Concerti*. The piano virtuoso Rudolf Serkin, now in his sixties, was performing as tirelessly and beautifully as ever. Glenn Gould, put off of concertizing by his perfectionism and terror of live audiences, was enthusiastic about the recording process. He returned to the studio to record, among other works, Beethoven's Piano Concerto Number Four in G Major, with Bernstein and the New York Philharmonic, and the first volume of Bach's *Art of the Fugue*. On New Year's Day, 1963, Bernstein substituted a sixteen-year-old protégé, André Watts, for the audience-skittish Gould to perform Liszt's Piano Concerto No. 1 at the new Philharmonic Hall. Watts brought down the house, and soon after, Columbia Masterworks released *The Exciting Debut of André Watts*, which included the Liszt concerto. When Watts turned twenty-one in 1967, he signed a long-term contract with Columbia and would remain on the label for the next two decades.

In 1961, Schuyler Chapin signed to Columbia Masterworks perhaps the finest classical pianist alive, Vladimir Horowitz. Long contracted to RCA Victor (along with the other great classical pianist of the era, Artur Rubenstein), Horowitz had become disappointed with RCA's promotion efforts and dismayed at its attempts to talk him into recording lighter classical material. Having stopped giving public performances in 1953—in part due to insecurity, in part due to boredom—he had come to depend on his recordings, yet now he felt unappreciated. The younger American-born piano virtuoso Gary Graffman, who had recently signed with Columbia, alerted Chapin, who arranged for Horowitz's signing. Beginning with his first recordings of selections from Chopin, Rachmaninoff, Schumann, and Liszt, Horowitz was happy. "The first record I made [for Columbia] sold one hundred and twenty thousand copies!" Horowitz later told a reporter. "RCA couldn't sell five thousand! It was Goddard Lieberson who did that!" Schuyler Chapin and Horowitz's producer, Tom Frost, also had something to do with it, but Columbia had certainly done well by Horowitz.

A year after he signed with Columbia, Horowitz began to reconsider his refusal to perform in concert. As an experiment, he rented Carnegie Hall and played to an empty house, "and it worked," he later recalled. "Everything sounded fresh." Two years later, Horowitz made his return on the same stage, to a clamorous reception. (Outside Carnegie Hall, looking at the 1,500 fans lined up for the night to buy tickets, a pedestrian was overheard asking a policeman, "Is this a Beatles thing?") Horowitz offered the public a recital that ranged from Busoni's transcriptions of Bach to Moritz Moszkowski. Columbia in turn produced a beautifully packaged two-album set, *An Historic Return: Horowitz at Carnegie Hall*, which reached retailers only a month after the concert. The recording would go on to win Grammys for best classical album, best solo instrumental classical performance, and best engineering of a classical recording.

Like the rest of Columbia's classical list, though, each recording by Horowitz was a *succès d'estime* and a source of great prestige that hurt the company's bottom line. On average, the company recouped less than half of the $100,000 it cost to produce and market a Horowitz album, despite the great pianist's mystique. Similarly, the less charismatic George Szell's albums with the Cleveland Orchestra won enormous acclaim but lost money, selling only five to ten thousand copies per release. Only recordings by the New York Philharmonic and the Philadelphia Orchestra could be counted on to sell reasonably well over the long run, particularly those aimed at a broad audience, such as their respective albums of Christmas music.

A low point came in 1967 when, amid artistic differences complicated by financial considerations, Eugene Ormandy and the Philadelphia Orchestra left Columbia for RCA Victor—the same label from whom Columbia had snatched Ormandy a quarter of a century earlier. Ormandy's arrival at Columbia Masterworks

Vladimir Horowitz

"The first record I made [for Columbia] sold one hundred and twenty thousand copies! RCA couldn't sell five thousand! It was Goddard Lieberson who did that!"

Isaac Stern

Vladimir Horowitz

in 1943, along with that of Frank Sinatra in the pop department, had been a landmark event in the company's history. When Columbia emerged as the premier LP recording company, its name became tightly entwined with the Philadelphia Sound. Now, with the departure of the Philadelphia Orchestra, another era had ended.

Thelonious Monk and Columbia Jazz

Like the classical catalog, jazz had long been a source of pride rather than profit for Columbia, and this remained true for most of the 1960s. Even Miles Davis, the label's most popular jazz artist, saw his sales decline in the early years of the decade to forty to fifty thousand per release, less than half of what they had been in the 1950s. As with Vladimir Horowitz, though, Columbia was willing to subsidize Davis, which kept him on the label—a decision that would pay off later when Davis began experimenting with electric instruments and fused jazz to rock. Dave Brubeck also remained with Columbia until his sales dropped, after which he disbanded his quartet and devoted himself to composing.

The most noteworthy addition to Columbia's jazz catalog was one of the select few geniuses of composition in jazz, Thelonious Monk. By the time Columbia signed him in 1962, Monk had been at the leading edge of jazz composition and performance for more than twenty years, beginning with his work at the start of the 1940s as the house pianist at Minton's Playhouse. As early as 1944, Monk would write what would become his most famous number, "'Round Midnight." He went on to make some important records for Blue Note and Prestige and then moved to Riverside, where he made his breakthrough album, *Brilliant Corners*, in 1956. A landmark six-month residency the following year at the Five Spot on the Bowery teamed Monk with a quartet that included John Coltrane on tenor saxophone and showcased Monk's evolving percussive, dissonant, angular style. Strains with Riverside over royalties then led Monk to undertake what turned into protracted negotiations with Columbia. He finally sat down to work with his producer Teo Macero at the Thirtieth Street studio on the last day of October 1962.

On his first Columbia album, Monk played in the same quartet with whom he had been working for two years, which included Charlie Rouse on tenor saxophone, John Ore on bass, and Frank Dunlop on drums. The selections consisted mostly of fresh versions of compositions Monk had recorded previously, including his take on "Body and Soul." But some stunning originals also appeared on the disc, including "Blues Five Spot" (retitled "Five Spot Blues" for the album), "Monk's Dream," which would become the title track, and Monk's revision of "Sweet Georgia Brown," which he renamed "Bright Mississippi," in honor of the civil rights struggle in the South.

Columbia heavily promoted *Monk's Dream* upon its release in 1963, and it became an instant best seller. *Criss-Cross* came along the same year, followed by eleven more albums, including several recorded in concert. Anything Monk performed and recorded was superior jazz—"carved sound," the critic Whitney Balliet called it—and so the albums were prize additions to the Columbia catalog. One standout, *It's Monk's Time*, released in 1964, included three new original compositions. Most of Monk's output, though, consisted of revisions of works that he had composed many years earlier. Not until *Underground*, released in 1968, did Monk release a Columbia album stocked chiefly with new compositions. Instead of a new musical revolution, Columbia got rearticulations of an older one, from an American master whose relatively small oeuvre of about seventy songs would be recorded by more artists than that of any other jazz composer, aside from the prolific Duke Ellington.

Ellington, meanwhile, continued to grace Columbia's list, his career energized by the response to *Ellington at Newport*. Working with the talented Columbia producer Irving Townsend, he undertook numerous innovative projects, such as a recording of the *Peer Gynt Suite*. He also set out to show he was the furthest thing from old hat by recording an album with John Coltrane.

But Ellington's imaginative, unconventional collaboration with Coltrane appeared not on Columbia but on Impulse! Records—one indication that Columbia was no longer at the forefront recording the latest in jazz. It was Verve that released the

Thelonious Monk, *Monk*.

Thelonious Monk

most important prebop jazz albums of the 1950s, including Ella Fitzgerald's overpowering renderings of the American popular songbook. Many of the greatest innovators in postbop jazz, including Coltrane, Bill Evans, Ornette Coleman, and the Modern Jazz Quartet, appeared on the other labels, including Impulse!, Blue Note, Riverside, and Atlantic.

Still, the future of popular music at Columbia would never have come from its jazz recordings. It arose out of Columbia's fitful and then frenetic embrace of rock and roll, and of a whole new generation of record buyers. Signs of change arrived as early as 1965, and they revolved, in one way or another, around the figure and the music of Bob Dylan— with Dion, one of the only Columbia recording artists who had grown up wanting to be a rock and roll star.

A Belated but Bold Entrance into Rock and Roll

Beatlemania, followed by the arrival of the Rolling Stones, the Animals, the Kinks, and the rest of the British Invasion, was the first explosive mass musical phenomenon of the baby-boomer generation—as important to the emerging counterculture of the 1960s as the rise of Sinatra had been during the 1940s and Presley in the 1950s. But unlike those earlier eruptions, the British Invasion caught the leading American record labels flatfooted. Capitol passed on its first chance to sign the Beatles, and only under enormous pressure did it release "I Want to Hold Your Hand." (The first Beatles album in America, *Introducing . . . the Beatles*, was released on the Vee-Jay label, a black-owned company founded to sell blues and R&B.) The rest of the very largest labels, with Columbia in the foreground, missed out completely. Columbia's subsidiary-turned-rival, Epic—now very much its own label, although attached to CBS—picked up the Dave Clark Five and the Yardbirds, but the other major British bands appeared on other labels—the Rolling Stones, for example, on London, an arm of British Decca, the Kinks on Reprise, and the Animals on MGM Records. The great cultural irony was that young men from Liverpool, Dartford, Muswell Hill, and Newcastle were making it big by reworking the kind of rhythm and blues music that had been appearing in the States for decades on independent labels like Excello, Chess, and Atlantic. And, once the British Invasion started, the biggest labels, including Columbia, were slow to make the most of it.

Columbia, though, did finally sit up and start to take notice. The Beatles and the other British acts were selling millions of 45-rpm singles and seizing command of Top 40 radio—but they were selling albums, too, which cut into Columbia's strength. An American group on Capitol, the Beach Boys, had already enjoyed success with LPs including *Surfin' USA* and *Surfer Girl* featuring their new California sound, but the British Invasion arrived on a tidal wave of new albums. Rock and roll had begun to pose a new challenge, commercially as well as artistically, to the fundamentals of Columbia's recording program in popular music.

And so Columbia made some significant moves toward reforming itself in the mid-1960s. One important step was to sign Paul Simon and Art Garfunkel, although their success took a little while to pan out. In 1957, the duo—still juniors at Forest Hills High School and calling themselves Tom & Jerry—scored a minor singles hit with "Hey Schoolgirl" on the tiny Big Records label. They later gravitated to the Greenwich Village folk scene and won attention in the clubs. Signed in 1964 by Columbia (which by now was on the lookout for the next Bob Dylan), they recorded an album called *Wednesday Morning, 3 AM*. Released in October 1964, the album flopped, but during the following summer, college stations in Boston and Florida began getting requests for one of its tracks, "The Sound of Silence," and the song received heavy air play. Tom Wilson, who had been overseeing Dylan's move toward playing with electrical instruments, quickly hired Dylan's session band to dub electric guitars, bass, and drum on the surprising hit track. At the end of the year, rereleased as a newly juiced-up single, "The Sound of Silence" reached number one on the *Billboard* pop chart.

Simon & Garfunkel had actually split up soon after *Wednesday Morning*'s release, but Simon immediately returned from England when "The Sound of Silence"

Simon & Garfunkel

took off, and the two reunited. With the Nashville-based producer Bob Johnston supervising, they recorded a second album, *Sounds of Silence*, which included, along with "The Sound of Silence," another hit, "I Am a Rock," which reached number three as a single in the summer of 1966. Johnston also produced Simon & Garfunkel's hit single "Homeward Bound," and their highly acclaimed, more musically ambitious album *Parsley, Sage, Rosemary and Thyme*. The duo succeeded because they had discovered and then honed a uniquely lyrical blend of folk music and rock and roll. Simon & Garfunkel's best work was yet to come.

Tom Wilson's inspiration to overdub electric instruments on "The Sound of Silence"—a revision that neither Simon nor Garfunkel much liked—came in part from Dylan's example but also from a Columbia band artistically indebted to Dylan that Columbia was fortunate to sign early. Toward the end of 1964, the label got word of an interesting new group in Los Angeles, the Jet Set, that was aiming to become an American version of the Beatles. The members' musical backgrounds ranged from the Brill Building pop of the 1950s and early 1960s to Greenwich Village folk, with guitarist and vocalist Jim McGuinn (who had played with the New Christy Minstrels) bridging the two. After changing their name to the Byrds, in obvious homage to the Beatles, they began recording at the end of January 1965 with an electrified version of Dylan's "Mr. Tambourine Man," a song that Dylan had yet to release himself. Released in April, the song reached number one, the first of a rapid string of Byrds' hits, including more covers of Dylan songs like "Chimes of Freedom" and "All I Really Want to Do." Over the next eight years, in different configurations but with McGuinn a constant presence, the band would take rock and roll into new permutations and combinations.

Dylan himself had tried recording for Columbia with rock and roll backing as early as 1962 on his misbegotten first single, "Mixed-Up Confusion." He returned to it anew, with his full powers, on the amplified songs, including "Maggie's Farm," which took up an entire side of *Bringing It All Back Home*, released in April 1965. But it was three months later, while recording his next album, *Highway 61 Revisited*, that Dylan opened up a new world for himself and for American popular music, when he recorded "Like a Rolling Stone." A mordant song in which Dylan took enormous pride, it was a rock and roller all the way, from the drummer Bobby Gregg's pistol shot opening through an intensifying six minutes and thirteen seconds (clipped by four seconds for the single). With its combination of intelligence and swelling sound, quite apart from its length, "Like a Rolling Stone" crashed through the teen-beat limits of mainstream rock and roll. Bruce Springsteen, later remembering hearing it for the first time on the radio, called it the song that "kicked open the door to your mind." It also rose to number two on the pop chart, marking Bob Dylan's crossover into a new kind of stardom, and showing, as even the Byrds' smooth electric version of "Mr. Tambourine Man" had not, that rock music fused to challenging lyrics could reach the pinnacle of Top 40 AM radio.

Dylan doubled down on his next album, *Blonde on Blonde*. Undertaken in New York barely weeks after *Highway 61*'s release, the sessions proceeded haltingly until, at Bob Johnston's suggestion, Dylan pulled up stakes for Nashville. He was accompanied by his organist and musical confidante, Al Kooper, and Robbie Robertson, the guitarist for his touring band, the Hawks. There, the New York hipsters met up with some of Nashville's finest young session men, led by Charlie McCoy, and created what Dylan later called the "wild mercury sound," and Kooper called "the sound of 3 A.M.," on gems like "Visions of Johanna," "Rainy Day Women #12 and 35," and "Sad-Eyed Lady of the Lowlands." Next came a frenetic, at times confrontational world tour, during which Dylan faced down hecklers who hated his new music. After his return home, he crashed his motorcycle outside of Bearsville, New York, and began a prolonged period of seclusion.

For a vital period of more than two years, from the middle of 1966 through 1968, Columbia could not look to Dylan as any sort of musical beacon. In his stead, the label's most successful rock band other than the Byrds, the underrated Paul Revere and the Raiders, recorded some conventional top-ten hits, fueled by appearances on teen music television shows like Dick Clark's *Where the Action Is*. But the Raiders also recorded some strong albums, produced, as the Byrds' had been, by Terry Melcher (the son of Doris Day) and featuring the band's fine lead singer, Mark Lindsay. Among the

The song that "kicked open the door to your mind."

Bruce Springsteen on hearing "Like a Rolling Stone" for the first time

Al Kooper

Paul Revere and the Raiders

Previous page:
The Byrds

Bob Dylan

group's best numbers was "Kicks," a song about drug addiction composed originally for the Animals by the successful husband-and-wife songwriting team of Barry Mann and Cynthia Weil. Yet the Raiders, even though they first became famous on the West Coast, were light years away in sensibility from the cultural changes that were taking shape in San Francisco, and that would soon turn Columbia into the premier major rock and roll label. The Columbia executive most responsible for that seismic shift was the one-time company lawyer, Clive Davis.

Clive Davis

Born in Brooklyn in 1934, Davis attended New York University and Harvard Law School supported by full scholarships, and joined Columbia Records in 1960. He quickly rose from general counsel to administrative vice president and finally to vice president and general manager in 1966. Goddard Lieberson, who had immense respect for lawyers, developed a particular respect for Davis's work, which included killing a complaint brought against Columbia's mail order club by the Federal Trade Commission. Lieberson also admired how Davis persevered in handling clients, particularly Streisand, Williams, Dylan, and their respective hard-nosed managers. Although not experienced in music production, Davis showed he had a talented ear and a sharp sense of timing when he helped bring the young Scottish folk singer Donovan to the Epic label in 1966, sealing the agreement just in time for Epic to release "Sunshine Superman." Lieberson was still the leader, but he had made Davis the number two man. By the end of the summer of 1967, Davis was named president of Columbia Records, still formally reporting to Lieberson (who took the title of president of the CBS-Columbia Group), but actually in charge of the label's day-to-day operations. The deal with Donovan was a strong indication of Davis's musical direction.

"For the first time, popular music is not just love ballads," Davis told the *New York Times* in August 1967. "It's expressing ideas, even leading the way on ideas." Davis had recently returned from the three-day Monterey International Pop Music Festival, which he would later say changed his life, and which certainly changed Columbia. Invited to the festival by his friend Lou Adler, late of Dunhill Records, Davis flew out to California knowing that two Columbia acts, the Byrds and Simon & Garfunkel, would appear. But he was unprepared for the vibes of peace and transcendence he felt pulsing everywhere around him, just as San Francisco's Summer of Love was beginning to blossom one hundred miles to the north. And Davis simply adored the music, performed by, among others, the Jimi Hendrix Experience and the Who (both groups making their first major American appearances), Jefferson Airplane, Country Joe and the Fish, the Mamas and the Papas, and the sensational soul singer Otis Redding. Artistically as well as spiritually, Davis believed, rock and roll had moved beyond where even the Beatles and Dylan had taken it.

"It was," he later wrote, "a glimpse of a new world." That new world, at its most utopian, utterly contradicted the corporate spirit of Black Rock. Yet Davis thought he could bring them together, using Columbia's enormous resources to spread the new musical consciousness—and at the same time rehabilitate Columbia's popular music program and make the company a fortune.

Davis's favorite act at the festival was Big Brother & the Holding Company, entirely because of Janis Joplin. As yet virtually unknown outside of the San Francisco scene, Joplin was a phenomenon ready to break out. A striking blues singer in the full-throated style, she brought a heavy dose of soul to psychedelic Haight-Ashbury rock (which had arisen largely out of San Francisco folk and bluegrass experiments). Her performances at Monterey, especially on "Combination of the Two" and "Ball and Chain," were electrifying. "She seemed bursting with emotion, and it seemed so *pure*" is how Davis later remembered it. By now the company's president, Davis worked through an expensive tangle of contractual snags, and Big Brother signed on early in 1968. In mid-August, *Cheap Thrills*, with its soon-to-be-famous cover by the cartoonist R. Crumb (who actually didn't much like Joplin's music but needed the money) was released. Within a month, one million copies had sold.

Clive Davis

"For the first time, popular music is not just love ballads. It's expressing ideas, even leading the way on ideas."

Janis Joplin with Clive Davis

Laura Nyro with Clive Davis

Santana with Clive Davis

Janis Joplin

A little more than two years later, Joplin was dead, consumed by an addiction to drugs and alcohol that ended in an overdose of heroin in a Los Angeles motel room. She had split from Big Brother late in 1968 and embarked on what proved an uneven solo career, although, poignantly, the best of her later solo recordings, a rendition of her then-boyfriend Kris Kristofferson's "Me and Bobby McGee," issued posthumously on the album *Pearl*, was one of the strongest she would ever release and by far the most popular. Joplin's fate, including the sad legend that attached to her troubled life, was one sign of the burnout that overtook parts of the counterculture at the very end of the 1960s and during the early 1970s. But the musical revolutions that Davis had glimpsed at Monterey had only begun, and, under Davis's direction, Columbia became the leading rock label in the world, overtaking and surpassing heavy competition from Warner Bros. and Capitol.

Rock and Roll Eclecticism

Looking back, one can see that it was the variety as well as the quality of Columbia's performers that made its rock catalog so impressive. The burgeoning rock and roll market actually embraced a wide range of styles, and the ability to dominate the market required understanding as much. Davis was smart but also eclectic, as were Columbia's A&R producers and advisers, including George Daly and, still active after all these years, John Hammond. A summary of Columbia's most auspicious rock acts in the late 1960s and early 1970s reads like a compendium of what rock and roll had become and a prediction of where it was headed.

Not that Columbia always performed flawlessly. Along with Big Brother, the label signed the excellent San Francisco psychedelic band Moby Grape. The group showed enormous potential and cut two successful albums, but it suffered badly because of a disastrous marketing decision to release five singles from the first album on the same day. In time, the band succumbed to drug abuse and sudden shifts in personnel. Generally, though, Columbia served its most talented rock artists well—and vice versa. A very different San Francisco band, Santana, cut its eponymous first album for Columbia in May 1969, offering a unique fusion of Latin music, jazz, and rock. Aided by the group's enormous exposure at the famous Woodstock Music and Art Fair in August, the album shot to number four on the Billboard pop chart. The group's next and best album, *Abraxas*, which featured "Black Magic Woman," proved even more popular.

Another innovative sound came from Blood, Sweat & Tears. Built from remnants of the pioneering New York band called the Blues Project (including, initially, Dylan's sometime organist, Al Kooper), BS&T mixed horn arrangements and jazz improvisation with rock, rhythm and blues, and pop. Revamped around the Canadian vocalist David Clayton-Thomas, the group released its self-titled second album in 1968, which became the first album ever to produce four hit singles, including "Spinning Wheel," and which went on to win the Grammy for Album of the Year in 1969—only the second rock album, after the Beatles' *Sergeant Pepper's Lonely Hearts Club Band* the year before, to capture that distinction. Columbia also released the albums of two similarly configured ensembles: the Electric Flag (which included the extraordinary guitarist Mike Bloomfield), and Chicago Transit Authority (which was soon known simply as Chicago), which scored big with its first release, a double album, and went on to record a string of hit albums over the decade to come, with songs like "25 or 6 to 4."

Leonard Cohen was something else altogether. John Hammond had learned about the Canadian poet and songwriter before the Monterey festival and Clive Davis's rise, and, in May 1967, Cohen recorded his first album, *Songs of Leonard Cohen*, with "Sisters of Mercy," "So Long, Marianne," and "Suzanne." Cohen's haunting verses and melodies were rooted in European and British folk traditions, and leading folk artists, notably Judy Collins, eagerly recorded their own versions. Through the 1970s, Cohen enlarged his musical territory to include pop and cabaret styling, while sustaining his singular literary intelligence.

The newcomer Laura Nyro, whose sound was more based on R&B than Cohen's, gave what some at the time called one of the few truly poor performances at Monterey.

"It was a glimpse of a new world."

Clive Davis
on rock and roll

Leonard Cohen

Leonard Cohen performing in New York's Central Park

But Nyro, who had initially recorded for Verve, had an impressive portfolio of songs, some of which would soon become major hits for groups that included the Fifth Dimension. Later, touted by Davis's fellow Brooklynite, the young agent David Geffen, Nyro came back to Davis's attention. After she auditioned for him with "Eli's Comin'," Davis was persuaded and presented her with a handsome recording contract. From *Eli and the Thirteenth Confession* in 1968 to *Gonna Take a Miracle* in 1971 (the year she abruptly announced she was retiring), Nyro honed a passionate sound that merged contemporary soul and elements of Brill Building pop.

In still another expansion of the rock genre, Columbia recorded Taj Mahal. Born Henry St. Clair Fredericks, Taj had begun concocting his own revision of Southern black blues styles with rock instrumentation as a member of the Rising Sons, a Los Angeles–based band whose original lineup included Ry Cooder and Ed Cassidy. In 1968, he recorded *Taj Mahal*, which included a rock version of Blind Willie McTell's "Statesboro Blues," which would go on to inspire Duane Allman. Soon after came *The Natch'l Blues* and a wonderful combination of two albums, the rock recording *Giant Step* and *De Ole' Folks at Home*, the latter being entirely acoustic. In 1972, Columbia lured the R&B funk ensemble Earth, Wind & Fire from Warner Bros. This band made superbly crafted songs out of their own material but also out of songs as disparate as Bread's "Make It With You" and Pete Seeger's "Where Have All the Flowers Gone?" An appearance at Fillmore East in 1968 with Al Kooper and Michael Bloomfield brought the Texas blues guitarist and vocalist Johnny Winter to Columbia's attention. His remarkable debut album for the label, *Johnny Winter*, appeared the following year, featuring Winter's brother Edgar on keyboards and the veteran Chicago bluesman Willie Dixon on upright bass.

Another success story involved two artists in yet another, entirely different musical camp. In 1971, the California singer-songwriter Jim Messina, formerly of the successful rock groups Buffalo Springfield and Poco, teamed up with the relatively unknown Kenny Loggins, to complete an album for Columbia that Loggins had begun. The result, *Sittin' In*, became a staple of the emerging, soothing, popular AM-radio style soon to be known as soft rock. Six more highly successful Loggins and Messina studio albums followed, featuring a versatile blend that ranged from sentimental pop to rockabilly.

Earlier arrivals to Columbia were also making waves. Two years after they reached a new artistic peak with *Bookends* in 1968, Simon & Garfunkel recorded *Bridge Over Troubled Water*, which became a massive hit thanks mainly to its title track, a smash single. (Soon after, though, tension between the two performers led them to go their separate ways). Amid several changes in personnel, the Byrds, led by McGuinn (who now called himself Roger) shifted from the psychedelia of *Eight Miles High* to, in 1968, the landmark country-rock album *Sweetheart of the Rodeo*. Bob Dylan, coming out of his seclusion, followed his own muse, as ever, and recorded a deceptively simple album of chorusless song parables, *John Wesley Harding* in 1967, which was about as far as one could get from the sounds of Santana or Chicago. Dylan followed with his own venture into country and western music, *Nashville Skyline*, which included a new version of "Girl of the North Country" recorded with his old friend Johnny Cash.

The critical rewards of Columbia's shift to rock and roll would take time to arrive, as the industry caught up fully with the rock revolution. But the staggering commercial rewards, foreshadowed by *Cheap Thrills*, were evident immediately, as sales figures went through the roof. *Blood, Sweat & Tears* sold 3.8 million copies and Santana's *Abraxas* sold 3.5 million. Chicago's first album, *Chicago Transit Authority*, was an astounding success that went double platinum in sales, and each of Chicago's new albums sold well over a million copies. Columbia's heavy investment in rock music, as well as its marketing ability, was plain to the world: between 1965 and 1969, the label's share of the rock music record market reportedly jumped from 15 percent to 60 percent. Other successful CBS labels, Epic especially, also moved heavily into rock and roll, signing and releasing major bands like Sly and the Family Stone and the Jeff Beck Group.

The fortunes to be made from rock affected the culture of Columbia, as leather-and-tie-dye-bedecked young musicians began turning up regularly on the twelfth floor of Black Rock. But the changes also ran deeper, affecting how Columbia did business

Blood, Sweat & Tears

Johnny Winter

Earth, Wind & Fire

with its leading artists. Davis understood that the emergence of the rock stars, and the competition for their services, compelled the recording companies to value their most popular performers far more than they ever had before, cultivating them as career artists. That is, he recalled and restated the old truth that recording companies rise or fall chiefly because of the talent they record. This now meant not just signing the best new acts but also promoting and then retaining them by spending on a scale unheard of in the early days, when recording companies had treated most performers, even stars, as hired help. Davis's enormous payouts for the rights to record the likes of Big Brother & the Holding Company, which were controversial at the time, would eventually turn out to be bargains. But in combination with the artists' insistence on retaining creative control, evident early on with Barbra Streisand and Bob Dylan, the competition for talent eventually shifted the balance of power in the leading sectors of the recording industry away from the companies and toward the most successful acts and their managers. With the increasing sophistication of expensive recording techniques, that shift permitted the label's very top earners to demand ever more, above and beyond promotion. And, from the 1960s on, Columbia's history, more than ever, would revolve around the stories of its star performers, both veterans and newcomers.

Country, Classical, and Jazz Amid the Rock Revolution

With Davis and Columbia so invested in rock music, and with rock now dominating the entire industry, it was, as it remains, easy to overlook Columbia's artistic successes with other musical styles during the late 1960s and early 1970s. Country and western music—which was, after all, one of the original components of rock and roll—continued to thrive at Columbia under Davis, even though it was not his major interest. The label had already committed considerable resources to its Nashville operation in the 1960s, overseen by Don Law and his successor, Bob Johnston, which helped lead to an explosion of popular acts, adding the likes of Claude King and Billy Walker to a roster that already included Flatt and Scruggs, Ray Price, and Marty Robbins. The growth continued into the 1970s. Among the highlights was "(I Never Promised You a) Rose Garden," written by Joe South (who was one of the Nashville musicians on Dylan's *Blonde on Blonde*). Performed by Lynne Anderson, and released in 1970, it became the largest-selling record ever by a female country singer, a distinction it would hold for nearly thirty years.

Most significant of all in the country field was Johnny Cash's breakthrough to superstardom. Cash, who had continued to struggle with his personal demons, moved into unexplored territory at the decade's close while he began putting his life in order. Ever since he had recorded "Folsom Prison Blues" for Sun Records in 1955, he had thought about one day recording an album in a prison, and in January 1967 he got his chance, backed by June Carter (whom he would marry later that year), Carl Perkins, and the Tennessee Three. Heavy on songs about prison life, including "The Wall" and "Green, Green Grass of Home," the two shows produced the album *Johnny Cash at Folsom Prison* in 1968—a collection of brilliant performances punctuated by the inmates' cheers that reached the top of the charts in pop as well as country music. Cash sang, according to a review in *Life* magazine, like "someone who has grown up believing he is one of the people that these songs are about." A year later, Columbia released something of a reprise, *Johnny Cash at San Quentin*, which also headed the pop and country charts in 1968 and 1969, and yielded "A Boy Named Sue," the biggest hit single of Cash's career. Then, in June 1969, ABC Television aired the first installment of *The Johnny Cash Show*. By now, Cash had become one of the greatest exponents of American balladry, cutting across boundaries of genre and taste.

The classical department at Columbia, which fared differently, hardly disappeared, but it certainly felt the shock waves of change. Leonard Bernstein, who had taken over Columbia Masterworks, recorded his cycle of Mahler symphonies, whose relentlessness and expressiveness had a certain psychedelic appeal. Meanwhile, Bernstein's successor as music director and conductor of the New York Philharmonic, the composer and pianist Pierre Boulez, recorded Bartók, Roussel, and Schoenberg as well as Handel and Wagner.

Johnny Cash at San Quentin

Johnny Cash, Folsom Prison

Moving well beyond the early modernists, Columbia also released the work of avant-garde composers like John Cage, Karlheinz Stockhausen, and Iannis Xenakis.

But to drive the point home, Columbia began marketing reissued Masterworks recordings with what now reads as a painfully contrived adaptation of "hippie" slang, proclaiming the albums as psychedelic wonders: "Charles Ives Sold Insurance, But His Real Gig Was The New Music," ran one advertisement. "Hector Berlioz Took Dope, And His Trips Exploded Into Out-of-Sight Sounds," ran another. Goddard Lieberson, who looked on as president of the CBS/Columbia group and was no prude, sighed deeply, but was pleased enough when Masterworks' sales figures momentarily rose. Another sign of the times was the enormous success of the keyboardist Walter (later Wendy) Carlos's *Switched-On Bach*, consisting of Bach compositions created on a Moog synthesizer. The goal, as veteran Masterworks marketer Peter Munves crudely put it, was to go out and grab the generation that was buying those tens of millions of rock albums: "This is an audience that doesn't know diddlysquat about Bach," Munves told one sales meeting, "so we'll do Bach on the synthesizer and we'll get 'em by the balls!"

Some critics blamed this attitude toward the public, at once condescending and clumsy, as well as the recording industry's new preoccupation with spending vast sums on rock music, for the overall decline in sales of classical music. And because Columbia Masterworks had been so distinguished until Davis changed Columbia's direction, Davis and Columbia received much of the blame. Yet to ascribe classical music's decline to the industry's (and Columbia's) new commercial priorities is simplistic. Given the relative decline of so much of its mainstream popular music program by the mid-1960s, Columbia might not have survived at all had Davis not made the shift into rock music. Even if the company had persevered, it is doubtful that it could have done any better than it did by its classical performers by trying to subsidize them with a weakened popular list. To focus on the supply side of the equation is to neglect the trends of consumer demand, especially as they were shaped and reflected by trends in radio programming.

Why the public's appetite for classical music was so much smaller in 1968 than it had been sixty years earlier—when Enrico Caruso was the equivalent of a modern rock star—remains a development in need of full explanation. Might a decline of classical musical education in the schools bear some responsibility—a decline, it should be added, that occurred despite efforts like Leonard Bernstein's Young People's Concerts? Much of the popular enthusiasm for classical music, and especially opera, in the early twentieth century came from immigrants. Might the cultural distance of their children and their later descendants from the heritage of Verdi and Wagner help explain the drop? All that is certain is that the decline was dramatic—and that Columbia's recording program both abetted and responded to it.

In jazz, the musical style favored by the youth of the 1920s and 1930s, continued commercial success came to depend largely on how eager artists were to incorporate rock sounds and techniques into their music. Clive Davis's attention focused chiefly on the evolution of Miles Davis's work into the fusion style that blended jazz and rock. The style appeared first on *In a Silent Way* in 1969 and, a year later, on *Bitches Brew*—the trumpeter's first gold record and a genuine artistic transformation that simultaneously reflected how much rock had changed Columbia and the entire musical landscape. "I let Miles have a free hand in the studio," the producer Teo Macero later recalled of the *Bitches Brew* sessions. "And I always encouraged him to use electronic equipment." According to Clive Davis, though, Miles had to be coaxed into enlarging his audience by appearing in venues like Bill Graham's Fillmore East. The young Fillmore audience, Davis insisted, was ready for his music, but Miles would have none of it. Certain that white promoters like Graham would cheat him, and convinced that the rock bands had ripped off his musical style, he vowed that he would never play for "those fucking long-haired white kids."

Clive Davis held steady, and he talked the artist into playing the Fillmore, where he performed on a double bill with Laura Nyro (a devoted Miles fan) in 1970. Thereafter, Miles toured with Santana and played numerous rock halls, ensuring the commercial success of *Bitches Brew*. And, in 1970, two of Davis's band members, the

Miles Davis
with producer
Teo Macero

Miles Davis

saxophonist Wayne Shorter and keyboardist Joe Zawinul, initiated the formation of a new fusion ensemble, Weather Report. The group's first, self-named album on Columbia both expanded on musical experimentation and reaffirmed the label's support for it.

Another variation of fusion came in the music of the Mahavishnu Orchestra and its leader, the guitarist John McLaughlin. A truly international ensemble—McLaughlin was British, and other group members hailed from Panama, Czechoslovakia, Ireland, and the United States—the orchestra originated in Davis's *Bitches Brew* sessions, which had included McLaughlin and drummer Billy Cobham. Its spirit, structure, and musical eclecticism also reflected McLaughlin's engagement in the teachings of the guru Sri Chimoy (who encouraged him to take the name Mahavishnu, meaning "divine compassion, power, and justice"). On *The Inner Mounting Flame*, released by Columbia in 1971, and *Birds of Fire* two years later, the group blended high-powered rock, funk, and classical music from both India and Europe. The recordings also were among the first to include a Moog synthesizer, which greatly expanded the instrumental possibilities. The group dissolved in 1973, only to reassemble under McLaughlin's direction with different musicians later that year, and (after a long break) again in 1984, to record five more studio albums, in addition to one concert recording and two compilations.

McLaughlin would in turn have great influence on the developing work of Carlos Santana. After Santana and his band released their third studio album, *Santana III*, in 1971, a rapid metamorphosis in style as well as personnel began. Bassist David Brown and percussionist Mike Carabello left the band, succeeded by, respectively, Tom Rutley, Doug Rauch, and Armando Peraza. Reflecting Carlos Santana's growing admiration for jazz fusion, the group's next album, *Caravanserai*, consisted chiefly of instrumentals with experimental jazz passages very different from the band's Latin rock. (Clive Davis objected, saying that the shift would destroy the band's popularity, but Santana stood frim and, although sales declined, the album did receive a gold record.) Santana in turn was drawn to the Mahavishnu Orchestra, and under John McLaughlin's initial guidance he became a disciple of Sri Chimoy. Taking the name Devadip (meaning "the lamp, light, and eye of God"), Santana would lead his band into complex and sprawling experiments with fusion. Their experimentation was capped by a studio album, *Welcome*, released in 1973 and, a year later, *Lotus*, a three-album set of "live" performances. Santana and McLaughlin also joined forces to record *Love, Devotion, Surrender*, again strongly influenced by their connections to Sri Chimoy.

Major Stars and New Techniques Appear, but Clive Davis Departs

By 1973, Davis had radically altered Columbia Records—and Columbia was by any measure the foremost company in the industry. The label's success was not limited to the United States. In 1967, just as Davis was taking over Columbia, CBS entered into negotiations with the giant Japanese corporation Sony to form a transpacific alliance, which led the following year to the inauguration of CBS/Sony, the first joint venture between Japan and the United States in the recording business. CBS/Sony emerged as the largest recording company in Japan, and the relationship would have a recurring impact on Columbia's history over the ensuing two decades. Davis's chief influence, however, was in changing the label's artistic makeup. To be sure, traditional vocal stylists who adjusted to the shift in public taste remained enormously creative as well as successful. Barbra Streisand, for one, had begun a second career as a major film star but also renewed her success as a recording artist, especially on the rock-influenced *Stoney End*, whose title track was written by Laura Nyro and was released in 1971. Others did not adjust so well, notably Tony Bennett, who left Columbia in 1971 and began a period of prolonged personal turmoil, although he would team up with Bill Evans to cut two strong albums for Fantasy Records in 1975 and 1976.

Columbia's priorities were clear, and the well of talent in rock and the rest of contemporary music seemed bottomless. Popular tastes, to be sure, were shifting again, in what sometimes seemed to be contradictory directions. The idealism of the 1960s

Laura Nyro

Santana peforming at Woodstock Festival

Carlos Santana

faltered as the Vietnam War dragged on, and as President Richard M. Nixon was reelected only to be consumed by the Watergate scandal. The intense introspection of successful artists such as Laura Nyro proved an early indication of a more general withdrawal from the flower-power, countercultural spirit that had originally attracted Davis to rock and roll. At the same time, the magnitude of rock's commercial success pushed other artists toward a more spectacular showmanship, to be promoted in enormous live venues that widened the distance between performers and their audiences. By the early 1970s, the first hints appeared of what came to be called arena rock—high-energy music meant to be performed in front of tens of thousands of fans at a time.

Continuing innovations in recording technology, particularly in connection with multitrack recording, also changed the character of rock music. The adoption of two-track (and later three-track) recording had enlarged the capacities of performers and producers to alter instrumentation and even the basic sound of commercial releases. Many of Motown Records' hits as well as Phil Spector's Wall of Sound productions were taped on three-track recorders (although Spector would then mix his recordings down to mono, which he thought sonically superior).

By the mid-1960s, though, four-track recording, pioneered a decade earlier at Atlantic Records, had become the norm in most studios. This development was succeeded by eight-track recording at the end of the decade and used to strong effect by the Beatles on *The White Album*, which in turn was quickly succeeded by sixteen-track recording. Columbia's artists and producers seized on these opportunities to create ever more complex layers of sound. One of the first sixteen-track recorders arrived at Columbia's New York studios in time to record the second album by Blood, Sweat & Tears, which appeared at the end of 1968. Technical virtuosity was getting to be as important—more so, it seemed to some—than musical abilities, a distant echo of the shift that John Philip Sousa had complained about six decades earlier. As performers, producers, and recording engineers spent more time in the studios overlaying tracks—soon, there would be twenty-four- and forty-eight-track machines—the intensity of multitracking began to inspire a backlash. Above all, the musicians' dependence on studio tools, combined with the inflated production style of arena rock and the cloying self-awareness of some of the singer-songwriters, would help ignite the hostile reaction in the mid- to late 1970s that became famous as punk rock.

Davis and Columbia, alert to the shifts, continued signing up fledgling talents with interesting styles, some of whom would only begin paying off after several years. In 1972, a pair of band managers invited Davis down to New York's au courant nightclub Max's Kansas City to hear a new group out of Boston. The band was not actually scheduled to appear, but the members had paid for a place on the bill out of their own pockets. They called themselves Aerosmith, they played a straight-ahead blues-influenced rock and roll, and Davis signed them up. Their debut album, released at the beginning of 1973, showed promise and included a big hit, "Dream On." Their second album, *Get Your Wings*—recorded after the band had tightened its musical chops by touring almost constantly for a year—included bluesier numbers, including a cover of "Train Kept A-Rollin" that came closer to defining a distinct blues-rock sound. And their third album, *Toys in the Attic*, released in 1975, would establish Aerosmith as a premier rock and roll band, led by guitarist Joe Perry's powerful riffs and vocalist Steven Tyler's raunchy intonations. Musical elements from the Rolling Stones and Led Zeppelin, as well as from proto-punk bands like the New York Dolls, all turned up in Aerosmith's work, but Perry in particular added a dirty blues spirit that came across as at once gleeful and tough.

Davis was also drawn to a band originally from Long Island, Blue Öyster Cult, which was helping to develop heavy metal rock. Starting out with the name Soft White Underbelly, the group had wanted to be an American answer to the British hard rock group Black Sabbath, featuring extended guitar-driven improvisations, dense drum-and-bass riffs, and songs with seemingly apocalyptic but often tongue-in-cheek lyrics. An eponymous debut album, released early in 1972, sold well. The band would enjoy strong if unspectacular critical and commercial success with its studio albums through the 1970s, with one standout, *Agents of Fortune*, released in 1976. As the enthusiasm of its audiences attested, the band's work was best appreciated in concert, which helps

Chicago

Joe Perry and
Steven Tyler
of Aerosmith

Billy Joel

explain why the "live" release from 1979, *Some Enchanted Evening*, would prove its most popular, even after Blue Öyster Cult continued its work into the 1980s.

Davis and Columbia also signed two very different artists with more introspective temperaments who showed exceptional potential. At the Mar y Sol music festival in Puerto Rico in spring 1972, Columbia executives heard a versatile young singer-songwriter from Long Island named Billy Joel and handed him a contract. In November 1973, Columbia released *Piano Man*, its hit title track a harbinger of things to come.

Also in 1972, John Hammond met a new performer from New Jersey, Bruce Springsteen, who turned up for a scheduled appointment alongside his manager, Mike Appel. Hammond found Appel's pushy manner to be obnoxious. "For God's sake, just stop it! You're gonna make me hate you," Hammond recalled telling the overbearing Appel. But then Springsteen performed a song, and Hammond would later write that he "reacted with a force I've felt maybe three times in my life." The producer got the newcomer and his mates, later dubbed the E Street Band, to record an album quickly (*Greetings from Asbury Park, N.J.*) followed by *The Wild, the Innocent & the E Street Shuffle*, which was released in September 1973. Springsteen was headed toward becoming a new style of singer-songwriter, one who melded highly intelligent lyrics with the kind of high-octane rock and roll that could fill an arena.

A new wave in Clive Davis's transformation of Columbia was beginning to swell. But by the time Joel's first and Springsteen's second album had appeared, Davis had been ousted from the label.

The full story behind Davis's downfall may never be told. In late May 1973, Columbia executives were called to a meeting on the thirty-fifth floor of Black Rock. The president and director of CBS, Arthur Taylor, introduced Irwin Segelstein, until now one of the top programmers at the television network, as the president of Columbia Records. A CBS press release charged Davis with improper use of company funds and announced further that Goddard Lieberson would be moving from his job at CBS to return as president of the CBS Records Group. Walter Yetnikoff, once the head of Columbia's legal office and lately a vice president in the international division, would take over as head of CBS Records International Group. Davis was accused of using Columbia funds to help pay for a lavish bar mitzvah he threw for his son at the Plaza Hotel. Davis eventually pleaded guilty to minor charges and paid a nominal fine. The allegation was, in the greater scheme of things, pretty small. Some believed that CBS had become overly vigilant about corruption, conflating borderline use of what amounted to petty cash with grand larceny. And there were plenty of personality conflicts, suspicions, and clashing ambitions around Columbia that, if they did not cause the coup, contributed to it. Among them was Lieberson's disillusionment with Davis, whom he thought had tried to supplant him instead of succeeding him: "The trouble with Clive Davis," he reportedly told friends, "is that he thought he was me."

But whatever skullduggery was involved, Davis's firing was an unprecedented turning point in Columbia's history. For decades an also-ran in the recording business—an enterprise that had at times lurched from point to point and lived under many different titles—Columbia had ascended during the 1940s until the mid-1960s with relatively little internal corporate disturbance. When Clive Davis came along, at first inspired by the spirit of the Aquarian age, he carried the label's mystique of tradition, sophistication, and elevated taste, cultivated by Lieberson, into the raucous jumble of rock-dominated contemporary music. And he did this without cheapening the label's reputation for musical quality. Columbia did not simply weather the revolutions of the 1960s, it mastered them, without losing its cachet of quality and class.

Black Rock, though, was not 799 Seventh Avenue. The upstart enterprise that had created the LP was now a gigantic corporation, with all the intrigue that went along with that way of doing business. Suddenly, shockingly, its chieftain was deposed. Although the changes Davis had made were responses to massive culture trends and not about to be reversed, the greatest leader from what now seemed a bygone age, Goddard Lieberson, would be back in charge, or so it seemed. Yet as far as Columbia's future over the coming decade was concerned, the man who mattered most would turn out to be Walter Yetnikoff.

Bruce Springsteen

Previous Page:
Steven Tyler of Aerosmith
at RFK Stadium

Janis Joplin

EARTH, WIND

HEAD TO TH

Lynn Anderson
Rose Garden

Snowbird
For The Good Times
Sunday Morning Coming Down
It's Only Make Believe
I Don't Want To Play House
Your Sweet Love Lifted Me
I Still Belong To You
I Wish I Was A Little Boy Again
Another Lonely Night
Nothing Between Us
Rose Garden

lly Joe
Royal

own in
the
docks

people

Her faces, her moods as many as the words used to describe her—hoyden and princess, vamp and torch-bearer, sophisticated and ingenuous, wistful and exuberant. She is utterly unique.

"Magnificent, sublime, radiant, electric—what puny little adjectives to describe Barbra Streisand," burbled one critic. He was right. Barbra's too much. "When she opened on Broadway," reported Life, "the entire, gorgeous, rattletrap showbusiness establishment blew sky-

high. Overnight, critics began raving, photographers flipping, flacks yakking and columnists flocking." Jule Styne said: "She carries her own spotlight."

You've heard her first three Columbia albums. Now you can bask in her glow when you hear her latest, People. It will make you feel like one of the "very special people" she sings about in the title song.

barbra streisand on columbia records

Barbra Streisand
People

TAJ MAHAL
THE NATCH'L BLUES

MILES DAVIS
BITCHES BREW

CHEAP THRILLS

Janis Joplin.
Big Brother and The
Holding Company.
They're going
to wipe you out.

It is a blues voice, ragged and painful but somehow beautiful and moving at the same time, a voice which has learned from Bessie Smith and Dinah Washington and Esther Phillips and Big Mama Thornton ... but it is a voice unique with Janis.

(She) totally abandons herself to each song, coming on very gutty and completely overpowering ... Each performance has the agonizing intensity of a woman giving birth. Pete Johnson—Los Angeles Times

Janis Joplin is the greatest white female singer around. Rat

Janis Joplin is where it's at, where it's been and where it will be. Hullabaloo

Her singing is a celebration—her voice and body hurled with lerraping power that leaves her limp. And this member of the audience feels that he has been in contact with an overwhelming life force. Part of that life force is an open sensuality.

Janis is fire ... one feels heat and sees red sundowns.
Janis sings with her body—rough, gutsy, possessed.
It is an incredible experience to hear Janis sing. Eye

From the sound in the grooves right on out to the cover of their new album, they kick and scratch and bite and work your ears over with unforgettable impact.

You've heard their fantastic "Piece of My Heart" new single on the air. So you know the talk is true.

On COLUMBIA RECORDS

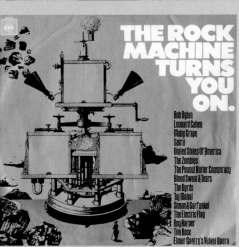

THE ROCK
MACHINE
TURNS
YOU
ON.

Bob Dylan
Leonard Cohen
Moby Grape
Spirit
United States Of America
The Zombies
The Peanut Butter Conspiracy
Blood, Sweat & Tears
The Byrds
Taj Mahal
Simon & Garfunkel
The Electric Flag
Roy Harper
Tim Rose
Elmer Gantry's Velvet Opera

ING
OF
IRE
ST OF

NY
ASH

BEL—JOHNNY YUMA
BONANZA
THE BIG BATTLE
EMEMBER THE ALAMO
NESSEE FLAT-TOP BOX
RING OF FIRE
WHAT DO I CARE
I'D STILL BE THERE
TILL MISS SOMEONE
TY SHADES OF GREEN
WERE YOU THERE
PEACE IN THE VALLEY

Billy Joel
Cold Spring Harbor

STEREO

I Left My Heart
IN SAN FRANCISCO

BLOOD, SWEAT & TEARS

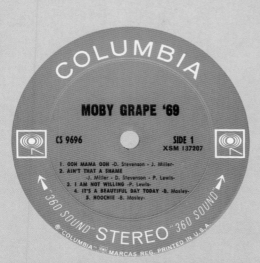

This man puts more thoughts, more ideas and images into one song than most people put into an album.

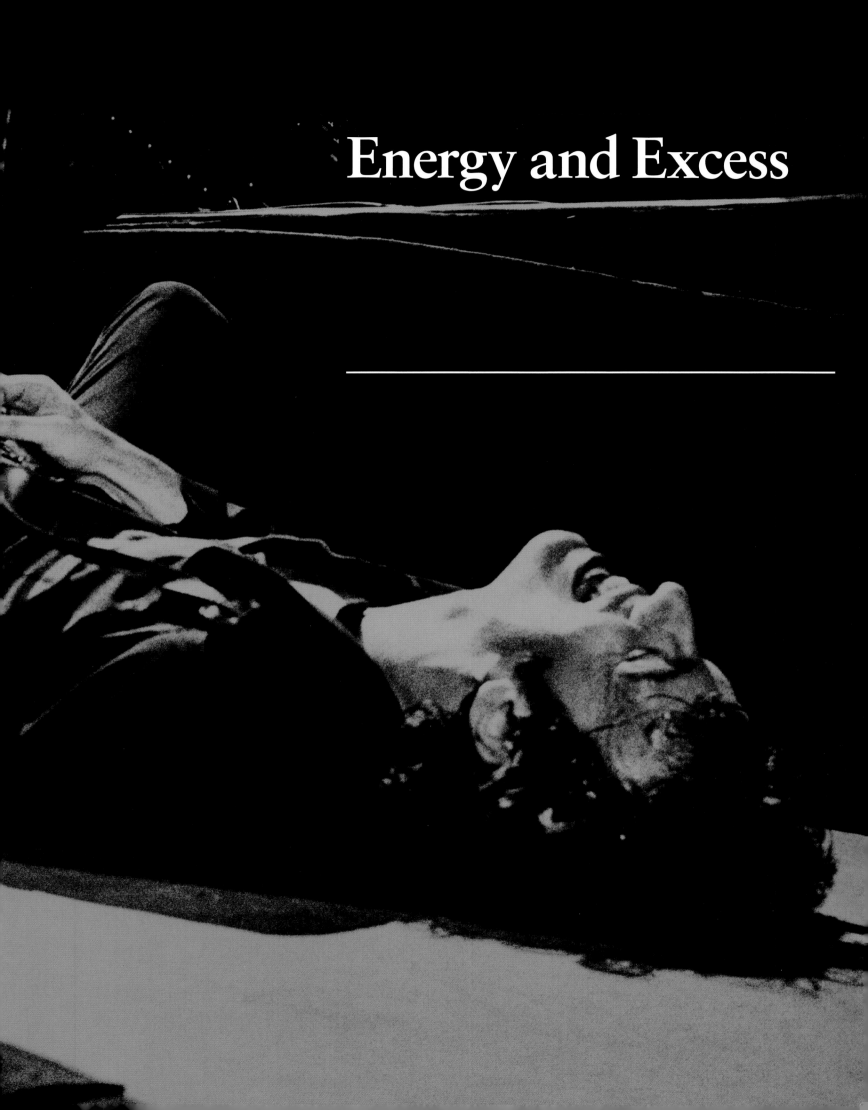

Energy and Excess

A year after he was appointed president of Columbia Records, Irwin Segelstein, the former CBS television programmer, told some reporters that, "We're going through some shock waves today and it will inevitably find its way into the drama and the music of tomorrow. But nobody can project it or predict it will happen." The shock waves Segelstein referred to were the alarming revelations about the Watergate scandal which, over the spring and early summer of 1974, were building toward President Nixon's resignation. The utopian dreams of the 1960s had largely subsided, and, though Segelstein could barely have known it yet, the mid- to late 1970s would bring economic uncertainty and political disquiet that culminated during Jimmy Carter's presidency, followed by Ronald Reagan's election to the White House. Although some of the best work from the mid-1970s onward built on and extended '60s rock, other styles, above all punk rock, aroused a rebelliousness that ripped into anything from the past that seemed complicit with a bloated and corrupt Establishment. The stylized decadence that showed up in still other phenomena like disco—advanced by the rise of an openly gay metropolitan night club scene, in the decade between Stonewall and the outbreak of the AIDS plague—would have shocked earlier generations of recording executives. The spirit of excess, indulgence, and ferocity that came to prevail in the corporate world would have caused a stir among them as well. And still, Columbia Records rode the waves, with some bemusing moments along the way.

Elvis Costello

An anecdote, drawn from the memoir of the man who succeeded Segelstein as the head of Columbia, illustrates the peculiar encounters of the time at and around the record label. In 1977, the Epic recording star Meat Loaf told Walter Yetnikoff (who was by now overseeing Epic as well as Columbia) that he was dying to meet, of all people, William Paley, in order, he said, to find out more about the history of CBS. Just as oddly, the impeccable Paley agreed to see him.

Meat Loaf, accompanied by Yetnikoff, arrived dressed in overalls and combat boots and carrying a box of glazed jelly doughnuts, which he offered to share. Paley, dressed in a bespoke business suit and sipping tea, accepted. The conversation then turned to Meat Loaf's new hit single.

"It's called 'Paradise by the Dashboard Light.'"

"I'm sorry to say I haven't heard it. What's the theme?" Paley inquired.

"Humping."

"Oh, I see."

"Phil Rizzuto is announcing a baseball game while me and this chick are getting it on. That's the paradise part."

"Paradise, indeed," Paley said, smiling broadly.

The single would become a classic rock staple. The album was an enormous success and would go on to sell more than forty million copies worldwide. The parent company CBS was delighted. And Yetnikoff, who had taken over Segelstein's job in 1975, would be the dominant power and personality at Columbia Records as well as Epic for more than a dozen years, leading the label through some of the wildest rides and most astounding commercial triumphs in its history.

Established Stars: Columbia Veterans and New Arrivals

The years immediately after Clive Davis's departure brought no dramatic change in Columbia's artistic priorities. Segelstein's appointment, coupled with Goddard Lieberson's return, signaled CBS's desire to create an air of probity after the upheaval of Davis's firing, but not a revamping of its recording program. Continued success by established major stars, including both long-time Columbia artists and newcomers to the label, proved one crucial source of stability—and affirmed Davis's emphasis on cultivating and retaining its leading acts.

By the mid-1970s, Barbra Streisand's recordings had become entwined with her career as a film actress, which had begun auspiciously in 1968 with an Oscar-winning reprise of her role as Fanny Brice in the Broadway hit *Funny Girl*. After starring with Robert Redford in *The Way We Were* in 1973, Streisand recorded, in addition to the soundtrack release, her own album for Columbia with the film's theme song as the title track. The album earned her another gold record, and "The Way We Were" became Streisand's first single to reach number one on the Billboard pop chart. Streisand's own composition from the film *A Star Is Born*, "Evergreen," with lyrics by Paul Williams, won her an Academy Award for Best Original Song as well as the Grammy for Best Pop Vocal Performance, Female in 1977. By the end of the 1970s, Streisand had established herself as the best-selling female recording artist of all time to that point; only the Beatles and Elvis Presley had sold more records. Over the ensuing decade, she blended her film work with a return to her musical roots for Columbia on 1985's *The Broadway Album*—another Grammy-winning popular hit. The dazzling newcomer of 1962 had made good on her promise to excel in a cluster of artistic endeavors.

Bob Dylan had started out at exactly the same time as Streisand, in MacDougal Street folk clubs like the Café Wha? and the Gaslight, which were only a few blocks away from her favorite Village *boîte*, Bon Soir. "Hammond's Folly" had become one of Columbia's greatest artistic triumphs. As his contract with the label was expiring in 1973, though, Dylan jumped to Asylum Records (run by Clive Davis's old friend David Geffen), for whom he recorded two albums, the underappreciated *Planet Waves* and a compilation from his concert touring with the Band in 1974. Columbia, in response, released a collection of studio outtakes to fulfill Dylan's last recording commitment, a move many critics saw as petty and churlish. Dylan, however, soon grew dissatisfied

Walter Yetnikoff (far left) with Carlos Santana, Bill Graham and Bruce Lundvall

Bruce Lundvall, Leonard Cohen, and Irwin Segelstein

Neil Diamond

with Asylum, and Columbia, under Segelstein, made an all-out effort to get him back. Dylan returned in 1975 in superb form, with a powerful album of heartache and rue, *Blood on the Tracks*, featuring songs that ran the emotional gamut from tender sorrow ("You're Gonna Make Me Lonesome When You Go") to fury ("Idiot Wind"). The following year, Dylan performed across the Northeast with his legendary caravan troupe, the Rolling Thunder Revue, and he released *Desire*, a collection of vibrant, at times cinematic, narrative songs. After experiencing a born-again religious conversion in 1979, he shifted gears to produce three gospel-drenched albums, working with Aretha Franklin's former producer, Jerry Wexler, on two of them, *Slow Train Coming* and *Saved*. He followed these three with another strong album, *Infidels*, in 1983. Then, in the mid-1980s, Dylan entered a prolonged period during which he released several comparatively undistinguished new recordings—a downturn only partially offset, in 1985, by a fine five-album retrospective compilation, *Biograph*, that included some excellent, previously unreleased work. Ever a seeker, willing to put himself and his art on the line, Dylan journeyed across great peaks and through deep valleys, and he seemed to make a habit of upsetting expectations. But he had settled in for the long haul as a Columbia recording artist.

Leonard Cohen went through his own changes in the late 1970s and 1980s. After a misbegotten pairing with Phil Spector produced *Death of a Ladies' Man* in 1977, released on Warner Bros., Cohen returned to his traditional musical roots, although influenced by Mediterranean and Asian sounds, on his 1979 Columbia album *Recent Songs*. In an astonishing misjudgment, Columbia refused the American release of Cohen's 1984 album of original material, *Various Positions*—a record that included "Dance Me to the End of Love" and "Hallelujah." Walter Yetnikoff, by now the head of Columbia, invited the artist to his office in Black Rock and informed him that the album was insufficiently contemporary and thus commercially unviable: "Look, Leonard," he explained, "we know you're great, but we don't know if you're any good." (The album appeared on the independent Passport Records label and was finally included in the Columbia catalog six years later.)

Yetnikoff and Columbia thought more highly of Cohen's next effort, *I'm Your Man*. Released early in 1988, the album included somber songs cowritten with Sharon Robinson, Jeff Fisher, and Jennifer Warnes, and another song with a translated poem by Federico Garcia Lorca for lyrics. It also featured a more up-to-date "synthpop" sound that was heavily reliant on the use of electronic keyboards.

Columbia's new signings in the mid-1970s included two veteran performers in different genres who would enjoy enormous success for decades to come. Neil Diamond, a long-proven star whose career dated back to his days working at the Brill Building, had actually been recruited by Clive Davis from MCA in 1971 but was only able to begin recording for Columbia in 1973. His first Columbia album, the soundtrack to *Jonathan Livingston Seagull*, won a Golden Globe and a Grammy and enjoyed excellent sales. Diamond's recording career quieted somewhat in the 1980s, but he remained a huge attraction, capable of selling out Madison Square Garden for thirteen consecutive nights in the mid-1980s. And, in the 1990s, he would record six new studio albums. Diamond remained one of Columbia's mainstays into the twenty-first century, even as one of his early releases on the label remained one of his best loved— his duet with Barbra Streisand, "You Don't Bring Me Flowers Anymore," which reached the very top of the Billboard pop chart in 1978.

Then there was the country music magician and self-styled "outlaw" Willie Nelson, whose success at Columbia began with Bruce Lundvall. Having worked his way up at the label since 1960 to become head of the domestic division, Lundvall remains best known for his work in jazz—but in 1975, he signed Nelson, who had previously recorded for Liberty, RCA Victor, and, more recently, Atlantic Records.

Having started out playing honky-tonks and working as a DJ in Texas, Nelson had met with great success as a songwriter in the 1950s and 1960s, composing songs that would become country standards, including "Funny How Time Slips Away" and "Crazy." In 1964, the same year he signed with RCA Victor, he joined the troupe of the *Grand Ole Opry*, and at the end of the decade, he recorded some midchart country hits. But amid frustrating financial dealings with Victor, Nelson broke off recording

Bruce Lundvall with Willie Nelson

Willie Nelson

and moved to Austin in 1972. The city's youth-culture scene rejuvenated him, and he began inventing a fresh sound, blending folk and jazz styles with Nashville country. After signing with Atlantic as the label's first country artist, Nelson recorded the critically acclaimed *Shotgun Willie*, followed by *Phases and Stages*, a concept album about divorce. Then Lundvall signed him up with Columbia.

Country musicians were still an important component of Columbia's roster, including major performers such as Mac Davis and the rock-influenced Charlie Daniels Band. But Nelson's debut album for Columbia, *Red Headed Stranger*, was entirely different: a collection of lean songs that told the story of a murderer on the lam, an album that completed his transition from the more commercial material he had recorded himself or written for other performers before his move to Austin. Columbia initially thought of the album as an original and interesting effort—Lundvall later called it a "collector's item"—that would extend the label's tradition in country music. But *Red Headed Stranger* turned into a blockbuster hit, and it instantly made Nelson's name as one of the creative country writers and performers in the nation. Over the next decade, Columbia released at least one Nelson album annually, and sometimes two, including his all-time best-seller, *Always on My Mind*, in 1982. Thirty years later, Nelson continues to tour as well as to record, long established as among the greatest and most beloved talents in the entire history of country music.

Bruce Springsteen's Breakthrough and Columbia's Rising Artists

Younger Columbia artists also contributed to the label's successful transition into the post-Davis years, above all John Hammond's find, Bruce Springsteen. In May 1974, Springsteen and the E Street Band played the Harvard Square Theater in Cambridge as the opening act for Bonnie Raitt, and the influential critic Jon Landau raved, "I saw rock and roll's future and its name is Bruce Springsteen." Fifteen months later, after bringing Landau in to assist with production, Springsteen released his breakthrough album, *Born to Run*. With its biting songs of entrapment, loss, and escape, the album introduced a more muscular texture to Springsteen's music, produced with an enveloping roar akin to Phil Spector's famous Wall of Sound, and featuring the full-blast tenor saxophone of Clarence Clemons. Springsteen later said that he wanted *Born to Run* to sound like "Roy Orbison singing Bob Dylan, produced by Spector."

Heavily promoted by Columbia, the album struck a few jaded writers, weary of grandiose publicity, as an overproduced and overhyped effort to sell the singer as the new Dylan. But *Born to Run*'s overpowering mix of intelligent lyrics and musical adrenaline helped push it to the number three position on the *Billboard* chart. It also secured for Springsteen a new fan base that would grow into one of the largest and most enthusiastic of any rock performer's. And after three years of protracted legal battles with his former manager, Mike Appel, Springsteen released a strong follow-up album, *Darkness on the Edge of Town*, which showed Springsteen deepening his musical reflections on adversity, hope, and despair.

Another highly successful younger group on Columbia emerged gradually out of the personnel changes in Carlos Santana's Latin jazz-rock fusion group. In 1973, former Santana band members Neal Schon and Gregg Rolie became the nucleus of Journey, originally devoted to its own fusion style. Neither of the group's first two albums, *Journey* and *Look into the Future*, enjoyed much success, but Columbia stayed loyal. The band dramatically changed its style to feature stunning power-ballad rock (while adding a new lead vocalist, Steve Perry, in 1977), and its popularity grew steadily. In 1981, after several more changes in personnel but still fronted by Perry, the band released *Escape*. The album, the group's eighth studio record, was a mammoth success, in time going platinum nine times over and generating three top-ten hits. Although the critics were not always kind to Journey's music, two more albums in the 1980s yielded several hits, including "Separate Ways (Worlds Apart)" and "Be Good to Yourself."

The band Toto started up in 1977, an ensemble of musicians who had worked with various headline acts including Boz Scaggs and Steely Dan. Initiated by the

"[I wanted it to sound like] Roy Orbison singing Bob Dylan, produced by [Phil] Spector."

Bruce Springsteen on *Born To Run*

Toto at the 25th Annual Grammy® Awards

Bob Dylan with Benny Goodman and John Hammond during a TV tribute to Hammond

Previous page: Clarence Clemons and Bruce Springsteen

Bruce Springsteen

keyboardist David Paich and the drummer Jeff Pocarno, Toto expertly combined elements of pop, rock, R&B, and jazz into a sound that bordered on soft rock and had enormous popular appeal. The group's eponymous first album, released in 1978, featured the hit single "Hold the Line," secured the band a Grammy nomination, and eventually went double platinum. Two less successful albums followed (the second an inauspicious move into arena rock), but *Toto IV*, released in 1982, would become one of the most commercially successful albums of the 1980s while also producing four hit singles and winning three Grammys, including Album of the Year. While the band experienced numerous changes in personnel, it would remain a reliable strong seller for Columbia through 1999 when it switched to Capitol.

Classical and Jazz in Difficult Times

As popular music flourished at Columbia during the mid-1970s, classical music seemed to fade further into the background, as it did throughout the recording industry. Still, Columbia Masterworks enjoyed a few bright moments. Tom Frost, Andrew Kazdin, and Paul Myers produced some fine new records. Masterworks also brought in new artists, including the mezzo-soprano Frederica von Stade (who, despite her Old World name, had grown up in a socially-prominent family in Somerville, New Jersey). Glenn Gould continued to record, chiefly in Toronto. The classical division produced a breakout album in 1975 that hit the *Billboard* pop chart, the flutist Jean-Pierre Rampal's *Suite for Flute and Jazz Piano*, recorded with its composer, Claude Bolling. Masterworks had already signed the violinist Pinchas Zuckerman, and before the 1970s were over it would begin recording the cellist Yo-Yo Ma.

Columbia's jazz division endured its own share of struggles. The label continued to package reissues of recordings long in the vault, but there was unpleasant bickering among the producers over credit and royalties. The troublesome avant-garde trumpeter Don Ellis, who had been recording for Columbia since 1967, gained attention in 1972 (and eventually won a Grammy), for his theme for the film *The French Connection*, but his volcanic temperament alienated musicians and producers alike. And Columbia's greatest jazz star, Miles Davis, hit the worst patch of his career in the mid-1970s, as drug addiction continued to plague him. Although he turned out some interesting work in his new fusion style (notably "Calypso Frelimo" on a studio album released in 1974, *Get Up with It*), most of Davis's recordings were extremely subpar. Still, Columbia was determined to continue its efforts in jazz, whether it meant signing established stars or encouraging new ones. The veteran saxophonist Stan Getz was one such established star. Long a Verve recording artist, Getz had become best known for his central role in introducing bossa nova to the United States in the 1960s. In 1975, Getz reunited with guitarist and composer João Gilberto to record *The Best of Two Worlds* for Columbia, the first of three albums he would record for the label over the next few years. And in 1976, when the legendary hard bop saxophonist Dexter Gordon ended fifteen years' residency in Europe with a homecoming at the Village Vanguard, Columbia was there to record it. For a decade to come, the label would record Gordon often, live and in the studio, as leader and session man.

Critics regard the Gordon homecoming album as an important boost for acoustic jazz after the heavily-promoted electric fusion releases of the early 1970s, but Columbia did not devote itself solely to older styles. Moving closer to a funk sound, Weather Report recorded an album a year in the 1970s, winning the *DownBeat* magazine's Readers Poll as Jazz Group of the Year seven years in a row, from 1973 through 1979. Columbia also had the great good fortune to acquire the services of the keyboardist Herbie Hancock, whom it backed strongly. For five years, beginning in 1963, Hancock had been a member of Miles Davis's working band, just as Davis was moving toward the experiments that would become *In a Silent Way*. In 1971, having formed his own sextet, Hancock cut the first of three experimental albums, on which he fully embraced electronic keyboards. The third of the albums, 1973's *Sextant*, was Hancock's first for Columbia. That same year, Hancock assembled a new band, which he called Head Hunters, in search of a funkier sound. Released by Columbia in October, *Head*

Yo-Yo Ma

Dexter Gordon

Stan Getz with Buddy Rich

Journey

Hunters was a major breakthrough both for Hancock and for electronic jazz, its guitar-less groove appealing to R&B fans who had shown little interest in jazz-rock fusion. Over the decades to come, the album would prove to be a lasting influence not simply on jazz but also on soul music, R&B, and, in time, hip-hop. More immediately, it sealed an artistic bond between Hancock and Columbia that would last for another decade and a half, through nearly thirty more albums.

A Changing of the Guard

Irwin Segelstein was a placeholder, and as president of Columbia Records he admirably restored calm to the label. Although Lieberson encouraged Segelstein to consult with him, Segelstein found himself leaning on Walter Yetnikoff for a good deal of advice and instruction. The great Lieberson, having returned to his old job as chairman of the CBS Records Group, might have been expected to provide the vast experience that Segelstein lacked. But Lieberson's return turned out to be mainly symbolic, engineered primarily to calm the nerves of CBS shareholders and impress Wall Street analysts. Lieberson himself, having already retired once, albeit with reluctance, was now looking forward to a well-deserved leisurely life with his wife in Santa Fe, where he would write and return to his first love, composing music. Sadly, soon after he finally stepped down in 1975, Lieberson was diagnosed with liver cancer and he died two years later. Meanwhile, it came as little surprise when CBS named Yetnikoff the new president of CBS Records Group in 1975.

One year younger than Clive Davis, Yetnikoff had a resumé that was startlingly similar to his predecessor's. Born and raised in Brooklyn, he had graduated from Columbia Law School in 1956 and worked for the Rosenman and Colin law firm, which represented CBS, and then joined Columbia's legal department. When Davis rose to become administrative vice president in 1965, Yetnikoff took over his job as general counsel. Although he did not get to share in Davis's Monterey epiphany, he underwent a similar transition from ambitious but culturally conventional young New York Jewish lawyer to 1960s corporate swinger. Or at least he had completed some of that transition, as he would candidly relate in his autobiography: "If we were square businessmen watching the sexual revolution play out in the music we sold," he recalled, "we sure as hell wanted free and easy sex for ourselves. Some execs were growing long hair, smoking pot and sporting love beads, but most were just Old School Horny." Yetnikoff was as horny as anyone, and his recollections of the late 1970s and 1980s include abundant tales of sexual intrigues and escapades fueled by alcohol, drugs, and egotism. But for all his wildness, Yetnikoff was a tough, street-smart businessman, which is why he would last as long as he did, and enjoy so much success. "I knew that, first and foremost, I had to make money for CBS," he writes. "The minute that stopped, I was out on my ass." That required not just finding the best new talent but also competing more fiercely than ever with other labels for the millions to be made from the recordings of established stars.

Yetnikoff's Early Signings

Yetnikoff's first significant signing as president, in 1975, would eventually prove his most momentous, though for Epic rather than Columbia. After churning out hits for Motown Records for years, the pop soul group the Jackson 5 was ready to move on. Looking nervously at the group's recent sales numbers, Yetnikoff cautiously approved a new deal with Epic, and the label assigned the performers to composers and arrangers Kenny Gamble and Leon Huff. Three albums followed, under the name the Jacksons, before Michael Jackson asked Yetnikoff for a chance to record solo with the producer Quincy Jones. The kid brother no more, Jackson followed the excellent *Off the Wall* with the astonishing *Thriller,* Jackson's finest single work of musical and performance art, an album that helped rearrange the connections between pop, soul, and rock, and that, by 2010, had sold enough copies to qualify for a platinum award twenty-nine times over.

Weather Report

Miles Davis

Herbie Hancock

Serendipity paid off. At the Columbia Records annual business conference in the summer of 1977—just as Michael Jackson was beginning to mull over going it alone—a very different artist, virtually unknown, also came to Yetnikoff's attention. The meetings were held at the Hilton Hotel in London, and one day a group of conventioneers (including Yetnikoff) stepped outside to see, on the sidewalk, a geeky man, oddly resembling Buddy Holly, who was singing and playing a guitar hooked up to a portable amplifier. A sandwich board sign beside him read, "Elvis Costello and Stiff Records Welcome CBS Records to London." Two bobbies quickly arrested the singer and hustled him away, but Columbia A&R vice president Gregg Geller, intrigued by what he had seen and heard, arranged a meeting in London several weeks later. As it happened, Geller arrived to find Costello's manager, Jake Rivera, on the phone with Clive Davis, who had formed his own company, Arista Records, but Geller landed the deal, and Elvis Costello moved to Columbia. The first of his albums, *My Aim Is True*, with its startling combination of punk rock attitude, musical virtuosity, and intense, cerebral word play, would prove to be one of the most popular of Costello's career. And over the ensuing decade, recording ten more albums with Columbia, Costello and his band, the Attractions, would lay the foundations for one of the most versatile, unpredictable, and distinguished bodies of work in contemporary rock and roll.

One important trend of the mid- to late 1970s that Columbia missed was harder-edged punk rock. Columbia had released one album by an important forerunner to punk, Iggy and the Stooges, but otherwise, punk's precursors, such as Lou Reed and the Velvet Underground, appeared on other labels. And when punk exploded in clubs like CBGB in New York between 1975 and 1977, most of its major artists were on other labels as well, including Patti Smith, the Ramones, Richard Hell and the Voidoids, Television, and the Sex Pistols, as well as the enormously influential punk-influenced avant-garde band Talking Heads. The premier British punk band the Clash signed with CBS Records in Britain early in 1977, but then appeared in the United States on Epic.

Columbia also largely bypassed the disco craze, which it dismissed as the latest passing fad geared to the singles market. A major exception was Cheryl Lynn's hit single "Got to Be Real," released in 1978, which went on to appear on Lynn's album of the same name released in 1978. With its bass-heavy dance beat and slickly arranged horns and piano accompaniment, the single was a tight embodiment of the disco style and reached the top of the R&B chart early in 1979; the album peaked at number eleven on the disco chart. Lynn went on to a major career as an R&B star, appearing on Columbia through 1985 and working closely with other talents, above all Luther Vandross. Another notable disco effort was a pairing of Barbra Streisand with the disco diva Donna Summer on the song "No More Tears (Enough is Enough)," which appeared, at Streisand's insistence, on Streisand's album *Wet* in 1979, quickly won a gold record as a single, and eventually went platinum.

The most prestigious signing early in Yetnikoff's tenure came at the opposite end of the rock and roll spectrum from punk, and at the end of the decade, when Paul McCartney left Capitol Records, the Beatles' longtime American label. CBS executives nearly nixed the proposed multimillion-dollar deal with McCartney, but Yetnikoff, expressing his exasperation using expletives, talked them into it. Five albums resulted over the ensuing five years, including the last recording by McCartney's group, Wings, and a soundtrack for the film *Give My Regards to Broad Street*. It was not McCartney's best work (which, to be sure, set the very highest standard), but every album was a strong seller.

Yetnikoff's early years also saw the appearance of Pink Floyd's first albums on the Columbia label, beginning with *Wish You Were Here*, in 1975. The band had released seven albums after its 1967 debut, *The Piper at the Gates of Dawn*, and its original leader, the troubled Syd Barrett, had long since departed, when Clive Davis helped persuade the group to defect from Capitol to Columbia in 1973. Despite continuing personal tensions and financial distractions, the quartet of David Gilmour, Nick Mason, Roger Waters, and Richard Wright hung together long enough to produce *The Wall* in 1979, one of the most important and enduring recordings in all

Pink Floyd's stage set during *Another Lapse of Reason* Tour of Europe

Pink Floyd onstage during rehearsal of *The Wall*, L.A. Sports Arena

rock music. A harrowing story of isolation and delusion, the work's grand scale (complete with full orchestral arrangement) perplexed some critics, their reactions summed up by the reviewer who wrote for *Melody Maker*: "I'm not sure whether it's brilliant or terrible, but I find it utterly compelling." But other critics warmly praised *The Wall*, and the public, stirred in part by the single "Another Brick in the Wall," made it the top album in the United States for fifteen weeks.

Two veteran R&B acts, also new to Columbia, further bolstered the label's sales in the later 1970s. Originally formed in Jersey City in 1962, the Manhattans had enjoyed some success on the small Carnival and DeLuxe labels. After several reformations, the group signed with Columbia in 1973 and hit pay dirt two years later with the single "Kiss and Say Goodbye," off its eponymous album, arranged and coproduced by the Philadelphia-based producer Bobby Martin. The group would record eight more albums with Columbia over the next decade, including two gold records, *It Feels So Good* in 1977 and *After Midnight* in 1980. The soul singer Johnnie Taylor had started out even earlier, as a member of the gospel group Highway QCs, founded in the 1950s by the young Sam Cooke. Between 1966 and 1973, known as "the Philosopher of Soul," Taylor recorded for Stax Records in Memphis and recorded a string of hits that made him one of Stax's biggest stars, alongside Isaac Hayes and the Staple Singers. But when Stax folded, Columbia quickly picked up Taylor, who rewarded the investment in 1975 with the single "Disco Lady," the first single ever certified as platinum, with sales of over two million copies.

One other important signing early in Yetnikoff's leadership was something of a family affair. Johnny Cash remained one of Columbia's most prized and popular artists, and all the while, Cash's eldest daughter, Rosanne, was inching toward her own recording career. Although literature and drama appealed to her, music finally captured her fancy. In 1978, she cut the demo with Emmylou Harris's sideman, Rodney Crowell, that started her career. By decade's end, Cash had signed with Columbia. Her second album for the label in 1981, *Seven Year Ache*, would be her first artistic breakthrough.

Facing New Competition: Enter James Taylor, Exit Paul Simon

Yetnikoff was not always so successful with Columbia's established stars. Having regained Bob Dylan in 1974 and retained Barbra Streisand and Johnny Cash, the label could boast of its long-term connections to three of the industry's greatest artists. But Yetnikoff had terrible relations with Paul Simon. After splitting from Art Garfunkel in 1970, Simon had recorded three excellent solo albums of original material, each one better than the one before. The third, *Still Crazy after All These Years*, which appeared in October 1975 and included the hit single "50 Ways to Leave Your Lover," topped the *Billboard* pop album chart and went on to win Grammy honors for Album of the Year and Best Pop Vocal Performance, Male. But there was turbulence between the artist and Columbia's new boss: Simon believed that the label was not supporting him strongly enough; Yetnikoff thought Simon pretentious and self-important. After much *sturm und drang*, the two nearly struck a deal in 1975, but Simon pulled back and moved to Warner Bros. Records.

Simon's departure was, in fact, part of a war that Yetnikoff and Columbia had been waging with Warner Bros. Records and its chief, Steve Ross. Having made his fortune operating funeral parlors and parking garages, Ross had taken over Warner Bros. and turned its record label into a dynamic part of a multimedia empire. With a stable that included the Grateful Dead, Van Morrison, Fleetwood Mac, James Taylor, and Black Sabbath—and having bought Atlantic Records to boot—Warner Bros. was now challenging the supremacy that Columbia had achieved in contemporary popular music in the late 1960s and early 1970s. Yetnikoff decided to make a name for himself early in his presidency by battling Ross, and he began by courting James Taylor. The switch took time to finalize, but after it was done, Taylor's first release on Columbia, the hit record "Handy Man," made it all seem worthwhile. Warner Bros.' subsequent signing of Paul Simon was to no small degree an act of retaliation.

"I'm not sure whether it's brilliant or terrible, but I find it utterly compelling."

Melody Maker review of *The Wall*

Paul Simon

Paul McCartney and Wings, Wembley Arena

James Taylor

The Heady Early 1980s: Bruce Springsteen, Billy Joel, and More

Into the 1980s, despite the competition from Warner Bros., Columbia held its own in rock and roll and other varieties of contemporary popular music. The years from 1982 through 1985 were particularly rich in powerful and popular releases. After *Darkness on the Edge of Town*, Bruce Springsteen had pushed his rhapsodies and sometimes-brutal elegies on working-class life in various musical directions, leading in 1982 to his stark collection, *Nebraska*. Springsteen and Jon Landau, now his manager, concluded correctly that the often bleak material on *Nebraska* sounded better performed solo, with acoustic guitar and harmonica, than with a full band. Columbia, now devoted to Springsteen, stood by the album, and the enthusiastic response it received from the critics further elevated Springsteen's artistic stature. Two years later, reunited with the E Street Band, he released *Born in the U.S.A.*, which seemed fully to bear out Landau's claim from nearly a decade earlier about Springsteen being the future of rock and roll. The album's title track combined bitter commentary on the fate of Vietnam veterans with an ironic, anthem-like chorus that sounded almost jingoistic and that fooled those listeners who would be fooled. With its seven hit singles (the most successful of which, "Dancing in the Dark," hit number two on the pop charts), *Born in the U.S.A.* sold fifteen million copies and secured Springsteen's place as one of the premier rock and rollers of his time or any other.

Springsteen's contemporary Billy Joel had stumbled a bit in the mid-1970s, although his jazzy epic, "New York State of Mind," on his 1976 album *Turnstiles*, became one of his signature tunes. Joel then released a series of major triumphs beginning with his 1977 breakthrough album, *The Stranger*, which joined him with the legendary veteran recording-engineer-turned-producer Phil Ramone. *The Stranger* included several enormous hits including "Movin' Out (Anthony's Song)" and "Just the Way You Are," the Grammy honoree for Record of the Year and Song of the Year. (Ramone reports that "Just the Way You Are" appeared on the album by chance, after he told Joel the record needed another ballad: "Well, here's a song we'll never record," Joel said. "But you should hear it.") After *52nd Street* the following year, which featured "My Life" and "Big Shot," and won the Grammy for Album of the Year, Joel hit another peak with *An Innocent Man* in 1983. A tribute to the music of Joel's youth, ranging from doo-wop to the sounds of Frankie Valli and the Four Seasons, the album included no fewer than four hits that would become popular classics: the title track, "Uptown Girl," "Tell Her About It," and "The Longest Time."

Also in 1983, the Australian band Men at Work's blockbuster second album, *Cargo*, although recorded a year earlier, finally appeared. The delay was due to the unexpected, late-blooming success of their first album, *Business as Usual*, first released in 1981. With its innovative use of woodwinds and brass, the band created a singular sound on such enormous hits as "Down Under." *Cargo* followed *Business as Usual* to the very top of the pop album charts. The band's third and final studio album, *Two Hearts*, appeared on Columbia in 1985; amazingly, with only three original albums to their credit, Men at Work would go on to sell thirty million records worldwide.

The list of other Columbia popular artists who hit a peak in the early 1980s defies categorization, a sign of the public's enthusiasm for a variety of sub-genres, and a result of Columbia's strategy to cast the widest possible net. In 1983 and 1984, the British pop duo of George Michael and Andrew Ridgeley, who called themselves Wham!, released back-to-back best-selling albums. In 1984, the all-female band Bangles released their successful first album, which attracted the attention of Prince, paving the way for the group's 1986 recording of his composition "Manic Monday."

In 1984, Columbia added to its eclectic catalog when it released *1100 Bel Air Place*, the first English language album by its longtime Latin star Julio Iglesias, which launched Iglesias's extraordinary career as both a Latin singer and crossover favorite. Over at Epic, further brightening the general mood around Black Rock, Michael Jackson's *Thriller* appeared in 1982, followed a year later by the newcomer Cyndi Lauper's smash solo album, *She's So Unusual*.

Finally, the grand old man of Columbia Records' jazz and blues recording, John Hammond, weighed in with one last find, although the act would end up recording for

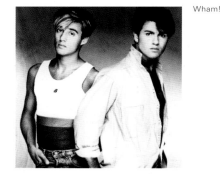

Wham!

Billy Joel

Epic. Hammond had retired from Columbia in 1975, written his autobiography, and undertaken a short-lived effort at running his own recording operation, John Hammond Enterprises. All the while, aspiring artists and their managers continued to seek him out. In 1982 Hammond received a tape of a Texas blues guitarist, Stevie Ray Vaughan, and his band, Double Trouble, that made him jump. The discovery, if that's the word for it, eventually led to Epic's 1983 release of Double Trouble's album *Texas Flood*, the first of several that Vaughan would record before his untimely death in a helicopter crash in 1990. With his intense fusion of blues, rock, and Texas swing, he is remembered today as one of the supreme modern guitar gods. But John Hammond, who lived until 1987, heard a hint of Columbia's glorious past in his playing, loud and clear. "He brought back a style that had died, and he brought it back at exactly the right time," he observed of Vaughan. "The young ears hadn't heard anything with this kind of sound."

Columbia's early-1980s heyday was in some ways a culmination of Clive Davis's move into rock and roll fifteen years earlier, but the label's success was not confined to conventional rock and pop albums. On the more serious side, late in 1984, Columbia released the single "Do They Know It's Christmas?" written by Midge Ure of Ultravox and Bob Geldof of the Boomtown Rats, and performed by the British charity supergroup Band Aid, to raise funds to help relieve a continuing famine in Ethiopia. The next year, an equivalent American all-star charity group, USA for Africa, recorded "We Are the World," written by Michael Jackson and Lionel Ritchie. The single, which also appeared on Columbia, sold twenty million copies. In a wholly different key, a bit of relief from the world's miseries came from Eddie Murphy, whose Columbia album of 1984, *Eddie Murphy: Comedian*, buttressed Murphy's rising career in films and won a Grammy for Best Comedy Recording. And in yet another field altogether, *Jane Fonda's Workout Record*, drawn from the actress's fitness routine video, appeared as a double album in 1982 and sold more than two million copies. By 1985, Columbia was going like commercial gangbusters.

Music Television and Yetnikoff's Complaint

The story of Columbia's successes of the early 1980s—indeed, the history of the entire recording industry—was inseparable from the rise of Music Television. MTV did nothing more than transform the public's enjoyment of popular music. The idea was not new, however. Efforts at marketing music acts through visuals had begun as early as the late 1920s, when performers appeared in brief films shown in movie theaters, including some memorable footage of Bessie Smith singing "St. Louis Blues" in a short subject released by Sack Amusement Enterprises of Dallas in 1929. During the 1940s, several production companies released so-called soundies—three-minute clips that covered every variety of music, from classical to hillbilly, and were viewed on a coin-operated film jukebox called the Panoram. Several small efforts in the 1970s, in the United States and abroad, to air promotional musical clips on television came to nothing but hinted at enormous possibilities.

MTV had its debut on August 1, 1981, as a network that would broadcast music videos twenty-four hours a day, seven days a week. At first, only a few thousand subscribers to a single cable system in northern New Jersey could receive it, and MTV continued to struggle over the next two years. But MTV hung on and a new art form was born—films intended for television that moved beyond mere promotion to become brief cinematic productions in their own right. By mid-decade, it was almost imperative for any artist who wanted to break a major hit to accompany the actual recording with a music video.

By 1983, criticism was growing among artists and record producers that MTV was slighting—indeed, purposefully excluding—black performers, except for a select few that included Donna Summer, Tina Turner, and Prince. The network replied that its format, which was dominated by rock and roll, ruled out soul and R&B acts, but many artists and record producers considered that a lame excuse. Among others, the performer Rick James (whose video for his Motown hit "Super Freak" was turned down for airing on MTV), publicly and vociferously demanded that the channel add more videos featuring black artists.

Julio Iglesias

Men at Work

George Michael

The breakthrough came in 1983 with the rise of Michael Jackson and the furious complaints by Walter Yetnikoff. Jackson, with his dance skills, was a natural for music videos, and he had great ambitions for the form as a showcase for his talents. But before 1983, Jackson had difficulty receiving airtime on MTV. Yetnikoff cried foul in his favorite blunt terms and threatened to retaliate unless the channel broadcast Jackson's video for "Billie Jean," from the album *Thriller*: "I'm pulling everything we have off the air," he told MTV's executives. "I'm not going to give you any more videos. And I'm going to go public and fucking tell them about the fact you don't want to play music by a black guy." MTV insisted it would have shown Jackson's video even without the pressure, a story that CBS disputed; in any event, MTV began showing the "Billie Jean" video in regular rotation, which greatly increased the network's credibility as well as its popularity—and greatly widened Jackson's audience.

The success of "Billie Jean" pushed MTV to broaden its repertoire to include more pop and R&B acts; it also helped lift Jackson to new heights. His fourteen-minute production for the song "Thriller" proved so popular that MTV ran it twice an hour. Subsequently regarded as the best effort ever in the genre, the video helped make the *Thriller* album a phenomenal success, but it also marked the coming of age of music videos as an art form. "It's difficult to hear the songs from *Thriller* and disengage them from the videos," the music critic Nelson George observed a decade later. "For most of us, the images define the songs." By the mid-1980s, Jackson's videos were helping to pave the way for the success on MTV of other black artists. The choreography on the videos for "Thriller" and "Beat It"—the latter in part a tribute to the dance sequences from *West Side Story*—also became an element of global pop culture, imitated as far away as the film studios of Bollywood. Closer to home, they also raised the music video's artistic standards for the entire range of rock and pop performers, for whom video productions became de rigueur.

The Walkman and the CD

While its artists were racking up sales and critical acclaim and beginning to adapt to the world of MTV, Columbia, through its ties abroad, was at least indirectly connected to two of the most important technological innovations in musical recording since the invention of the LP. After the introduction of stereo sound on commercial recordings in the 1950s, several new products hit the market that had the potential to change the listening habits of the world. Eight-track players caught on and lasted though the early 1980s; the tape cassette, so easily adaptable for use both at home and in automobiles, lasted even longer; but quadraphonic sound bombed. In the late 1970s, Columbia's overseas partner, Sony, developed a portable stereo listening device, originally at the request of its cofounder, Akio Morita, who wanted to be able to listen to operas on his frequent airplane flights across the Pacific. At the very end of the decade, Sony introduced the Walkman, a low-cost portable stereo cassette player whose output was designed to be heard through headphones—the first step in the long journey toward the portable recorded music we take for granted today. The Walkman, as later adapted to other formats, was revolutionary, allowing consumers to listen to music any place and any time they wanted. It also made the entire experience an individual one, in which the listener could walk around sonically sealed off from the rest of the world.

Soon after the Walkman appeared, another revolution in both the recording and manufacturing of music hit the industry, the introduction of the compact disc. Toward the end of the 1970s, Sony in Japan, along with another Columbia partner, Philips in the Netherlands, had been working on major innovations in adapting laser and digital technology to audio reproduction. The two corporations joined forces in 1979, and a year later they presented their new product—a small and easily portable disc that could contain an LP's worth of digitized music unblemished by needle scratches. Thanks to its partnership with Sony, Columbia had an instant advantage over the other labels. The first Sony CD commercially released to the public (in Japan) in October 1982 was Billy Joel's *52nd Street*, marketed along with Sony's first CD

Sony Walkman advertisement

Sony Compact Disc advertisement

Leonard Bernstein

As a composer, Bernstein was an eclectic ball of energy

Leonard Bernstein was never anywhere near the biggest record seller at Columbia, except with *West Side Story.* He was, however, a household name and one of the most important cultural forces in the United States. As much as even the Beatles, he brought down barriers between high culture and popular culture, and not only to the benefit of high culture. He wrote hit songs. He loudly championed the early work of teenage singer-songwriter Janis Ian, a significant find, and Ian wasn't the only pop artist with whom Bernstein developed a creative relationship. When he presented the Young People's Concerts, he did so with generous enthusiasm, not condescension. He taught a generation to love not only the big names but also Mahler, Copland, and other composers he cherished. He may have been a pioneer of "radical chic," but that was an outgrowth of a commitment to true humanism.

He was an entertainer as well as an educator. Leonard Bernstein was not just any entertainer, though. He was an artist first, which is why he could take a simple request from Jacqueline Kennedy Onassis to write a mass for the opening of the Kennedy Center for the Performing Arts and turn it into *Mass,* a multimedia extravaganza. As a composer, Bernstein was an eclectic ball of energy whose works include not only theater pieces and a mass, but ballets, symphonies, chamber music, operas, and operettas. This was in addition to conducting one of the world's great orchestras.

Leonard Bernstein combined emotion and ambition in a very personal way. He reached for the stars, because in music, he heard the heavens speak. For many, he was the face of classical music in his time and he did it proud.

Dave Marsh

Leonard Bernstein

player. The following March, CD players and discs hit the American market, including sixteen Columbia titles on CD, the largest number from any label.

Interestingly, CDs initially seemed most important to the classical music division, much as had been true for the LP when it was first released, albeit for different reasons. Recordings of the finest classical performances dating from the 1930s and 1940s were marred by noise inherent in the analog formats, and the CD promised audiophiles the same performances with a much cleaner sound. As many of those older recordings had gone out of print, the CD offered an additional boon to classical-record buyers. Those buyers, moreover, seemed more likely than others to care enough about the finest aural nuances to make the investment. "It will be like hearing the tapes that [Bruno] Walter's recording engineer heard," Andrew Kazdin told the *New York Times*. The CD looked like a strong shot in the arm for Columbia's classical records division, which had been slumping for decades.

The general manager of Columbia Masterworks at the time, Joseph Dash, had been working for Columbia since 1969, and was doing his best to update the division's offerings. He commissioned a new logo, and he signed new artists, including the tenor Placido Domingo and the composer Philip Glass (whose avant-garde opera masterwork, *Einstein on the Beach*, with its nonsense libretto by Bob Wilson, appeared on Columbia in 1979). Dash also searched for opportunities to record crossover albums. He gave proper recognition to the label's established roster as well: Isaac Stern, Leonard Bernstein, and Rudolf Serkin each received the title of Artist Laureate, in order to draw fresh attention to them. In 1981, Glenn Gould recorded a new version of Bach's *Goldberg Variations*, completing a circle begun on his debut album for Columbia a quarter century earlier. Dash's biggest commercial success, though, was in getting RCA Victor to permit their pop star John Denver to perform for Columbia his song "Perhaps Love" in a duet with Domingo, which produced an international hit after its release in 1981. And when the CD was developed, Dash pursued digital technology wholeheartedly, approving, in addition to digital reissues of older analog recordings, new recordings by Yo-Yo Ma, the conductor Michael Tilson Thomas, the pianist Emanuel Ax, and the violinist Midori, among others.

By the late 1980s, the prices of CDs and CD players had dropped precipitously, and most popular music buyers began to throw away their turntables. Capitalizing on this trend, Dash continued both to remaster old analog recordings and make entirely new classical recordings for CD, while he kept his eyes open for new crossover opportunities. A big one materialized in 1983, when George Butler, of Columbia's jazz A&R division, presented him with a tape of the young jazz trumpeter Wynton Marsalis playing the Haydn Trumpet Concerto.

Wynton Marsalis and Traditions Made New

Marsalis was the son of one of New Orleans' first families of jazz. (He received his first trumpet, when he was six years old, from Al Hirt.) He moved to New York in 1978 to attend Juilliard, but he quickly took up an apprenticeship as one of Art Blakey's Jazz Messengers. After touring and recording with Herbie Hancock as well as Blakey, Marsalis started recording jazz for Columbia, which would lead to his winning eight Grammy awards in five years, beginning in 1983 with his album *Think of One*. Also in 1983, Columbia Masterworks issued a recording of the versatile Marsalis playing trumpet concerti by Mozart and Hummel as well as Haydn, which won the Grammy for Best Instrumental Soloist Or Soloists (With Orchestra). The following year, Marsalis won the same award for an album of Handel, Purcell, and others, recorded with the English Chamber Orchestra.

In time, Marsalis would concentrate primarily on jazz, including composing and teaching as well as concertizing and recording, all of which would lead to his cofounding the first jazz program at Lincoln Center for the Performing Arts in New York City in 1987. But with the broad musical reach of his early years at Columbia, Marsalis, like, before him, Benny Goodman commissioning Béla Bartók and Duke Ellington performing Edvard Grieg, broke down persistent barriers that isolated jazz

Branford Marsalis

Wynton Marsalis

from classical music. In fact, far from abandoning his classical interests, Marsalis went on to create some major triumphs in third stream composition, including ballet, chamber music, and, most impressively, his oratorio *Blood on the Fields*, which won a Pulitzer Prize in 1997. Marsalis would never find much of interest in the style of fusion of jazz and rock that Miles Davis continued to pursue in the 1980s; indeed, a famous feud between the two began when, after the 1985 release of Davis's final album for Columbia, *You're Under Arrest*, Marsalis dismissed it and the rest of Davis's fusion recordings as "not really jazz." A changing of the guard was underway—but this time, unlike in the bebop 1940s, Columbia recorded both sides of the change.

Often enough, though, the two sides converged. Through the mid-1980s, until he decided to leave Columbia in 1988, Herbie Hancock, alongside various combinations of musicians, recorded numerous albums of jazz-influenced disco and pop fusion. These involved experiments using electrical instruments, synthesizers, and even computers. But Hancock also recorded in his older acoustic style, to the point of recording an album of piano solos (although it initially appeared only in Japan and was not released in the United States until 2004). In 1981, Wynton Marsalis joined a group organized by Hancock with Tony Williams and Ron Carter, and they recorded *Quartet*; with the further addition of Marsalis's saxophonist brother Branford, the group toured before appearing on Wynton Marsalis's self-named first Columbia album. Thereafter, Columbia released Branford Marsalis's first album, *Scenes in the City*, in 1984, beginning a long association that would in time include his serving as director of Columbia Jazz Records. All the while, Branford was either appearing or recording with a variety of musicians that included the rock singer Sting, Dizzy Gillespie, and Miles Davis. Jazz had other important and distinctive faces at Columbia in the early 1980s as well. Through 1986, Weather Report, with Wayne Shorter and Joe Zawinul, turned out five more albums. In 1986, by taking over Elektra's contract with saxophonist Grover Washington Jr., an all-time jazz fusion giant, Columbia put a punctuation mark on its reputation as the preeminent fusion label.

An Unquiet Lull: Def Jam and Hip-Hop

Columbia and its subsidiary labels had created such a rare degree of artistic achievement as well as commercial success in the years immediately preceding 1985 that it became all too easy to view the succeeding years as a lull. By 1990, some competitors and journalists would even claim that Columbia had lost its steam and become, in industry parlance, a "cold" label.

Yet Columbia artists continued to excel with high-profile new albums, notably Barbra Streisand's *The Broadway Album* and Wynton Marsalis's *Black Codes (From the Underground)* and *J Mood*—artistic successes that also won Grammy awards. In a major coup, Yetnikoff worked out a US distribution deal with Rolling Stones Records and released two solo albums by Mick Jagger, *She's the Boss* in 1985 and *Primitive Cool* in 1987. Although the albums received mixed reviews—and infuriated Keith Richards, who thought Jagger was slighting his obligations to the Rolling Stones—they generated strong sales.

In 1987, a young hard-rock singer named Michael Bolton, whom Columbia had signed away from RCA Victor in 1983, began to deliver on his promise with a soulful album, *The Hunger*. That same year, the young jazz pianist Harry Connick Jr. began gaining notice with a self-titled album of instrumentals. Country stars Johnny Cash and Willie Nelson joined with Waylon Jennings and Kris Kristofferson to form a super group eventually known as the Highwaymen; their first album, released in 1985, topped the country charts and generated two hit singles. Columbia also scored heavily with the soundtrack album from the Tom Cruise movie *Top Gun*. But the most important new development had been taking shape for more than a decade in New York City's poor black neighborhoods and become the most exciting new movement in all popular music—the rise of urban hip-hop.

As with rock and roll in the 1950s, most of the major recording companies were slow to recognize hip-hop as an emerging musical wave—but Columbia's neglect,

Glenn Gould

Philip Glass

given the label's strong and longstanding ties to New York was, in retrospect, especially striking. The city had fallen on hard times in the 1970s, and the combination of economic stagnation, fiscal crisis, widespread drug addiction and rising crime rates afflicted the poorer areas of the outer boroughs with particularly severe cruelty. The hip-hop scene originated at block parties in black neighborhoods in the South Bronx, in part as an imaginative reaction to the mounting, hollowed-out grimness of the environment—sometimes angry, sometimes insistently exuberant, but always forceful. With its DJ record scratching, beat juggling, and sampling, frenetic b-boy and b-girl dancing, and clever, rhyming raps, hip-hop performance evolved from an outlet for frustrated inner-city youth into a distinctive and powerful new musical form. The scratching alone amounted to something of a revolution in recorded music, as the DJs turned the records into musical instruments.

Early hip-hop was performance-based, live, and extended, and hence not conducive to records or to radio play. The DJs, proud of their outsider status, also resisted taking their acts out of the clubs and into recording studios. Yet at the very end of the decade small independent labels like Sugar Hill figured out how to capture the energy on records like the Sugarhill Gang's "Rapper's Delight," a 12-inch, 33⅓-rpm released in 1979, with its famous opening lyric, "I said a hip-hop, a hippie, a hippie to the hip-hop." That same year, Mercury Records, then headquartered in Chicago, released a hip-hop recording, Kurtis Blow's "Christmas Rappin'." Yet even after Blow's "The Breaks" began selling a million copies for Mercury the following year, most hip-hop was left to the smaller, independent labels.

In 1983, the versatile Herbie Hancock awakened mainstream music listeners to some of the innovations of hip-hop on his single, "Rockit," from the album *Future Shock*, which featured record scratching. But it took a little longer for Columbia, Hancock's own label, to catch on fully, by which time the New York hip-hop scene had long since expanded beyond the South Bronx downtown to Greenwich Village. In 1984, a New York University student named Rick Rubin established a new independent label, Def Jam Recordings, inside his dormitory room in Weinstein Hall. Soon joined by the independent impresario Russell Simmons (the older brother of the well-known rapper Joseph Simmons, better known as "Run" in the group Run-D.M.C.), Rubin became the latest hot hip-hop producer. Within a year, Def Jam was enjoying such strong sales of releases by LL Cool J ("I Need a Beat") and the Beastie Boys ("Rock Hard") that Columbia seized an opportunity to become the label's distributor.

The returns to Columbia came swiftly—and they were stunning. Recorded late in 1986, the Beastie Boys' *Licensed to Ill*, which featured the hit "(You Gotta) Fight for Your Right (to Party!)," became the fastest-selling debut album to date in Columbia's history. It went on to hit number one on the *Billboard* Top 200 chart, the first hip-hop album to do so. With Columbia, Def Jam also established a subsidiary label, OBR Records, catering chiefly to R&B artists. The label would be short lived, but it enjoyed considerable success with Oran "Juice" Jones's single "The Rain." And in 1987, Def Jam/Columbia signed what would soon become one of the most acclaimed and controversial hip-hop groups, Public Enemy.

With its Def Jam connection, Columbia seemed to be moving well beyond its successes of the early to mid-1980s, once again slowly aligning itself with evolving trends in popular music, much as it had twenty years earlier when Clive Davis pushed the label to embrace rock and roll.

More broadly, Columbia's prestige had never been greater. "To be at Columbia, to be there in the tradition that had been started by John Hammond and the others . . ." Landau now recalls. "The image Columbia had at the time was synonymous with the highest quality." Landau tells of when Bruce Springsteen turned up at Black Rock for the ceremonial signing of a new Columbia contract in 1985. Surrounded by executives and producers, Springsteen sat down, Landau recalls, and "just started reminiscing." At the heart of his reveries was the Columbia Records insignia: "You know the old red label with the black type—he said he always loved that label," Landau relates.

That image of superior quality would last. But by the late 1980s, big changes were also afoot on the business side that would change Columbia Records and its sister labels forever.

"You know the old red label with the black type—he said he always loved that label."

Jon Landau quoting Bruce Springsteen

Harry Connick Jr.

Sony

In 1986, Columbia's Japanese partner, the gigantic electronics firm Sony, began making serious efforts to acquire Columbia and the rest of CBS Records outright. Having pioneered the transition to compact discs, Sony was eager to obtain as much of the back catalog it could, in order to sell music to go along with its CD players. Sony's initial offer of $1.25 billion made clear just how much Akio Morita wanted the deal to succeed. But Sony's pursuit didn't come out of the blue. It actually stemmed from various difficulties and intrigues that had arisen earlier within CBS and Columbia.

The swashbuckling American capitalism of the 1980s—eclipsing the preceding decade of stagflation and diminished expectations—peaked in the aftermath of Ronald Reagan's landslide reelection in 1984. Corporate raiding was rampant, and CBS was by no means immune. To ward off continuing attempts at hostile takeover, William Paley turned to his friend, the self-made billionaire and stock player Lawrence Tisch—a situation that Tisch was able to turn to his own advantage.

Born in Brooklyn in 1923, Tisch had made his fortune developing hotels in New Jersey and the Catskills with his brother, Robert, before they took over the Loews movie chain. By diversifying into several other industries, from tobacco to watchmaking, the Tisch brothers turned Loews into a megacorporation, with assets of more than $3 billion by 1980. But just as Tisch understood the logic of enlargement through shrewd acquisition, he understood the perils of corporate overextension, especially in predatory times. He also understood how to turn a profit by purchasing troubled firms, improving their value, and then selling them off. In May 1986, seeing CBS's stock price as badly undervalued, Tisch bought 24.9 percent of the company for $800 million, a bargain, and then was appointed president and CEO of CBS by Paley. Tisch duly geared up for ruthless cost-cutting, including the divestiture of nonbroadcasting assets, which would help to drive up the price of CBS's undervalued stock. This strategy would certainly deter a hostile takeover of CBS by another firm or corporate raider, but it would also enable Tisch eventually to cash out with a handsome profit. And it would cut CBS Records off from CBS to make do on its own.

Ordinarily, the record division would have been off limits to Tisch's downsizing. Columbia and Epic were turning enormous profits. There was also a profound sense of attachment among CBS's directors, Paley in particular, to the CBS-Columbia connection, which now dated back nearly half a century. But despite the label's artistic and commercial success, the business corridors of CBS Records were beclouded. Tisch, who was chiefly interested in slicing and dicing CBS into its constituent parts, demeaned the record company in particular as superfluous to CBS's core mission which, supposedly, was broadcasting. Tisch and Yetnikoff took an instant dislike to each other, personally as well as professionally. A breaking scandal worsened the situation. The entire record industry, long dependent on independent tipsters to promote sales and airplay, had become increasingly reliant on a small group of expert promoters who would tell radio networks what music they should play. The arrangements raised the possibilities of a rerun of the politicized payola scandals of the 1950s, as investigative journalists focused on two of the promoters with whom Yetnikoff and his counterparts at the other labels often worked, Joe Isgro in Los Angeles and Fred DiSipio of New Jersey.

Yetnikoff angrily declared himself innocent of any wrongdoing and demanded solid proof of criminal activity. Playing their parts well, the other companies affected shock and dismay, and Yetnikoff and CBS Records suddenly looked tainted. It was all the more reason, in Tisch's view, to dump the record division. Stories began circulating about how the infuriated Yetnikoff was now doing his best to annoy Tisch at company meetings, in an effort to plague him into selling off the company. Tisch decided to go ahead and put it on the market.

As soon as he learned that CBS Records was being sold, Yetnikoff cast about for a friendly buyer who, unlike Tisch's CBS, would be easy to work with. Among those he turned to was Sony, with whom he had negotiated the partnership with Columbia twenty years earlier. Yetnikoff knew that Sony could block the sale of CBS's interest in CBS/Sony and thus had veto power over any deal Tisch might want to make. But Yetnikoff also wondered if Sony might be interested in simply purchasing CBS Records,

Beastie Boys

while keeping himself and his management team in place. When he contacted Sony's American subsidiary, headed by Norio Ohga, Sony turned out to be very interested, and its management persisted against competing bidders. However, the CBS executive board, which shared Paley's skepticism about the necessity of the sale, overruled Tisch and killed the deal. Sony would not be dissuaded, even when Tisch returned to them with a price of $2 billion; meanwhile, Paley and the CBS board remained reluctant and dragged their feet. Finally, the stock market crash of October 1987 gave Tisch all the arguments he required about the urgent need for CBS to retrench, and he cleared away all opposition. On November 19, CBS Records, Inc., formally became a wholly owned subsidiary of the Sony Corporation of Tokyo, through its US subsidiary, Sony Corporation of America.

A glow of adventurous expectations emanated from the label as the new regime began. Yetnikoff spread the word among his leading stars that it was a time to rejoice: they had been delivered, he said, from what he called "Tisch's tarnished Tiffany" into the hands of a great international corporation. (CBS television had long been known as the classy "Tiffany network.") Sony, for its part, was delighted to have taken command of an iconic American cultural institution. But the transition would turn out to be more wrenching than expected, especially for Yetnikoff.

At decade's end, less than two years after Sony's purchase, Columbia Records' closest competitor, Warner Bros. Records, compiled figures from *Billboard* showing that between May 1988 and May 1989 Warner Bros. had placed more than twice as many albums in the top twenty as CBS had. Even more dramatically, in the first quarter of 1989, Warner boasted a 56.5 percent share of the market, compared to 12.7 percent for CBS. According to a report in the *New York Times*, the scuttlebutt around the industry was that CBS had concentrated too much on courting and keeping older stars, instead of breaking in younger acts at a relatively lower cost. The top tier of Columbia's talent—including Barbra Streisand, Bob Dylan, Bruce Springsteen, James Taylor, and Billy Joel—seemed to be past its prime and aging fast.

Yetnikoff conceded that his company had very recently fallen behind, but he blamed the problems on CBS's spending priorities. "We need more A&R people," he told the *New York Times*, and he claimed that, under Sony, it would take only a year of concerted effort to reverse the situation. In fairness, the dismal reports about Columbia's artistic decline were exaggerated and panicky. To his credit, Yetnikoff could point, for starters, to *Licensed to Ill*, released fairly recently. He could also point to Columbia's success with the boy group New Kids on the Block. Originally signed in 1985, their first album disappointed artistically and commercially, but their second album, *Hangin' Tough*, released late in 1988, became a surprise smash early in 1989—just as Columbia was supposedly falling into its tailspin. Above all, he could point to *Faith* by George Michael, late of Wham!, an astoundingly successful solo album whose six Top Five singles dominated the charts for the entirety of 1988. In 1989, in the midst of what Columbia's critics were calling the company's dry spell, *Faith* won Grammy honors as Album of the Year, and the record eventually went platinum ten times over.

As it happened, though, in a little more than a year, Yetnikoff was out, no longer the favorite of Sony executives in Tokyo, his reputation marred by continuing investigations into the alleged corruption by the independent promoters whom he had defended. After a brief interim period, he would be succeeded by a former management company director whom he had mentored and brought into the CBS organization, Tommy Mottola.

The closing decade and a half of CBS/Columbia, from 1973 through 1987, had been unsettling years of energetic expansion and excess, highlighted by the successes of the mid-1980s. In part, that turbulence had been an extension of the appetites and business acumen of the man in charge, Walter Yetnikoff. But it was chiefly the product of the buccaneer business practices of the Reagan years, the early advent of digital technology and the CD, and the continuing revolution in popular music. These developments, in combination, fed a noisy and expensive search for the next new blockbuster, the next new wave, that in turn made first-week sales figures and lists of Grammy (much expanded since the first awards in 1959) the surest signs of validation. Begun in uncertainty, the period ended in uncertainty, and with an entirely new corporate structure in place. The years to come would bring even greater turbulence.

New Kids on the Block

Public Enemy

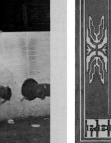

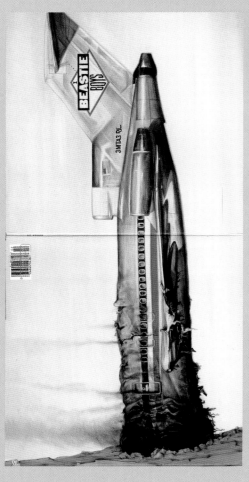

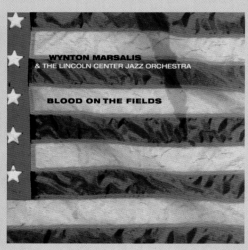

Bruce Springsteen.
"Darkness on the Edge of Town."
On Columbia Records and Tapes.

HANGIN'
TOUGH

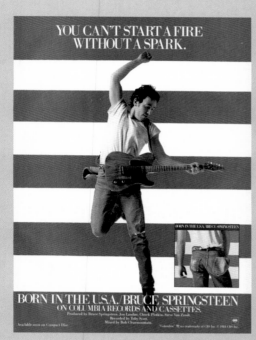

YOU CAN'T START A FIRE
WITHOUT A SPARK.

BORN IN THE U.S.A./BRUCE SPRINGSTEEN
ON COLUMBIA RECORDS AND CASSETTES.

BOB
DYLAN
BLOOD
ON
THE
TRACKS

Weather Report   Heavy Weather

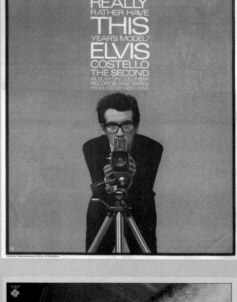
Blue Öyster Cult: Some Enchanted Evening

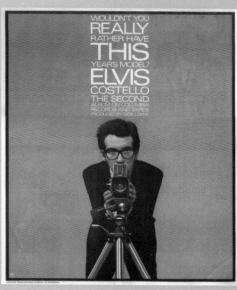

WOULDN'T YOU
REALLY
RATHER HAVE
THIS
YEAR'S MODEL?
ELVIS
COSTELLO
THE SECOND
ALBUM ON COLUMBIA
RECORDS AND TAPES
PRODUCED BY NICK LOWE

LOVE
DEVOTIO
SURREN

ESCAPE INTO A NEW JOURNEY.
"ESCAPE," JOURNEY'S LATEST BREAKTHROUGH.
FEATURING "WHO'S CRYING NOW."
ON COLUMBIA RECORDS AND TAPES.

'Do They Know It's Christmas?'

LOVERBOY'S BACK.
The most successful new band in years
returns with "Get Lucky."

The band that let rock & roll go with "Turn Me Loose," from
their platinum debut album, is back with a record that's
even hotter, even tighter!

Now, all the fans who've been demanding, "Lover, come back,"
can come and get "Get Lucky." Loverboy's second album.

Featuring the single, "Working For The Weekend."
Loverboy. "Get Lucky." On Columbia Records
and Tapes.

Look for Loverboy on their cross-country journey with Journey.

MICK JAGGER
PRIMITIVE COOL

Prestige and Pop

Columbia Records marked two milestones in 2012: the 125th anniversary of the formation of the American Graphophone Company and the 25th anniversary of Sony's purchase of Columbia from CBS. For one-fifth of its history, Columbia had been, in one way or another, under Sony's aegis. No longer headquartered at Black Rock, the company took up residence in 1992 at the decidedly postmodern Sony Tower on Madison Avenue, originally designed for AT&T by Philip Johnson. The history of Columbia's Sony years is still being written. Yet certain patterns show where the label's catalogs have been strong, especially in mainstream pop music, and where they have been either weak or inconsistent. As during much of the label's history, those patterns have reflected the changing tastes and preferences of the company's top management.

Destiny's Child

After 1987, Columbia's managerial history became a puzzle of corporate permutations and personnel shuffles. Adding to the difficulties, at the turn of the millennium the label, along with the entire music industry, had to reckon with the challenges of the continuing digital revolution and the explosion of music-downloading on the Internet. Bewildering as these transitions were, though, Columbia clearly witnessed a shift at the highest levels away from ex-lawyers and toward artist managers and promoters, who accelerated the long-term shift toward packaging blockbuster acts. And new trends were apparent in the music itself, some of them contradictory. Traditional mainstay sections of the Columbia Records catalog, including classical music and jazz, were not what they once were, as listeners turned to a proliferation of smaller recording companies devoted to these genres. The partial disintegration within the industry of all-embracing general interest labels, of which Columbia and RCA Victor had once been the major examples, told of a dispersal of listeners and marketers into well-defined and easily targeted niches.

The music that popular music fans favored also changed, notably with the enormous growth of hip-hop, and in line with what, in retrospect, was a fitful rearrangement of American musical form that had begun decades earlier. In the 1950s and 1960s, the advent of rhythm and blues along with rock and roll simplified Tin Pan Alley's chord constructions, but songs were still highly structured blends of melody and lyrics. Then, starting with funk, disco, and hip-hop in the 1970s, the approach shifted again, with even greater emphasis on rhythmic groove and word play. Melody hardly disappeared, least of all in disco, but beat and lyrical rhyming became featured all the more—to the point where, in some hip-hop music, songs resembled incantations. Just as Columbia had once resisted rock and roll only to become the preeminent rock and roll label in the late 1960s, so its response to these new changes in popular music became an important part of its history during the first quarter century of Sony's ownership.

By the same token, though, all was not brand new in the recording business, and some of what was new defied easy classification. Columbia's well-established stars like Streisand and Dylan, far from over the hill, retained and even expanded their followings. In the 1990s, Columbia's hottest new performers, including Mariah Carey and the group Destiny's Child, specialized in a fresh, R&B-influenced reworking of familiar forms of contemporary pop. And among younger and older artists alike, interesting experiments cracked through barriers of style, language, and generation, to create collaborations, crossovers, and hybrids of established styles that were previously unimaginable and defied existing categories. These new experiments also brought together audiences who were previously unfamiliar with one another.

There have been two distinct phases in Columbia's history since 1987. The first brought the rise and fall of a corporate regime unlike any the label had ever known. That regime's unraveling began in 2003; two years later, a second phase commenced in which Columbia belatedly started coming to grips with the demands of the new digital era. By then, the recording industry that had emerged during the 1940s and 1950s and went in new directions during the 1960s and 1970s—in large part through the efforts of Columbia Records—no longer existed. The test, for Columbia, would be in how much influence it would have over the reconfigured industry.

Tommy Mottola, Don Ienner and the "New" Columbia

Even a bare-bones history of Columbia's post-CBS management history must begin with Tommy Mottola. Yet another outsized figure in the history of Columbia Records, Mottola operated in a street-wise style very different from John Hammond, Goddard Lieberson, or Clive Davis. And, although he and Yetnikoff were the best of pals, they evoked different types of New York ethnic toughness. With his lavish lifestyle and Mafia-style mannerisms, Mottola could come across as menacing and slightly unsavory. A gifted judge of competitors as well as musical talent, Mottola shrugged off the unsubstantiated suspicions: "Hey," one reporter quoted him as saying, "if that gives me an edge, OK. All I want to do is win, man. Period." Mottola was smart—much too smart to get mixed up with criminals—and he was certainly good at winning:

System of a Down

The Offspring

Steven Tyler and Joe Perry of Aerosmith

by boosting the careers of numerous newly discovered talents and pressing hard to expand Columbia's marketing presence around the world, he wiped out any loose talk about Columbia as a "cold" label. Mottola also impressed his own tastes on Columbia, shifting the company toward a heavier investment in updated versions of more traditional pop styles, with an emphasis on vocal virtuosity.

A native of the Bronx, born in 1949, Mottola was raised in comfortable, suburban New Rochelle in a close-knit Italian family where an interest in music was strongly encouraged. Having gained a reputation as the baddest kid in New Rochelle, and singing under the name T. D. Valentine, he cut a pair of 45-rpm singles for Epic in the early 1970s that went nowhere. ("I was really mediocre," he later admitted.) But the experience got Mottola into contact with the wider world of professional music. While working as a song plugger for the Chappell music publishing firm, he ran across the performing duo of John Hall and Daryl Oates, and he switched to the field of artist representation. With Mottola as their manager, Hall and Oates became one of the premier acts in rock.

In 1975, Mottola formed a management company with the immodest gangland name of Don Tommy Enterprises (which he later changed to Champion Entertainment), where he aided the careers of various other performers, including Carly Simon and John Cougar Mellencamp. Deeply dedicated to reinstating New York (as opposed to Los Angeles, home to Warner Bros., Capitol, and MCA) as the national center of the recording industry, Motolla devised for Champion Entertainment what one journalist called "a total management concept," offering strong marketing and promotion skills directly to his artists, above and beyond what the record labels had to offer. By the mid-1980s, Mottola had gained a measure of insiders' fame. In one example, Dr. Buzzard's Original Savannah Band, one of Mottola's acts, opened their one hit, the disco sensation "Cherchez la Femme/C'est Si Bon," with a line about him: "Tommy Mottola lives on the road." Mottola also became close personal as well as professional friends with Walter Yetnikoff. In the mid-1980s, wanting to conquer new frontiers, Mottola became deeply interested in joining the CBS Records group. In 1988, five months after the Sony purchase, Yetnikoff named him as the group's president, replacing Al Teller, a seasoned veteran who had previously headed Columbia Records.

The appointment of an artist manager with no background inside a recording company to the job of president at any label would have struck the industry as odd. To do so at Columbia—where (with the rare and only partial exception of Irwin Segelstein) top executives had long been promoted from within—seemed bizarre. "Walter could have done better by opening the L.A. phone book and choosing at random," one manager remarked. But Yetnikoff had confidence in Mottola's ear for music as well as his toughness in business. As head of the entire CBS Records operation for the United States (which included Epic as well as Columbia), Mottola stood beside the head of the international division, Bob Summers, with both of them working under Yetnikoff. When Yetnikoff departed in 1990 (or, according to several reports, was pushed out, partly at Mottola's instigation) the operation of CBS Records fell temporarily to Mottola, Summers's, and the longtime head of Columbia's record club, Neal Keating. These three reported to Norio Ohga, the head of Sony's American subsidiary, with Sony executive Michael Schulhof handling day-to-day operations. Once he was elevated to Yetnikoff's old job in 1990, Mottola and his team would guide the destiny of Columbia and its sister labels for thirteen years.

In charge at Columbia was Don Ienner, known to almost everyone in the business as "Donnie," who in 1989, at the age of thirty-six, became the youngest president in the label's history. In 2002, he would become chairman of Columbia and, a year later, head of Sony Music North America. Despite his youth, Ienner had been involved in the record business, in one way or another, for twenty years. He had started working as a teenager in the Capitol Records mailroom in New York at the end of the 1960s, a job arranged by his brother, Jimmy, an independent record producer. After working with Jimmy for a few years in their production, publishing, and management firm, C.A.M. U.S.A. (where he worked with bands that included Grand Funk Railroad and the Bay City Rollers), Ienner joined Clive Davis's Arista Records as head of promotion. At Arista, Ienner's musical horizons broadened: the label's early artists included the Kinks, Patti Smith, the Thompson Twins, and, in time, Whitney Houston.

"All I want to do is win, man. Period."

Tommy Mottola

Joe Perry, Steven Tyler, and Brad Whitford of Aerosmith with Michele Anthony and Tommy Mottola

Billy Joel with Don Ienner and John Mayer

Tony Bennett

Ienner became Davis's protégé, and in 1987 he was named Arista's executive vice president and general manager. By then, Ienner later recalled, his experience placed him "next in line for the presidency of a record company." Once Mottola had tapped him to lead Columbia, Ienner had to deal with telling Davis where he was headed: even fifteen years after his firing from Columbia, Davis still bore hard feelings. Still, Ienner hit the ground running at Columbia and did not look back. Already a big fan of Bruce Springsteen—whose manager, Jon Landau, had encouraged Ienner to move to Columbia—Ienner was especially eager to sign younger talent playing new forms of alternative rock, a field, he later said, in which Columbia was "nowhere."

Another vital figure at the top was Michele Anthony, who in the 1990s and the early years of the new millennium was the most powerful woman in the recording industry. A daughter of the talent manager Dee Anthony (who had represented Tony Bennett and Jerry Vale, as well as the rock and rollers Peter Frampton, Ten Years After, and Joe Cocker), the younger Anthony had a distinguished early career as an entertainment lawyer and then joined Sony in 1990 as senior vice president. She was charged with the responsibility of overseeing regional A&R offices, special projects, and new artistic opportunities. Rising steadily thereafter, eventually to the post of president and chief operating officer of Sony Music Label Group US, she played a pivotal role in guiding Sony Music's industry and government relations, providing a liaison with Sony's other divisions and companies (including Sony Pictures Entertainment), and signing some acts for Sony, notably Pearl Jam for Epic and the Offspring for Columbia, and re-signing others, most importantly Aerosmith. Thanks to her professional bond with Mottola, Anthony had particularly close working relations with Columbia Records.

Mel Ilberman, a veteran of the recording industry, was Mottola's chief *consigliere* as well as a key Sony executive. At age sixty, nearly a generation older than Mottola, Ilberman came to Sony in 1988 after a long and colorful career at Polydor and RCA. As the experienced senior man, Ilberman helped Mottola rein in the usual rivalries among the label's senior management, while overseeing business affairs and all deal making—earning the nickname "Doctor No." Above all, Ilberman offered Mottola the kind of financial and business expertise he badly needed. According to one unnamed executive, quoted in *New York* magazine, Ilberman "was Tommy's brains"—an unkind exaggeration, but a sign of how important Ilberman had become among the inner circle. Mottola, according to the then-head of Sony Europe, Paul Russell, was "a great A&R guy," but he lacked high-level business experience and was too tied to New York to oversee effectively a worldwide conglomerate on the scale of Sony music and Columbia. Ilberman, named head of Sony International in 1992, filled both gaps, and he proceeded to restructure Sony's international operation into an integrated, truly global company.

During the 1990s, Mottola and Ienner eliminated the misperception that Columbia had become an aging label, out of touch with current tastes. With their expertise in managing, packaging, and promoting musical acts, Mottola and Ienner actually helped to manufacture certain trends, while turning individual artists into major stars. Yet what some came to call the "new" Columbia also retained the enormous prestige provided by the label's well-established artists. Columbia, Paul Russell recalls, was still very much "the premier label" in the early 1990s; artists clamored to join its ranks. Earlier charges by critics and rivals that Columbia's top-tier performers were past their prime had proved grossly mistaken. They continued to prove so through the first years of the new millennium.

The Heritage Artists

Tumultuous though Columbia's corporate history was—and successful as Mottola and Ienner were in redefining the label after 1990—the careers and output of Columbia's established stars, sometimes called the label's heritage artists, made little concession to age or changing popular tastes. Barbra Streisand began the 1990s immersed in her film work as well as philanthropic and fund-raising activities, and appeared to have left the concert stage and recording studio behind. But in 1993,

Don Ienner with Destiny's Child

Mel Ilberman, Don Ienner, Dave Glew, and Tommy Mottola

Bruce Springsteen

following up on her Broadway album of eight years earlier, she recorded *Back to Broadway*, which headed the pop charts and included an especially lovely duet with Johnny Mathis, who had returned to Columbia in 1967, on "I Have a Love/One Hand, One Heart." Soon after, Streisand announced her first public concert appearances in twenty-seven years. Her tour the following summer, breathlessly previewed by *Time* magazine as "the music event of the century," was a smashing success, as was the film version televised by HBO.

Johnny Mathis had re-signed with Columbia after only three years on Mercury. Although he would never repeat the hit-making success of his early career, his unique sound (Streisand called him one of her favorite singers when they joined forces in 1993) had kept his work current and popular, notably on recordings of Christmas songs, with which he became particularly identified. Mathis held the distinction of having had the longest tenure in total number of years of any Columbia recording artist. His honors piled up, including a Grammy for Lifetime Achievement in 2003.

Billy Joel's career followed a different arc. After surviving personal and business upheavals that began after the release of his album *Storm Front* in 1989, Joel released *River of Dreams* in 1993, which was followed by a long hiatus from releasing original pop material. But Joel branched out into new areas, recording a collection of original classical piano pieces entitled *Fantasies and Delusions* in 2001. Even though his pop-music composing all but ceased, Joel remained a perennial favorite on the concert trail, notably in a series of periodic tours with Elton John that had begun in 1994. *Movin' Out*, a so-called jukebox musical conceived by the choreographer Twyla Tharp that featured Joel's music, ran for more than three years on Broadway beginning in 2002, winning the 2003 Tony Awards for orchestration and choreography. Joel's emotional show at Shea Stadium in July 2008—the final rock concert before the stadium's demolition, at the site of the Beatles' historic concert more than forty years earlier—yielded an acclaimed CD/DVD set as well as a full-length documentary film, *Last Play at Shea*.

Bruce Springsteen's career had its ups and downs in the 1990s, one high point coming with the release of his song "Streets of Philadelphia," written for the Tom Hanks film about the AIDS plague, *Philadelphia*. The song won the Academy Award for Best Original Song in 1994 as well as four Grammies. Many years later, Springsteen would describe the decade as his "lost" years: "I didn't do a lot of work. Some people would say I didn't do my best work." But he rebounded in 2002 with the critical and commercial success of *The Rising*, a series of reflections on the terrorist attacks of September 11, 2001, which was also his first studio effort with the full E Street Band since *Born in the U.S.A.* Thereafter, Springsteen's involvement with classic American folk music and political causes deepened.

Bob Dylan's work, as ever, broke free of any expectations. Largely written off as a has-been at the end of the 1980s, Dylan recorded two acoustic albums of older folk songs and blues in the early 1990s, *Good as I Been to You* and *World Gone Wrong*, which reconnected him with his muse. By the winter of 1996, he was back to writing new material; the album that followed, *Time Out of Mind*, released in 1997, marked a major comeback, featuring some of Dylan's best songs in more than a decade, including "Not Dark Yet" and "Cold Irons Bound." *Time Out of Mind* won three Grammies, including Album of the Year. It also began a renaissance of Dylan's career, affirmed four years later with *"Love and Theft"*—a commercial as well as critical success that built on a dense style of allusion and appropriation, merged vaudeville jokes with apocalyptic imagery, and drew on sources as disparate as Donizetti and Charlie Patton.

Other older artists, including veteran Columbia performers as well as newcomers, also thrived, especially after the turn of the millennium. Neil Diamond built greatly on his productivity in the 1990s when he released *12 Songs*, produced by Rick Rubin. Having left Def Jam records in 1988 following a power struggle within the company, Rubin had gone his own way and made a new reputation as a producer who brilliantly revitalized or redirected the recording careers of older artists, most notably Johnny Cash (who now recorded for Rubin's own American Recordings label). For *12 Songs*, Rubin teamed up Diamond with the likes of organist Billy Preston and guitarist Mike Campbell of Tom Petty's band, the Heartbreakers. Released in 2005, it became the

Barbra Streisand,
Back to Broadway

best-selling and most acclaimed album of Diamond's in many years, and it also launched Diamond's latest tour of sold-out shows.

Leonard Cohen spent five years, from 1994 to 1999, in seclusion at the Mount Baldy Zen Center near Los Angeles, where he was ordained a Rinzai Buddhist monk in 1996. However, before and after his retreat, he continued to work hard on his musical projects and poetry. *The Future*, released in 1992, included a diverse collection of melodic styles, including gospel, country, and even marching band music, melded to prophetic lyrics of grimness and perseverance. And, despite rumors at decade's end that he had abandoned songwriting completely, he returned to music in 2001 with a superb album, *Ten New Songs*, including "In My Secret Life" and "Alexandra Leaving," the latter based on verse by the modern Greek poet Constantine Cavafy. No contemporary musical artist, Dylan included, made richer use of religious, and especially Jewish, imagery to explore contemporary tangles of love, infidelity, depression, and endurance.

Columbia also continued to pick up veteran artists from other labels, including some who had previously departed its own ranks. After being dropped by Warner Bros. Records, Bette Midler recorded her first album for Columbia in 2003, a highly successful collection of songs previously made famous by the Columbia star Rosemary Clooney. This was followed by a similar tribute to Peggy Lee. In an entirely different corner of the pop music field, the rock megastar David Bowie teamed his own ISO label with Columbia in 2002 and released *Heathen*, his most acclaimed studio album since the early 1980s. A year later, Bowie kicked off the release of a follow-up album, *Reality*, with a concert beamed via satellite to movie theaters around the world, featuring some of his classic older numbers as well as songs from the new release. Columbia also welcomed back Aerosmith in 1997 after the band's relationship with Geffen Records ended. Three studio albums followed, including *Nine Lives*, an instant top seller, and an underappreciated album of reinvented blues covers, *Honkin' on Bobo*, released in 2004. But the most extraordinary story of an established artist was a revival that took Columbia back to its golden years of mid-century.

"That man's amazing," Elvis Costello said, in obvious wonder. "A pro. Truly great! His rhythm, his styles, the way he grabs a tune . . ." It was late in 1994, and Costello was on the set of *MTV Unplugged*, where he had just performed a duet with the singer he was praising, Tony Bennett. After he departed Columbia in 1972, Bennett had recorded his two fine albums with Bill Evans and started his own short-lived record company, but otherwise his career had started to crumble. At the end of the 1970s his second marriage was coming apart, he had succumbed to drug abuse, and he was in trouble with the Internal Revenue Service—yet he had no contract, had no manager, and was not performing outside Las Vegas. His family, especially his sons Danny and Dae, came to his rescue, helping him to get his life in order, and reassembling his career. In 1986, newly re-signed with Columbia, Bennett recorded *The Art of Excellence*, his first album to appear on the charts in fourteen years.

Bennett's revival was fortuitously well timed. In the mid-1980s, the older members of the baby boom generation were reaching their forties, and amid the rise of disco, punk, and New Wave rock, they were newly receptive to evergreens from the American popular songbook. Bennett's son Danny made sure his father was booked on late-night television shows popular with baby-boomer audiences. His vocal talents mellowed but undimmed, Bennett recorded two songbook albums, a tribute to Frank Sinatra in 1992 and one to Fred Astaire in 1993, both of which won him Grammys for Best Traditional Pop Vocal Performance. Yet despite his tendency to stick with the standards, Bennett remained a cosmopolitan and open-minded man. He admired the talents of younger artists and was happy to work with them.

Bennett reached a turning point with his *MTV Unplugged* appearance. "I've been unplugged my whole career," he quipped, performing a solo set and singing duets with Costello, k.d. lang, and J. Mascis of the band Dinosaur, Jr. The show vastly expanded Bennett's appeal; the album made from it, in addition to enjoying instant heavy sales, earned Album of the Year honors as well as Bennett's third Grammy in a row in the traditional pop category.

Bob Dylan

Billy Joel at
Shea Stadium

Heavy Pop

The recruiting and promotion of new acts by Columbia under Mottola and Ienner was heavily shaped by Mottola's preference for young, mainstream pop performers whom Columbia would expertly package and market abroad as well as in the United States. One successful younger pop holdover from the Yetnikoff years, New Kids on the Block, expanded on their success with *Hangin' Tough* by releasing a Christmas album, followed by the wildly successful *Step By Step* and a stand-alone hit single, "If You Go Away." By 1991, the group was one of the hottest acts in Britain and Japan as well as the United States, appealing to younger listeners who wanted their own version of the next new thing, blending pop, R&B, and elements of rap. New Kids on the Block was also one of the acts made all the more successful by its appearances on MTV. The group's fortunes began to decline around 1993, amid the rising popularity of gangsta rap and grunge rock, and it would disband late in 1994. (One of its very early members, Donnie Wahlberg's brother, Mark, went on to enjoy a brilliant career first as a rapper in Marky Mark and the Funky Bunch and then as a film actor.) By then, though, Columbia boasted an array of exceptionally successful pop acts.

Among the other holdovers, the rocker, now turned soul singer, Michael Bolton enjoyed the greatest successes of his career in the early 1990s with his albums *Time, Love, and Tenderness* and *Timeless: The Classics*, and he remained a stalwart of Columbia's pop roster for the rest of the decade. After an interlude playing funk in the mid-1990s, Harry Connick Jr. returned to his piano jazz style. Alongside a burgeoning career, which had him acting in films and on television as well as writing music for Broadway, Connick released several fine albums on Columbia through the first decade of the new millennium, notably a 2004 collection of standards aimed directly at the aging baby boomers, *Only You*. The most prominent new pop acts in the Sony orbit, though, were female. At Epic, the French-Canadian soprano Céline Dion crossed over to the English language market to become the most popular female pop singer of her generation. Columbia, meanwhile, boasted no less of a talent, Mariah Carey.

The story of Carey's arrival and early years at Columbia had the makings of a modern, true-life Cinderella tale. Born in 1970, the daughter of an Irish-American mother and an African-Venezuelan father, Carey had been singing since the age of three. While in high school, she had worked as a demo singer for local recording studios near her home on Long Island. After graduation, she moved to New York and wound up working as a backup singer for the Puerto Rican salsa and freestyle singer Brenda K. Starr. In 1988, Starr introduced Carey to Mottola at a party and handed him a tape of Carey's singing. Mottola departed and flipped the tape on in his car. Impressed by what he had heard, he returned to the party to find Carey, but she had departed. Undaunted, Mottola tracked her down and signed her to a Columbia contract. Two years later, Carey would be a star; five years later, she would be Mottola's wife.

Carey, with a coloratura voice, was blessed with great technical virtuosity and a stunning range. Her style, although shaped by her mother, a former opera singer, was also influenced by R&B, particularly Motown's recordings of the 1960s and 1970s. Yet a smooth pop sensibility in her singing widened her appeal. Her first album, *Mariah Carey*, for which she cowrote the music, received heavy promotion from Columbia and topped the *Billboard* chart upon its release in 1990. Mottola was determined to make Carey a star, and he succeeded. The album also won praise from some influential critics (*Billboard* called it an "extremely impressive debut"), which helped earn Carey the Grammy for Best New Artist. Her second album, *Emotions*, conceived as a tribute to the Motown sound, fared less well with the critics, although the title-track single was a number one hit. Thereafter, Carey moved from one hit recording to another, beginning with an EP based on her appearance on *MTV Unplugged* (which convinced some of the harsher skeptics who thought her singing abilities had been enhanced and even simulated by studio equipment). Her successes continued with *Music Box*, still her best-selling album, in 1993, on through her seventh studio album, *Rainbow*, in 1999.

By decade's end, though, the Cinderella story was going haywire. Carey, the pop phenomenon, edged steadily closer to a rap and hip-hop style. (*Rolling Stone* called

Michael Bolton

Mariah Carey

Rainbow "a sterling chronicle of accessible hip-hop balladeering.") But as her singing evolved, unbearable tensions afflicted Carey's and Mottola's marriage, ending a romance that had always been an aspect of Carey's astonishing rise. The two announced their separation in 1997, and their divorce was made final a year later. Carey finally left Columbia in 1999.

In the same year that Carey released her debut album, 1990, a chance meeting in Houston, Texas, triggered a chain of events that would produce another great pop sensation. At an audition for a girl group, nine-year-old Beyoncé Knowles met another nine-year-old, LaTavia Roberson—not, on its face, an especially auspicious encounter. But over the next six years, after much shuffling of personnel (including the addition of Kelly Rowland and LeToya Luckett), as well as several changes of the group's name, the ensemble Destiny's Child emerged, managed by Beyonce's father, Matthew Knowles. Signed by Columbia in 1997, the group's first single, "No, No, No," was released late in that year. It then reappeared on their first, self-titled album a few months later, only to hit number one as a single in a remixed version. A year and a half later came *The Writing's on the Wall*, which would sell fifteen million copies world-wide. Further reshuffling left the group as a trio of Knowles, Rowland, and Michelle Williams—and in 2001, *Billboard* named them "Duo/Group of the Year." Often compared to 1960s Motown superstars the Supremes, the group survived considerable wrangling, as well as a three-year hiatus, to release three more studio albums before the remaining members agreed to go their separate ways in 2005. By then, the group had sold more records than any girl group other than the Spice Girls. And by then, the Motown comparisons had deepened; although she dismissed the notion, lead singer Beyoncé Knowles found herself being likened to Diana Ross. Her solo career, though, which began well before the group officially dissolved, suggested that the comparisons might have had merit. She was quickly emerging as the latest pop diva.

Knowles—soon to become celebrated simply as Beyoncé—started acting in films and recording soundtracks in 2001. She also collaborated with prominent R&B and rap performers, including Grammy-winning duet recordings with her then boyfriend, the rapper Jay-Z, and veteran soul singer Luther Vandross. And in 2003, after other members of Destiny's Child had released their own solo efforts before they went their separate ways, Columbia released Beyoncé's *Dangerously in Love*. A mixture of slow jam and up-tempo songs, the album sold more than three hundred thousand copies in its first week, a formidable figure in view of the general fall in CD sales since 2000. It also spun off four top hit singles, including "Crazy in Love," which featured a guest rap verse by Jay-Z, and won multiple Grammys. The comparisons to Diana Ross would become unavoidable four years later, when Beyoncé won a Golden Globe nomination for her portrayal of the Ross-based character Deena Jones in the film version of the 1981 Broadway musical *Dreamgirls*. On the verge of an exceptional career as a movie actress as well as a recording and touring star, Beyoncé was a seasoned professional who had been hard at work for seventeen years—yet she was only twenty-six.

The Mottola and Ienner years brought another major crossover from records to films and television and back again—the rapper-turned-television-star-turned-film-star Will Smith, whose debut album on Columbia, *Big Willie Style*, sold six million copies and generated four hit singles, including "Getting Jiggy wit' It." Mottola and Ienner also widened Columbia's pop offerings to include more Hispanic and Hispanic-influenced talent, to go along with the continuing success of Julio Iglesias. The Puerto Rican singer Ricky Martin, already a major Latin star, recorded his self-titled debut album in English for Columbia in 1999. A single from the album, the catchy dance number "Livin' la Vida Loca," became an international sensation that propelled Martin into a highly successful career as a crossover artist. Encouraged by Martin's breakthrough, another Puerto Rican male star, Marc Anthony, left RMM Records for Columbia in 1999 and recorded his first English-language Latin pop album. Epic became the recording home to the singer-actress Jennifer Lopez, soon to be recognized by her nickname JLo (and who later married Marc Anthony), as well as to the crossover Colombian singer and songwriter Shakira.

Will Smith

Marc Anthony

Ricky Martin

Hip-hop

Well outside of mainstream pop was the alliance Columbia had already formed with Def Jam Recordings. Thanks to that connection, Sony and Columbia, under Tommy Mottola, somewhat surprisingly ended up releasing some of the most charged, creative, and controversial hip-hop music of the late 1980s and early 1990s.

After Rick Rubin left Def Jam in 1988, Sony continued to hold a 50 percent share of the enterprise. From 1988 through 1992, Def Jam/Columbia produced major hip-hop releases, including, in 1990, LL Cool J's "Mama Said Knock You Out." Above all, in 1988, came the politically charged group Public Enemy's *It Takes a Nation of Millions to Hold Us Back*, followed two years later by *Fear of a Black Planet*, which included "Fight the Power," one of the most influential songs in all hip-hop. Originally released in a slightly different version on the soundtrack to Spike Lee's film *Do the Right Thing*, "Fight the Power" was inspired in part by the Isley Brothers' funk protest song, "Fight the Power, Parts 1 & 2" from 1975. In the hip-hop style, the song drew on samples from the work of other artists, including James Brown. But, thanks to new digital technology, it also included extensive looping and layering of the sound that transformed the samples into something completely new. The song emerged as an angry recording that berated such American icons as Elvis Presley and John Wayne but was also musically exhilarating. Condemned for their support of the Nation of Islam Supreme Minister Louis Farrakhan, as well as for anti-Semitic statements made by the group's "Minister of Information," Professor Griff, Public Enemy marked a particularly lurid moment for a slice of African American culture that equated racial pride with a bellicose black nationalism and Afro-centrism. But even after that mood receded later in the 1990s, the group's musical sophistication and technical daring strongly influenced hip-hop's subsequent development.

Columbia, though, faced some new difficulties with its hip-hop offerings. In 1992, Def Jam fell into serious financial difficulties, and PolyGram Records took over Sony's share in the company. From this point on, Columbia and its sister labels would miss out on some of the more interesting hip-hop talents and innovations, from the heyday of gangsta rap through the diversification of styles that would lead, after 2000, to the rise of innovative artists and crossover successes like OutKast, Kanye West, Eminem, and Jay-Z. Columbia did sign the gangsta rapper 50 Cent and released his outrageous single "How to Rob," but dropped him after violent feuding among hip-hop factions led to his being shot and nearly killed in 2000—after which he recovered and became a major star.

Still, Columbia released work by some major hip-hop artists in the 1990s and later. In 1991, in association with Ruffhouse Records, Columbia signed the Latino hip-hop group from California Cypress Hill, which achieved substantial crossover success with eight albums in connection with Columbia. Ruffhouse and Columbia teamed up again in 1996 to release Fugees' landmark second and final album, *The Score*, which included three hit singles (including a reworking of Roberta Flack's "Killing Me Softly"). With its intelligent lyrics and expert employment of the latest digital technology, the album hit number one on the *Billboard* chart. Its use of sampling to merge many far-flung styles, including contemporary Irish folk music, with hip-hop helped make it, in turn, an international sensation.

Columbia and Ruffhouse also released additional landmark albums by two of the three members of Fugees, Wyclef Jean and Lauryn Hill. Jean's hit *The Carnival* was a seamless blend of hip-hop, soul, R&B, reggae, and Haitian music, which featured "We Trying to Stay Alive" (based on the Bee Gees' disco classic "Stayin' Alive") and "Gone till November," performed with the New York Philharmonic. *The Carnival* pushed hip-hop into new, more cosmopolitan and tuneful directions; Hill's widely acclaimed and richly honored *The Miseducation of Lauryn Hill* did the same, although its island connections were with Jamaica, not Haiti—and much of its emotional power originated in Hill's difficult romance and painful breakup with Jean in the mid-1990s.

Hill had helped write and also performed on *The Carnival* in 1996, but she took time off to prepare for the birth of a child by her new lover, Bob Marley's son,

Cypress Hill

Public Enemy

Public Enemy,
Fear of a Black Planet

Previous page:
Beyoncé

LL Cool J

Rohan. Working in the attic of her house in South Orange, New Jersey, and gripped by an intense creative rush, she completed thirty songs before the child was born; two years later, her album was finished. Shifting from gritty defiance to dazed vulnerability, *The Miseducation of Lauryn Hill* powerfully described the hurt and redemption of love, drawing on literary sources as diverse as the Doors' Jim Morrison and the Bible. Musically, it was as ambitious in its eclecticism as anything from hip-hop, R&B, or the then-emerging genre of neo-soul. In a hip-hop world dominated by men, Hill's was a female voice of unusual subtlety and intelligence.

Topping both the pop and R&B charts in the United States—its sales in the United States alone would reach the platinum level eight times over—*Miseducation* made Hill an instant media icon. A nominee for ten Grammys (and the winner of five, including Album of the Year), she was hailed in a cover story in *Time* as the artist who had finally taken hip-hop into the musical mainstream without compromising its musical or emotional integrity. Hill herself, though, largely withdrew from the music scene into her private life, which has included mothering five more children, and she has not recorded another studio album since.

Columbia was also the home of one of the premier East Coast hip-hop stars, Nas. A buzz around Nas had started after his appearance on "Live at the Barbecue" (a track on an album by Main Source) in 1991. Columbia signed him only after Russell Simmons passed on him—a sign of where Columbia still stood in the hip-hop pecking order compared to the smaller independents. Beginning, though, with his own landmark first album, *Illmatic*, in 1994, Nas rewarded Columbia's support. Conveying the grimness of inner-city life without hopelessness, and doing so cohesively with fluid, sophisticated rhymes, *Illmatic* quickly won a following, and it has won some critics' praise as the very best hip-hop album yet recorded. Nas reinforced his reputation in 2001 with *Stillmatic*, in which he returned to the social and philosophical themes of his debut release. Nas's outspokenness embroiled him in various controversies, including a feud with Jay-Z that lasted nearly five years. But Nas burnished his reputation with a string of new Columbia releases that began with *God's Son* in 2002, followed by the double disc *Street's Disciple*, two years later.

Columbia also fared well in conventional R&B and soul music during the 1990s, some of it influenced by hip-hop. Born in Brooklyn in 1973, the son of a Puerto Rican father and Haitian mother, Gerald Maxwell Rivera would become known to listeners simply as Maxwell. He recorded his first album with Columbia in 1994, in a distinctive neo-soul style. Doubts among company executives about its commercial potential led the label to shelve it for two years. When finally released, the album, *Maxwell's Urban Hang Suite*, only began to capture attention when its second single "Ascension (Don't Ever Wonder)" became a hit. The album would sell two million copies and receive a Grammy nomination, but Maxwell's career took some odd turns. A clash with Columbia over material taped for *MTV Unplugged* led to the release of a truncated extended-play (EP) record with only seven songs (including a reworking of British singer Kate Bush's "This Woman's Work") instead of a proper album. Then, in 1998 and 2001, he released highly successful new studio albums, the second of which, *Now*, reached the top of the *Billboard* pop chart. A long break would follow—the singer said there was too much competition in the record industry, and he felt no rush—before he released his next album, *BLACKsummer'snight*, in 2009, with acclaimed songs of toughness and vulnerability that evoked the 1970s recordings of Marvin Gaye.

Rock's Offspring

Rock and roll, the core of Columbia's popular music program since the late 1960s, seemed to fade in importance compared to mainstream pop in the 1990s and after, but the appearance was deceptive. A new generation of rock and roll artists came of age in the late 1980s and early 1990s, their work rooted in earlier styles but blending these in fresh ways that broke down the stylistic distinctions of twenty years earlier. Columbia recorded some of the best of them.

Wyclef Jean

Nas

Maxwell

On Monday nights during the summer of 1992, limousines crowded outside a small Irish café, Sin-é, on St. Mark's Place in the East Village, as record executives came to listen to a sensational new act. The son of Tim Buckley, the doomed troubadour of the 1960s, Jeff Buckley was performing a mix of rock, folk, blues, and R&B, singing solo and playing on a borrowed Fender Telecaster. Signed by Columbia in October, Buckley recorded a live EP of his Sin-é material, assembled a band, and spent six weeks at Bearsville Studios outside Woodstock, New York, laying down the basic tracks for what would become his first album, *Grace*, released in 1994.

Combining original compositions with covers—including an exquisite rendition of Leonard Cohen's "Hallelujah"—*Grace*, with its gentle, aching vocals and elegant rock arrangements, was singular among the loud and dissonant rock bands of the day. The album won Buckley praise from some of the most discerning artists alive, including Bob Dylan and David Bowie. The album did not merge styles as much as it constantly changed shape, turning from the almost psychedelic imagery of "Mojo Pin" to Buckley's choir-voiced rendition of Benjamin Britten's interpretation of "Corpus Christi Carol."

After two years of touring heavily and collaborating with, among others, Patti Smith and Tom Verlaine, Buckley went to work on his second album, which he was calling *My Sweetheart the Drunk*, but never finished it to his satisfaction. In May 1997, he drowned accidentally in the Mississippi River near Memphis, where he and his bandmates were about to work on some new material—an enormous loss to American music. On the strength of his only album, he would be remembered as one of the finest popular recording artists of his generation.

Even before Buckley released *Grace*, other, very different rock styles had begun appearing on Columbia. In 1989, based on a demo tape prepared a year earlier, Columbia signed the band Alice in Chains and made them a top priority. A promotional EP, *We Die Young*, quickly appeared in 1990 in advance of a full-scale album. Recorded between December 1989 and April 1990, the album, *Facelift*, tried to convey what the guitarist Jerry Cantrell called the "moody aura" and "the brooding atmosphere and feel of Seattle." With hit tracks that included "Man in the Box," and with strong touches of heavy metal, it was the first grunge album to break through to the top 50 of the *Billboard* Top 200. Its success was due, in good measure, to MTV's decision to put the video of the latter in its daily schedule.

In 1996, Columbia, having neglected punk rock two decades earlier, signed the Offspring and released the band's fourth studio album, *Ixnay on the Hombre*, early the following year. Having originated in Huntington Beach, California, in the mid-1980s, the group had broken through with its previous album, *Smash*, released by Epitaph Records in 1994. This album was widely credited (along with the work of Green Day, Bad Religion, and other California bands) with reviving and updating the punk style that had first surfaced twenty years earlier. Less politically charged than *Smash*, *Ixnay on the Hombre* was also somewhat less successful commercially— although, by selling four million copies and generating three singles, it was successful enough. Over the ensuing decade and a half, the Offspring would release four additional highly successful albums with original material, as well as a greatest hits album, and establish itself as one of the premier punk rock bands of all time. Indeed, the band's enormous mainstream success led some critics to question whether it still could be appropriately labeled "punk." "I guess I just think of us as a rock band now, although we're still coming from the same theme we came from," the group's bassist Greg Kriesel responded in 2010. "Punk rock is so different today, though; now it's much more commercial whereas before punk rock was really underground."

The Armenian-American group System of a Down had built on the success of its first, self-named alternative-metal collection with the enormously successful *Toxicity*, released in 2001. In 2005 would come a double album, the first half released six months before the second; both *Mesmerize* and *Hypnotize* debuted at number one, making System of a Down one of a handful of groups, including the Beatles, to have two albums enter the charts in the top slot in the same year. While enjoying critical success, including a Grammy in 2006 for Best Hard Rock Performance for their anti-military song "B.Y.O.B.," the group also campaigned to increase popular awareness of the systematic mass slaughter of Armenians in the Ottoman Empire during and just after World War I.

Jeff Buckley

Previous page:
Fugees

Alice in Chains

282 | 283

Chapter 7 : Prestige and Pop

360 Sound : The Columbia Records Story

Columbia Record Club

A letter from Columbia Records to its dealers dated August 12, 1955, explained it all. Record clubs, like book clubs, were proliferating. The major labels didn't participate because it would alienate the dealer base. Charged with pleasing everyone, Columbia vice-president Norman Adler devised the Columbia Record Club. Consumers would not only benefit from a mail order service but would have access to name artists; dealers would sign up new members in exchange for 20 percent of the member's purchases in perpetuity; and Columbia could sell its catalog directly to the consumer. Budgeting $1 million dollars for advertising and promotion, the Columbia Record Club offered one free LP to new subscribers, and a wide selection of jazz, easy-listening, and Broadway show LPs. By the end of 1955, it boasted 128,000 members, and was making plans to move its operation to Terre Haute, Indiana, where Columbia's central pressing plant was located. By 1960, membership exceeded 1.25 million earning Adler a promotion to executive vice-president, second in command to Goddard Lieberson. By 1963, the club accounted for 10 percent of the entire recorded music market.

From 1958, the Columbia Record Club offered albums on other labels. Two notable holdouts, RCA and Capitol, had followed Columbia's lead in launching their own clubs. Generally, retailers had a six-month window before a record was offered for sale by the clubs. By the time the Columbia Record Club, by then Columbia House, celebrated its twentieth anniversary in 1975, membership stood at three million. The teaser (ten, eleven, twelve albums for a penny) was followed by a monthly catalog showing the Selections of the Month by genre together with hundreds of alternates. Consumers had ten days to decline altogether or choose an alternate; otherwise they'd receive the selection.

Membership grew exponentially after the CBS Video Library was added in 1982. In 1990, Columbia House reportedly shipped its one billionth record. The following year, Warner Bros. Records partnered with Columbia's new owner, Sony, and membership peaked at ten million before Internet retailers and big box stores took a bite out of sales. In 2002, Sony and Warner sold 85 percent of Columbia House to the Blackstone venture capital group for $410 million, and ownership has changed several times since then. The last Columbia House CD was shipped on June 30, 2009. It is now the Columbia House DVD Club.

Colin Escott

Columbia Record Club solicitation

A punk original unfettered by her mainstream success, Patti Smith joined Columbia in 2004 to release her ninth album, *Trampin'*. Smith made it clear that she was proud to join "so many artists I admire, including Bob Dylan, Miles Davis, and Glenn Gould." A collection of poetic songs that ranged in theme and style from hoe-down exuberance to Blakean mysticism, *Trampin'* was, not unlike much of the poetry of another of Smith's heroes and friends, the late Allen Ginsberg, at once political and undogmatic. "Smith lives the vocation of a poet in the old-fashioned sense of the work," the critic Thom Jurek wrote in a review. "Once bards *were* the gadflies of society."

A major new artist, the guitarist and vocalist John Mayer surfaced in 2000 and, although obviously influenced by rock, defied easy categorization. Signed by the Columbia subsidiary label Aware, Mayer cut his first album, *Room for Squares*, in 2000; eventually, Columbia picked it up, remixed, and rereleased it. By the end of 2002, several of the album's blues- and pop-influenced rock numbers had become hits on the radio, including "Your Body Is a Wonderland," which won Mayer a Grammy for Best Male Pop Vocal Performance. These were only the first breakthroughs for an artist whose music would range widely over the years to come.

Country and Folk amid the Trend toward Pop

Country music, important to Columbia and its associated labels since the efforts of Gid Tanner and Charlie Poole in the 1920s, went through some major shifts during the pop-oriented 1990s. The label had the good fortune to record Dolly Parton from 1987 to 1995, years that saw Parton back away from her earlier forays into pop music and return to her country roots. The best of her albums for Columbia, *White Limozeen* produced a pair of number one singles in 1989, "Why'd You Come in Here Lookin' Like That" and "Yellow Roses." But country music audiences were starting to favor what became known as contemporary country music, with a slicker, rock and roll- as well as pop-flavored sound, a turn that knocked even established stars like Parton out of the charts. Parton would record her most powerful work of these years, including her 2001 album for Sugar Hill Records, *Little Sparrow*, after she left Columbia. The label's most dependable country artist, Mary Chapin Carpenter, had started out with Columbia in 1987 and recorded some major hit albums and singles in the early 1990s, mixing up-tempo country rock songs about toughness and perseverance with slower, introspective ballads. But, after 2004, even though her albums continued to score well in the country charts, she too departed Columbia, for Rounder Records and then Rounder's Zoë Records label.

The most attention-grabbing country act in Columbia's catalog, as well as by far the best selling, were the Dixie Chicks, who exemplified the shift to a country sound that merged pop with traditional country music. Originally a bluegrass quartet, the group had evolved into the trio of Natalie Maines, Martie Maguire, and Emily Robison. The Dixie Chicks built a following in the early 1990s with their high-profile concert appearances on the folk and country circuit and two records from a small independent company. Signed by Sony in 1995 for its newly revived Monument Records label, the group's next album, *Wide Open Spaces*, climbed to the top five of both the pop and country charts, and in 1998 the Dixie Chicks sold more CDs than all other country groups combined. Their next two albums, *Fly* and *Home*—the second released on the group's own subsidiary label after the Chicks sued Sony in a royalties dispute—won strong reviews as well as generating excellent sales.

A huge controversy erupted, though, when, at a concert in London during the run-up to the US invasion of Iraq in 2003, Natalie Maines, who like the rest of the band was raised in Texas, declared that the group opposed the coming war and that they were ashamed to share their home state with President George W. Bush. The Dixie Chicks' more conservative country fans were outraged, and a storm of retaliation ensued, which included everything from public rallies organized to smash the band's CDs to canceled corporate sponsorships. Various artists, including the country music legend Merle Haggard, came to the group's defense. But many other country singers

John Mayer

expressed anger at Maines's remark, and country radio stations ceased playing Dixie Chicks' music. The controversy would continue for years to come.

Otherwise, although its country and folk acts were not numerous, Columbia boasted some major talents in different subgenres. Shawn Colvin recorded a superb debut album, *Steady On*, in 1989, and through the rest of the 1990s she established herself as one of the leading lights (along with Mary Chapin Carpenter and Suzanne Vega) in a younger cohort of folk singers. Her best-selling album, *A Few Small Repairs*, featured songs about the travails and heartache of divorce, including the wrenching single "Sunny Came Home," which earned the Grammys for Song of the Year and Record of the Year in 1997. The contemporary country star Travis Tritt recorded two albums with Columbia between 2002 and 2005 only to leave, citing creative differences over the second album, *My Honky Tonk History*. The very different avant-garde country sounds of banjo wizard Béla Fleck and his ensemble the Flecktones, with their melding of bluegrass and jazz, also appeared temporarily on Columbia. Beginning with the group's eighth album, *Outbound*, in 2000, their relationship with Columbia would last through four more releases, until 2006. In 2004, Columbia released the first self-titled studio album by one of the most exciting new country groups (and certainly one of the finest ever to come out of New York's Lower East Side), Olabelle, produced by the great T Bone Burnett.

Burnett, meanwhile, had been a force of nature from the late 1980s onward, producing scores of artists ranging from Tony Bennett to the Japanese jazz musician Akiko Yano, overseeing the stunning soundtrack for the film *O Brother, Where Art Thou?*, contributing Oscar-winning songs to *Cold Mountain*, and winning a large clutch of awards. His first collection of new songs on Columbia, *The Criminal Under My Own Hat*, appeared in 1992, a favorite of the critics that enjoyed little commercial success. Nevertheless, it was a source of prestige for the label that, in the business strategy established decades earlier, would be underwritten by the enormous profits generated by its pop and mainstream R&B recordings.

Culture Shifts

By 2003, those pop and mainstream R&B performers, along with the heritage artists, were the jewels in the crown of Tommy Mottola's and Don Ienner's new Columbia. And under Mottola, the label became known for its swagger, born of Mottola's own devotion to ceaseless work on behalf of his artists mixed with what one critic called his "larger than life" persona. He was, the critic said, "one of those old-line music guys who passed out perks and took them himself." The "old-line" style, though, with its gaudy rewards of cars, vacations, and expensive watches, was quickly becoming unsustainable. Dependent on what had become unrealistic expectations of a constant cavalcade of blockbuster hits, caught unprepared by the rise of peer-to-peer sharing of music files on the Internet, Sony and Columbia suddenly awakened to how badly its business foundations had eroded. Columbia was hardly alone: across the industry, album sales actually declined by 11 percent between 2001 and 2003. But Columbia's losses were staggering—reported at $132 million during the first half of fiscal year 2002–2003—and suddenly the swagger disappeared.

The dissonance between the Mottola and Ienner regime's presumptions and the emerging realities of the recording industry had become untenable. A major house-cleaning by Sony was in the offing. But the pressures had been building for years. And the adjustments demanded of Columbia involved far more than cutting back on perks and paying greater heed to the bottom line. The rise of new media, of which file sharing proved to be a startling harbinger, called for entirely new ways of thinking about how record labels might reposition themselves to do what they did best, which was to nurture and bring attention to gifted artists. A certain humility seemed in order as the boom times of the 1990s became the lean times of the 2000s. But so, too, a new boldness was required if Columbia was to negotiate successfully the digital era.

Shawn Colvin

Lauryn Hill

DELUXE EDITION
MARIAH **THE BALLADS**

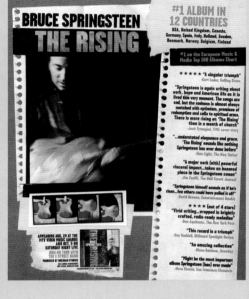

BRUCE SPRINGSTEEN
THE RISING

#1 ALBUM IN 12 COUNTRIES

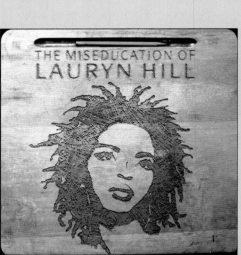

THE MISEDUCATION OF
LAURYN HILL

MICHAEL BOLTON

Timeless
THE CLASSICS

CypressHill
Black Sunday

PARENTAL ADVISORY
EXPLICIT LYRICS

Still the #1 *solo* act in the business.

#1 in total albums
sold both physically and digitally
for the sixth straight year*.
The Streak Continues.

COLUMBIA RECORDS.

MIB
MEN IN BLACK
THE ALBUM

20 years from now, we'll be reserving this

JOHN MAYER **ROOM F**

JOHN MAYER **HEAVIER THINGS**

BEYOND COMPARISON

6 GRAMMY NOMINATIONS

TONY BENNETT

JEFF BUCKLEY

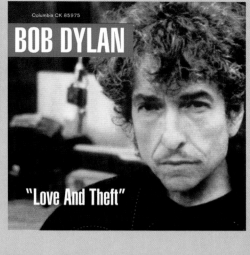

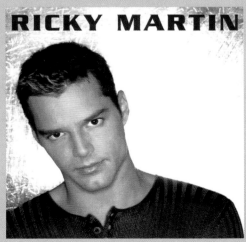

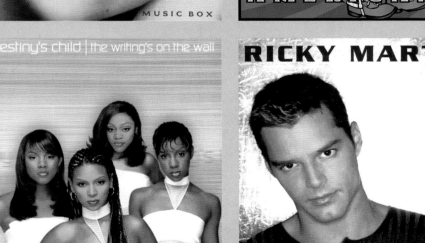

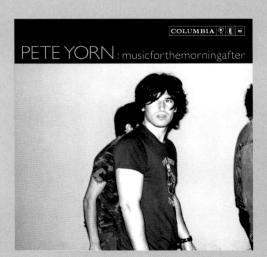

Turbulence and Opportunity in the Digital Age

During the years just before and after the turn of the millennium, business tumults, intensified by the ever accelerating pace of global capitalism, repeatedly unsettled Columbia Records, at times even threatening to overshadow the label's musical output. In 1997, the parent Sony Corporation named Howard Stringer of Columbia Broadcasting as president of its American subsidiary. After emigrating from Britain in the early 1960s, Stringer had had a glittering career in broadcasting at CBS as a journalist, producer, and executive. Now he would oversee an entirely different kind of media empire.

Bob Dylan

Nobuyuki Idei,
Tommy Mottola, and
Howard Stringer

Howard Stringer, Clive
Davis, Michele Anthony,
and Andy Lack

Steve Barnett, Beyoncé,
Rob Stringer, and Jay-Z

Neil Diamond

New Sony management in Tokyo under Nobuyuki Idei was coming to disdain Tommy Mottola's flashy and expensive style, as well as his enormous personal income (which would reportedly reach $20 million per year by 2002, even as the label's earnings were plummeting). Back home, Stringer and Mottola simply disliked each other, not least because Mottola was ill suited to serving as anyone's subordinate. Columbia was hardly the only recording company to suffer dramatic declines in revenues after 1999, but Columbia's run of heavy losses sealed Mottola's fate. Stringer made his move in January 2003, naming Andrew Lack, the former head of NBC News (with whom Stringer had previously worked at CBS), to replace Mottola as chairman and chief executive officer of Sony Music Entertainment. To provide some continuity, Don Ienner was promoted from head of Columbia to chairman of Sony Music US, and Michele Anthony from Sony Music Entertainment executive vice-president to chief operating officer of the Sony Music Label Group, US.

Further major corporate changes followed. In March 2004, Sony Music Entertainment entered into a 50/50 partnership with the giant German-based transnational media giant Bertelsmann AG and its Bertlesmann Music Group, with Andrew Lack named as CEO of the new partnership. The merger brought under one umbrella numerous recording companies besides Columbia and Epic: observers with a taste for historical irony would have appreciated that Columbia was now part of the same outfit as its venerable archrival, RCA Victor, as well as Clive Davis's Arista Records. The competition between Columbia and Victor, dating back to 1901, was finally over, and the longtime underdog, Columbia, had completed its triumph. But the Sony-BMG partnership was unstable, in part because it was not always clear which partner was in charge. Continued decline in market share and revenues contributed to Bertelsmann's decision to replace Andrew Lack early in 2006 with the Bertelsmann executive Rolf Schmidt-Holtz. Soon after the new regime was in place, Don Ienner and Michele Anthony resigned, reportedly under pressure from the top.

Finally, in August 2008, Sony agreed to buy back Bertelsmann's share of the music company for $1.2 billion. The deal left the revived Sony Music Entertainment, Inc., in control of all the record labels it had acquired as part of the merger, including RCA Victor and Arista.

As of 2012, Columbia's chairman and chief executive officer was Rob Stringer, Howard Stringer's younger brother by two decades. Rob had followed his own path in Britain, working in a rock club in his hometown of Aylesbury, graduating from art school, and finding a job with CBS records in 1985. He rose to become, first, managing director of Epic Records in 1993 and then, seven years later, chief executive officer of Sony-BMG UK. Stringer was alert, as many record executives were not, to how the rapid reshuffling of all existing media could affect the recording industry. In particular, while at Sony-BMG, he noticed the potential importance of the reality-television programming being pioneered by the British impresario and entrepreneur Simon Cowell, both as an opportunity to expand the market for recorded music and as a source of new talent. At his core, though, Stringer held fast to the idea that the recording labels' primary responsibility was to collaborate with the greatest talents they could find. In 2006, charged with the task of combining business innovation and artistic preeminence while also leaving behind past excesses, Stringer took over as chairman of the Sony Music Group.

One year earlier, Steve Barnett had been named chairman of Columbia, a position he still held in 2012, along with the position of chief operating officer. Barnett had begun his music career in 1972 when, at age twenty, he started working as an agent and then as a manager. In 1988, he moved over to the recording side of the business as senior vice president international at Epic. Over the ensuing eight years, Barnett played a vital role in encouraging and marketing numerous successful campaigns for Epic. In 1994, he was named the label's president. Barnett's success at Epic in turn recommended him to assume the chairmanship of Columbia after the Mottola and Ienner operation's downfall. Once Stringer arrived in the United States, he and Barnett began working out a new strategy for Columbia at a time when many observers were forecasting the entire industry's collapse.

There were strong reasons to be pessimistic. The late 1980s and 1990s had been commercial boom times for the major record labels, in part because the CD revolution led listeners to replace their old vinyl libraries. Profit margins for the industry averaged above

30 percent during the decade of 1985–1995, and total annual sales in the United States reached a peak of $14.6 billion in 1999. But that peak year was precisely when Internet file sharing became popular, threatening all conventions of copyright and intellectual property. It took time for the recording labels to awaken to the threat. The extent to which Internet downloading, distinct from other factors, actually caused the companies' difficulties remains in dispute. But the bottom line was clear, and the situation only worsened as the decade dragged on. By 2008, five years after Sony dismissed Mottola, total sales, industry wide, had tumbled to $10 billion and would continue to fall thereafter.

In attempting to reverse the tide, Columbia embraced all sorts of innovations, including new alliances and coproduction ventures. The experiments did not all turn out happily, least of all the ill-fated placement of the brilliant and mercurial Rick Rubin as Columbia's cochairman. Impressed by Rubin's success as a record producer for established artists as well as recent discoveries—a striking combination of old and new—Stringer gambled that Rubin might provide Columbia with a jolt of unconventional genius that would benefit the entire label. Barnett went along with the idea of a cochairmanship and helped persuade Rubin to come aboard in 2007. Very quickly, though, it became clear that Rubin had been miscast, his unorthodox operational style—which included an aversion to working at Columbia's offices—putting him at odds with how the rest of the label's management worked. By 2011, Rubin's tenure at Columbia was over.

Still, in line with the inspiration behind Rubin's appointment, Columbia sought to recombine old and new. If Columbia were to succeed in the new digital world, it would have to look to the unfamiliar, including untried business models appropriate to the rapidly changing technological and marketing climate. It would, as ever, have to look for new performers. But it would also have to recommit itself to an exceptional group of artists who had been preserving and expanding the label's prestige since the 1960s.

Enduring Greatness

As it approached its 125th anniversary, Columbia Records had achieved something extraordinary with its established stars. Throughout the history of musical recording, the norm had been for popular artists to switch labels at least once, and often several times. Bing Crosby's long association with Decca after 1931 was a rare exception; Benny Goodman recorded for several labels but kept returning to Columbia over a span of fifty years. Generally, though, it was uncommon for musicians or singers to stick with the same label for more than a decade. Yet by 2005, several of the greatest popular musical performers in modern times had recorded exclusively for Columbia, or nearly so, for more than thirty years, and in some cases for more than forty. No matter what innovations it might undertake, Columbia was determined to sustain those connections, both by promoting the work of the label's established artists and in some cases—including Barbra Streisand, Bob Dylan, Neil Diamond, Tony Bennett, and Harry Connick Jr.—making all-out efforts to re-sign them.

In September 2000, Streisand, who was absorbed in an array of activities, gave some farewell concerts and announced her retirement from the stage—only to return and tour sixteen cities in 2006. During these years, she also recorded three albums and a fine one-off duet with Tony Bennett on "Smile." Then, in 2009, Columbia released an album of Streisand singing standards, *Love Is the Answer*, produced by the outstanding jazz vocalist and pianist Diana Krall. Promoted with a one-night performance at the Village Vanguard, which was filmed and released on DVD, the album debuted at number one in *Billboard*, making Streisand the only artist ever to have released number one albums in five consecutive decades. But, quite apart from its commercial success and the career milestones it set, *Love Is the Answer* marked a return to the standards songbook that Streisand had mined in her youth, her voice deeper but her range and prowess still exceptional. At age sixty-seven, performing classics such as "In the Wee Small Hours of the Morning," Streisand remained the leading female vocalist of her era. She affirmed that position two years later with the release of *What Matters Most*, a collection of songs written by her longtime friends Alan and Marilyn Bergman, which debuted at number four on the *Billboard* albums chart.

Barbra Streisand

Leonard Cohen

Harry Connick Jr.

Tony Bennett

Johnny Mathis dramatically cut back his concert and recording schedule after 2000, but he could still surprise. In September 2010, Columbia released *Let It Be Me: Mathis in Nashville*, an album of country songs—and, at age seventy-five, Mathis found himself nominated for a Grammy for Best Traditional Pop Vocal Album. In 2008, Billy Joel followed up on his earlier move into classical composition by performing a new piece, "Waltz No. 2 (Steinway Hall)," with the Philadelphia Orchestra as part of a celebration of the Philadelphia Academy of Music's 151st anniversary. Joel's most popular older recordings, some of them collected with outtakes and demos and released by Columbia as *My Lives* in 2005, remained securely fixed in the classic rock canon.

Bruce Springsteen's output shifted between new work in rock and roll and explorations into traditional American music, some of it tied to his interest in political campaigns and causes. In 2006, he released *We Shall Overcome: The Seeger Sessions*, a collection of thirteen songs plus two bonus tracks popularized by the legendary radical folk singer Pete Seeger, who had released more than a dozen albums on Columbia between 1961 and 1974. In 2008, Springsteen, who had supported John Kerry's presidential candidacy four years earlier, strongly supported Barack Obama's campaign. And, in November, shortly after Obama's election, Springsteen announced the release of *Working on a Dream*, which had taken shape during the 2007–2008 campaign, its optimistic tone a contrast to *Magic*, released the previous year. Although the critics were not unanimous in their praise, *Rolling Stone* gave the new album its highest rating and likened its ambition and scope to Springsteen's best recordings of the 1970s. Ever a rock and roll icon, Springsteen further mingled his music with social concerns. *Wrecking Ball*, released in 2012, spoke directly to the continuing effects of the devastating Great Recession that began in 2008. It also featured arrangements that recalled Springsteen and the E Street Band in the mid–1980s, including two tracks that featured Springsteen's great sidekick saxophonist, Clarence Clemons, who died suddenly of complications from a stroke in 2011.

Bob Dylan's renaissance, signaled by *Time Out of Mind* and *"Love and Theft,"* turned into one of the most talked-about developments in contemporary music. Two of his albums, *Modern Times* (released in 2006) and *Together through Life* (released three years later) topped the popular album chart, the first Dylan albums to do so since *Desire* in 1975. *Modern Times*, which actually debuted at number one (a feat Dylan had not previously achieved), seems to have had the most powerful impact in winning him a following among the younger generation of music fans; it also won the Grammy for Best Contemporary Folk/Americana Album. Writing in his new, dense style that consciously compacted literary as well as musical references from far and wide into a new whole, Dylan composed songs that contemplated disconnection and mortality with poignancy, defiance, humor, and sometimes with all three. Accompanying a heavy touring schedule of roughly one hundred shows a year, as well as the completion of numerous other projects (including his acclaimed memoir, *Chronicles: Volume One*; his three-year run as the host of *Theme Time Radio Hour*; Martin Scorsese's television documentary of his early career, *No Direction Home*; and some high-profile museum exhibitions of his paintings), Dylan's recordings were stunning displays of energy and creativity. He received a special Pulitzer Prize, as well as, in 2012, the Presidential Medal of Freedom. Yet Dylan also remained elusive, resistant to any easy definition. In 2009, as he approached his sixty-ninth year, he released an album of carols and holiday standards, *Christmas in the Heart*, that left many critics and long-time fans scratching their heads and wondering what would come next.

Leonard Cohen's postmonastery work, notably the 2004 album *Dear Heather*, marked a shift away from the bleakness that haunted *Ten New Songs*—although *Dear Heather* did conclude with a cover of the country music heartbreak classic "Tennessee Waltz." (Cohen added a new verse of his own.) The album was also notable for its strong, sympathetic collaborations with the jazz singer Anjani Thomas, Cohen's latest romantic partner. Two years later, Cohen and Thomas cowrote the songs on Thomas's *Blue Alert*, which included musical settings of much older verse by Cohen as well as Thomas's rendition of a coauthored song, "Nightingale," which Cohen had sung on *Dear Heather*. Then, in 2008, at age seventy-three, Cohen returned to touring for the first time in fifteen years, mounting a strenuous series of shows that carried on

Bob Dylan,
Modern Times

Bruce Springsteen,
*We Shall Overcome:
The Seeger Sessions*

298 | 299

Chapter 8 : Turbulence and Opportunity in the Digital Age

360 Sound : The Columbia Records Story

After Top 40

The twenty-first-century challenge will be to learn how to expose music

The challenge in running a record company has never been in deciding what to record. There are many answers to that, and expertise in finding which performers do each type of music best, while not common, isn't all that rare.

The challenge is how to find an audience, how to unlock the barrier between the sounds being made and the people who might—maybe, probably, surely—want or even need to hear them.

From about 1920 to the end of the century, there were just two important answers. One was live performance. The other was radio (and to a lesser extent, television) broadcasts. But by the dawn of the twenty-first century, radio had become a very narrow channel, and for some kinds of music, live performance was no longer central. There were other kinds of exposure now available, largely through the Internet and other forms of digitized media, but these are very hard to control all the way to a final purchase, to say the least. In economic terms, this devalues the music. In business terms, it makes it a hell of a lot harder to sell.

The twenty-first-century challenge will be to learn how to expose music, in its many varieties, in a way that makes sure that musicians and the people who support them can make their living at it. Some large part of this will still be played by live music, and another part, whose scope isn't yet known, will still be played by broadcasting. Listening on the Internet has already assumed a major portion of broadcasting's role, which has the salutary effect of making a much larger variety of sounds more easily available, and the downside of that pesky matter of economics.

The long-term answers should be as fascinating as the rest of the story has been.

Dave Marsh

Jeff Buckley

into 2009 and 2010. He produced two remarkable CD/DVD sets, *Live in London* (capturing a performance of more than two and a half hours) and *Songs from the Road*. Cohen also won numerous awards, including, in 2011, two especially prestigious honors, the Glenn Gould Prize and the Prince of Asturias Award for Literature. And in 2012, he would release another new album, the haunting collection *Old Ideas*.

Over the decade and a half after his triumph on *MTV Unplugged*, Tony Bennett enjoyed a string of successful concerts and recording projects and received numerous accolades, including nine more Grammys. One musical highlight out of many was the album *Duets*, its release timed to coincide with Bennett's eightieth birthday in 2006. The album featured his performance of "Smile" with Barbra Streisand, along with eighteen other pairings. (Bennett's partners for the duets ranged from Sting to the Dixie Chicks.) A second album of duets appeared in 2011, to help mark his eighty-fifth birthday. What had been Bennett's comeback in the 1990s evolved into a new career, as his personal triumph helped to meld the tastes and talents of younger generations to a classic style of early to mid-twentieth-century American song. For Columbia, Bennett's success represented a remarkable, unexpected revival of what had once been the label's strongest suit in popular music.

Established stars who had come later to Columbia also completed major projects after 2005. Working once again with Rick Rubin, Neil Diamond followed up *12 Songs* three years later, in 2008, with *Home before Dark*, his first number one album ever. The previous year, Columbia had released Patti Smith's *Twelve*, a tribute to some of the finest rock songs of the 1960s, 1970s, and after, from the Rolling Stones' "Gimme Shelter" to Nirvana's "Smells like Teen Spirit." Jakob Dylan and his band the Wallflowers had made a breakthrough in 1996 with their second album, *Bringing Down the Horse*, released on Interscope Records, but when Dylan set off on a solo career in 2006, he signed with Columbia. He went on to record two albums, the mostly acoustic *Seeing Things*, produced by the ubiquitous Rick Rubin, and the electric *Women + Country*, overseen by another major producer (and sometime Columbia artist), T Bone Burnett.

The most explosive new album by a veteran act appeared in 2008. The iconic Australian hard rock band AC/DC had capped its own comeback during the 1990s by signing a long-term, multirecord deal with Epic in 2002. Obtaining the band's catalog as well as the band itself was a major coup for Sony and for AC/DC's former manager Steve Barnett. Several successful remasterings and DVD releases followed, but it took six years for the band to be ready with a new album of original material. Released in October 2008, the fifteen-track *Black Ice* was sold in the United States exclusively at Wal-Mart and Sam's Club's outlets, as well as on the band's Web site—a fresh promotion and marketing strategy. The album wound up becoming Columbia's most successful release by an act new to its catalog since 1991, when accurate sales data were first assembled. With more than 7 million copies of *Black Ice* sold worldwide, combined with 5.5 million in catalog sales, AC/DC surpassed the Beatles as the top-selling catalog act of the year and stood, overall, as the best-selling act of the year. At the end of 2011, more than 40 million AC/DC albums had been sold since the group signed with Sony Music.

Mottola and Ienner's Musical Legacy

Although Tommy Mottola and (after 2006) Don Ienner were gone, some of the artists who had arrived at Columbia during their tenure remained among the label's and the industry's premier performers. The completion of Beyoncé's second solo album, *B'Day*, was delayed by her appearance in *Dreamgirls*, but it debuted in 2006 at number one in the charts and sold more than five hundred thousand copies in its first week. The new album included one of her biggest hit singles, "Irreplaceable," and it impressed industry experts strongly enough to win the Grammy for Best Contemporary R&B Album. Two years later, Columbia released *I Am . . . Sasha Fierce*, which, along with three of its tracks, won a total of five Grammys. And *4*, released in 2011, debuted at number one. Enjoying an exceptional career in films and on concert tour as well as with her recording, Beyoncé, before reaching the age of thirty, had become a unique success story of her generation, bringing to mind the young Barbra Streisand as well as Diana Ross.

"Hip-hop is where rock used to be."

John Mayer

Patti Smith

Previous page:
Bruce Springsteen with the E Street Band (left), and with Seeger Sessions Band (bottom right)

John Mayer

The San Francisco-based pop rock band Train had enjoyed one of the greatest rock hits of the Mottola-Ienner years with the single "Drops of Jupiter (Tell Me)," which won two Grammys in 2002 and helped the band's second studio album, *Drops of Jupiter*, gain double-platinum sales in the United States and Canada. *My Private Success*, Train's follow-up album released in 2003, sustained the band's commercial popularity; three years later, a rearranged lineup released *For Me, It's You* to positive reviews but disappointing sales; but in 2009, Train enjoyed a major comeback with *Save Me, San Francisco*, which yielded three hit singles, including the best-selling single of the year in 2010, "Hey, Soul Sister."

John Mayer's second album, *Heavier Things*, included a number one Adult Top 40 single, "Daughters," which won Song of the Year honors as well as the Grammy for Best Male Pop Vocal Performance in 2004. By then, though, Mayer, who enjoyed working with other premier artists, was already on the move. After collaborations with Kanye West and Common, he declared that "hip-hop is where rock used to be." Soon, he began working with blues guitarists Buddy Guy, B. B. King, and Eric Clapton, as well as with Herbie Hancock. After forming the John Mayer Trio with bassist Pino Palladino and drummer Steve Jordan (which led to a highly acclaimed live album, *Try!*), Mayer sharpened his work as a guitar virtuoso, winning praise from *Rolling Stone* in 2007 as one of the "New Guitar Gods." In addition to recording two acclaimed solo albums—the Grammy-winning, double-platinum record *Continuum* in 2006, followed three years later by another major commercial success, *Battle Studies*—Mayer threw himself into extramusical enterprises that ranged from philanthropy to writing a music column for *Esquire* magazine.

The Dixie Chicks remained embroiled in the row kicked up by their outspoken stance on the invasion of Iraq in 2003. "We don't feel a part of the country scene any longer, it can't be our home anymore," band member Martie Maguire remarked as the furor continued. Finally, with Rick Rubin producing, the band recorded a new album in 2006, *Taking the Long Way*, which included a hit single whose title summed up the trio's defiant attitude: "Not Ready to Make Nice." Despite a lack of radio airplay, the album sold more than half a million copies in its first week; "Not Ready to Make Nice" won three Grammys, including Song of the Year and Record of the Year, and *Taking the Long Way* won for Best Country Album.

Thereafter, the group starred in a film documentary, *Shut Up and Sing*, for which NBC, citing "public controversy," refused to run an advertisement. The trio then took an extended break, and at decade's end it remained uncertain whether the three would reunite. Still, with the success of "Not Ready to Make Nice," the Dixie Chicks had earned a measure of vindication and clear recognition of the importance of their music. Despite the wrangling, the group sold thirty million albums in the United States, the most by any all-female band in the United States since the Neilsen Sound Scan era began in 1991. Then, during the summer of 2010, the group conducted a stadium concert tour with the Eagles. Early in that year came word that new music by the trio was on the way.

In hip-hop, Nas continued to enjoy artistic success, even as he continued to run into his own controversies. The appearance of the critically acclaimed *Hip-Hop Is Dead* (released by Def Jam but cofinanced by Columbia), followed by a free concert at Virginia Tech after a mass shooting there in 2007, led to attacks by the commentator Bill O'Reilly of the conservative Fox News Network, who denounced Nas as a purveyor of violence. (Nas eventually challenged O'Reilly to a public debate, but O'Reilly declined.) The pattern deepened with Nas's next release in 2008, which featured strongly political tracks. Civil rights leaders as well as O'Reilly and other conservatives denounced the rapper's decision to call the album *Nigger*; Nas finally relented and the album was simply titled *Nas*. Yet despite the flap, the album debuted at number one on the *Billboard* album charts, earned favorable reviews, and was nominated for a Grammy.

Just prior to Ienner's departure, a fresh twist on R&B and soul music, as influenced by hip-hop, emerged in the work of John Legend. Born John Stephens in 1978, Legend attended the University of Pennsylvania and was asked by Lauryn Hill to play piano on one track of her solo album. After graduating in 1999, Legend tried to break into the music business and along the way supplied backup vocals for a number of top-shelf performers, including Kanye West, Alicia Keys, and Jay-Z. In 2004, Sony

"We don't feel a part of the country scene any longer, it can't be our home anymore."

Martie Maguire,
Dixie Chicks

Dixie Chicks

Previous page:
Dixie Chicks

John Legend

released Legend's first proper album, *Get Lifted*, in conjunction with West's G.O.O.D. label. Combining old-fashioned soul-style singing with rap and pop, Legend developed his own blend. Over the rest of the decade, he would record two more studio albums, try his hand at acting on television, and lend his talents to political causes (including the Obama campaign in 2008) and philanthropic efforts. His musical interests also took him outside the conventional limits of R&B and hip-hop, including collaborations with the Brazilian singer Ana Carolina and Noel Schajris, formerly of the Mexican duo Sin Bandera ("Without a Flag"). The most auspicious of the collaborations, with the neo-soul/R&B band the Roots, produced the album *Wake Up!* in 2010, which went on to win Grammy awards for Best R&B Album and Best Traditional R&B Vocal Performance (for the track "Hang on in There").

Across the Genres

In other areas where Columbia had once set the standard, the label's long-diminishing recording programs continued to diminish in the face of changing tastes and hard business realities. The relation between supply and demand in the recording industry has always been complicated, but the figures were dismaying for genres that had already been marginalized. Between 1999 and 2007, while rock releases rose from about one-quarter to nearly one-third of all sales, and hip-hop held steady with a little more than 10 percent of the market, jazz recordings declined from 3 percent to a shade over 1 percent, and classical declined from 3.5 to 1.9 percent.

In jazz, the wave of the future turned out to be the so-called smooth jazz style that Grover Washington Jr. had helped initiate as part of his fusion experiments and continued to record for Columbia until his untimely death in 1999. Performers such as Kenny G and David Sanborn became the best-known jazz performers in the country. Apart from a few exceptions, chiefly in metropolitan areas as well as on satellite radio outlets, most of the remaining radio stations that played jazz at all featured a smooth jazz format. (To differentiate themselves, the exceptions claimed to play "real jazz," or words to that effect.)

Steadily, most of the major figures of Columbia jazz, including some of the strongest young lions, fell away to join jazz-oriented labels. From the mid-1990s on, Herbie Hancock recorded for Verve and various other companies, before he started his own label, Hancock Records, in 2010. Wynton Marsalis issued his Pulitzer Prize–winning oratorio, *Blood on the Fields*, in 1997, as well as, five years later, his massive *All Rise (Symphony No. 1)*, commissioned by the New York Philharmonic, but thereafter he recorded mainly for Blue Note. His brother Branford, after ending his stint as director of Columbia Jazz Records in 2002, moved to his own outfit, Marsalis Music. The gifted pianist Marcus Roberts and his trio moved to J-Master; the trumpeter Terence Blanchard moved to Blue Note and other labels. Columbia was not the only major label affected, but the change was all the more dramatic given the label's historic commitment to recording jazz. Diana Krall, the single-greatest breakout jazz artist in the late 1990s, first gained major attention and then thrived recording for Impulse! and Verve. Later young jazz sensations such as Esperanza Spalding made their names on small niche labels.

Still, Columbia could boast a small, highly talented list of jazz artists, headed by the tireless Harry Connick Jr. (whose 2009 album, *Your Songs*, was produced by Clive Davis). In 2005, Sony's classical division released the first album by the eighteen-year-old jazz pianist wunderkind Eldar Djangirov. Born in Kyrgyzstan, heavily influenced by masters such as Art Tatum and Oscar Peterson, Djangirov (best known as Eldar) would go on to record a live album at the respected New York club the Blue Note, as well as fine collections of his own compositions. The trumpeter and composer Chris Botti, whom Columbia picked up from Verve, won a strong following with eleven albums released between 2001 and 2012, playing in a crossover style that was just as accessible as smooth jazz.

Classical music, its relative importance having dwindled steadily since the 1960s, underwent several makeovers during the first two decades of Sony's

Beyoncé, *B'Day*

Beyoncé

ownership—powerful testimony to the dramatic shifts that had overtaken American musical culture during the previous half century. Soon after Columbia's sale to Sony in 1988, the entire classical division, including what had been Columbia Masterworks, was renamed Sony Classical and removed to Hamburg, Germany, where, under the direction of Günther Breest, the label continued to release new recordings of the traditional classical repertoire. In 1995, Sony Classical moved back to New York, now under the leadership of Peter Gelb, who in later years would serve as the managing director of the Metropolitan Opera. Gelb was more drawn to a business model based on crossover releases as well as Broadway original cast recordings and film soundtracks, all complementing the familiar classical catalog. Few if any noted it at the time, but most of the main interests that had driven Goddard Lieberson from the 1940s through the 1960s were now combined in one of Sony's smaller divisions.

Yo-Yo Ma remained at the center of Sony Classical's program, releasing fresh recordings of Bach, Mendelssohn, Brahms, and Strauss, sometimes in collaboration with two other stars, Emanuel Ax (who also recorded for Sony) and Itzhak Perlman— but Ma, too, undertook crossover efforts in which he teamed up with, among others, Bobby McFerrin. (In a very different hybrid, he formed a trio with the bassist Edgar Meyer and violinist Mark O'Connor for two albums, *Appalachia Waltz* and *Appalachian Journey*.) In 1999, Sony Classical picked up the contract of the young violinist Joshua Bell, and, over the ensuing decade, he blossomed into one of the most important new classical stars. Bell recorded works of composers ranging from Beethoven and Debussy to contemporaries including John Corigliano, while he also participated in crossover projects such as the bluegrass-classical album *Short Trip Home*, recorded with Edgar Meyer, Sam Bush, and Mike Marshall. But Sony Classical's bread and butter was its soundtrack releases, including the soundtrack to the blockbuster film *Titanic* (its theme song performed by Céline Dion), as well as original cast recordings of *Hairspray*, *The Producers*, and other Broadway shows.

In 2004, the division became Sony-BMG Masterworks, the one recording department where there was truly a merger between the two corporate giants. Directed by Gilbert Hetherwick , the new Masterworks found itself in charge of the RCA Victor and RCA Victor Red Seal labels—a major addition that remained under Sony's purview after the partnership with BMG ended in 2008. Renamed once again as Sony Masterworks, the division continued to release the work of exciting new performers. Much of this work—including that of the pianist Simone Dinnerstein and the tenor Vittorio Grigolio— was acquired through Sony's global classical department, Sony Classical International, headed by Bogdan Roscic. Still, for all its artistic vitality, classical music, although more commercially viable than jazz, continued to represent just a sliver of the market. Sony Masterworks accordingly stayed alert for the best opportunities for Broadway releases— which would include, in another closing of a circle, an original cast recording of the award-winning Lincoln Center revival in 2008 of *South Pacific*, the same show that had been Columbia's first great original cast LP success nearly sixty years earlier.

Gold in the Vaults

Where Columbia knew it could make good—and ended up doing better than that—was in reissuing older material in its vaults. There was nothing new, of course, about reissues; the label had been exploiting its rich backlist by reissuing recordings by Bessie Smith, Benny Goodman, and others for decades. From 1970 to 1980, Columbia sponsored a series of special John Hammond reissues, whose highlights included important five-volume collections of work by Bessie Smith and (with various orchestras) Lester Young. But with the emergence of the CD came new, comprehensive collections of great artists, complete with extended liner notes. And as the baby-boomer generation aged, there was renewed interest in reissued recordings from the 1960s, including tracks that had been previously unreleased and outtakes of alternate versions of landmark recordings.

The label's expanded CD reissue program kicked off in 1986 and then began anew in 1990 under the name Legacy Recordings. And in the latter year, Columbia

AC/DC

AC/DC receiving plaques to commemorate sales of more than seven million copies of *Black Ice*

Angus Young of AC/DC

issued an important two-CD boxed set containing virtually every surviving bit of music that the blues great Robert Johnson had recorded for Vocalion in 1936 and 1937, including twelve alternate takes. The Johnson project proved to be something of an outlier, even within Legacy's ambitious program. Like the recording industry as a whole, Columbia was generally more interested in reissuing material recorded within relatively recent memory than music dating back to the 1930s and earlier. Much of the Johnson material, meanwhile, had already appeared on two separate reissue collections in 1961 and 1970, both readily available on CD. But Johnson's deep impact on rock, blues, and folk artists, most famously Bob Dylan, Eric Clapton, and the Rolling Stones, made him different—more like a contemporary artist than other performers of his vintage. (An unverifiable but much repeated story told of a midlevel Sony promotion man in the Midwest, arranging for local media interviews, who called New York to ask "if Robert could do a few phoners.") By 1990, meanwhile, Johnson's reputation had extended far beyond music insiders—and the chance to own previously unreleased takes and the remastered originals (as well as copies, included in the accompanying notes, of the only two known photographs of the mysterious genius) brought his old fans in for more. The unanticipated excitement generated by the collection's release and strong early sales in turn redoubled its popularity. Columbia had hoped to sell twenty thousand copies of the set, but the collection would wind up selling more than one million and win a Grammy for Best Historical Recording.

Thereafter, under the leadership of Jeff Jones and with an expert staff that included Steven Berkowitz and Adam Block, Legacy established itself as the preeminent reissue program in the industry. Collections of Bob Dylan's work became a model. The success of the five-album *Biograph* in 1985, with its mixture of old favorites and previously unreleased recordings, may have been Dylan's finest achievement between the mid-1980s and the early 1990s, but it also foreshadowed the Bob Dylan Bootleg series, undertaken in 1991, consisting of previously unreleased material and important concert recordings. Some of this material had long been circulating among collectors and fans as illicit bootlegs (hence the name for the series). By bringing to listeners optimally produced recordings of such landmark concerts as the stormy, shocking "electric" performance at the Manchester Free Trade Hall in 1966 and the acoustic concert at Philharmonic Hall two years earlier, the series did a great deal to reignite interest in Dylan's work.

Among Legacy's most remarkable reissue endeavors was its rerelease of Miles Davis's *Kind of Blue* (on vinyl as well as CD), to commemorate the fiftieth anniversary of the album's original appearance in 1959. By including false starts, studio sequences, and other bonus tracks, Legacy showed something of how Davis and his band put the recording together, offering listeners a historical document as well as a retrospective of the best-selling album in jazz history. Nine years earlier, in 2000, Legacy released the complete recordings of Louis Armstrong with the Hot Five and Hot Seven, a four-CD set (also including alternate takes) of what many critics still regard as the most creative recording sessions in jazz history. Longstanding Columbia traditions—dating to 1939, when George Avakian mulled over discarded masters in Bridgeport, and even further back, to Armstrong and his bandmates recordings for OKeh in Chicago in the late 1920s—had been updated as well as revived.

Meanwhile, in 2008, Legacy gained access to recordings not originally released on Columbia or Epic, including releases on RCA Victor, Arista, and Buddah Records, and began to supplement Columbia's original rich holdings with reissues of work by artists ranging from Jefferson Airplane to the classical guitarist Christopher Parkening. In line with their earlier collections, Legacy's producers supplemented tracks already officially released with alternate takes and rehearsal material.

The Latest Revolution: Grappling with the New Digital World

If the past looked and sounded richer than ever, though, the future still seemed nebulous and sometimes even gloomy, not just for Columbia but for the entire recording

Yo-Yo Ma

industry. Efforts by the labels to stamp out file sharing failed dismally to halt the decline in sales, despite some victories in the courts for the recording companies along the way. Indeed, those court battles, on balance, were public relations debacles, pitting the recording industry Goliaths against scrappy Davids like Napster—and ultimately against the industry's own consumers, who were downloading eagerly.

The effects of Internet distribution, as well as of increasingly accessible digital technologies, proved to be intense. Giant record store chains, which were once important arbiters of taste and commerce, went bankrupt as customers started making their purchases online. Recording artists began depending on their tour revenues (and related income from merchandise like T-shirts and posters), which made the major tour promoters more important than ever. New and inexpensive recording techniques enabled performers to bypass studios altogether and record in their living rooms, although without the expertise of experienced professionals. By decade's end, the basic structures of recording music seemed to be crumbling: in Los Angeles alone, reportedly half of the city's recording facilities failed in 2009. Listeners began buying the bulk of their music in the form of digital downloads. Sony's Andrew Lack, alone among the recording company heads, saw how Apple and iTunes, especially, stood to take undue advantage, but his efforts to secure profits from iPod sales failed. Early in 2010, Apple announced that ten billion tracks had been downloaded from its iTunes store, to which Columbia had made its material available since the store began in 2003.

The rise of the Swedish-based music streaming service Spotify further accelerated the Internet revolution. Launched in the United States in July 2011, Spotify offered some fifteen million songs and other pieces of music from the major record companies (including Sony) as well as most of the important independents, either free of charge or with a nominal monthly fee for enhanced service. Open fully for integration with iTunes and the various new so-called social media, including Facebook and Twitter, Spotify promised to make virtually the entire universe of recorded music accessible to computers and smartphones at the touch of a few buttons.

The benefits to consumers of peer-to-peer sharing and direct purchase were enormous, maximizing choice and minimizing expense. By giving listeners that unprecedented choice in obtaining recorded music, the changes spurred the growth of niche labels, which permitted performers to reach markets previously inaccessible to them. The ease with which virtually any performer, right down to semi-amateur garage bands and guitar pickers, could bypass the recording companies and produce digital recordings of reasonable and even excellent quality meant that an overwhelming abundance of recorded music was suddenly everywhere. As Internet downloading began supplanting the purchase of CDs, thereby ending the exchange of a physical object, it became less clear exactly what it was the recording industry was selling. The technology could not be undone or controlled. In 2012, all of the major labels are still struggling to adapt. Talk of the recording industry's imminent demise has grown louder.

Yet today is hardly the first time that observers from inside as well as outside the recording industry have forecast the industry's doom. At the beginning of the 1920s, and even more so during the Great Depression, radio's eradication of commercial recordings seemed assured. And even if it provides little instruction, let alone comfort, the long history of Columbia Records affirms that volatility and uncertainty, sometimes extreme, have been the rule and not the exception for the recording industry from the start. Apart from the confident years between 1945 and 1960, when it established its ascendancy in part because of the LP, Columbia has had to face fundamental changes, technological as well as artistic, that, in the moment, seemed to threaten the company's future severely—from the switch from cylinder to discs, to the rise of radio, to the musical revolutions of the late 1960s. Although it struggled for much of its first half century, Columbia survived and then flourished, in part because of its hardnosed business maneuvering, and in part because it tried to stay at the vanguard of technical and institutional as well as artistic change.

Two great advantages that the major recording labels continue to enjoy, none more so than Columbia, are their respected imprimaturs as well as the resources at their command to record and then market artists with broad appeal. It is one thing to record music inexpensively and make it readily available in cyberspace; it is quite

Chris Botti

Joshua Bell

another to make that music stand out from the enormous new field of competition and bring it the attention it deserves. Columbia has aimed to build on these advantages by remaining at the forefront in as many areas as it can. To augment its executive talent, the label in 2010 added Ashley Newton, formerly of Island Records, Virgin Records, U.K. and RCA, as president of Columbia Records. And Columbia has sought out an eclectic collection of younger performers, while it has aggressively pursued new business and marketing strategies.

Perhaps the most promising of these new acts is the British singer-songwriter Adele, signed in partnership with the British independent label XL. Born in north London in 1988, Adele Laurie Blue Adkins began singing as a young girl, impersonating the Spice Girls, and she wrote her first recorded song, "Hometown Glory," at age sixteen. The success of that single, released in October 2007, led to her first album, *19*, released by Columbia in the United States, which featured another powerful single, "Chasing Pavements" as well as a moving rendition of Bob Dylan's "Make You Feel My Love." The album would go on to win two Grammys in 2009, for Best New Artist and Best Female Pop Vocal Performance (for "Chasing Pavements").

As adept in jazz and pop styling as in folk and country, Adele has fashioned a distinct sound, which she describes as "heartbroken soul." Her alluring blend initially lacked any obvious musical niche, especially for radio airplay. So Columbia decided, early on, to publicize her work gradually, with carefully selected appearances on television as well as touring engagements that would build her appeal at the grassroots. The strategy worked—and Adele's second album, *21*, topped the charts in more than thirty countries and sold more than ten million copies in the U.S.

Columbia has also pursued deals with other media outfits, both in and out of music recording. In 2009, the company began a joint venture with Jay-Z's new Roc Nation label; two years later, the first artist signed, the charismatic young rapper J. Cole, debuted at number one on the *Billboard* Album chart. In 2010, Sony formalized its association with Simon Cowell and began moving heavily into new departures in television programming. Recalling its expansion of its audience base, decades earlier, on radio, Columbia now attempted to capitalize on the boom in cable television that had accompanied the proliferation of the Internet.

In June 2007, Columbia announced an expansive global partnership with the young viewers' cable network Nickelodeon to combine pop music and television in fresh ways, which allowed Columbia to produce and finance music-themed TV shows. Columbia has also been alert to other developments in television, signing Susan Boyle, the overnight sensation from the reality program *Britain's Got Talent*, who released an extremely successful album, *I Dreamed a Dream*, in 2009—very nearly the best-selling album of the year even though it only appeared at the end of November. Boyle's second album, a Christmas collection titled *The Gift*, debuted at number one in both the United States and Great Britain, only the third album ever to do so. A Simon Cowell creation, the multinational operatic pop group Il Divo, sold more than 26 million albums and DVDs worldwide by the end of 2011, blending classical favorites with contemporary songs.

Columbia's involvement in the Fox Network's musical comedy-drama series *Glee*, beginning in 2009, has been even more remarkable as a business success. Focused on a fictional high school glee club, the series depicts individual characters dealing with perennial problems of love and sex as well as social issues against the backdrop of their club's efforts to compete on the championship choral group circuit. A carefully crafted blend of edgy drama and music, *Glee* quickly became an entertainment phenomenon, creating spin-offs in books, DVDs, apparel, greeting cards, and other merchandise along with musical recordings. The music's commercial success, though (with Columbia releasing the album versions of *Glee*'s recordings), has been astonishing. In 2009 alone, 25 songs by the *Glee* cast reached *Billboard*'s Hot 100 list, the most by any artist since the Beatles had 31 in 1964. Two years later, *Glee* surpassed Elvis Presley's record of 108 entries in the Hot 100. And while thirteen million copies of the singles were downloaded digitally through iTunes, the cast's soundtrack albums sold more than twelve million copies worldwide by May 2012, to go along with forty-five million singles sold worldwide.

Jack White

Doug Morris, Steve Barnett, Rob Stringer, and Jonathan Dickins presenting a plaque to Adele commemorating sales of *21*

Women Take Center Stage

The songs took a tough look at reality and kept an eye on what it cost to shake free

As the age of rock waned in the late eighties and early nineties, women stepped up to claim the center of pop music.

In the first hundred years of recorded music, there had never been a time when a group of female artists had occupied the creative center. But the female artists who emerged from the late nineties onward defined what the pop of the next twenty years sounded like, and what its songs talked about. Singing was the focus. The songs took a tough look at reality and kept an eye on what it cost to shake free.

Four Columbia acts were key to this change: Mariah Carey; Destiny's Child and its lead figure, Beyoncé; the Dixie Chicks; and Adele.

More than any female vocalist since Aretha Franklin, Mariah Carey, with her extreme phrasing and pitch—she went to the highest heights in her falsetto, and stayed there while extending syllables until they droned—inspired a new generation of singers. (A listen to any televised talent contest will prove it.) Carey's career was way ahead of this trend: she began making records in 1990, when rock still ruled, but she fits in here because she stayed hot for seven consecutive years.

Destiny's Child, the most important female vocal group since the Supremes, appeared in 1997, broke up in 2004, and took a feminist stance all the way through. The solo career of its lead singer Beyoncé now overshadows the group's accomplishments, but she operates individually on the same feminist principle.

In 1998 came the Dixie Chicks, a trio with pop-bluegrass harmonies who scored far more with pop audiences than country ones. Their militancy resulted in a platinum single, "Goodbye Earl," in 2000, and the near-destruction of their career due to opposition to President George W. Bush in 2004. Natalie Maines possesses an amazing voice but the Chicks are a group in sound and spirit.

Adele has made only two albums, the first, *19*, in 2008, and the second, *21*, in 2010. The first was a hit, the latter a massive one. At her best, she has a barbed tone that recalls Janis Joplin and Bob Dylan, but with more finesse. She belongs with this group because she's an original, and she's an original because she's herself.

Dave Marsh

Adele

"Synergy" became an overused word early in the new millennium, but the *Glee* craze has shown exactly how synergy might work—and offered one business model for how Columbia and the other labels could adapt to the digital age. Yet how, exactly, the pursuit of profits will continue to mesh with the pursuit of musical excellence—what sorts of musical sounds the new synergy will encourage and endorse—remain unknowable. So does the future of the nonspecialized, general-music recording labels of the sort Columbia has been for its entire existence.

One indication of Columbia's future direction came in March 2011, when Howard Stringer appointed the industry veteran Doug Morris as CEO of Sony Music Entertainment. Morris had helped to shape the recording industry's development for more than forty years, as a songwriter and producer as well as executive. His appointment by Stringer made Morris the only person to date to head the three largest recording companies, Warner Music, Universal Music, and Sony.

Further signs about where Columbia was headed, as well as remembrances of its glorious past, came during the early months of 2012. Among the heritage artists, Leonard Cohen's *Old Ideas*, released on January 31, received rave reviews and reached the top of the sales charts in more than a dozen countries around the world—the highest charting debut of Cohen's career. A few weeks later, Bruce Springsteen's *Wrecking Ball*, another great success with the critics, debuted at number one in sixteen countries, Springsteen's fifth number one in ten years. In February 2012, Columbia extended what had become the longest and most successful connection in the history of recorded music when it announced the re-signing of Barbra Streisand. In the tradition of adding major established artists to its list, Columbia reached an agreement with the dazzling, at times enigmatic, multi-talented rocker Jack White. In April 2012, the label released *Blunderbuss*, which debuted at number one, in conjuction with White's own Third Man Records. White could have had his pick of record labels but chose Columbia because, he told one interviewer, "[its] history is amazing. They're the first record label. The first." Columbia, he remarked, has been the home of so many artists he admires, above all Bob Dylan; it also has "the kind of muscle" required to gain the widest possible audience. Another reminder of the label's legacy, now poignant, came with the passing of the banjo pioneer and country music artist supreme Earl Scruggs at age 88, in late March.

Heading into the 2012 Grammys, Columbia's executives could look back over the previous year with great satisfaction, having ended 2011 as the number one record label overall with a 9.39 percent share of the current U.S. album market. But the new year continued to bring commercial affirmations of Columbia's approach to the new digital age, combining its heritage artists with fresh new acts, including some that had evolved in other media. In March, the new British pop boy quartet One Direction, having emerged out of Simon Cowell's U.K. television showcase *X-Factor*, saw their album *Up All Night* debut at number one on the *Billboard* chart, the first British group ever to claim that distinction. With unprecedented buzz on social media, some ten thousand young fans mobbed the *Today* show's outdoor plaza in Rockefeller Center for the group's American television debut, the frenzy evoking to some observers long-ago memories of Beatlemania. Overall, Columbia claimed the top spot on the album charts for the first twelve weeks of 2012.

The 2012 Grammy Awards, meanwhile, became something of a celebration of Columbia's popular recording program. At 85, Tony Bennett, the grand master of Columbia recording stars, won his fifteenth and sixteenth awards, the first for *Duets II* in the category of Best Traditional Pop Vocal Album, and the second for the rendition off of that album of "Body and Soul" with the late Amy Winehouse, as Best Pop Duo/Vocal Performance. And at the other end of the chronological spectrum, Adele swept all six categories in which she was nominated, including the recording industry's triple crown of Album of the Year (for *21*), Song of the Year, and Record of the Year (both for "Rolling in the Deep"). It capped a year in which *21* was also the most popular album in the world, selling twenty million copies worldwide.

For decades, Columbia's emphasis on combining tradition and innovation has been a key to its overall achievements. Another key has been its accumulated prestige. But there is still another factor, a delicate balance among commercial imperatives,

Simon Cowell (center) with One Direction

The cast of *Glee* receiving plaques to commemorate sales

The cast of *Glee*

artistic discrimination, and sheer love of music, which the label has managed to sustain. "Signing to Columbia was a no-brainer really," Adele has remarked, given, she says, that Rob Stringer and Steve Barnett are "still huge fans of the music. Of course, they have their responsibilities and targets to meet but they still love music for the same reason everybody else does, and I haven't met many record company execs of huge labels that still feel like that." Times and tastes have changed enormously, but as in the days of Frank Walker, John Hammond, Art Satherley, Goddard Lieberson, and their contemporaries, so, today, Columbia heeds the principle that if you get the music right, the business comes right. Or, as Adele has put it, Columbia remains a singular musical enterprise in an industry where "most artists can't stand the suits."

Columbia at 125: The Label of Modern Life

In 1889, when Columbia began seriously recording music, the United States was only beginning to establish itself as an international power; most Americans still lived in rural areas; slavery had been dead for barely more than a generation (and racial segregation was about to be given federal sanction); and Americans were still striving to produce music and art that was worthy of international notice. A cultural eon has passed since then.

From the start, though, Columbia Records was a force for cultural change as well as a source of entertainment. Beginning with the perceptive and aggressive businessman Edward Easton, the label pioneered in turning recorded sound into a form of mass musical enjoyment. Over the decades that followed, it recorded many of the greatest artists of modern times, who redefined entire genres of musical composition and performance from classical to every conceivable form of popular music. While pursuing profits, Columbia helped open up vital cultural channels that once were blocked, breaking down walls of cultural ignorance and prejudice. Beginning with its experiments during the cylinder era, Columbia also made vital contributions to the technology of recorded sound that transformed the ways in which artists conceived of their works and their listeners experienced them.

It is impossible to think of America—or, for that matter, to think of modern life—without the music of Al Jolson, Bessie Smith, Louis Armstrong, Frank Sinatra, Leonard Bernstein, Miles Davis, Barbra Streisand, Bob Dylan, and dozens of other giants. And so it is impossible to imagine modern life without Columbia Records, the graphophone company that survived depressions, wars, and, more than once, near-extinction to bring all that music to the world. There are other great recording labels, but none with a longer or richer history of accomplishment.

Now, in its anniversary year, Columbia faces challenges involving nothing less than whether the recording industry will survive. Columbia is still the home to some of the foremost musical performers of our time, and it is still the label that many emerging stars would like to call home. Fulfilling its commitments to musical excellence as well as financial success will require unprecedented acuity and innovation in the digital era. But the label has had to redefine itself many times before, going all the way back to when recorded talk and music consisted of scratches on wax cylinders. Experience since then suggests that however future soundscapes may sound and however people may listen to them, Columbia, in one form or another, will enjoy many more anniversaries to come.

—April 30, 2012

Adele

Adele with Howard Stringer, Steve Barnett, Rob Stringer, and Doug Morris

Previous page:
Adele

Bruce Springsteen

BRUCE SPRINGSTEEN WORKING ON A DREAM

train
SAVE ME, SAN FRANCISCO

I Dreamed A Dream
SUSAN BOYLE

h

Passion Pit
MANNERS

AC/DC
BLACK ICE

BRUCE SPRING STEEN WRECKING BALL

WN

DIXIE CHICKS
TAKING THE LONG WAY

J COLE COLE WORLD THE SIDELINE STORY

olvin

Born AND Raised
Music BY JOHN MAYER
IN STEREO Recorded SOUND

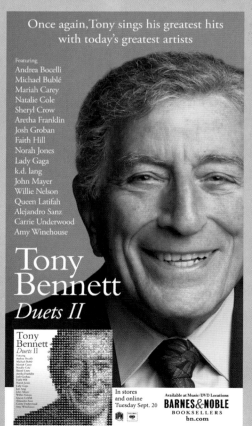

Once again, Tony sings his greatest hits with today's greatest artists

Featuring
Andrea Bocelli
Michael Bublé
Mariah Carey
Natalie Cole
Sheryl Crow
Aretha Franklin
Josh Groban
Faith Hill
Norah Jones
Lady Gaga
k.d. lang
John Mayer
Willie Nelson
Queen Latifah
Alejandro Sanz
Carrie Underwood
Amy Winehouse

Tony Bennett
Duets II

In stores and online Tuesday Sept. 20

Available at Music/DVD Locations
BARNES & NOBLE
BOOKSELLERS
bn.com

MGMT

ISRAEL
HOUGHTON

AEROSMITH
HONKIN' ON BOBO

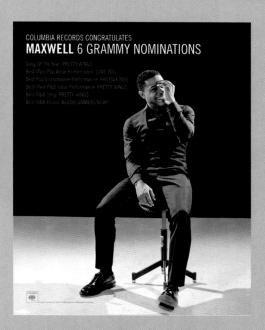

GRAMMY Awards

1960

Best Musical Composition First Recorded and Released in 1959: "Anatomy of a Murder," No Artist

Best Performance by a Vocal Group or Chorus: "Battle Hymn of the Republic," Richard Condie

Best Soundtrack Album, Original Cast—Motion Picture or Television: *Porgy and Bess*, Ken Darby/ Andre Previn

Best Performance by a Dance Band: "Anatomy of a Murder," Duke Ellington

Song of the Year: "The Battle of New Orleans," Johnny Horton

Best Country & Western Performance: "The Battle of New Orleans," Johnny Horton

Best Broadway Show Album: *Gypsy*, Ethel Merman

Best Performance, Documentary, or Spoken Word (Other Than Comedy): "A Lincoln Portrait," Carl Sandburg

Best Soundtrack Album, Background Score from Motion Picture: *Anatomy of a Murder*, Soundtrack

1961

Best Jazz Composition of More Than Five Minutes' Duration: "Sketches of Spain," No Artist

Record of the Year: "Theme from *A Summer Place*," Percy Faith

Best Performance by a Chorus (Seven or More): "Songs of the Cowboy," Norman Luboff Choir

Best Country & Western Performance: "El Paso," Marty Robbins

Best Show Album (Original Cast): *The Sound of Music*, Soundtrack

Best Comedy Performance, Musical: *Jonathan and Darlene Edwards in Paris,* Jo Stafford/ Paul Weston

1962

Best Documentary or Spoken Word Recording (Other Than Comedy): *Humor in Music*, Leonard Bernstein

Album of the Year, Classical: *Stravinsky Conducts 1960: Le Sacre Du Printemps; Petrouchka*, Columbia Symphony Orchestra (Igor Stravinsky)

Best Contemporary Classical Composition: *Stravinsky: Movements for Piano and Orchestra*, Columbia Symphony Orchestra (Igor Stravinsky)

Best Country & Western Recording: "Big Bad John," Jimmy Dean

Best Gospel or Other Religious Recording: "Everytime I Feel the Spirit," Mahalia Jackson

Best Performance by a Vocal Group: "High Flying," Lambert, Hendricks & Ross

Best Recording for Children: *Prokofiev: Peter and the Wolf*, New York Philharmonic (Leonard Bernstein)

Best Soundtrack Album or Recording of Original Cast from Motion Picture: *West Side Story*, Soundtrack

Best Classical Performance, Instrumental Soloist(s) (With Orchestra): *Bartok: Violin Concerto No. 1*, Isaac Stern

1963

Best Background Arrangement: "I Left My Heart in San Francisco," No Artist

Best Solo Vocal Performance, Male: "I Left My Heart in San Francisco," Tony Bennett

Record of the Year: "I Left My Heart in San Francisco," Tony Bennett

Best Classical Composition by a Contemporary Composer: *Stravinsky: The Flood*, Columbia Symphony Orchestra & Chorus (Igor Stravinsky)/ Various Artists

Best Classical Performance, Orchestra: *Stravinsky: The Firebird Ballet*, Columbia Symphony Orchestra (Igor Stravinsky)

Best Classical Performance, Vocal Soloist (With or Without Orchestra): *Wagner: Gotterdammerung— Brunnhilde's Immolation Scene/Wese*, Eileen Farrell

Best New Artist: Robert Goulet

Album of the Year, Classical: *Columbia Records Presents Vladimir Horowitz*, Vladimir Horowitz

Best Classical Performance, Instrumental Soloist or Duo (Without Orchestra): *Columbia Records Presents Vladimir Horowitz*, Vladimir Horowitz

Best Gospel or Other Religious Recording: *Great Songs of Love and Faith*, Mahalia Jackson

Best Performance by a Chorus: *Presenting the New Christy Minstrels*, New Christy Minstrels

Best Recording for Children: *Saint-Saens: Carnival of the Animals/Britten: Young Person's Guide to the Orchestra*, New York Philharmonic (Leonard Bernstein)

Best Classical Performance, Instrumental Soloist(s) (With or Without Orchestra): *Stravinsky: Violin Concerto in D*, Isaac Stern

1964

Best Album Notes: *The Ellington Era*, Duke Ellington

Best Classical Performance, Instrumental Soloist or Duo (Without Orchestra): *The Sound of Horowitz*, Vladimir Horowitz

Best Recording for Children: *Bernstein Conducts for Young People*, New York Philharmonic (Leonard Bernstein)

Album of the Year: *The Barbra Streisand Album*, Barbra Streisand

Best Album Cover: *The Barbra Streisand Album*, Barbra Streisand

Best Vocal Performance, Female: *The Barbra Streisand Album*, Barbra Streisand

Most Promising New Classical Recording Artist: Andre Watts

1965

Best Accompaniment Arrangement: "People," No Artist

Best Classical Composition by a Contemporary Composer, Piano: *Barber: Piano Concerto*, John Browning

Best Album Notes: *Mexico (Legacy Collection)*, Carlos Chavez

Best Chamber Performance, Instrumental: *Beethoven: Trio No. 1 in E Flat, Op. 1 No. 1*, Jascha Heifetz/ Gregor Piatigorsky

Best Classical Performance, Instrumental Soloist(s) (Without Orchestra): *Vladimir Horowitz Plays Beethoven, Debussy, Chopin*, Vladimir Horowitz

Album of the Year, Classical: *Bernstein: Symphony No. 3 Kaddish*, New York Philharmonic (Leonard Bernstein)

Best Album Cover: *People*, Soundtrack

Best Classical Performance, Instrumental Soloist(s) (With or Without Orchestra): *Prokofiev: Violin Concerto No. 1 in D*, Isaac Stern

Best Vocal Performance, Female: *People*, Barbra Streisand

1966

Best Classical Performance, Orchestra: *Ives: Symphony No. 4*, American Symphony Orchestra (Leopold Stokowski)

Best Composition by a Contemporary Classical Composer: *Ives: Symphony No. 4*, American Symphony Orchestra (Leopold Stokowski)

Song of the Year: "The Shadow of Your Smile," Tony Bennett

Album of the Year, Classical: *Horowitz at Carnegie Hall (An Historic Return)*, Vladimir Horowitz

Best Classical Performance, Instrumental Soloist(s) (Without Orchestra): *Horowitz at Carnegie Hall (An Historic Return)*, Vladimir Horowitz

Best Engineered Recording, Classical: *Horowitz at Carnegie Hall (An Historic Return)*, Vladimir Horowitz

Best Classical Chamber Music Performance, Instrumental or Vocal: *Bartok: The Six String Quartets*, Juilliard String Quartet

Best Spoken Word or Drama Recording: *John F. Kennedy— As We Remember Him*, Goddard Lieberson

Best New Country & Western Artist: The Statler Brothers

Best Contemporary (R&B) Group Performance, Vocal or Instrumental: "The Flowers on the Wall," The Statler Brothers

Best Vocal Performance, Female: *My Name Is Barbra*, Barbra Streisand

1967

Best Classical Choral Performance (Other Than Opera): *Ives: Music for Chorus*, George Bragg/Gregg Smith/Columbia Chamber Orchestra/Ithaca

Best Performance by a Chorus: "Somewhere My Love," Ray Conniff Singers

Best Vocal Performance, Female: "If He Walked into My Life," Eydie Gorme

Best Spoken Word, Documentary, or Drama Recording: *Edward R. Murrow— A Reporter Remembers, Vol. 1 the War Years*, Edward R. Murrow

Best Score from an Original Cast Show Album: *Mame*, Original Broadway Cast

1968

Album of the Year, Classical: *Berg: Wozzeck*, Pierre Boulez/Paris National Opera

Best Opera Recording: *Berg: Wozzeck*, Pierre Boulez/Paris National Opera

Best Country & Western Performance, Duet, Trio, or Group (Vocal): "Jackson," June Carter/Johnny Cash

Best Album Cover, Photography: *Bob Dylan's Greatest Hits*, Bob Dylan

Best Classical Performance, Instrumental Soloist(s) (With or Without Orchestra): *Horowitz in Concert*, Vladimir Horowitz

Album of the Year, Classical: *Mahler: Symphony No. 8 in E Flat Major*, London Symphony Orchestra (Leonard Bernstein)

Best Classical Choral Performance (Other Than Opera): *Mahler: Symphony No. 8 in E Flat Major*, London Symphony Orchestra (Leonard Bernstein)

Best Score from an Original Cast Show Album: *Cabaret*, Original Cast

Best Classical Choral Performance (Other Than Opera): *Orff: Catulli Carmina*, Eugene Ormandy/ Robert Page/Temple University Chorus/ Philharmonic Orchestra

Best Classical Performance, Orchestra: *Stravinsky: Firebird & Petrouchka Suites*, Igor Stravinsky

1969

Best Chamber Music Performance: *Gabrieli: Canzoni for Brass, Winds, Strings & Organ*, E. Powers Biggs/ Edward Tarr Brass/Vittorio Negri/Gabrieli Consort

Best Choral Performance (Other Than Opera): "The Glory of Gabrieli," George Bragg/ Vittorio Negri/ Gregg Smith Singers/Texas Boys

Best Male Country Vocal Performance: "Folsom Prison Blues," Johnny Cash

Best Album Notes: *Johnny Cash at Folsom Prison*, Johnny Cash

Best Country Performance by a Duo or Group, Vocal or Instrumental: "Foggy Mountain Breakdown," Flatt & Scruggs

Best Classical Performance, Instrumental Soloist(s) (With or Without Orchestra): *Horowitz on Television*, Vladimir Horowitz

Best Album Cover: *Underground*, Thelonious Monk

Best Classical Performance, Orchestra: *Boulez Conducts Debussy*, New Philharmonic Orchestra/ Pierre Boulez

Best Contemporary Pop Performance, Vocal Duo, or Group: "Mrs. Robinson," Simon & Garfunkel

Record of the Year: "Mrs. Robinson," Simon & Garfunkel

Best Country Song: "Little Green Apples," O.C. Smith

Song of the Year: "Little Green Apples," O.C. Smith

Best Original Score Written for a Motion Picture or a Television Special: *The Graduate*, Soundtrack

1970

Best Choral Performance (Other Than Opera): *Berio: Sinfonia*, Luciano Berio/ Ward Swingle/Swingle Singers/New York Philharmonic

Album of the Year: *Blood, Sweat & Tears*, Blood, Sweat & Tears

Best Arrangement Accompanying Vocalist(s): "Spinning Wheel," Blood, Sweat & Tears

Best Contemporary Instrumental Performance: "Variations on a Theme by Eric Satie," Blood, Sweat & Tears

Best Country Song: "A Boy Named Sue," Johnny Cash

Best Male Country Vocal Performance: "A Boy Named Sue," Johnny Cash

Best Chamber Music Performance: *Gabrieli: Antiphonal Music of Gabrieli*, Chicago Brass/ Cleveland Brass/Philadelphia Brass

Best Classical Performance, Orchestra: *Boulez Conducts Debussy, Vol. 2 "Images Pour Orchestre,"* Cleveland Orchestra (Pierre Boulez)

Best Album Notes: *Nashville Skyline*, Bob Dylan

Best Contemporary Performance by a Chorus: "Love Theme from *Romeo & Juliet*," Percy Faith Orchestra & Chorus

1971

Best Female Country Vocal Performance: "Rose Garden," Lynn Anderson

Best Country Vocal Performance by a Duo or Group: "Rose Garden," June Carter/Johnny Cash

Best Engineered Recording, Classical: *Stravinsky: Le Sacre Du Printemps*, Cleveland Orchestra & Chorus (Pierre Boulez)

Best Classical Performance, Orchestra: *Stravinsky: Le Sacre Du Printemps*, Cleveland Orchestra & Chorus (Pierre Boulez)

Best Jazz Performance, Large Group or Soloist with Large Group: *Bitches Brew*, Miles Davis

Best Chamber Music Performance: *Beethoven: The Complete Piano Trios*, Eugene Istomin/Leonard Rose/ Isaac Stern

Best Recording for Children: *Sesame Street*, The Muppets

Best Score from an Original Cast Show Album: *Company*, Original Cast

Best Male Country Vocal Performance: "For the Good Times," Ray Price

Best Country Song: "My Woman, My Woman, My Wife," Marty Robbins

Album of the Year: *Bridge over Troubled Water*, Simon & Garfunkel

Best Engineered Recording, Non-Classical: *Bridge over Troubled Water*, Simon & Garfunkel

Best Arrangement Accompanying Vocalist(s): "Bridge over Troubled Water," Simon & Garfunkel

Record of the Year: "Bridge over Troubled Water," Simon & Garfunkel

Song of the Year: "Bridge over Troubled Water," Simon & Garfunkel

Best Album Notes: *World's Greatest Blues Singer*, Bessie Smith

Best Choral Performance (Other Than Opera): *Ives: New Music of Charles Ives*, Gregg Smith/ Gregg Smith Singers/Columbia Chamber Ensemble

Best Contemporary Song: "Bridge over Troubled Water," Simon & Garfunkel

1972

Best Jazz Performance by a Group: *The Bill Evans Album*, Bill Evans Trio

Best Jazz Performance by a Soloist: *The Bill Evans Album*, Bill Evans Trio

Album of the Year, Classical: *Horowitz Plays Rachmaninoff (Etudes—Tableaux Piano Music)*, Vladimir Horowitz

Best Classical Performance, Instrumental Soloist(s) (Without Orchestra): *Horowitz Plays Rachmaninoff (Etudes—Tableaux Piano Music)*, Vladimir Horowitz

Best Chamber Music Performance: *Debussy: Quartet in G Minor/Ravel: Quartet in F*, Juilliard String Quartet

Best R&B Song: "Ain't No Sunshine," Bill Withers

1973

Best Instrumental Arrangement: "Theme from *The French Connection*," Don Ellis Big Band

Best Classical Performance, Instrumental Soloist(s) (Without Orchestra): *Horowitz Plays Chopin*, Vladimir Horowitz

1974

Best Album Notes, Classical: *Hindemith: Sonatas for Piano (Complete)*, Glenn Gould

Best Classical Performance, Instrumental Soloist(s) (Without Orchestra): *Scriabin: Horowitz Plays Scriabin*, Vladimir Horowitz

Best R&B Instrumental Performance: "Hang on Sloopy," Ramsey Lewis

Album of the Year, Classical: *Bartok: Concerto for Orchestra*, New York Philharmonic (Pierre Boulez)

Best Classical Performance, Orchestra: *Bartok: Concerto for Orchestra*, New York Philharmonic (Pierre Boulez)

Best Engineered Recording, Classical: *Bartok: Concerto for Orchestra*, New York Philharmonic (Pierre Boulez)

Best Score from an Original Cast Show Album: *A Little Night Music*, Original Cast

Best Recording for Children: *Sesame Street Live*, Sesame Street Cast/Various Artists

Album of Best Original Score Written for a Motion Picture or Television Special: *Jonathan Livingston Seagull*, Soundtrack

1975

Best Gospel Performance: "The Baptism of Jesse Taylor," The Oak Ridge Boys

Best Score from an Original Cast Show Album: *Raisin*, Original Cast

Album of Best Original Score Written for a Motion Picture or Television Special: *The Way We Were*, Soundtrack

Song of the Year: "The Way We Were," Barbra Streisand

1976

Best Classical Vocal Soloist Performance: *Mahler: Kindertotenlieder*, Janet Baker

Best Engineered Recording, Classical: *Ravel: Daphnis Et Chloe (Complete Ballet)*, Camarata Singers/New York Philharmonic (Pierre Boulez)

Best Album Notes: *Blood on the Tracks*, Bob Dylan

Best R&B Vocal Performance by a Group: "Shining Star," Earth, Wind & Fire

Best Female Pop Vocal Performance: "At Seventeen," Janis Ian

Best Engineered Recording, Non-Classical: *Between the Lines*, Janis Ian

Best Male Country Vocal Performance: "Blue Eyes Crying in the Rain," Willie Nelson

Best Classical Performance, Orchestra: *Ravel: Daphnis Et Chloe (Complete Ballet)*, New York Philharmonic (Pierre Boulez)

Best Choral Performance, Classical: *Orff: Carmina Burana*, Robert Page/ Michael Thomas/Cleveland Orchestra & Choirs

Best Album Notes, Classical: *Footlifters*, Gunther Schuller

Album of the Year: *Still Crazy After All These Years*, Paul Simon

Best Male Pop Vocal Performance: *Still Crazy After All These Years*, Paul Simon

1977

Best Album Package: *Chicago X*, Chicago

Best Arrangement Accompanying Vocalist(s): "If You Leave Me Now," Chicago

Best Pop Vocal Performance by a Duo, Group, or Chorus: "If You Leave Me Now," Chicago

Best Engineered Recording, Classical: *Gershwin: Rhapsody In Blue*, Columbia Jazz Band (Michael Tilson Thomas)

Best Soul Gospel Performance: "How I Got Over," Mahalia Jackson

Best Gospel Performance (Other Than Soul Gospel): "Where the Soul Never Dies," The Oak Ridge Boys

Best R&B Song: "Lowdown," Boz Scaggs

1978

Album of the Year, Classical: *Concert of the Century*, Bernstein/Fischer-Dieskau/Horowitz/Menuhin/Stern

Best R&B Vocal Performance by a Group: "Best of My Love," The Emotions

1979

Best Album Notes: *A Bing Crosby Collection, Vols. 1 & 2*, Bing Crosby

Best R&B Vocal Performance by a Duo, Group, or Chorus: "All 'n All," Earth, Wind & Fire

Best Arrangement Accompanying Vocalist(s): "Got to Get You into My Life," Earth, Wind & Fire

Best R&B Instrumental Performance: "Runnin'," Earth, Wind & Fire

Record of the Year: "Just the Way You Are," Billy Joel

Song of the Year: "Just the Way You Are," Billy Joel

Best Male Country Vocal Performance: "Georgia on My Mind," Willie Nelson

Best Cast Show Album: *Ain't Misbehavin'*, Original Cast

Best Historical Repackage Album: *Lester Young Story Vol. 3*, Lester Young

1980

Best Male Rock Vocal Performance: "Gotta Serve Somebody," Bob Dylan

Best R&B Song: "After the Love Has Gone," Earth, Wind & Fire

Best R&B Vocal Performance by a Duo, Group, or Chorus: "After the Love Has Gone," Earth, Wind & Fire

Best Latin Recording: *Irakere*, Irakere

Album of the Year: *52nd Street*, Billy Joel

Best Male Pop Vocal Performance: *52nd Street*, Billy Joel

Best Rock Instrumental Performance: "Rockestra Theme," Paul McCartney/Wings

1981

Best Pop Performance by a Duo or Group with Vocals: "Guilty," Barry Gibb/Barbra Streisand

Best Pop Instrumental Performance: "One on One," Bob James/ Earl Klugh

Best Male Rock Vocal Performance: "Glass Houses," Billy Joel

Best Male Pop Vocal Performance: "This Is It," Kenny Loggins

Best R&B Performance by a Duo or Group with Vocals: "Shining Star," The Manhattans

Best Country Song: "On the Road Again," Willie Nelson

Best Engineered Recording, Non-Classical: *The Wall*, Pink Floyd

1982

Best Album of Original Score Written for a Motion Picture or Television Special: *Raiders of the Lost Ark*, Soundtrack

1983

Best Jazz Instrumental Performance, Soloist: *We Want Miles*, Miles Davis

Best R&B Performance by a Duo or Group with Vocals: "Wanna Be with You," Earth, Wind & Fire

Best Male R&B Vocal Performance: "Sexual Healing," Marvin Gaye

Best R&B Instrumental Performance: "Sexual Healing," Marvin Gaye

Best New Artist: Men at Work

Best Country Song: "Always on My Mind," Willie Nelson

Song of the Year: "Always on My Mind," Willie Nelson

Best Male Country Vocal Performance: "Always on My Mind," Willie Nelson

Best Vocal Arrangement for Two or More Voices: "Rosanna," Toto

Record of the Year: "Rosanna," Toto

Album of the Year: *Toto IV*, Toto

Best Engineered Recording, Non-Classical: *Toto IV*, Toto

Best Recording for Children: *In Harmony 2*, Various Artists

Best Spoken Word, Documentary, or Drama Recording: *Raiders of the Lost Ark: The Movie on Record*, Tom Voegeli

1984

Best R&B Instrumental Performance: "Rockit," Herbie Hancock

Best Jazz Instrumental Performance, Soloist: "Think of One," Wynton Marsalis

1985

Best R&B Instrumental Performance: *Sound-System*, Herbie Hancock

Best Arrangement on an Instrumental: "Grace (Gymnastics Theme)," Quincy Jones

Best Jazz Instrumental Performance, Soloist: "Hot House Flowers," Wynton Marsalis

Best Country Song: "City of New Orleans," Willie Nelson

Best Recording for Children: "Where the Sidewalk Ends," Shel Silverstein

Best Country Instrumental Performance: "Wheel Hoss," Ricky Skaggs

Best Instrumental Composition: *The Natural*, Soundtrack

Best Male Rock Vocal Performance: "Dancing in the Dark," Bruce Springsteen

Best Instrumental Composition: "Olympic Fanfare and Theme," John Williams

1986

Best Country Instrumental Performance: "Cosmic Square Dance," Chet Atkins/Mark Knopfler

Best Reggae Recording: *Cliff Hanger*, Jimmy Cliff

Best Pop Performance by a Duo or Group with Vocals: "We Are the World," Quincy Jones/Prince/USA for Africa

Record of the Year: "We Are the World," Quincy Jones/Prince/USA for Africa

Best Jazz Instrumental Performance, Group: "Black Codes (From the Underground)," Wynton Marsalis

Best Jazz Instrumental Performance, Soloist: "Black Codes (From the Underground)," Wynton Marsalis

Song of the Year: "We Are the World," USA for Africa

Best Chamber Music Performance: *Schoenberg: Quartets for Strings (Complete)*, Juilliard String Quartet

Best Cast Show Album: *Annie*, Original Cast

Best Arrangement Accompanying Vocalist(s): "Evergreen (Love Theme from *A Star is Born*)," Barbra Streisand

Best Female Pop Vocal Performance: "Evergreen (Love Theme from *A Star is Born*)," Barbra Streisand

Song of the Year: "Evergreen (Love Theme from *A Star is Born*)," Barbra Streisand

Best Male Pop Vocal Performance: "Handy Man," James Taylor

1987

Best Pop Instrumental Performance, Orchestra, Group, or Solo: "Top Gun Anthem," Harold Faltermeyer/Steve Stevens

Best Pop Performance by a Duo or Group with Vocals: "That's What Friends Are For," Elton John/Gladys Knight/Dionne Warwick/Stevie Wonder

Song of the Year: "That's What Friends Are For," Elton John/Gladys Knight/Dionne Warwick/Stevie Wonder

Best Jazz Instrumental Performance, Group: "J Mood," Wynton Marsalis

Best Jazz Vocal Performance, Male: "'Round Midnight," Bobby McFerrin

Best Album Notes: *The Voice, the Columbia Years 1943–1952*, Frank Sinatra

Best Female Pop Vocal Performance: *The Broadway Album*, Barbra Streisand

1988

Best Album Package: *King's Record Shop*, Rosanne Cash

Best Jazz Instrumental Performance, Group: *Marsalis Standard Time, Vol. 1*, Wynton Marsalis

Best Rock Vocal Performance, Male or Female: "Tunnel of Love," Bruce Springsteen

Best Gospel Performance, Female: "I Believe In You," Deniece Williams

Best Comedy Recording: *A Night at the Met*, Robin Williams

1989

Album of the Year: *Faith*, George Michael

Best Album Package: *Tired of the Runnin'*, The O'Kanes

1990

Best Male Pop Vocal Performance: "How Am I Supposed to Live Without You," Michael Bolton

Best Country Song: "After All This Time," Rodney Crowell

Best Gospel Vocal Performance, Male: "Meantime," Bebe Winans

Best Gospel Vocal Performance, Female: "Don't Cry," Cece Winans

1991

Best New Artist: Mariah Carey

Best Historical Album: *The Complete Recordings*, Robert Johnson

1992

Best Male Pop Vocal Performance: "When a Man Loves a Woman," Michael Bolton

Best Female Country Vocal Performance: "Down at the Twist and Shout," Mary Chapin Carpenter

Best Rap Solo Performance: "Mama Said Knock You Out," LL Cool J

Best Contemporary Jazz Performance: "Sassy," The Manhattan Transfer

Best Musical Show Album: *The Will Rogers Follies*, Original Cast

1993

Best Country Instrumental Performance: "Sneakin' Around," Chet Atkins/Jerry Reed

Best Traditional Pop Performance: *Pefectly Frank*, Tony Bennett

Best Female Country Vocal Performance: "I Feel Lucky," Mary Chapin Carpenter

Best Jazz Instrumental Performance, Individual or Group: "I Heard You Twice the First Time," Branford Marsalis

1994

Best Jazz Vocal Performance: "'Round Midnight," Bobby McFerrin

Best Traditional Pop Vocal Performance: "Steppin' Out," Tony Bennett

Best Country Song: "Passionate Kisses," Mary Chapin Carpenter

Best Female Country Vocal Performance: "Passionate Kisses," Mary Chapin Carpenter

Best Rock Song: "Runaway Train," Soul Asylum

1995

Best Country Instrumental Performance: "Young Thing," Chet Atkins

Album of the Year: *MTV Unplugged*, Tony Bennett

Best Traditional Pop Vocal Performance: *MTV Unplugged*, Tony Bennett

Best Pop Instrumental Performance: "Cruisin'," Booker T. & the MG's

Best Female Country Vocal Performance: "When Love Finds You," Mary Chapin Carpenter

Best Traditional Folk Album: *World Gone Wrong*, Bob Dylan

Best Rock Instrumental Performance: "Marooned," Pink Floyd

Best Male Rock Vocal Performance: "Streets of Philadelphia," Bruce Springsteen

Best Rock Song: "Streets of Philadelphia," Bruce Springsteen

Best Song Written for a Motion Picture/TV/Other Visual Medium: "Streets of Philadelphia," Bruce Springsteen

Song of the Year: "Streets of Philadelphia," Bruce Springsteen

1997

Best Country Instrumental Performance: "Jam Man," Chet Atkins

Best Traditional Pop Vocal Performance: "Here's to the Ladies," Tony Bennett

Best Album Notes: *The Complete Columbia Studio Recordings*, Miles Davis/Gil Evans

Best Historical Album: *The Complete Columbia Studio Recordings*, Miles Davis/Gil Evans

Best Recording Package—Boxed: *The Complete Columbia Studio Recordings*, Miles Davis/Gil Evans

Best R&B Performance by a Duo or Group with Vocals: "Killing Me Softly with His Song," Fugees

Best Rap Album: *The Score*, Fugees

Best Contemporary Folk Album: *The Ghost of Tom Joad*, Bruce Springsteen

1998

Best Traditional Pop Performance: *Tony Bennett on Holiday: Tribute to Billie Holiday*, Tony Bennett

Record of the Year: "Sunny Came Home," Shawn Colvin

Song of the Year: "Sunny Came Home," Shawn Colvin

1999

Best Male Rock Vocal Performance: "Cold Irons Bound," Bob Dylan

Album of the Year: *Time Out of Mind*, Bob Dylan

Best Contemporary Folk Album: *Time Out of Mind*, Bob Dylan

Best Rap Solo Performance: "Men in Black," Will Smith

Best Engineered Album, Non-Classical: *Hour Glass*, James Taylor

Best Pop Album: *Hour Glass*, James Taylor

1999

Best Rock Performance by a Duo or Group with Vocals: "Pink," Aerosmith

Best Country Collaboration with Vocals: "Same Old Train," Black/Diffie/Haggard/Harris/Krauss/Loveless/Scruggs/Skaggs

Best New Artist: Lauryn Hill

Best Female R&B Vocal Performance: "Doo Wop (That Thing)," Lauryn Hill

Best R&B Song: "Doo Wop (That Thing)," Lauryn Hill

Album of the Year: *The Miseducation of Lauryn Hill*, Lauryn Hill

Best Rap Solo Performance: "Gettin' Jiggy Wit It," Will Smith

2000

Best Traditional Pop Vocal Performance: *Bennett Sings Ellington—Hot and Cool*, Tony Bennett

Best Country Album: *Fly*, Dixie Chicks

2001

Best Historical Album: *Louis Armstrong: Complete Hot Five and Hot Seven Recordings*, Louis Armstrong

Best R&B Song: "Say My Name," Destiny's Child

Best R&B Performance by a Duo or Group with Vocals: "Say My Name," Destiny's Child

Best Contemporary Jazz Album: *Outbound*, Bela Fleck & the Flecktones

Best Jazz Instrumental Album, Individual or Group: *Contemporary Jazz*, Branford Marsalis

Best Contemporary Soul Gospel Album: *Thankful*, Mary Mary

Best Instrumental Arrangement Accompanying Vocalist(s): "Both Sides Now," Joni Mitchell

2002

Best Traditional Pop Vocal Album: *Songs I Heard*, Harry Connick Jr.

Best R&B Performance by a Duo or Group with Vocals: "Survivor," Destiny's Child

Best Contemporary Folk Album: *Love and Theft*, Bob Dylan

Best Historical Album: *Lady Day: The Complete Billie Holiday on Columbia, 1933–1944*, Billie Holiday

Best Rock Song: "Drops of Jupiter (Tell Me)," Train

Best Instrumental Arrangement Accompanying Vocalist(s): "Drops of Jupiter (Tell Me)," Train

2003

Best Traditional Pop Vocal Album: *Playin' with My Friends: Bennett Sings the Blues*, Tony Bennett

Best World Music Album: *Mundo*, Ruben Blades

Best Country Album: *Home*, Dixie Chicks

Best Recording Package: *Home*, Dixie Chicks

Best Male Pop Vocal Performance: "Your Body Is a Wonderland," John Mayer

Best Rock Song: "The Rising," Bruce Springsteen

Best Rock Album: *The Rising*, Bruce Springsteen

Best Male Rock Vocal Performance: "The Rising," Bruce Springsteen

Best Spoken Comedy Album: *Robin Williams—Live 2002*, Robin Williams

2004

Best Traditional Pop Vocal Album: *A Wonderful World*, Tony Bennett/k.d. lang

Best Contemporary R&B Album: *Dangerously in Love*, Beyoncé

Best Female R&B Vocal Performance: "Dangerously in Love 2," Beyoncé

Best R&B Song: "Crazy in Love," Beyoncé/Jay-Z

Best Rap/Sung Collaboration: "Crazy in Love," Beyoncé/Jay-Z

Best Remixed Recording, Non-Classical: "Crazy in Love (Maurice's Soul Mix)," Beyoncé/Jay-Z

Best R&B Performance by a Duo or Group with Vocals: "The Closer I Get to You," Beyoncé/ Luther Vandross

Best Boxed or Special Limited Edition Package: *The Complete Jack Johnson Sessions*, Miles Davis

Best Song Written for a Motion Picture/TV/Other Visual Medium: "A Mighty Wind," The Folksmen/ Mitch & Mickey

Best Instrumental Arrangement Accompanying Vocalist(s): "Woodstock," Joni Mitchell

2005

Best Country Performance by a Duo or Group with Vocals: "Top of the World," Dixie Chicks

Song of the Year: "Daughters," John Mayer

Best Male Pop Vocal Performance: "Daughters," John Mayer

Best Male R&B Vocal Performance: "Call My Name," Prince

Best Traditional R&B Vocal Performance: "Musicology," Prince

2006

Best Pop Instrumental Album: *At This Time*, Burt Bacharach

Best Traditional Pop Vocal Album: *The Art of Romance*, Tony Bennett

Best Instrumental Arrangement Accompanying Vocalist(s): "What Are You Doing for the Rest of Your Life?," Chris Botti/Sting

Best Long Form Music Video: *No Direction Home*, Bob Dylan

Best New Artist: John Legend

Best R&B Album: *Get Lifted*, John Legend

Best Male R&B Vocal Performance: "Ordinary People," John Legend

Best Rock Vocal Performance, Solo: "Devils & Dust," Bruce Springsteen

Best Hard Rock Performance: "B.Y.O.B.," System of a Down

2007

Best Traditional Pop Vocal Album: *Duets: An American Classic*, Tony Bennett

Best Instrumental Arrangement Accompanying Vocalist(s): "For Once in My Life," Tony Bennett/ Stevie Wonder

Best Pop Collaboration with Vocals: "For Once in My Life," Tony Bennett/Stevie Wonder

Best Contemporary R&B Album: *B'day*, Beyoncé

Record of the Year: "Not Ready to Make Nice," Dixie Chicks

Song of the Year: "Not Ready to Make Nice," Dixie Chicks

Best Country Performance by a Duo or Group with Vocals: "Not Ready to Make Nice," Dixie Chicks

Album of the Year: *Taking the Long Way*, Dixie Chicks

Best Country Album: *Taking the Long Way*, Dixie Chicks

Best Contemporary Folk/Americana Album: *Modern Times*, Bob Dylan

Best Rock Vocal Performance, Solo: "Someday Baby," Bob Dylan

Best Contemporary Jazz Album: *The Hidden Land*, Bela Fleck & the Flecktones

Best Male R&B Vocal Performance: "Heaven," John Legend

Best Pop Vocal Album: *Continuum*, John Mayer

Best Male Pop Vocal Performance: "Waiting on the World to Change," John Mayer

Best Traditional Folk Album: *We Shall Overcome: The Seeger Sessions*, Bruce Springsteen

Best Long Form Music Video: *Wings for Wheels: The Making of Born to Run*, Bruce Springsteen

2008

Best Pop/Contemporary Gospel Album: *A Deeper Level: Live*, Israel & New Breed

Best R&B Performance by a Duo or Group with Vocals: "Disrespectful," Chaka Khan/Mary J. Blige

Best Male R&B Vocal Performance: "Future Baby Mama," Prince

Best Metal Performance: "Final Six," Slayer

Best Rock Vocal Performance, Solo: "Radio Nowhere," Bruce Springsteen

Best Rock Song: "Radio Nowhere," Bruce Springsteen

2009

Best New Artist: Adele

Best Female Pop Vocal Performance: "Chasing Pavements," Adele

Best Album Notes: *Kind of Blue*, Miles Davis

Best Gospel Performance: "Get Up," Mary Mary

Best Rock Vocal Performance, Solo: "Gravity," John Mayer

Best Male Pop Vocal Performance: "Say," John Mayer

Best Remixed Recording, Non-Classical: "Electric Feel (Justice Remix)," MGMT

Best Rock Song: "Girls in Their Summer Clothes," Bruce Springsteen

2010

Best Hard Rock Performance: "War Machine," AC/DC

Best Traditional Pop Vocal Performance: "At Last," Beyoncé

Best Female Pop Vocal Performance: "Halo," Beyoncé

Best Contemporary R&B Album: *I Am . . . Sasha Fierce*, Beyoncé

Song of the Year: "Single Ladies (Put a Ring on It)," Beyoncé

Best Female R&B Vocal Performance: "Single Ladies (Put a Ring on It)," Beyoncé

Best R&B Song: "Single Ladies (Put a Ring on It)," Beyoncé

Best Pop/Contemporary Gospel Album: *The Power of One*, Israel Houghton

Best Gospel Song: "God in Me," Mary Mary/ Kierra "Kiki" Sheard

Best R&B Album: *Blacksummers'night*, Maxwell

Best Male R&B Vocal Performance: "Pretty Wings," Maxwell

Best Rock Vocal Performance, Solo: "Working on a Dream," Bruce Springsteen

2011

Best Pop Performance by a Duo or Group with Vocals: "Hey Soul Sister," Train

Best Traditional R&B Vocal Performance for solo, duo, group or collaborative performances, with vocals: "Hang On In There," John Legend/The Roots

Best R&B Song: "Shine," John Legend/The Roots

Best R&B Album: "Wake Up!," John Legend/ The Roots

Best Engineered Album, Non-Classical: "Battle Studies," John Mayer

Best Pop/Contemporary Gospel Album: "Love God. Love People." Israel Houghton

2012

Record of the Year: "Rolling In The Deep," Adele

Album of the Year: *21*, Adele

Song of the Year: "Rolling In The Deep," Adele

Best Pop Solo Performance: "Someone Like You," Adele

Best Pop Vocal Album: *21*, Adele

Best Short Form Music Video: "Rolling in the Deep," Adele

Best Pop Duo/Group Performance: "Body and Soul," Tony Bennett and Amy Winehouse

Best Traditional Pop Vocal Album: *Duets II*, Tony Bennett

Best Instrumental Arrangement Accompanying Vocalist: "Who Can I Turn To (When Nobody Needs Me)," Tony Bennett

Best Boxed or Special Limited Edition Package: *The Promise: The Darkness On the Edge of Town Story*, Bruce Springsteen

Billboard #1 Albums
1955 – May 1st, 2012

Love Me or Leave Me, Doris Day/Soundtrack, 1955

My Fair Lady, Original Cast, 1956

Johnny's Greatest Hits, Johnny Mathis, 1958

Sing-along with Mitch, Mitch Miller, 1958

Christmas Sing-along with Mitch, Mitch Miller, 1958

Flower Drum Song, Original Cast, 1959

Heavenly, Johnny Mathis, 1959

The Lord's Prayer, Mormon Tabernacle Choir, 1960

The Sound of Music, Original Cast, 1960

Camelot, Original Cast, 1961

Stars for a Summer Night, Various, 1961

Holiday Sing-along with Mitch, Mitch Miller, 1962

West Side Story, Soundtrack, 1962

Days of Wine and Roses, Andy Williams, 1963

People, Barbra Streisand, 1964

Bookends, Simon & Garfunkel, 1968

Cheap Thrills, Big Brother & The Holding Company/
Janis Joplin, 1968

The Graduate, Simon & Garfunkel/Soundtrack, 1969

Blood, Sweat & Tears, Blood, Sweat & Tears, 1969

Johnny Cash at San Quentin, Johnny Cash, 1969

Bridge over Troubled Water, Simon & Garfunkel, 1970

Blood, Sweat & Tears 3, Blood, Sweat & Tears, 1970

Abraxas, Santana, 1970

Pearl, Janis Joplin, 1971

Santana III, Santana, 1971

Chicago V, Chicago, 1972

Chicago VI, Chicago, 1973

The Way We Were, Barbra Streisand, 1974

Chicago VII, Chicago, 1974

Blood on the Tracks, Bob Dylan, 1975

Chicago VIII, Chicago, 1975

That's the Way of the World, Earth, Wind & Fire, 1975

Between the Lines, Janis Ian, 1975

Still Crazy After All These Years, Paul Simon, 1975

Greatest Hits, Chicago, 1975

Gratitude, Earth, Wind & Fire, 1976

Desire, Bob Dylan, 1976

A Star Is Born (Soundtrack), Barbra Streisand/Kris
Kristofferson, 1977

52nd Street, Billy Joel, 1978

Greatest Hits, Vol. 2, Barbra Streisand, 1979

The Wall, Pink Floyd, 1980

Glass Houses, Billy Joel, 1980

Guilty, Barbra Streisand, 1980

The River, Bruce Springsteen, 1980

Escape, Journey, 1981

Tug of War, Paul McCartney, 1982

Business as Usual, Men at Work, 1982

Footloose, Soundtrack, 1984

Born in the U.S.A., Bruce Springsteen, 1984

Make It Big, Wham!/George Michael, 1985

We Are the World, USA for Africa, 1985

The Broadway Album, Barbra Streisand, 1986

Top Gun, Soundtrack, 1986

Bruce Springsteen & The E Street Band Live 1975–85,
Bruce Springsteen & The E Street Band, 1986

Licensed to Ill, Beastie Boys, 1987

Tunnel of Love, Bruce Springsteen, 1987

Faith, George Michael, 1989

Hangin' Tough, New Kids on the Block, 1989

Storm Front, Billy Joel, 1989

Step by Step, New Kids on the Block, 1990

Mariah Carey, Mariah Carey, 1991

Time, Love and Tenderness, Michael Bolton, 1991

Totally Krossed Out, Kris Kross, 1992

Timeless (The Classics), Michael Bolton, 1992

Back to Broadway, Barbra Streisand, 1993

Black Sunday, Cypress Hill, 1993

The River of Dreams, Billy Joel, 1993

Music Box, Mariah Carey, 1993

Jar of Flies, Alice in Chains, 1994

The Division Bell, Pink Floyd, 1994

Greatest Hits, Bruce Springsteen, 1995

Pulse, Pink Floyd, 1995

Daydream, Mariah Carey, 1995

Alice in Chains, Alice in Chains, 1995

The Score, Fugees, 1996

It Was Written, Nas, 1996

Nine Lives, Aerosmith, 1997

Men in Black: The Album, Soundtrack, 1997

Butterfly, Mariah Carey, 1997

Higher Ground, Barbra Streisand, 1997

Armageddon, Soundtrack, 1998

The Miseducation of Lauryn Hill, Lauryn Hill, 1998

I Am . . . , Nas, 1999

Ricky Martin, Ricky Martin, 1999

Fly, Dixie Chicks, 1999

Survivor, Destiny's Child, 2001

Now, Maxwell, 2001

Toxicity, System of a Down, 2001

God Bless America, Various Artists, 2001

The Rising, Bruce Springsteen, 2002

Home, Dixie Chicks, 2002

Dangerously in Love, Beyoncé, 2003

Heavier Things, John Mayer, 2003

Devils & Dust, Bruce Springsteen, 2005

Mezmerize, System of a Down, 2005

#1's, Destiny's Child, 2005

Hypnotize, System of a Down, 2005

Ancora, Il Divo, 2006

Taking the Long Way, Dixie Chicks, 2006

Now 22, Various Artists, 2006

Modern Times, Bob Dylan, 2006

B'day, Beyoncé, 2006

Dreamgirls, Soundtrack, 2007

Magic, Bruce Springsteen, 2007

Home Before Dark, Neil Diamond, 2008

Black Ice, AC/DC, 2008

I Am . . . Sasha Fierce, Beyoncé, 2008

Working on a Dream, Bruce Springsteen, 2009

Together Through Life, Bob Dylan, 2009

Blacksummers'night, Maxwell, 2009

Love Is the Answer, Barbra Streisand, 2009

Battle Studies, John Mayer, 2009

I Dreamed a Dream, Susan Boyle, 2009

Glee: The Music, The Power of Madonna, Soundtrack/
Glee Cast, 2010

Glee: The Music, Volume 3: Showstoppers,
Soundtrack/Glee Cast, 2010

Glee: The Music, Journey to Regionals, Soundtrack/
Glee Cast, 2010

The Gift, Susan Boyle, 2010

21, Adele, 2011

4, Beyoncé, 2011

Duets II, Tony Bennett, 2011

Cole World: The Sideline Story, J. Cole, 2011

Wrecking Ball, Bruce Springsteen, 2012

Up All Night, One Direction, 2012

Blunderbuss, Jack White, 2012

Acknowledgments

I did most of the research and writing of this book while in residence as a fellow at the Huntington Library in San Marino, California, to whose staff, scholars, and recently-retired director, Roy Ritchie, I am enormously grateful. Limitations of space and format preclude full notes and a bibliography, but there have been a few works about Columbia that helped me enormously and deserve special mention: Gary Marmorstein's *The Label: The Story of Columbia Records* (2007); the multi-authored *Sony Music 100: Soundtrack for a Century*, published in 1999 in conjunction with the multi-CD commemorative collection of the same name; and the various articles on Columbia's early history by Tim Brooks, available at Brooks's Web site, www.timbrooks.net. Steve Barnett and Peter Fletcher offered extraordinary assistance from start to finish, eager to help in every way possible and with no strings attached. Columbia Records has been especially professional as well as forthcoming, giving me access to recordings, archives, and every other kind of source without influencing in any way what I chose to write about or how I chose to write it. Thanks also to Chloe Ballatore, the late Robert Bower, Howard Few, Judy Fiskin, Nick Goldberg, Dov Weinryb Grohsgal, Miriam Hernandez, Virginia Hernandez, Michael Ochs, Marilinda Perez, Lorraine Sciarra, Derek Shearer, Michael Simmons, Susan Toigo, Ian Whitcomb, Jon Wiener, Amy Wilentz, and Carla Zimowsk. Special thanks to Steve Berkowitz, Michael Brooks, Tim Brooks, Marty Erlichman, Colin Escott, Bill Flanagan, Gregg Geller, Marc Kirkeby, Jon Landau, Steve Mockus, Paul Russell, Phil Schaap, Emily Thompson, and Warren Zanes, as well as to Leigh Saffold, Beth Weber, and the entire staff at Chronicle Books. James Wilentz has been irreplaceable. I owe the most, once again, to Jeff Rosen.

—Sean Wilentz

The following people provided invaluable assistance in the production of the book:

Steve Barnett and Rob Stringer

Peter Fletcher, Project Manager

Mark Farrow and Gary Stillwell at Farrow, Design and Art Direction

Mary Maurer, Photo Editor / 2310 Design

Greg Allen, Image and Print Production / 2310 Design

Joyce Fletcher, Manager Photo Rights Clearance

Marcia Edelstein, Photo Rights Clearance

Crystal Singh-Hawthorne, Manager, Design Administration, Sony Music Creative Group

Andrew Ross, Business Affairs

Visual Research: Mary Maurer, Peter Fletcher, Marcia Edelstein, Joyce Fletcher, Cheryl Pawelski, and Greg Allen

Thanks to Colin Escott, John Tefteller, and Cheryl Pawelski for sharing ephemera from their collections.

Special thanks to Tom Tierney and Che Williams in the Sony Music Archives.

Thanks also to Dave Marsh, Greg Linn, Scott Greer, Nancy Marcus-Seklir, Dave Bett, Eric Taylor, Richard Story, Adam Block, John Jackson, Steve Berkowitz, Arnold Levine, Mark Wilder, Michael Brooks, Stephen Russo, Clinton McConnell, Greg Young, Jay Gress, Jono Medwed, Vinnie Maressa, Sheryl Afuang, and Khal Chirwa.

Photography Credits

Evan Agostini/Getty Images: Steven Tyler, Joe Perry, Brad Whitford of Aerosmith with Michele Anthony and Tommy Mottola (p. 265)
Robert Agriopoulos: Joe Perry and Steven Tyler of Aerosmith (p. 213)
Greg Allen: Beastie Boys (p. 252)
Kwaku Alston: Branford Marsalis (p. 247)
Eve Arnold/Magnum Photos: Rosemary Clooney (p. 136)
Artists & Friends: Journey (p. 232)
Erich Auerbach/Hulton Archive/Getty Images: Aaron Copland (p. 131)
Marc Baptiste: Fugees (pp. 280-281), Lauryn Hill (p. 286)
Michael Benabib: Public Enemy (p. 276)
Paul Bergen/Redferns/Getty Images: Wyclef Jean (p. 279)
Alan Berliner/Berliner Photography: Mel Ilberman, Don Ienner, Dave Glew, and Tommy Mottola (p. 266)
Bredell/Hulton Archive/Getty Images: Moran and Mack (p. 75)
Andrew Brusso: Cypress Hill (p. 276)
Larry Busacca/Wire Image/Getty Images: Steve Barnett, Beyoncé, Rob Stringer, and Jay-Z (p. 294), AC/DC plaque presentation (p. 310), Adele with Howard Stringer, Steve Barnett, Rob Stringer, and Doug Morris (p. 320)
Stephanie Cabral: Glee plaque presentation (p. 316)
Danny Clinch: Bob Dylan (p. 269), John Mayer (p. 285), Seeger Sessions Band (p. 301), Bruce Springsteen (pp. 267, 300, 301)
Bob Cato: Leonard Cohen (p. 202), Laura Nyro (p. 211), Andy Williams (p. 175)
John Cohen/Hulton Archive/Getty Images: Bill Monroe (p. 138)
Lorca Cohen: Leonard Cohen (p. 297)
Fin Costello/Redferns/Getty Images: Steven Tyler (pp. 214-215)
C. Taylor Crothers: AC/DC (p. 310)
Chris Cuffaro: George Michael (p. 243)
Merri Cyr: Jeff Buckley (pp. 282, 299)
Gregg DeGuire/Wire Image/Getty Images: Dixie Chicks (p. 306)
Jesse Diamond: Neil Diamond (p. 295)
Lauren Dukoff: Adele (p. 315)
Alfred Eisenstaedt/Time & Life Pictures/Getty Images: Leonard Bernstein (p. 123)
Thomas S. England/Time & Life Pictures/Getty Images: Bob Dylan with Benny Goodman and John Hammond (p. 230)
Fabrizio Ferri: Chris Botti (p. 313), Destiny's Child (p. 261)
Photography © Glen E. Friedman, courtesy Glen E. Friedman Archive: System Of A Down (p. 263)
Freidman-Abeles ©The New York Public Library for the Performing Arts: Barbra Streisand (p.179)
Chris Gallo: Columbia LP Spines (pp. 8-9), Columbia Cylinders (p. 22)
Gerschel/Hulton Archive/Getty Images: Pablo Casals (p. 36)
Greg Gex: Beyoncé (pp. 290-291)
Guy Gillette: Louis Armstrong with W. C. Handy and George Avakian (p. 144)
William P. Gottlieb/Redferns/Getty Images: Billie Holiday (p. 86), Frank Sinatra (p. 112)
William P. Gottlieb/Ira and Leonore S. Gershwin Fund Collection, Music Division, Library of Congress: George Avakian (p. 102), Cab Calloway (p. 78), Fifty-Second Street (p. 99), Frank Sinatra with Axel Stordahl (p. 114), Alex Steinweiss (p. 115), Art Tatum (p. 78)
Charles L. Granata/KEG Productions, Inc.: Frank Sinatra (p. 108)
Steve Granitz/Wire Image/Getty Images: Adele (p. 320)
Don Hunstein: Louis Armstrong (p. 144), Tony Bennett (pp. 120-121, 135, 177), Leonard Bernstein (pp. 157, 245), Dave Brubeck (pp. 152-153, 164), The Byrds (pp. 196-197), Johnny Cash (pp. 186, 187), Rosemary Clooney (p. 137), John Coltrane with Cannonball Adderley and Miles Davis (p. 147), Ray Conniff (p. 136), Robert Coote, Julie Andrews with Rex Harrison (p. 163), Miles Davis (pp. 148-149, 168, 208), Miles Davis with Ted Macero (p. 209), Bob Dylan (pp. 172-173, 184, 185), Flatt and Scruggs (p. 140), Aretha Franklin (p. 182), Erroll Garner (p. 143), Robert Goulet (p. 177), Glenn Gould (p. 156, 158-159, 248), Vladimir Horowitz (p. 191), Mahalia Jackson (p. 142), Billy Joel (p. 212), Yo-Yo Ma (p. 233), Johnny Mathis (p. 145), Mitch Miller (pp. 155, 178), Charles Mingus (p. 150), Thelonius Monk (p. 193), Eugene Ormandy (p. 111), Paul Revere & the Raiders (p. 199), Carlos Santana with Walter Yetnikoff, Bill Graham and Bruce Lundvall (p. 224), Simon & Garfunkel (p. 194), The Sound Of Music (p. 128), Isaac Stern (pp. 156, 190), Igor Stravinsky (p. 126), Barbra Streisand (pp. 176, 178), Bruno Walter (p. 127), Weather Report (p. 235), West Side Story (pp. 160, 161)
Eric Johnson: Maxwell (p. 278)
Naomi Kaltman: Michael Bolton (p. 270), Mariah Carey (pp. 258-259)
Steven Klein: Ricky Martin (p. 273)
Photography by Markus Klinko and Indrani: Beyoncé (pp. 274-275)
Palma Kolansky: Harry Connick Jr. (p. 297)
Urve Kuusik: Miles Davis (p. 235)
© Elliott Landy/Landyvision.com: Janis Joplin (p. 217)
Elliott Landy/Premium Archive/Getty Images: Janis Joplin with Clive Davis (p. 201)
Chris Lee: Joshua Bell (p. 313)
Russell Lee/Archive Photos/Getty Images: Lonnie Johnson (p. 60)
Michael Levine: Will Smith (p. 272)
Peter Lindbergh: Beyoncé (p. 308)
© Frederick Lombardi: Chicago (p. 213)
Art Maillet: Dexter Gordon (p. 233), Willie Nelson with Bruce Lundvall (p. 226), Bruce Springsteen (p. 216)
Jonathan Mannion: Nas (p. 279)
© Jim Marshall Photography LLC: Johnny Cash (p. 207), Johnny Cash with Bob Dylan (p. 188), Leonard Cohen (p. 203), Janis Joplin (p. 200), Santana (p. 210)
Kevin Mazur/Wire Image/Getty Images: Billy Joel (p. 269), Billy Joel with Don Ienner and John Mayer (p. 265)
Jo McCaughey: Jack White (p. 314)
Jim McCrary/Redferns/Getty Images: Herbie Hancock (p. 234)
Melodie McDaniel: Patti Smith (p. 303)
Eric Meola: Bruce Springsteen (pp. 228-229)
Gjon Mili/Time & Life Pictures/Getty Images: Larry Adler (p. 107), New York Philharmonic (p. 110), Paul Robeson (p. 106)
Estate of Keith Morris/Redferns/Getty Images: Elvis Costello (p. 223)
Tom Munro: John Mayer (p. 302)
Frank Ockenfels: Shawn Colvin (p. 287)
Michael O'Neill: Yo-Yo Ma (p. 312)
Hank Parker: Bob Dylan (p. 183)
Nigel Parry: Tony Bennett (p. 264)
Gilles Petard/Redferns/Getty Images: Louis Armstrong (p. 73), Count Basie (p. 88), Big Maybelle (p. 154), Duke Ellington (p. 67), Benny Goodman (p. 100), Billie Holiday (p. 104), Paul Whiteman (p. 69)
Stephanie Pfriender: Marc Anthony (p. 272)
Robin Platzer/Twin Images/Getty Images: Nobuyuki Idei, Tommy Mottola and Howard Stringer (p. 294)
Anthony Pidgeon/Redferns/Getty Images: Aerosmith (p. 262)

© Neal Preston: Pink Floyd (p. 236), Bruce Springsteen (p. 321)
Michael Putland: Angus Young of AC/DC (p. 311)
Midwest Auction Galleries: Columbia Disc Graphophone (p. 21)
Aaron Rapoport: Men At Work (p. 242)
David Redfern/Redferns/Getty Images: Stan Getz with Buddy Rich (p. 233), Julio Iglesias (p. 242), Wynton Marsalis (p. 246), Paul McCartney (p. 238)
Ebet Roberts/Redferns/Getty Images: Phillip Glass (p. 249)
George Rose/Getty Images: Bruce Springsteen (pp. 220-221)
Walter Sanders/Time & Life Pictures/Getty Images: Phonograph (p. 24)
Eric Schaal/Time & Life Pictures/Getty Images: Peter Goldmark (p. 129)
F. Scott Schaefer: The Offspring (p. 263)
Steve Schapiro: Barbra Streisand (pp. 180-181)
Jerry Schatzberg/trunkarchive.com: Bob Dylan (p. 198)
Rocky Schenck: Alice In Chains (p. 283)
Mark Seliger: Tony Bennett (p. 296), Dixie Chicks (pp. 304-305), Bob Dylan (p. 293)
Tom Sheehan/Sony Music Archive/Getty Images: Billy Joel (p. 241)
© Vernon L. Smith: Miles Davis with Gil Evans (p. 146), Ethel Merman with Jack Klugman (p. 162), Mitch Miller (p. 151)
W. Eugene Smith/Time & Life Pictures/Getty Images: Mary Martin and Ezio Pinza (p. 132)
Sandy Speiser: Bob Dylan (p. 182), Laura Nyro with Clive Davis (p. 201), Johnny Winter (p. 204)
Frank Stefanko: Bruce Springsteen (p. 231)
Dennis Stock/Magnum Photos: Frank Sinatra (p. 116)
Syco/Rex Features: Simon Cowell with One Direction (p. 316)
Michael Thompson: Mariah Carey (p. 271)
© 2009 Twentieth Century Fox Television. All rights reserved: Glee (p. 317)
Rob Verhorst/Redferns/Getty Images: Pink Floyd (p. 237)
Mark Von Holden/Getty Images: Adele plaque presentation (p. 314)
Lawrence Watson: LL Cool J (p. 277), Public Enemy (p. 254)
© Bruce Weber: Harry Connick Jr. (p. 251)
Matthew Welch: John Legend (p. 307)
Timothy White: New Kids On The Block (p. 255)
Andrew Yee: Adele (p. 318)
Firooz Zahedi: Barbra Streisand (p. 297)

COLLECTIONS:
American Stock Archive/Getty Images: Al Jolson (p. 45)
Archive Photos/American Stock Archive/Getty Images: W. C. Handy (p. 47)
Archive Photos/FPG/Getty Images: Vernon and Irene Castle (p. 46)
Archive Photos/Frank Driggs Collection/Getty Images: Louis Armstrong and His Hot Five (pp. 70-71), Jimmy Dickens (p. 141), Duke Ellington (p. 74), Golden Gate Quartet (p. 105), Benny Goodman with Count Basie and John Hammond (p. 84), Screamin' Jay Hawkins (p. 154), Blind Willie Johnson (p. 64), Original Dixieland Jass Band (p. 49), Bessie Smith (p. 63), Mamie Smith (p. 61), Victoria Spivey (p. 60), Bob Wills (p. 80)
Archive Photos/Hulton Archive/Getty Images: Louis Armstrong (p. 66)
Archive Photos/Metronome/Getty Images: Andre Kostelanetz (p. 103)
Archive Photos/Pictorial Parade/Getty Images: Sarah Vaughan (p. 142)
Archive Photos/Transcendental Graphics/Getty Images: Benny Goodman (p. 90)
Mark Berresford Rare Records: Wilbur Sweatman (p. 57)
CEA/Cache Agency: Roy Acuff (p. 83)
CBS Photo Archive/Getty Images: Gene Autry (p. 76), James Conkling with Mitch Miller (p. 134)
© Bettmann/CORBIS: Early Recording Session (p. 32), Thomas Edison (p. 19)
Courtesy of Colin Escott, © Bear Family Archives: Columbia Race Catalog (p. 62), Jimmy Dean with Johnny Cash and Don Law (p. 189)
Everett Collection: James Taylor (p. 239), Ethel Waters (p. 65), Wham! (p. 240)
Gamma-Keystone/Getty Images: Al Jolson (p. 25)
Hulton Archive/Getty Images: Al Jolson (p. 44), Frank Sinatra (p. 113), Sophie Tucker (p. 75)
Hulton Archive/Evening Standard/Getty Images: Guy Lombardo (p. 77)
Hulton Archive/Keystone/Getty Images: William Paley (p. 109)
Hulton Archive/Keystone Features/Getty Images: Jitterbug (p. 117)
Hulton Archive/Topical Press Agency/Getty Images: Ted Lewis (p. 56)
© Lebrecht Music & Arts/CORBIS: Edison Standard Phonograph (p. 21)
Library of Congress: Alexander Graham Bell (p. 19), Emile Berliner (p. 34), Art Gillham (p. 58), John Philip Sousa (p. 28), U.S. Marine Band (pp. 30-31)
Michael Ochs Archives/Getty Images: Bix Beiderbecke (p. 68), Boswell Sisters (p. 78), Count Basie (p. 89), Blood Sweat & Tears (p. 204), Al Jolson (p. 45), Lefty Frizzell (p. 141), Willie Nelson (p. 227), Paul Simon (p. 238)
Michael Ochs Archives/Frank Driggs Collection/Getty Images: Charlie Christian with Benny Goodman (p. 109)
© Minnesota Historical Society/CORBIS: Gramophone Picnic (pp. 14-15)
Moviepix/John Kobal Foundation/Getty Images: Gene Autry (p. 81)
New York Daily News Archive/Getty Images: Frank Sinatra (pp. 96-97)
Photofest: Andre Kostelanetz (p. 102)
Pictorial Press/Cache Agency: Johnnie Ray (p. 154), Stanley Brothers (p. 139)
Popperfoto/Getty Images: Bing Crosby (p. 93)
Redferns/Echoes/Getty Images: Earth, Wind & Fire (p. 205)
Redferns/GAB Archive/Getty Images: Duke Ellington (pp. 52-53), Kay Kyser (p. 104), Patsy Montana (p. 80), Kate Smith (p. 92)
Redferns/JP Jazz Archive/Getty Images: Benny Goodman (p. 91), Billie Holiday (p. 87)
Redferns/PALM/RSCH/Getty Images: Mary Garden (p. 40), Ernestine Schumann-Heink (p. 37), Bert Williams (p. 39)
From the Collection of Kinney Rorrer: Charlie Poole (p. 60)
Science & Society Picture Library/Getty Images: Chichester Bell (p. 18), Bell and Tainter's Graphophone (p. 20), Columbia Graphophone (p. 20)
Courtesy of the Sony Music Archives: Gene Autry with Don Law (p. 79), Bill Bachman and Peter Goldmark (p. 129), Leonard Bernstein with Goddard Lieberson (p. 125), Dave Brubeck with Goddard Lieberson (p. 125), Leonard Cohen with Bruce Lundvall and Irwin Segelstein (p. 224), Miles Davis with Goddard Lieberson (p. 124), Destiny's Child with Don Ienner (p. 266), Doris Day (p. 134), Edward Denison Easton (p. 17), Neil Diamond (p. 225), Duke Ellington (p. 167), Benny Goodman (p. 101), John Hammond (p. 85), Don Hunstein (p. 130), Al Kooper (p. 199), Mary Martin with Goddard Lieberson (p. 133), Phonograph (p. 24), Santana with Clive Davis (p. 201), Art Satherley (p. 139), Howard Stringer, Clive Davis, Michele Anthony and Andy Lack (p. 294), George Szell (p. 130), Charles Sumner Tainter (p. 18)
Time & Life Pictures/Getty Images: Toto (p. 230)

Index

Trademarks

50 Cent musical entertainment is a registered trademark of Curtis Jackson. AC DC musical entertainment is a registered trademark of Leidseplein Presse BV. Academy Award, Grammy award, and Oscar award are registered trademarks of the National Academy of Motion Picture Arts and Sciences. Adele musical entertainment is a registered trademark of Adele Laurie Blue Adkins. Aerosmith musical entertainment is a registered trademark of Rag Doll Merchandising, Inc. American Telephone and Telegraph is a registered trademark of AT&T Intellectual Property. American Top 40 radio programs is a registered trademark of Premiere Radio Networks, Inc. Arista Records is a registered trademark of Arista Records LLC. Art Blakey & the Jazz Messengers musical entertainment is a registered trademark of The Art Blakey Estate. Asylum phonograph records and Elektra phonograph records are registered trademarks of Elektra Entertainment Group Inc. Atlantic musical sound recordings is a registered trademark of Atlantic Recording Corporation. Bay City Rollers musical entertainment is a registered trademark of BCR Entertainment, Inc. Beastie Boys musical entertainment is a registered trademark of Beastie Boys, composed of Michael Diamond, Adam Horowitz, and Adam Yauch. Bee Gees musical entertainment is a registered trademark of the Estate of Maurice Gibb. Beyoncé musical entertainment is a registered trademark of BGK Trademark Holdings, LLC. Big Brother and the Holding Company musical entertainment is a registered trademark of Big Brother and the Holding Company, composed of Sam Andrew, Peter Albin, James Gurley, and David R. Getz. Billboard magazine is a registered trademark of VNU Business Media, Inc. Black Sabbath musical entertainment is a registered trademark of Anthony Frank Iommi. Blood Sweat and Tears musical entertainment is a registered trademark of Robert Wayne Colomby. Blue Note phonograph records, Capitol Records, and Liberty phonograph records are registered trademarks of Capitol Records, Inc. Boston Symphony Orchestra is a registered trademark of Boston Symphony Orchestra, Inc. Broadcast Music, Inc. is a registered trademark of Broadcast Music, Inc. Bruce Springsteen & The E Street Band musical entertainment is a registered trademark of Bruce Springsteen. Brunswick phonographs and phonographic records is a registered trademark of Brunswick Record Corporation. Buddah sound recordings and Red Seal musical sound recordings are registered trademarks of BMG Music. Buffalo Springfield musical entertainment is a registered trademark of Stephen Stills, Neil Young, and Paul Richard Furay. Café Wha? is a registered trademark of R.O.N. Entertainment Inc. Carnegie Hall performance venue is a registered trademark of Carnegie Hall Corporation. CBGB club and performance venue is a registered trademark of the Estate of Hillel Kristal. Chess phonograph records, Clef Records, Decca musical sound recordings, Interscope Records, Jackson 5 musical entertainment, Motown phonograph records, and The Supremes musical entertainment are registered trademarks of UMG Recordings, Inc. Country Joe and the Fish musical entertainment is a registered trademark of Country Joe and the Fish, composed of Joseph A. McDonald and Barry Melton. Cypress Hill is a registered trademark of Cypress Hill, composed of Larry Muggerud, Senen Reyes, and Louis Freese. Def Jam Recordings is a registered trademark of DJR Holdings, LLC. Destiny's Child musical entertainment is a registered trademark of Mathew Knowles. Dictaphone graphophones is a registered trademark of Dictaphone Corporation. Dixie Chicks musical entertainment is a registered trademark of Dixie Chicks, composed of Emily Erwin Robins, Martha Eleanor Maguire, and Natalie Maines Pasnar. Double Trouble musical entertainment is a registered trademark of Stevie Ray Vaughan Estate. Down Beat periodical is a registered trademark of Maher Publications, Inc. Earth, Wind & Fire musical entertainment is a registered trademark of Maurice White DBA Earth, Wind & Fire Productions. Eminem musical entertainment is a registered trademark of Marshall B. Mathers III. Epitaph records is a registered trademark of Epitaph. Esquire magazine is a registered trademark of Hearst Magazines Property, Inc. Facebook is a registered trademark of Facebook, Inc. Fantasy musical sound recording, Prestige musical sound recording, Riverside phonograph records, and Stax phonograph records are registered trademarks of Concord Music Group, Inc. Fifth Dimension musical entertainment is a registered trademark of Fifth Dimension, composed of Florence La Rue and Lamonte MacLemore. Fisk Jubilee Singers musical entertainment is a registered trademark of Fisk University. Fleetwood Mac musical entertainment is a registered trademark of John McVie and Michael Fleetwood. Fox News and Glee television series is a registered trademark of Twentieth Century Fox Film Corporation. Frankie Valli and the Four Seasons musical entertainment is a registered trademark of Frankie Valli and Bob Guadio DBA The Four Seasons Partnership. Golden Globe award is a registered trademark of Hollywood Foreign Press Association. Grand Funk Railroad musical entertainment is a registered trademark of GFR Ltd. Grand Ole Opry radio program broadcasting services is a registered trademark of Gaylord Entertainment Company. Grateful Dead musical entertainment is a registered trademark of Grateful Dead Productions. Green Day musical entertainment is a registered trademark of Green Day, Inc. Harold Melvin & The Bluenotes musical entertainment is a registered trademark of Ovelia Melvin. His Master's Voice and RCA Victor phonographs are registered trademarks of RCA. Island records, Mercury records, Polygram records, and Verve records are registered trademarks of Universal International Music Company. Itunes is a registered trademark of Apple Computer, Inc. Jay-Z musical entertainment is a registered trademark of Shawn Carter. Jefferson Airplane musical entertainment is a registered trademark of Jefferson Airplane, Inc. Journey musical entertainment is a registered trademark of NM Productions. Kenny G musical entertainment is a registered trademark of Kenneth Gorelick. Led Zeppelin musical entertainment is a registered trademark of Joan Hudson as trustee of the Estate of John H. Bonham, Robert A. Plant, James P. Page, and John Baldwin a.k.a. John Paul Jones. Life magazine and Time magazine are registered trademarks of Time Inc. Light Crust Doughboys is a registered trademark of Frank Arthur Greenhaw. Lincoln Center performance venue is a registered trademark of Lincoln Center for the Performing Arts, Inc. LL Cool J musical entertainment is a registered trademark of James Todd Smith. Madison Square Garden performance venue is a registered trademark of Madison Square Garden Corporation. Marsalis Music records is a registered trademark of Marsalis Music LLC. Max's Kansas City nightclub and restaurant is a registered trademark of MXKC Holdings LLC. MCA entertainment services is a registered trademark of MCA Inc. Meat Loaf musical entertainment is a registered trademark of Platinum Enterprises, Inc. Metropolitan Opera is a registered trademark of Metropolitan Opera Association. MGM phonograph records is a registered trademark of Metro-Goldwyn-Mayer Lion Corp. Moby Grape musical entertainment is a registered trademark of Moby Grape, composed of Jerry A. Miller Jr., Peter C. Lewis, Alexander Lee Spence, James Robert Mosley, and Donald J. Stevenson. Moog synthesizers is a registered trademark of Moog Music Inc. MTV Music Television and Nickelodeon entertainment broadcasting is a registered trademark of Viacom International, Inc. Napster is a registered trademark of Napster, Inc. NBC radio sound and television broadcasting is a registered trademark of NBC Universal Media. New Kids on the Block musical entertainment is a registered trademark of NKOTB, Inc. New York Dolls musical entertainment is a registered trademark of Island Boys Mambo, Inc. New York Philharmonic symphony orchestra is a registered trademark of Philharmonic-Symphony Society of New York, Inc. Nirvana musical entertainment is a registered trademark of Nirvana LLC. North Carolina Ramblers musical entertainment is a registered trademark of Charlie Poole Publishing Inc. and Original Rambler Music Inc. OutKast musical entertainment is a registered trademark of OutKast, Inc. Paramount sound recordings is a registered trademark of Paramount Pictures Corporation. Paul Revere and the Raiders musical entertainment is a registered trademark of RRR, Inc. Pearl Jam musical entertainment is a registered trademark of Pearl Jam, LLC. Philips phonographs is a registered trademark of Koninklijke Philips Electronics N.V. Pink Floyd musical entertainment is a registered trademark of Pink Floyd Limited. Polydor records is a registered trademark of Polydor International. Prince musical entertainment is a registered trademark of Paisley Park Enterprises. Public Enemy musical entertainment is a registered trademark of Carleton Ridenhour. Rickenbacker electric guitars is a registered trademark of Rickenbacker International Corporation. Rolling Stone magazine is a registered trademark of Straight Arrow Publishers, Inc. Rolling Stones musical entertainment and Rolling Stones phonograph records are registered trademarks of Musidor B.V. Run-DMC musical entertainment is a registered trademark of Darryl McDaniels. Sam's Club stores and Wal-Mart stores are registered trademark of Wal-Mart Stores, Inc. Sears retail department store is a registered trademark of Sears Brands, LLC. Sex Pistols musical entertainment is a registered trademark of Glitterbest Limited. Shakira musical entertainment is a registered trademark of Shakira Isabel Mebarak. Sly and the Family Stone musical entertainment is a registered trademark of Even St. Productions, Ltd. Spice Girls musical entertainment is a registered trademark of Spice Girls Limited. Spotify is a registered trademark of Spotify Limited. Steely Dan musical entertainment is a registered trademark of Steely Dan, Inc. Sugar Hill phonograph records is a registered trademark of Sugar Hill Records, Inc. Sugarhill Gang musical entertainment is a registered trademark of Joseph R. Robinson, Jr. Sun Record Company is a registered trademark of Sun International Corporation. Taj Mahal musical entertainment is a registered trademark of Henry Fredericks. Ten Years After musical entertainment is a registered trademark of Richard Lee, Leo Lyans, and Michael G. Churchill. The Allman Brothers Band is a registered trademark of The ABB Merchandising Co., Inc. The Beach Boys musical entertainment is a registered trademark of Brother Records, Inc. The Beatles musical entertainment is a registered trademark of Apple Corps Limited. The Boston Symphony Orchestra is a registered trademark of Boston Symphony Orchestra, Inc. The Brothers Four musical entertainment is a registered trademark of Robert L. Flick. The Byrds musical entertainment is a registered trademark of David Van Cortlandt Crosby. The Clash musical entertainment is a registered trademark of Dorisimo Limited. The Dave Clark Five musical entertainment is a registered trademark of Dave Clark London Ltd. The Doors musical entertainment is a registered trademark of The Doors and the Estate of James Morrison. *The Ed Sullivan Show* television program is a registered trademark of Sullivan Productions, Inc. The Highwaymen musical entertainment is a registered trademark of The Highwaymen, LLC. The Manhattans musical entertainment is a registered trademark of Edward Bivens. The Nation weekly publication is a registered trademark of Nation Associates, Inc. The New Christy Minstrels musical entertainment is a registered trademark of Randy Sparks. The New Republic periodical is a registered trademark of TNR II, LLC. *The New York Times* newspaper is a registered trademark of The New York Times Company. The Offspring musical entertainment is a registered trademark of The Offspring, composed of Bryan Holland, Gregory Kriesel, and Kevin Wasserman. The Philadelphia Orchestra is a registered trademark of Philadelphia Orchestra Association. The Royal Conservatory of Music is a registered trademark of The Royal Conservatory of Music. The Village Vanguard night club is a registered trademark of Deborah Gordon, Rebecca Gordon, and Lorranine Gordon. Tom Petty and the Heartbreakers musical entertainment is a registered trademark of Thomas Earl Petty a.k.a. Tom Petty DBA Tom Petty and the Heartbreakers. Tony award is a registered trademark of American Theatre Wing, Inc. Toto musical entertainment is a registered trademark of Toto Corporation Twitter is a registered trademark of Twitter, Inc. Universal Music Group is a registered trademark of Universal City Studios LLC. US Marine Band musical entertainment is a registered trademark of US Marine Corps. Vanguard Records is a registered trademark of Welk Music Group, Inc. Variety weekly newspaper is a registered trademark of Reed Properties Inc. Vee-Jay musical sound recordings is a registered trademark of Vee-Jay Limited Partnership. Victor talking machines and records is a registered trademark of Victor Talking Machine Company. Wall of Sound is a registered trademark of Monster, LLC. Weather Report musical entertainment is a registered trademark of Weather Report, composed of Wayne Shorter and Joe Zawinul. Western Electric is a registered trademark of Lucent Technologies Inc. WLS radio broadcasting services is a registered trademark of WLS, Inc. WSM radio broadcasting services is a registered trademark of Opryland Usa, Inc. Zoë records is a registered trademark of Rounder Records Corp.

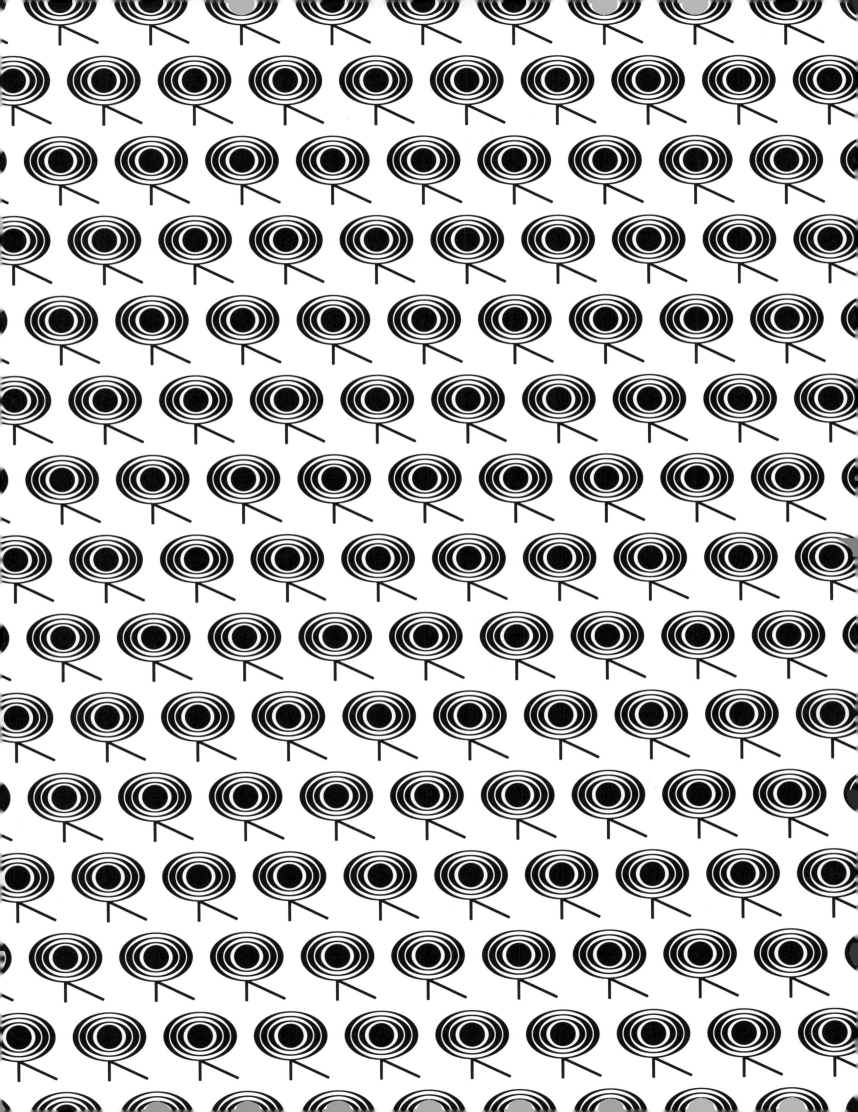

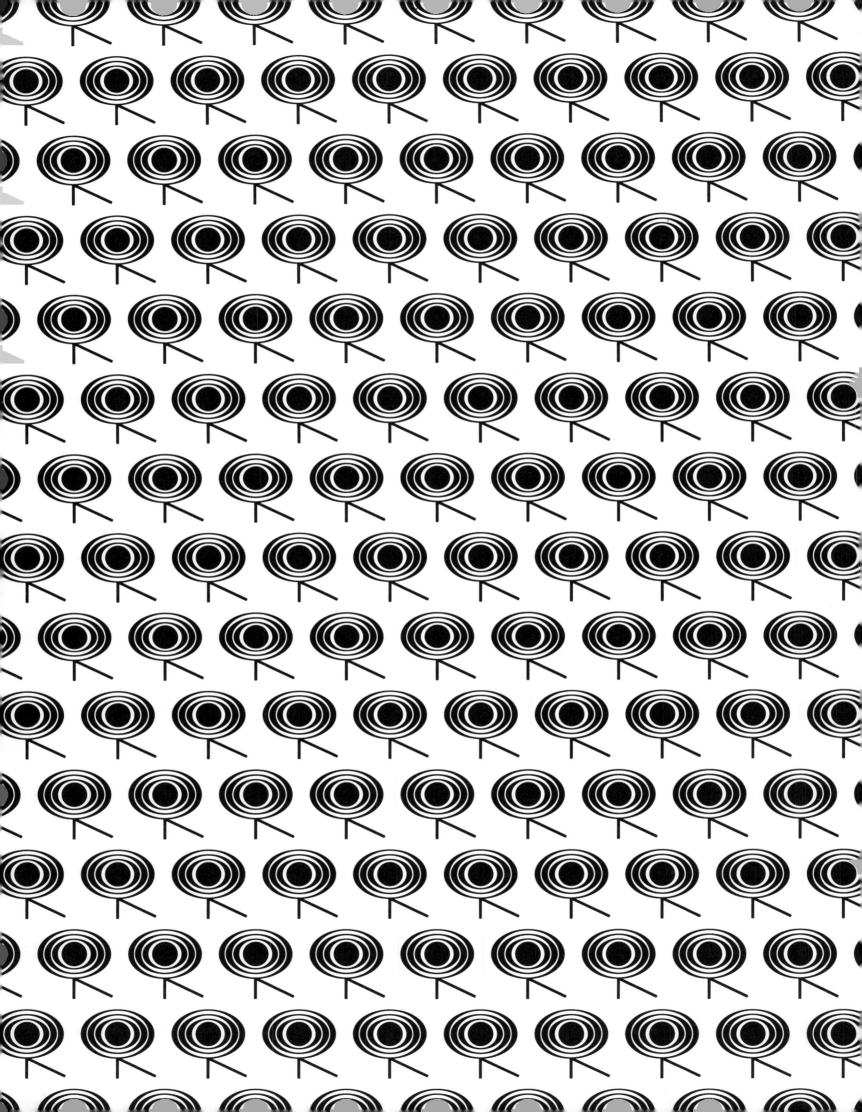